D0788714

THE HISTORIAN'S LINCOLN

"NOW WE SEE THROUGH A GLASS DARKLY. . . ." Broken original glass collodion negative made by Alexander Hesler, in Springfield, Illinois, June 3, 1860. Reproduced from gelatin silver prints at the Smithsonian Institution. This and all subsequent photographs of Lincoln in Chapter 2 are from James Mellon, *The Face of Lincoln* (New York: Viking Press, 1979).

973.7092
L638 bg

WITHDRAWI

THE
HISTORIAN'S
LINCOLN

*Pseudohistory, Psychohistory,
and History*

GABOR S. BORITT
Editor

NORMAN O. FORNESS
Associate Editor

UNIVERSITY OF ILLINOIS PRESS

Urbana and Chicago

178304

© 1988 by the Board of Trustees of the University of Illinois
Manufactured in the United States of America
C 5 4 3 2

This book is printed on acid-free paper.

$23.20 MWW 4-10-90 (X.R.B.)

Library of Congress Cataloging-in-Publication Data

The Historian's Lincoln.

Papers presented at a conference held at Gettysburg
College.
  Bibliography: p.
  Includes index.
  1. Lincoln, Abraham, 1809-1865—Congresses.
I. Boritt, G. S. (Gabor S.), 1940-   . II. Forness,
Norman O.
E457.4.H65   1988   973.7′092′4   88-1349
ISBN 0-252-01527-4 (alk. paper)

For Judith and Adam

And whensoever the vessel that he made of the clay was marred in the hand of the potter, he made it again another vessel, as seemed good to the potter to make it.

—Jeremiah 18:4

Contents

Preface and Acknowledgments

For much of a year before Lincoln's 175th birthday, and during the anniversary year itself, my family and I worked at restoring a long-abandoned Pennsylvania stone house that was older than Lincoln. With school out, in the summer afternoons and evenings we worked on the house, and from very early morning until the early afternoon, while the children played, I worked on organizing an ambitious gathering of the Lincoln scholars of the nation. Since February 12, 1984, "The Lincoln Image" exhibition of mid-nineteenth-century popular prints had been in place at the new art gallery of Gettysburg College and the proposed Lincoln conference was to occur in the fall, when the exhibition closed to move on to Brown University.

"Lincoln 175" took place as planned. Its goal was to make available to the general public the fruits of a decade of vigorous Lincoln scholarship from the mid-1970s to the mid-1980s. The authors of the most important books were invited to summarize, update, or revise their findings. Other outstanding historians of Lincoln or his era were asked to comment critically on these papers, and the original authors were given an opportunity to reply.[1]

Substantial emphasis was placed on reaching the literate public without abandoning solid scholarly moorings, though it was clear from the beginning that some scholars would be more successful than others in this endeavor. Professional historians, too, were to benefit, for they rarely have the time to read widely outside their own areas of specialization; they tend to rely on historiographical essays that synthesize such fields. These essays, as the introduction that follows demonstrates, have severe limitations. So the conference, and subsequently this volume, was to offer a halfway stop between the harsh abbrevi-

---

1. Some of the most sparkling and revealing moments of the conference came from the rebuttals by the principal authors to the critiques of the commentators. However, the readers for the University of Illinois Press recommended that these not be included in the book. The rebuttals are available from the editor.

ations of the historiographical summary and the often insurmountable obstacle of reading a dozen books in a particular field. One also hopes that many a reader of *The Historian's Lincoln* will be inspired to follow further the trail that begins here.

Perhaps even specialists on the Civil War and on Lincoln himself will learn from this book, which makes clear that, to a degree, Lincoln studies are disjointed just as the study of American history is disjointed. Scholars do not study each other's work carefully enough or talk to each other enough. They did talk at Gettysburg at "Lincoln 175." The dialogue needs to continue.

In the acknowledgment of debts Gettysburg College, the host of the conference, must come first. Under President Charles E. Glassick the College enthusiastically encourages creative, hard work. Vice President Richard P. Allen suggested the conference as a useful contribution to both scholarly and community relations. Others at Gettysburg whose support was welcome include former Dean David B. Potts as well as my congenial colleagues in the History Department: former chairman Basil L. Crapster, Bruce W. Bugbee, George H. Fick, Charles H. Glatfelter, Jean Holder, and J. Roger Stemen.

One colleague must be singled out beyond all others. Norman O. Forness helped organize the conference and later served as an associate editor of the book. He gave the first editorial reading to the manuscript, corresponded with contributors, read galleys, page proofs, and created for the end of the book the contributors' vitae and part of the index. I am grateful for his hard work and friendship.

The bulk of the index is the product of the painstaking work of Peter Sandler.

Tina Fair, my secretary, served as the History Department's secretary during the conference and consistently performed beyond the call of duty. She worked evenings, weekends, and more, often at a moment's notice. She typed the manuscript, saw it through its several stages, and was cheerful and prompt.

During the conference Bill Lagle served as chief of staff with good humor, energy, and efficiency. Student assistants who helped with the conference and the book included Karin Hagen-Fredricksen, John Stoudt, Tim Gelsinger, John Deeben, and Cathy Hancock.

Charlton Heston attended "Lincoln 175" and gave a brilliant but unrecorded rendering of the Gettysburg Address that lives in the memory of the more than two thousand people who heard it.

The National Endowment for the Humanities made the conference and, in part, the book financially possible and I especially wish to thank Andrea Anderson for her encouragement and good counsel. The Pennsylvania Humanities Council made a planning grant available and my indebtedness to Craig R. Eisendrath and Carol Coren must be specially noted.

The photographs in this book are all from James Mellon. Nearly all of the lithographs and engravings are courtesy of the Louis A. Warren Lincoln Library and Museum and its director Mark E. Neely, Jr. A few of the popular prints, however, are reproduced through the courtesy of the Library of Congress, the New York Public Library, and the Old Print Shop in New York City. Carol Saller, my editor at the University of Illinois Press, performed her task with admirable expertise.

The "Lincoln 175" conference was successful beyond all hope — "The best I ever attended," said a former president of the Organization of American Historians in a moment of enthusiasm, to which a future winner of the Pulitzer Prize added his happy assent. Spirits were heady; scholarship seemed full of excitement and good fellowship. Only the years to come will tell, however, whether through this book that gathering of scholars has also made a lasting and worthwhile contribution to the study of Lincoln. Soon after the conference a devastating fire swept my family's less than fully restored stone house. We were displaced for more than four months and the editing of this book was delayed much longer. But the home was rebuilt, more beautiful than ever. This book, too, was finished. And so my final thanks is to my family, who gave support—and whom I had the privilege to support—through good times and bad: my wife, Liz, and our three sons, Norse, Jake, and Daniel.

The book is dedicated to my sister and brother: with gratitude for a lifetime together.

G. S. B

Acknowledgments to Publishers

The contributors of the principal papers to this book wish to express their thanks for permission to publish previously printed materials: Dwight G. Anderson thanks Alfred A. Knopf; Gabor S. Boritt thanks Macmillan, Southern Illinois University Press, Memphis State University Press, Charles Scribner's Sons, and the *New York Times Book Review*; LaWanda Cox thanks the University of South Carolina Press; George B. Forgie thanks W. W. Norton and Co.; William Hanchett thanks the University of Illinois Press; Harold Holzer and Mark E. Neely, Jr., thank Charles Scribner's Sons; David A. Nichols thanks the University of Missouri Press; Charles B. Strozier thanks Basic Books; Glen E. Thurow thanks the State University of New York Press; Thomas Reed Turner thanks Louisiana State University Press.

Introduction
LOOKING FOR LINCOLN

AT THE GETTYSBURG CEMETERY the Lincoln of Gore Vidal's novel barely gets through his first sentence—about the events in America "four score and seven years ago"—when the young presidential secretary, John Hay, cynically observes that such rhetoric "will please the radicals." Though the national commitment to the noble notion that "all men are created equal," particularly in its Civil War black-white context, is thereby dismissed, the Gettysburg Address itself is not. In Vidal it is "a rifle salute to the dead." Each word is fired across the battlefield. The aim—that the "nation might live." Vidal thus pledges himself to one side of the controversy among historians concerning the meaning of Lincoln for our times.[1]

Scholarly debate in the historical profession, however gentlemanly and ladylike most of the time, is endemic, as it should be. History, after all, attempts to imitate life. In the field of Lincoln studies during the past decade, life has been full and the arguments lively.

One of the most fundamental issues for scholars has been whether Lincoln's ultimate commitment was to union or liberty. In the first view, Lincoln becomes the great nationalist whose devotion to the union of the states reached the level of religious mysticism—someone rather in the mold of Italy's Camillo Benso di Cavour, Germany's Otto von Bismarck or, to point to Edmund Wilson's far-fetched choice, Russia's Vladimir Ilyich Lenin. Lincoln's words from his 1862 letter to *New York Tribune* editor Horace Greeley can be seen as carved in marble: "My paramount object in this struggle *is* to save the Union, and is *not* either to save or to destroy slavery. If I could save the Union without freeing *any* slave I would do it, and if I could save it

A somewhat different version of this essay appeared in the *New York Times Book Review,* Feb. 8, 1987, pp. 1, 34-35.

by freeing *all* the slaves I would do it; and if I could save it by freeing some and leaving others alone I would also do that."[2] Though even during the Civil War questions of liberty encompassed much more than slavery, that institution provided the litmus test. Not surprisingly, it also provided the most heatedly fought-over subject of Lincoln studies during the past generation.

Those who understand Lincoln's commitment to liberty as paramount point out that by the time of the Greeley letter, he had decided in favor of emancipation. They see in that letter, and in much similar evidence, less an oath of allegiance to the Union than a political stratagem addressed to that antiblack majority of Northerners without whose support slavery could not be abolished. Lincoln did greatly prize the Union. Yet as he explained in New York in 1861, the Union was a ship that carried "the prosperity and the liberties of the people." He continued, "I understand a ship to be made for the carrying and preservation of the cargo, and so long as the ship can be saved, with the cargo, it should never be abandoned."[3]

Quibbling about the supremacy of union and liberty may seem intellectually arcane; after all it is obvious that Lincoln fought America's bloodiest war for both. Yet the distinction between union and liberty held fateful meaning for the world. The idea of one is essentially national, that of the other is universal. We dare not gainsay the achievements of Cavour or Bismarck, nor do we dare forget that their degenerate twentieth-century descendents in the worship of the nation as an end in itself were Mussolini and Hitler. Could America have followed a road more like theirs if its unification had come about under the leadership of a man who did not rank liberty first among his values? Asking the question thus places me on one side of the debate. Warning the reader is enough. It must also be said that the field can be conceived in other ways as well.

The need for a unified, believable portrait of Lincoln raised a second fundamental problem for historians. Ever since the moment of martyrdom in 1865 there have been two Lincolns: the man and the god. One was the crafty backwoods lawyer, "the crude small-time politician," to cite Stephen Vincent Benét;[4] the other, the immortal statesman, "the Great Emancipator" who partook of divinity. The two have coexisted with each other and battled each other, and still do. Whatever the public thought, the compromise whereby the common man captured the Illinois years and the divine one the presidency could not be satisfactory for scholars, since it suggested an inexplicable transfiguration. Accordingly, they have labored through much of this century to bridge the gap.[5]

Perhaps their best success during this past decade came with the psychohistorians through the very nature of psychoanalytic theory, which stresses intricate connections among the child, youth, and adult. It should be added quickly that some of the psychohistory of Lincoln is little more than well-written and well-argued mythmaking, which brings to mind the grumbling of novelist John Gardner's crusty old professor Sven Agaard in *Freddy's Book.* " 'Pseudo-history,' he said, with a scornful little headshake. I blinked, not sure whether it was a joke or a slip of the tongue, and tentatively corrected him, my tone ironic: 'Psycho-history.' "[6]

Yet the success of the genre is especially visible in the work of Charles B. Strozier, coeditor of an essay collection, *The Public and Private Lincoln* (1979), and author of *Lincoln's Quest for Union* (1982).[7] The latter book, questionable interpretations notwithstanding, often sheds brilliant new light on Lincoln's relations with his mother, father, stepmother, best friend, longtime law partner, wife, and eldest son, creating an image historians must reckon with. It suggests ways in which private experiences shaped the public figure. When Lincoln's search for inner unity is turned into a search for the union of Americans, Strozier makes a case that the idea of the Union was central to Lincoln's very being.

A quite able George B. Forgie disagrees. In *Patricide in the House Divided* (1979),[8] he finds liberty more important than union in understanding Lincoln. But Forgie's sophisticated work is less a study of a man than of a society whose most ambitious sons are oppressed by the fame of the revolutionary fathers. The sons therefore find their path to glory through war.

One shudders; psychohistory can exact a heavy price for the continuity it creates. Yet Forgie respects Lincoln. Not so Dwight G. Anderson, whose protagonist in *Abraham Lincoln: The Quest for Immortality* (1982)[9] lives in something of a Forgie-like world. It might be argued that Anderson, more than Forgie, shows the courage of his convictions, for he labels Lincoln a "tyrant," a "demon" who would destroy the United States created by the Constitution "to gratify his own ambition." Neither liberty nor union was sacred to him.

Anderson holds the Civil War president, as the founder of modern

America, partly responsible for his successors' attempts to save the world in places like Vietnam, and considering that most of the new Lincoln scholars were trained in the 1960s and cut their professional teeth in the 1970s, it is surprising that not more of them are anti-Lincoln. A significant part of their generation has replaced a sense of virtue and pride in the nation's history with guilt—"The Fall of the American Adam," as the imposing scholar C. Vann Woodward speaks of it.[10] That generation's views are changing now. Yet during the civil rights era, so ironically, even scholars wondered whether to lean toward the portrait of Lincoln as the Emancipator or as the honky. For a time, Don E. Fehrenbacher has noted, Lincoln's disavowal of social and political equality for whites and blacks in his debates with Stephen Douglas in 1858 seemed to become the most quoted of "all Lincoln's writings, outstripping even the Gettysburg Address and the Second Inaugural."[11] Without such a disavowal, Lincoln would have disappeared into a footnote to history.

Instead he went to the White House. A masterly study of what he called "the most difficult question" of those years is LaWanda Cox's *Lincoln and Black Freedom* (1981).[12] The book suggests that at last it is possible to look at the subject without stressing its relevance to the contemporary world. Her complex, minutely researched study can be summed up simply: Lincoln was the most effective friend of black freedom during the Civil War. This much of the Lincoln legend is true. So it lives. Cox's answer to what she called "the nagging questions"[13] seems all the more trustworthy because she had been a leader of the past generation's radical revision of Reconstruction historiography, which, for scholars at least, went a long way toward turning a misguided, tragic era into one of great promise and some achievement. If thus Cox struck a most sturdy blow for Lincoln and liberty, her work would have been even better had it dealt thoroughly with the Illinois years and so also struck a blow for continuity in the Lincoln image.

Peyton McCrary's *Abraham Lincoln and Reconstruction* (1978)[14] covers similar ground but focuses more on an experiment in liberty in Louisiana than on the president. Differing interpretations of detail notwithstanding, the book reaches a conclusion essentially identical with Cox's, presaging her work. In contrast, David A. Nichols in *Lincoln and the Indians* (1978)[15] portrays a president consumed with saving the Union and largely ignoring not only the chaotic, corrupt, and brutal system for dealing with Indians but also his own humanitarian instincts. Nichols might concede that by saving the Union Lincoln tried to save liberty, but that was small comfort for the thirty-eight Indians executed in Minnesota just after Christmas 1862 following an uprising, or for Indian people as a whole.

Yet, the tragedy of the Indian is dwarfed among Lincoln scholars by the vaster tragedy of the nation swallowed up in civil war. Religion provided solace for the suffering. Glen E. Thurow's *Abraham Lincoln and American Political Religion* (1976)[16] is a demanding philosophical analysis of major Lincoln texts, principally of the recently much-studied 1838 Lyceum Address, the Gettysburg Address, and the Second Inaugural. Thurow's president unites American political and religious traditions and stresses both continuity and liberty. So does David Hein's fine essay, "Lincoln's Theology and Political Ethics" (1983).[17]

Continuity and liberty are also highlighted in my own *Lincoln and the Economics of the American Dream* (1978).[18] The book examines, often in dreadfully dull detail, the development of the Illinoisan's growth-oriented economic persuasion. The work also argues that Lincoln defined liberty above all as the right to rise—a commitment that was central to his public, and private, life.

Economics of course can be difficult stuff and at the level of popular culture the most enticing Lincoln story has always been his murder. Yet until the current generation, professional historians have turned up their noses at the assassination, and the subject fell mostly into the hands of speculators, historical or financial, or honest paranoids, producing a vast array of pseudohistories: conspiracy theories purveyed by cheap paperbacks, book clubs, cinema, television, video, and more. Superior sleuth William Hanchett's *The Lincoln Murder Conspiracies* (1983),[19] complemented by Thomas Reed Turner's study of public opinion, *Beware the People Weeping* (1982),[20] at last sets the record straight. Unlike in most detective novels, but as in all historical research, untied knots remain. But it is also reasonably clear that Lincoln's assassination was the work of a small group of conspirators spawned by a society deeply disturbed and divided by war. Lincoln's last speech, pointing to black suffrage, appears to have been the final straw for John Wilkes Booth. "That means nigger citizenship," he declared upon hearing the president. "Now, by God, I'll put him through." And so he did—to apotheosis.[21]

The most popular historical interpreter of the man today is Stephen B. Oates, and the most popular public lecturer in the field — for there is a steady Lincoln public — is Mark E. Neely, Jr. Oates's *With Malice toward None* (1977)[22] is the standard biography today. Its very likeable Lincoln stands for liberty, and his story has continuity from the log cabin to Ford's Theatre. The sprightly book has very real strengths, but how long it will endure depends on when, or whether, a historian with talents equal to those of Oates — no mean requirement — will come forth with a new biography. The literature discussed here began to date Oates almost immediately. That he, too, sensed this can be gathered from *Abraham Lincoln: The Man behind the Myths* (1984),[23] in part a summary of what Oates had learned since his earlier work, interpreting for the general public the work of the specialists.

Neely is perhaps the most knowledgeable expert in the field and one awaits a major book from him. He has already authored the capable *Abraham Lincoln Encyclopedia* (1982),[24] and coauthored a number of works, including (with R. Gerald McMurtry) *The Insanity File* (1986),[25] a fascinating study based on a newly discovered cache of materials about Mary Todd Lincoln, who in 1875 was committed to an asylum by her son. Neely, in addition to doing a monthly piece in the *Lincoln Lore,* has written important articles; Lincoln studies are also nurtured by scholarly fare less imposing than books. Shorter pieces are sometimes collected, and the best of the recent crop of such volumes came from two great elder statesmen of Lincoln studies, Richard N. Current and Don E. Fehrenbacher, each bringing forth a collection of a lifetime of writing. (A third eminent figure, Robert V. Bruce, makes less frequent but ever telling contributions to Lincoln studies, and a fourth, David Herbert Donald, fell silent on Lincoln years ago, though his considerable prestige lingers.) Among other prizes, Current has won the Bancroft, and Bruce, Fehrenbacher, and Donald the Pulitzer, the last named twice. Current's *Speaking of Abraham Lincoln* (1983)[26] suggests with rare common sense answers to the perennial question so uncomfortable to historians, "What would Lincoln do today?" Fehrenbacher's *Lincoln in Text and Context: Collected Essays* (1987)[27] displays a sure grip on minute detail and broad interpretation, and also perhaps the most penetrating mind in the field. Current and Fehrenbacher served as mentors to many of the young scholars discussed in this essay who also are the principal contributors to this book, and Bruce had two of them study directly under him: Boritt and Turner.

Two distinguished lecture series focus on Lincoln. One is the annual R. Gerald McMurtry Lecture of the Louis A. Warren Lincoln Library and Museum of Fort Wayne, Indiana. See for example: Robert V. Bruce (*Lincoln and the Riddle of Death*, 1981), Harold Hyman (*Lincoln's Reconstruction: Neither Failure of Vision nor Vision of Failure*, 1980), Herman Belz (*Lincoln and the Constitution: The Dictatorship Question Reconsidered*, 1984), and John V. Simon (*House Divided: Lincoln and His Father*, 1987).[28] The other series is Gettysburg College's Robert Fortenbaugh Memorial Lecture, delivered each November 19 on the anniversary of the Gettysburg Address. Though the theme of the lecture is mid-nineteenth-century American history and the Civil War, scholars are often seduced by the locale to speak on Lincoln, as were for example Jacques Barzun (*Lincoln's Philosophic Vision*, 1982), James M. McPherson (*Lincoln and the Strategy of Unconditional Surrender*, 1984), Marcus Cunliffe (*The Doubled Images of Lincoln and Washington*, 1987), and Arthur Schlesinger, Jr. (*War and the Constitution: Abraham Lincoln and Franklin Delano Roosevelt*, forthcoming).[29]

Who are the authors of the new Lincoln studies? The large majority are young, in their forties, and all but two are men. One of the women, LaWanda Cox, whose book is such a sparkling "affair with Mr. Lincoln,"[30] refers to herself as "an old lady" and has been retired for many years. The other woman, Jean Baker, has just published a biography of Mary Todd Lincoln which makes excellent use of the development of women's studies.[31] Why write about Lincoln? Motives surely vary and one can only speculate. Most institutions of higher learning have experts on the Civil War president and his era, but making a name vis-à-vis Lincoln is difficult. Nor have recent scholarly trends encouraged the study of great men. Yet the graduate students who decide to lose themselves for long years in libraries and archives and master the literature—more has been written in English on Lincoln than on any other figure but Jesus—these students must instinctively sense that somewhere on their road acclaim might be waiting with its rewards. After all, they hitch their scholarly lives to the unequaled man of American history. Most students may also sense quickly that whatever the outcome of their quest, they would be spending their time in the company of one of the most attractive human beings of history.

A remarkable fact about Lincoln studies today, as in the past, is the number of prominent nonspecialists who wish to have their say about him. John P. Diggins's *Lost Soul of American Politics* (1984)[32] illustrates the point, as does *Abraham Lincoln and the American Political Tradition* (1986), edited by John L. Thomas, which includes, among others, contributions from Robert H. Wiebe, Michael F. Holt, James M. McPherson, and William E. Gienapp.[33] The same appears to be true abroad, where the well-known East German social historian Jurgen Kuczynski recently published *Abraham Lincoln: Eine Biographie* (1986).[34]

The work of the nonspecialist is at times thought-provoking; at times, merely provoking. An example of the latter is Oscar and Lilian Handlin's *Abraham Lincoln and the Union* (1980),[35] in the popular Library of American Biography, edited by Oscar Handlin. In the late nineteenth and early twentieth centuries, Boston's John T. Morse, Jr., the editor of the influential American Statesmen Series, made the mistake of reserving the Civil War president for himself.[36] Oscar Handlin did the same. The book adds little to the field, though the disfavor with which young Lincoln scholars greeted it, one suspects, stemmed partly from their chagrin for not gaffing the assignment for themselves.

For historians, however, the most troubling recent Lincoln book is Mr. Vidal's very engaging 1984 novel,[37] which has also become a radio feature and a television miniseries. To the general public, Vidal's is the most influential Lincoln image of our time. It is also the most insidiously ahistorical. The book's factual errors are a minor problem in a novel, and its seeming participation in scholarly debates matters not at all. But the cynical, amoral world it creates with a comfortable Lincoln at its center is surely the worst literary blow against Lincoln's reputation on record and, to a Watergate-tempered generation, all too acceptable.

In the realm of fiction, even as this book goes to press, Vidal is being challenged by William Safire, the *New York Times*'s Pulitzer Prize–winning political columnist, with his massive novel, *Freedom*.[38] Safire takes the story of Lincoln, the struggling but superior politician, through the Emancipation Proclamation. Though he provides a substantial "underbook" of sources, thus carefully separating fact from fiction, a perhaps unprecedented device for a novel, and though he will force scholars to rethink some issues, no small achievement for the genre, what he writes is not history. Both Safire and Vidal also serve history, however, by enchanting a large public that historians cannot hope to reach.

There is promising—as well as other—work among scholars, too. Don Fehrenbacher is bringing out a new selection of Lincoln's writings for the Library of America. Harry V. Jaffa is working on a sequel to his philosophically grounded study of the Lincoln-Douglas debates.[39] Less happily, M. E. Bradford, who may have been denied the chairmanship of the National Endowment for the Humanities in part because of his articles on Lincoln, and who has seen fit to compare Lincoln to Hitler, is threatening to do a full-length study.[40] Neely is working on civil liberties and the Constitution. Both McPherson and Hanchett have outlined volumes of interpretive essays. Lous Einhorn is studying Lincoln's speech. Frank S. Williams is producing a two-volume selected bibliography. Thomas Schwartz is planning a massive update of the standard but dated two-volume bibliography of all writings about Lincoln.[41] Roger D. Bridges, under the auspices of the Abraham Lincoln Association, is assembling at last all of Lincoln's legal papers. There are always rumblings about new biographies: Robert W. Johannsen and William Gienapp appear to be at work on brief volumes, and Donald on a full-length life. I am working on a comparative study of Lincoln with Jacques Portes of the Sorbonne, and also on the computerization of Lincoln's writings, which may lead both to a concordance and to authorship studies and so to a new definition of the Lincoln canon.

Lincoln once pleaded that he not be represented "as a man of great learning, or a very extraordinary one in any respect,"[42] and we can leave him here among the ordinary people with whom he felt most comfortable—and where this book will begin. His trip to Gettysburg is chronicled in Philip B. Kunhardt, Jr.'s *A New Birth of Freedom* (1983).[43] Lincoln's humorous yarns are collected in P. M. Zall's *Abe Lincoln Laughing* (1982).[44] Nearly all of these stories have come down to us through an oral tradition, and Zall is the first scholar to attempt to separate the authentic from the apocrypha. This wonderful collection is in a class by itself among the many Lincoln joke books, but the sad fact remains that we do not know for certain how many of these stories Lincoln actually told, much less how many originated with him.

Photographs, too, helped make Lincoln the common people's

chief magistrate, but it took a most uncommon amount of money, and much work, to hunt down the finest surviving negatives and prints and coax from them, through modern technology, *The Face of Lincoln* (1979).[45] The stunning, detailed new likenesses of James Mellon's album make even veteran scholars feel as if they have seen Lincoln for the first time. (The standard catalogue of photographs remains Charles Hamilton and Lloyd Ostendorf *Lincoln in Photographs*, which in its updated 1985 edition includes the newest discoveries.)[46] Humble Abe Lincoln had nearly eighty photographs taken during his presidency—in contrast to proud Jefferson Davis's one.[47] But only one daguerreotype was taken before the slavery dispute broke, and only two others before the year he debated Douglas; one wonders to what extent photographs have contributed to the historian's long-fractured image of Lincoln.

And how much have the photos contributed to Lincoln's apotheosis? These are questions for future students. That popular prints did aid deification, and therefore also the fracturing, is shown in *The Lincoln Image* (1984)[48] which employs the term narrowly to refer to engravings and lithographs. This book—by Holzer, the leading expert on Lincoln iconography, Neely, and myself—takes readers back to a time when visual images were rare and precious, rather than pervasive and frequently cheap, as today, and when pictures of political heroes were given honored places in both public places and the home.

There is an identical pair of Currier and Ives lithographs in this book—but whiskers have been added to one to transform it into the bearded statesman. The viewer realizes quickly, perhaps with the beginnings of a smile, that the beard is not quite right; Lincoln never wore anything quite as thick and bushy. And so we have a metaphor for the work of the Lincoln scholars. If most of them labor with infinitely greater care than the Currier and Ives artist did, and if the work of some historians is substantially better than that of others, the collective end result is no better than that bearded Lincoln. One knows it is Lincoln, no doubt about it, and one also knows that somehow it is not quite right. Of course some scholars with youthful spirit would quickly add, "at least not yet."

So the work goes on. Lincoln is the central figure of American mythology and—so far as historians can admit to such—of American history. The mythology is fed by best-selling novels, plays, cartoons, films, television shows, miniseries, videos, talk shows, advertisements,

THE PRESIDENTIAL CONTENDER GROWS INTO THE BEARDED STATESMAN. *Hon. Abraham Lincoln, Republican Candidate for Sixteenth President of the United States* (14 x 18¾) in the hands of the Currier and Ives artists becomes *Hon. Abraham Lincoln, Sixteenth President of the United States* (14 x 18¾). That Lincoln never quite had a beard like this seemed not to bother the unsophisticated print-buying public of mid-nineteenth-century America. Today such lithographs are treasured by collectors.

the shrines visited each year by millions, the humble penny, the postage stamps (three since 1984), an oral tradition, and much more. The historian's work in turn spills over into the culture at large—though the relationship of the two is symbiotic—and affects the myth through which Americans see Lincoln. And since Americans for a century and more have seen themselves at their best in Lincoln, what they see affects their future.

G. S. B.

NOTES

1. Gore Vidal, *Lincoln: A Novel* (New York: Random House, 1984), pp. 489-91.

2. Roy P. Basler, ed., Marion Dolores Pratt and Lloyd A. Dunlap, asst. eds., *The Collected Works of Abraham Lincoln*, 9 vols. (New Brunswick, N.J.: Rutgers University Press, 1953-55), 5: 388.

3. Ibid., 4: 233.

4. Stephen Vincent Benét, *John Brown's Body* (New York: Rinehart, 1928), p. 60.

5. The issues discussed in the previous paragraphs are also considered in G. S. Boritt, *Lincoln and the Economics of the American Dream* (Memphis: Memphis State University Press, 1978), especially "A Historiographical Essay: Lincoln, Man and God," pp. 289-311.

6. John Gardner, *Freddy's Book* (New York: Knopf, 1980), p. 31.

7. Cullom Davis, Charles B. Strozier, Rebecca Monroe Veach, and Geoffrey C. Ward, eds., *The Public and Private Lincoln: Contemporary Perspectives* (Carbondale: Southern Illinois University Press, 1979); Charles B. Strozier, *Lincoln's Quest for Union: Public and Private Meanings* (New York: Basic Books, 1982).

8. George B. Forgie, *Patricide in the House Divided: A Psychological Interpretation of Lincoln and His Age* (New York: Norton, 1979).

9. Dwight G. Anderson, *Abraham Lincoln: The Quest for Immortality* (New York: Knopf, 1982).

10. C. Vann Woodward, "The Fall of the American Adam," *American Academy of Arts and Sciences Bulletin* 35 (1981): 26-34.

11. Don E. Fehrenbacher, *Lincoln in Text and Context: Collected Essays* (Stanford: Stanford University Press, 1987), p. 101.

12. LaWanda Cox, *Lincoln and Black Freedom: A Study in Presidential Leadership* (Columbia: University of South Carolina Press, 1981).

13. Ibid., p. viii.

14. Peyton McCrary, *Abraham Lincoln and Reconstruction: The Louisiana Experiment* (Princeton: Princeton University Press, 1978).

15. David A. Nichols, *Lincoln and the Indians: Civil War Policy and Politics* (Columbia: University of Missouri Press, 1978).

16. Glen E. Thurow, *Abraham Lincoln and American Political Religion* (Albany: State University of New York Press, 1976).

17. Kenneth W. Thompson, ed., *Essays on Lincoln's Faith and Politics,* by Hans J. Morgenthau and David Hein (Lanham, Md.: University Press of America, 1983).

18. See note 5.

19. William Hanchett, *The Lincoln Murder Conspiracies: Being an Account of the Hatred Felt by Many Americans for President Abraham Lincoln during the Civil War and the First Complete Examination and Refutation of the Many Theories, Hypotheses, and Speculations Put Forward since 1865 Concerning Those Presumed to Have Aided, Abetted, Controlled, or Directed the Murderous Act of John Wilkes Booth in Ford's Theater* [sic] *the Night of April 14* (Urbana: University of Illinois Press, 1983).

20. Thomas Reed Turner, *Beware the People Weeping: Public Opinion and the Assassination of Abraham Lincoln* (Baton Rouge: Louisiana State University Press, 1982).

21. Quoted in Hanchett, *The Lincoln Murder Conspiracies,* p. 37.

22. Stephen B. Oates, *With Malice toward None: The Life of Abraham Lincoln* (New York: Harper and Row, 1977).

23. Stephen B. Oates, *Abraham Lincoln: The Man behind the Myths* (New York: Harper and Row, 1984).

24. Mark E. Neely, Jr., *The Abraham Lincoln Encyclopedia* (New York: McGraw-Hill, 1982).

25. Mark E. Neely, Jr., and R. Gerald McMurtry, *The Insanity File: The Case of Mary Todd Lincoln* (Carbondale: Southern Illinois University Press, 1986).

26. Richard Nelson Current, *Speaking of Abraham Lincoln: The Man and His Meaning for Our Times* (Urbana: University of Illinois Press, 1983).

27. See note 11.

28. All the lectures are published by the Lincoln National Life Foundation, in Fort Wayne, Indiana, under the editorship of Mark E. Neely, Jr.

29. All the lectures are published by Gettysburg College under the editorship of Gabor S. Boritt.

30. Cox, *Lincoln and Black Freedom,* p. xiii.

31. Jean Baker, *Mary Todd Lincoln: A Biography* (New York: Norton, 1987).

32. John P. Diggins, *The Lost Soul of American Politics: Virtue, Self-Interest, and the Foundations of Liberalism* (New York: Basic Books, 1984).

33. John L. Thomas, ed., *Abraham Lincoln and the American Political Tradition* (Amherst: University of Massachusetts Press, 1986).

34. Jürgen Kuczynski, *Abraham Lincoln. Eine Biographie* (Berlin: Akademie-Verlag, 1986).

35. Oscar Handlin and Lilian Handlin, *Abraham Lincoln and the Union* (Boston: Atlantic/Little, Brown, 1980).

36. John T. Morse, Jr., *Abraham Lincoln,* 2 vols. (Boston: Houghton Mifflin, 1895).

37. See note 1.

38. William Safire, *Freedom: A Novel of Abraham Lincoln and the Civil War* (New York: Doubleday, 1987).

39. Harry V. Jaffa, *Crisis of the House Divided: An Interpretation of the Lincoln-Douglas Debates* (New York: Doubleday, 1959).

40. The comparison to Hitler is in M. E. Bradford, *A Better Guide than Reason: Studies in the American Revolution* (La Salle, Ill.: Sherwood, 1979), p. 56. For three discussions of the chairmanship of the NEH see Suzanne Garment, "The NEH Becomes a Storm Center One More Time," *Wall Street Journal*, Oct. 30, 1981; Eric Foner, "Lincoln, Bradford, and the Conservatives," *New York Times*, Feb. 13, 1982; and [M. E. Bradford], "For the Chair of NEH: A Southern Candidate Recalls His Struggle," *Humanities in the South* 56 (1982): 1, 12-13.

41. Jay Monogham, comp., *Lincoln Bibliography, 1839-1939*, Collections of the Illinois State Historical Library, vols. 31-32, Bibliographical Series, vols. 4-5 (Springfield: Illinois State Historical Library, 1943-45).

42. Basler, *Collected Works of Lincoln*, 4: 127.

43. Philip B. Kunhardt, Jr., *A New Birth of Freedom: Lincoln at Gettysburg* (Boston: Little, Brown, 1983).

44. P. M. Zall, ed., *Abe Lincoln Laughing: Humorous Anecdotes from Original Sources by and about Abraham Lincoln* (Berkeley: University of California Press, 1982).

45. James Mellon, ed. and comp., *The Face of Lincoln* (New York: Viking, A Studio Book, 1979).

46. Charles Hamilton and Lloyd Ostendorf, *Lincoln in Photographs: An Album of Every Known Pose* (Dayton: Morningside, 1985).

47. Mark E. Neely, Jr., Harold Holzer, and Gabor S. Boritt, *The Confederate Image: Prints of the Lost Cause* (Chapel Hill: University of North Carolina Press, 1987), p. 179. John O'Brien is working on a study of Davis which may suggest that two photographs have been taken of the Confederate president.

48. Harold Holzer, Gabor S. Boritt, and Mark E. Neely, Jr., *The Lincoln Image: Abraham Lincoln and the Popular Print* (New York: Scribner's, 1984).

PART I

The Common People's Lincoln

☆ ☆
☆

CHAPTER 1

ABE LINCOLN LAUGHING

P. M. ZALL

THEY USED TO SAY that George Washington was first in war, first in peace, first in the hearts of his countrymen, and Ben Franklin was first in everything else. But we now know better. Recent polls of professional historians in 1948, 1968, and again in 1983 concur in placing Abraham Lincoln first among American presidents.[1] More significantly, when twenty-five years ago the Gallup poll asked common Americans to name three persons past or present they wished they could take home to dinner, Lincoln led all the lists.[2] And in an "anecdotal test of greatness," James David Fairbanks counted the number of pages devoted to each president in Paul Boller's *Presidential Anecdotes*. Lincoln led again: twenty-five pages to Washington's twenty-one pages and Ronald Reagan's nine.[3] At age 175, Lincoln still is living witness to the power of humor to hide the pain, heal the hurt, sustain the spirit.

The extent to which Lincoln transfused this power to his people may be seen in these initial responses to his death reported in *Harper's Magazine*: Vermont—"Upon reading that 'the assassin leaped from the box on to the stage and escaped in the rear of the theatre,' our friend cried out, in a most excited manner. 'Why didn't they stop the stage? The driver ought to be arrested and shot!'"

Iowa— A four-year-old Davenport girl exclaimed, " 'I wish that rebel was dead—I wish he was hung.' Having heard these two words before, and not *exactly* understanding their meaning, and thinking perhaps it was better to add an opinion of her own, she said, 'I wish he was put on top of the house and the ladder taken away!'"[4]

More than any of the numberless classical eulogies recited across the land, these homestyle anecdotes reflect the real depth of affection shared by Lincoln and his people. Herndon said their sympathy was Lincoln's most valuable asset: Lincoln and his people "became one

3

in thought, one in will, one in action."[5] We ought to take this not in an abstract sense but as a mutual transfusion of sympathy, literally "feeling with," the same mutual infusion evident between revivalist preachers and their congregations. Consider this interchange recorded at Pittsburgh en route to the inaugural: Lincoln is standing on a chair in the hotel lobby acknowledging the crowd's welcome—

> I acknowledge with all sincerity the high honor you have conferred on me. ["Three cheers for Honest Abe," and a voice saying, "It was no accident that elected you, but your own merits"] I thank you, my fellow citizen, for your kind remark, and trust that I feel a becoming sense of the responsibility resting upon me. ["We know you do."]
>
> I could not help thinking, my friends, as I traveled in the rain through your crowded streets, on my way here, that if all that people were in favor of the Union, it can certainly be in no great danger—it will be preserved. [A voice—"We are all Union men." Another voice—"That's so." A third voice—"No compromise." A fourth—"Three cheers for the Union."]
>
> But I am talking too long, longer than I ought. ["Oh, no! go on; split another rail." Laughter.] You know that it has not been my custom, since I started on the route to Washington, to make long speeches; I am rather inclined to silence, ["That's right"] and whether that be wise or not, it is at least more unusual now-a-days to find a man who can hold his tongue than to find one who cannot [laughter, and a voice— "No *railery*, Abe."][6]

Even making allowances for what the shorthand reporter left out, the synergetic give-and-take sounds like a revival meeting.

That is no coincidence. These people grew up with the great religious revival.[7] Abe Lincoln's stepsister recalled how, as children, they would gather around him after their parents had gone to church Sunday mornings. Abe would play preacher: he'd "read a verse, give out a hymn, we would sing. He would preach and we would do the crying."[8] That is the "crying" we hear echoing in the Pittsburgh hotel lobby. And there Lincoln typically responds in his concluding remarks: " 'I have made my appearance now only to afford you an opportunity of seeing, as clearly as may be, my beautiful countenance!' [Loud laughter, and cheers]."[9]

In thus turning the joke upon himself Lincoln employs a technique developed in public activities most closely allied to camp preaching — namely, stump speaking and circuit riding. These, rather than camp meetings, were the ultimate sources of his art, particularly the art of storytelling, which would become inseparable from his reputation as lawyer, legislator, politician, president. Like the giant Antaeus who retained his invincible strength only so long as he touched the earth that gave him birth, Lincoln relied on his stories for contact with his people. An example of his losing touch is his sober lecture on the subject of "Man" at the Wisconsin State Fair. The *Milwaukee Daily National* complained that "his backwoods and homespun oratory, the wit, pungency, and sharpness were wanting." The people came to hear plain "Abe" but, getting instead "the honorable Abraham Lincoln," they wandered away to the cow pens and the sideshows.[10]

As his generation had grown up with the great revival so they had also come to age with stump speaking. Like state fairs and camp meetings, elections gave backwoods people what Tom Clark calls "the excellent excuse for being in a crowd." The more frequently public offices changed hands, the better the people liked the democratic process. Judge John Test, seeking reelection, tried to seduce voters of Allenville, Indiana, with his views on the tariff. He knew he had lost when one old man allowed he had never seen a tariff but believed "it was hard on sheep."[11]

Stump speaking peaked with the celebrated "log cabin campaign" of 1840, marvelous training for Lincoln, especially because the acknowledged King of the Stump was his Whig colleague Tom Corwin of Ohio (who would become Lincoln's ambassador to Mexico). Corwin's reputation as a storyteller matched Lincoln's: he tells of a Frenchman complaining that America's been sending the wrong kind of diplomats abroad. "Why don't you send . . . good-looking men who speak some language?" Corwin: "Don't they all speak *some* language?" Frenchman: "No . . . I met a gentleman at Copenhagen who speaks no language at all. He speaks some *patois* which they call Ohio."[12]

The few recorded performances of Corwin on the stump make clear the close connection with camp-meeting preaching, especially with respect to biblical allusions. Stumping for Tip Harrison, he accosts one skeptical Democrat: " 'Oh, my unsanctified brother!' — his eye again fixed upon his unbelieving auditor, his body bent over, and his hands lifted imploringly — 'I will not repeat to you the curse that was pronounced when "Noah awoke from his wine and knew what his younger son had done unto him." I pray you, be warned by it. Turn from your evil ways. Quit your ridicule and abuse of your good pioneer father protector, General Harrison.' "[13] He went on like this for a hundred days and more, speaking in as many places for two to three hours at a time, stump speaking's finest hours.

Lincoln learned from the master and came to succeed him as King of the Stump because the public came to favor a more home-style oratory. Corwin's most quoted speech is a satire of a Democrat in Congress who had dared impugn Tip Harrison's military record. The Democrat, a general in the Michigan militia, is depicted after a hard day's drill: retreating to "a neighboring grocery," he unsheaths his eighteen-inch blade and "with an energy and remorseless fury he slices the watermelons that lie in heaps around him . . . Whiskey, Mr. Speaker, is here also, and the shells of watermelons are filled to the brim."[14] Corwin slides easily into mythological allusions: "As the Scandinavian heroes of old, after the fatigues of war, drank wine from the skulls of their slaughtered enemies in Odin's Halls, so now our militia general and his forces from the skulls of melons thus vanquished, in copious draughts of whiskey assuage the heroic fire of their souls, after the bloody scenes of a parade day."

Also in Congress, eight years later, Lincoln attacked another militia general, Democrat Lewis Cass, contrasting him with the Whig presidential candidate Zachary Taylor. Lincoln dispenses with Corwin's biblical or classical allusions and drives directly to the point— General Cass had an innocuous military record: he "*invaded* Canada without resistance, and he *outvaded* it without pursuit. . . . He was a volunteer aide to General Harrison on the day of the battle of the Thames; and . . . Harrison was picking huckleberries just two miles off while the battle was fought. I suppose," said Lincoln, "it is a just conclusion with you, to say Cass was aiding Harrison to pick huckleberries."[15] The difference between the attacks is not merely that Lincoln avoids scholarly allusions. He typically uses the vernacular, and even more typically turns the joke on himself: "By the way, Mr. Speaker, did you know I am a military hero? Yes, sir, in the days of the Black Hawk war, I fought, bled, and came away." The draft shows the next sentence was inserted as an afterthought: "If Gen. Cass went in advance of me in picking huckleberries, I guess I surpassed him in charges upon the wild onions." Lincoln concludes the episode: "If he saw any live, fighting Indians, it was more than I did; but I had a good many bloody struggles with the mosquitoes; and, although I never fainted from loss of blood, I can truly say I was very hungry." This technique of ridiculing an adversary while effacing himself reflects lessons Lincoln learned on the Eighth Judicial Circuit, backcountry Illinois, where the periodic visits of judges and lawyers provided settlers another "excellent excuse for being in a crowd." Herndon describes the festive holiday atmosphere. After the courthouse closed, the judges, lawyers, litigants, and natives congregating from the country around all trooped to the tavern. There the most celebrated storytellers would compete in front of standing-room-only crowds cheering them on:

> The barroom, windows, halls, and all passageways would be filled to suffocation by the people eager to see the "big ones" and to hear their stories told by them. Lincoln would tell his story in his very best style. The people, all present, including Lincoln, would burst out in a loud laugh and a hurrah at the story. The listeners . . . would cry out: "Now, Uncle Billy (William Engle), you must beat that or go home." . . . And thus this story-telling, joking, jesting, would be kept up till one or two o'clock in the night, and thus night after night till the court adjourned for that term.[16]

Night after night for six months out of the year, year after year, in county seat after county seat, across eight counties, this was Lincoln's training. Is it any wonder that spinning stories became second nature to him?

Circuit lawyers in the backcountry employed stories the way Eastern lawyers used eloquence. When one of the latter, visiting, opined that Lincoln was wasting time telling the jury stories, his host corrected him, explaining that Lincoln, like a good racehorse, "breaks to win."[17] At statewide conventions, opponents would accuse him of putting on "a sort of assumed clownishness." In Congress, even friends would scorn his awkward pacing up and down or wild gestures, which stump speakers called "doing the motions."[18] Yet the Whigs brought him to tour New England for Zachary Taylor in 1848 and he captivated the effete Easterners. At Worcester, "whenever he tried to stop, the shouts of 'Go on! go on!' " brought down the house.[19]

Earlier the log cabin theme of the Harrison campaign made his home-style oratory a natural attraction, but an added element was

7

the swiftly developing fad for frontier sketches in the popular press. William T. Porter's sporting weekly, the *Spirit of the Times*, came to serve as a national clearinghouse, reprinting stories from other newspapers and magazines, inviting submissions from doctors, lawyers, and especially soldiers on the frontier. So far as Easterners knew, those were the authentic voices of the frontier. This is a sample of "Stump Speaking in Arkansas" according to the *Spirit of the Times* (for April 13, 1844): "Feller citizens—I'm going to sand my speech with quotation from Seizem the celibrated Latin cricket, when addressed the Carthagenions and Rocky Mountain Cods at the battle of the Cow Pens! Look Out! — I'm comin'—cock your rifles and be ready! 'Eat ye burute E' as the immaculate feller said, when he got stabbed in the back in the House of Representatives!" If this is what they expected and Lincoln is what they got, who can blame the Easterners for bringing down the house?

At the same time, he rudely upset their expectations in other respects. Lincoln's dress, manners, and speech brought frontier sketches to life for some. For others, the initial culture shock was indelible. Consider the first impressions recorded by the novelist Nathaniel Hawthorne, sophisticated New Yorker George Templeton Strong, and Harriet Beecher Stowe. Hawthorne, finding him "about the homeliest man I ever saw," called him "the essential representative of all Yankees"—by which he meant the comical cartoon character of a Yankee that still survives in our elongated Uncle Sam. Hawthorne's greatest disappointment was that Old Abe had not told one of his famous stories.[20]

Strong did not know how to describe him even in a private diary—"a barbarian, Scythian, yahoo or gorilla." Charmed during their first meeting, Strong returned to the diary trying to reproduce a Lincoln story and recording what it must have sounded like to Eastern ears tuned to more dulcet tones:

> Wa-al that reminds me of a party of Methodist parsons that was traveling in Illinois when I was a boy thar, and had a branch to cross that was pretty bad-ugly to cross, ye know, because the water was up. And they got considerin' and discussin' how they should git across it, and they talked about it for two hours, and one on 'em thought they had ought to cross one way when they got there, and another another way, and they got quarrelin' about it, till at last an older brother

8

put in and he says, says he, "Brethren, this here talk ain't
no use. I never cross a river until I come to it."

This is hardly a phonetic transcription. Strong confessed that he
despaired of capturing the story's "intense provincialism and rusticity,"
and had to be satisfied with a weak approximation.[21]

Harriet Beecher Stowe had trouble adjusting Lincoln's appearance to her preconception of what a president ought to look like. At
their first meeting he greeted her with the famous: "So you're the
little woman who wrote the book that made this great war!" Then
he invited her to sit by the hearth. "I do love an open fire," he
confided; "I always have one to home."[22] In reporting the visit to her
children, Stowe was most impressed not by the famous greeting, but
by the bucolic expression "to home."

Lincoln's pronunciation also struck Easterners as rustic. He would
call "Meester Chairman," or say "unly" for "only" or rhyme "again"
with "skin."[23] How much of this was put on as assumed clownishness?
Some evidence may be found in revisions of his papers: when he
drafted the autobiographical sketch for his first presidential campaign,
he revised the expression "reading, writing, and Arithmetic" to
"readin, writin, and cipherin."[24] In print, then, as on the platform,
he deliberately adapted his style to the homespun oratory his people
expected. Stephen Douglas called him "the best stump speaker in the
West" doubtless because of his chameleonlike quality of becoming a
part of the atmosphere that surrounded him.[25]

In the East, however, he found that print-oriented audiences also
had nonverbal preconceptions and so he capitalized on his appearance.
Although a corporation lawyer and a leading Republican in his state,
he nevertheless showed up at the Cooper Institute wearing a new suit
showing the creases from a suitcase and carrying a pencil behind his
ear. His platform presence became legendary. The *New York Tribune*
despaired of describing it: "The tones, the gestures, the kindling eye
and the mirth-provoking look defy the reporter's skill."[26] The reporter
for the *Janesville Morning Gazette* described an animated cartoon: "A
shrug of his shoulder, an elevation of his eyebrows, a depression of
his mouth, and a general malformation of countenance so comically
awkward that it never fails to bring down the House." Writers for
the comic magazines had a field day: "When walking he resembles
the offspring of a happy marriage between a derrick and a windmill.

9

When speaking he reminds one of the old signal-telegraph that used to stand on Staten Island." One skilled observer managed to catch him in full flight: "He commenced his speech in a rather diffident manner, even seemed for a while at a loss for words, his voice was irregular, a little tremulous at first." Then came a remarkable transformation as Lincoln told two or three stories: "His body straightened up, his countenance brightened, his language became free and animated."[27]

Democrats insisted he was playing to the masses: "He possessed the rare art of assuming an extra uncouthness or rusticity of manner and outward habit, for the purpose of securing particular favor with the masses."[28] And Douglas knew only too well that Lincoln had mastered the art. Douglas claimed he never feared Lincoln's logic or his arguments, but "every one of his stories seems like a whack upon my back."[29] The home-style stories of the stump, the courthouse, and the newspaper humor columns had become a formidable weapon in national politics, such as the one about the candidate who, losing an election for town supervisor, comes home to find his wife all dressed up to go out. "I'm going down to Mr. Brown's house," says she. "When you left this morning you told me tonight I should sleep with the new town supervisor."[30]

His friends sensed that Lincoln's "homely illustrations" were what attracted the people[31] — even sophisticated Easterners. With hindsight we can guess that his old-fashioned stories evoked nostalgia for a simpler life that never was. Yet even so cynical a reporter as Henry Villard marveled at Lincoln's seemingly inexhaustible stock of stories and the way he could adapt them to varied audiences — "rough looking Sangamon County farmers . . . sleek and pert commercial travellers, staid merchants, sharp politicians, or preachers, lawyers, or other professional men."[32]

His celebrity as a teller of funny stories preceded him to the presidency. He knew the risks. He liked to quote the two Quaker ladies on a train discussing prospects of the war. "I think," affirms one, "that Jefferson Davis will succeed." "And why does thee think that?" "Because Jefferson is a praying man." "Abraham is a praying man." "Yes, but the Lord will think Abraham is joking."[33] When critics objected that his always telling stories demeaned the dignity of the presidency, he countered: "I have found that common people—" and he repeated, "common people—take them as you find them, are more easily influenced by a broad and humorous illustration than in any other way."[34] "In a Government of the people," he also said, "what lies at the bottom of all of it, is public opinion."[35]

His stories were proven effective in keeping a house divided from falling apart. Responding to critics of his war policy, he said, put him in the fix of a traveler back home lost in a terrific thunderstorm. Flashes of lightning showed the way but the peals of thunder took him to his knees. "By no means a praying man, his petition was short and to the point—'O Lord, if it is all the same to you, give us a little more light and a little less noise.' "[36]

Such stories were not mere abstractions, like classical myths or Aesop's fables, but living expressions of a people who swapped them among friends and relations even as he told them anew—and better than most. Another traveler back home is caught in a driving rain. He whips up his horse seeking shelter. He passes a farmhouse, and a man sticks his head out an upstairs window shouting, "Hello! Hello!" The traveler reins up: "What you want?" "Nothing." "Then what in tarnation are you shouting 'Hello' for when people are passing by?" "Well, what in tarnation are you passing by for when people are shouting 'Hello'?"

With the modern premium on being original, it is hard to appreciate that the real power behind this and stories like it derives from its being an old favorite. The story about shouting "Hello!" had appeared only recently in the mass-circulating *Harper's Weekly* (May 23, 1857) and heaven knows how many newspapers had been reprinting it: "Boy," said an ill-tempered old fellow to a noisy lad, "what are you hollerin' for when I am going by?" "Hmph," said the boy, "what are you going by for when I am hollerin'?" In transforming this old joke into a down-home story, Lincoln endowed it with the authenticity of the human voice. Even when recorded in cold print, his stories take on a dramatic quality from his use of commonplace details, colloquial language, and a seeming spontaneity as though improvised on the spot. We seem to share the process of his remembering them as they come to him, a double pleasure in the story and the storyteller.[37]

As he cultivated the deceptively simple homespun stance of a stump speaker in the East, so he also cultivated the artlessness of the circuit-riding storyteller. He would memorize those stories, walking around with clippings from newspapers or magazines or even with a comical book until he had them by heart and could slip them into conversations, interviews, or speeches on any occasion. He confided his secret to the family minister: "If you have an auditor who has the time and is inclined to listen, lengthen it out slowly as if from a jug. If you have a poor listener, hasten it, shorten it, shoot it out of a pop-gun."[38]

These stories had practical, everyday value. As president, Lincoln used them to save time and temper. Under prodding from reporters, his secretary John Hay often tried to pry stories for the sake of stories,[39] but in the White House Lincoln listened. When he had to talk, stories helped keep that talk short, sweet, and to the point—as when he diverted one delegation who came complaining about the way the war was being waged in the West. He addresses one of their leaders: "Judge List, this reminds me of an anecdote which I heard a son of yours tell in Burlington in Iowa. . . ." It is his story about the chickens of a pioneer household who became so used to pulling up stakes and moving on that "whenever they saw the wagon sheets brought out they laid themselves on their backs and crossed their legs, ready to be tied" to the back of the wagon. If he listened to every delegation like theirs, he told them, "I had just as well cross my hands and let you tie me."[40]

He could very well have heard that story from Judge List's son out in Burlington, Iowa, but he could more easily have found it in that old favorite repository for frontier sketches, William T. Porter's *Spirit of the Times* back in 1857. Because he used so many of these old favorites so frequently, people would naturally attach his name to any old chestnut: The farmer tells his son that it is time to take a wife, and the sons asks, "Whose?"[41] By the same token, however, the popular press would recycle stories he did tell and attribute them to somebody else. In an 1858 debate Lincoln described his reaction to Douglas's blandishments by declaring himself "not very much accustomed to flattery, and it came all the sweeter to me. I was rather like the Hoosier who reckoned he loved gingerbread better than any other man, and got less of it." This appeared in *Harper's Magazine* three years after his death, with the gingerbread changed to "wheat biscuit" and no mention of Lincoln at all.[42]

Nevertheless by the time of the second presidential campaign, his storytelling had become a political issue. Witness titles of some campaign pamphlets of 1864: *The Royal Ape,* and *The Humors of Uncle*

Abe—The Second Joe Miller. The anti-Lincoln *Old Abe's Joker* balanced the pro-Lincoln *Old Abe's Jokes*. The avalanche of old jokes obscured their origins to the extent that Lincoln himself was unsure of which stories he had and had not told: a citizen comes complaining about Secretary Stanton's meanness. Lincoln tells him about the owner of a large dog who comes complaining to the owner of a small dog. How is it that the small dog whips every dog in town? "That is no mystery . . . your dog and the other dogs get half through a fight before they get mad. My dog is always mad."[43]

The symbiotic relation with the press continued. He would quip and they would clip; they would quip and he would clip. In this way the stream of Lincoln stories swelled inexhaustibly: at a field hospital, the damsel asks a soldier where he was wounded and the soldier blushes and avoids answering. She appeals to Mr. Lincoln to ask him. Lincoln blushes too: "Ma'am the bullet that wounded him would not have wounded you."[44] Or, consider this remarkable switch: when Lincoln was postmaster of New Salem, reading the newspapers before passing them on, a favorite in the humor columns was the story of Benjamin Franklin traveling through northwest Pennsylvania on a cold winter's night and coming to an inn where the natives had monopolized the fireplace. Franklin cooly orders oysters for his horse. The landlord is incredulous, but Franklin persists, and the landlord troops out to the stable followed by the crowd of curious natives while Franklin takes his choice of seats by the fire. In the Democrats' pamphlet of 1864 called *Lincolniana, or the Humors of Uncle Abe,* the plot remains the same but the scene has shifted to Indiana, Franklin has changed to Lincoln, and the oysters have miraculously transformed to catfish.[45]

Would that we could as easily recreate the symbiotic relation Lincoln enjoyed with his national audience. Together they had grown up with the religious revival, stump speaking, circuit riding, and more recently with unprecedented technological advances in communications that made for a truly national press and a nation of newspaper readers.[46] Lincoln was thus able to reach unprecedented millions of readers with words recorded by shorthand reporters, transmitted over telegraph lines, and reproduced in inexpensive newspapers within reach of all who could read. We can only guess the extent to which the wire services, for example, supplanted the earlier flesh-and-blood audiences who responded with the fervor of camp meetings. You know, for instance, that the earlier drafts of the Gettysburg Address did not have the phrase "under God," until the Associated Press included that phrase in its transcript. Lincoln's subsequent drafts included "under God" also. Conceivably he had used the phrase unconsciously, responding to the audience's applause or to the rhythm of his carefully controlled cadences—conceivably he responded to a supernatural power. In any event, I believe he did not write it down till the Associated Press printed it.[47]

In the popular press Harriet Beecher Stowe linked Lincoln to Moses, "leading his Israel through the wilderness."[48] She said he rejected fine writing for the same reason that motivated St. Paul: "Because he felt that he was speaking on a subject which must be made clear to the lowest intellect." The urgency of this mission of course increased with the access afforded by the communication revolution, and Lincoln was eminently capable of handling it. "He was," said Horace Greeley, "simply a plain, true, earnest, patriotic man, gifted with eminent common sense."[49] That common sense, said Greeley, bonded "shrewdness on the one hand, humor on the other" and "allied him intimately, warmly, with the masses of mankind." He was a man speaking to the masses of mankind, and everybody listened. They still do.

In his 175th year, politicians of all parties once more invoked his stories as token of their being on the right side. A Democratic party spokesperson tried to reassure us of harmony on the platform committee. What looked like squabbling reminded him of what Lincoln said about cats on the back fence: they sound like they're killing each other when all the time they are only making more cats.[50] In the normal course of events such stories, apocryphal or not, will become embroidered in our national heritage, like "Don't swap horses in . . ." or "You can fool. . . ." They take on the force of proverbs because they speak to the condition of humankind. Dear Abby recently published an old Lincoln story about the preacher saying the Bible never mentions a perfect woman, which proves none exist. A woman in the back stands up: "I know a perfect woman, and I've heard of her about every day for the last six years." "Who was she?" "My husband's first wife."[51]

Very early in his career, Lincoln says he has decided never to marry because he wouldn't want to marry anyone blockhead enough to have him.[52] Nearing its close, somebody asks how he likes being president: He feels "like the man who's tarred and feathered and being rid out of town on a rail, 'If it wasn't for the honor of the thing I'd rather walk.' "[53] Is it any wonder he left his people laughing?

NOTES

1. Polls of experts by A. M. Schlesinger in 1948 for *Life* (Nov. 1), and in 1962 for the *New York Times* (July 29) ranked the top five: Lincoln, Washington, F. Roosevelt, Wilson, and Jefferson. Gary Maranell in 1970 polled the Organization of American Historians for *Journal of American History* 57 (June 1970), 104-13, and concurred in the ranking except for inserting T. Roosevelt before Wilson under "General Prestige." R. K. Murray and T. H. Blessing in 1983 polled the same organization, ranking as "Great" only Lincoln, F. Roosevelt, Washington, and Jefferson (*Time*, Dec., 19, 1983, p. 18). See also "The Presidential Performance Study," *Journal of American History* 70 (1983): 535-55.

2. Peter Karsten, *Patriot-heroes in England and America: Political Symbolism and Changing Values over Three Centuries* (Madison: University of Wisconsin Press, 1978), p. 105.

3. James David Fairbanks, "Review of Paul Boller, *Presidential Anecdotes*," *Presidential Studies Quarterly* 12 (1982): 457.

4. *Harper's New Monthly Magazine* 31 (July 1865): 269.

5. William H. Herndon, *Herndon's Life of Lincoln*, ed. Paul M. Angle (Cleveland: World Publishing Co., 1949), p. 489.

6. Roy P. Basler, ed., Marion Dolores Pratt and Lloyd A. Dunlap, asst. eds., *The Collected Works of Abraham Lincoln*, 9 vols. (New Brunswick, N.J.: Rutgers University Press, 1953-55), 4: 208-9.

7. The firm connection between national politics and the religious revival is shown in Paul Kleppner, *The Evolution of American Electoral Systems* (Westport, Conn.: Greenwood Press, 1981), pp. 118-19. The connection with stump speaking is touched upon by Mildred Freburg Berry, "Abraham Lincoln: His Development in the Skills of the Platform," in *A History and Criticism of American Public Address*, ed. William Norwood Brigance, 2 vols. (New York: Russel and Russel, 1960), 2: 841-43. This delightful essay sparked my interest in the present study, along with the work of two old friends, Robert G. Gunderson and Lewis O. Saum, who ought to know the depth of my gratitude.

8. Ward H. Lamon, *The Life of Abraham Lincoln* (Boston: J. R. Osgood and Co., 1872), p. 40.

9. Basler, *Collected Works of Lincoln*, 4: 209-10. Similar self-effacing remarks on the "ugly man" theme could be multiplied many times over. My favorite remains the one Lincoln told at the Anti-Nebraska Editors' Convention in 1856: Riding through a wood the ugly man meets a woman who stops—"Well, for land sake, you are the homeliest man I ever saw." "Yes, madam, but I can't help it" . . . "No, I suppose not," she observed, "but you

might stay at home." Otto R. Kyle, "Mr. Lincoln Steps Out," *Abraham Lincoln Quarterly* 5 (1948): 37.

10. *Milwaukee Daily National*, Oct. 1, 1859.

11. Thomas D. Clark, "The American Backwoodsman in Popular Portraiture," *Indiana Magazine of History* 42 (1946): 23. Oliver Hampton Smith, *Early Indiana Trials and Sketches* (Cincinnati: Moore, Wilstach, Keys and Co., 1856), p. 80. For a picturesque report of stump speaking at Parkersburg, Va., see Mrs. Arthur G. Beach, "An Example of Political Oratory in 1855," *Ohio Archaeological and Historical Publications* 39 (1930): 673-82; especially the description of the bald-headed old man who sat directly in front of the speaker, Henry A. Wise, "who always speaks with tobacco in his mouth" (p. 678).

12. Josiah Morrow, *Life and Speeches of Thomas Corwin: Orator, Lawyer, and Statesman* (Cincinnati: W. H. Anderson and Co., 1896), p. 386.

13. Addison P. Russell, *Thomas Corwin: A Sketch,* (Cincinnati: R. Clarke and Co., 1882), p. 41.

14. *Congressional Globe*, Feb. 15, 1840, 26th Cong. 1st sess., 785-86.

15. Basler, *Collected Works of Lincoln*, 1: 509.

16. Emanuel Hertz, ed., *The Hidden Lincoln: From the Letters and Papers of William H. Herndon* (New York: Viking Press, 1938), p. 101.

17. This and the next statement summarize my discussion in P. M. Zall, ed., *Abe Lincoln Laughing: Humorous Anecdotes from Original Sources by and about Abraham Lincoln* (Berkeley: University of California Press, 1982), p. 4.

18. Berry, "Abraham Lincoln," in Brigance, ed., *American Public Address*, pp. 844-53, compiles contemporary reports.

19. Contemporary report quoted in R. H. Luthin, "Abraham Lincoln and the Massachusetts Whigs in 1848," *New England Quarterly* 14 (1941): 619. The *Boston Daily Advertiser*, Sept. 14, reported that he had been "interrupted by warm and frequent applause"; James Schouler, "Abraham Lincoln at Tremont Temple in 1848," *Massachusetts Historical Society Proceedings* 42 (1909): 86. See also William F. Hanna, *Abraham among the Yankees* (Taunton, Mass.: Old Colony Historical Society, 1983).

20. J. T. Fields, *Yesterday with Authors* (New York: Houghton Mifflin, 1900), pp. 98-99, reprints Hawthorne's original article for the *Atlantic Monthly* of which Fields had been editor, along with Fields's request that he ameliorate the caricature of the president to avoid giving comfort to his enemies.

21. Strong was speaking of his "outside polish," finding him otherwise "a most sensible, straightforward, honest old codger"; George Templeton Strong, *Diary*, vol. 3, ed. Alan Nevins and M. H. Thomas (New York: Macmillan, 1953), p. 204. The dialect story is from pp. 204-5, dated Jan. 20, 1862.

22. Charles Edward Stowe and Lyman Beecher Stowe, *Harriet Beecher Stowe* (Boston: Houghton Mifflin Co., 1911), p. 203.

23. Berry, "Abraham Lincoln," in Brigance, ed., *American Public Address*, pp. 857-58, discusses the vexing question of Lincoln's pronunciation, piecing together a description from scattered sources.

24. Basler, *Collected Works of Lincoln*, 3: 512, n. 2.

25. Benjamin P. Thomas, *Abraham Lincoln: A Biography* (New York: Alfred A. Knopf, 1952), p. 182.

26. This and the next two quotations are from Berry, "Abraham Lincoln," in Brigance, ed., *American Public Address*, pp. 850, 829, in that order.

27. Jeriah Bonham, *Fifty Years' Recollections* (Peoria, Ill.: Franks, 1883), pp. 159-60.

28. *Abraham Africanus I: His Secret Life as Revealed Under Messmeric Influence* (New York: J. F. Feeks, 1864), p. 39.

29. Robert Hitt interview in Stewart scrapbook, Huntington Library accession 151179, 5: 64.

30. Adapted from *Old Abe's Jokes* (New York: T. R. Dawley, 1864), pp. 109-10.

31. Quoted in Robert G. Gunderson, "Reading Lincoln's Mail," *Indiana Magazine of History* 55 (1959): 388.

32. Henry Villard, *Memoirs of Henry Villard, Journalist and Financier, 1835-1900* (New York: Houghton Mifflin, 1904), pp. 142-43.

33. "Mint of Lincoln's Wit," *Magazine of History* 32, extra no. 125 (1926): 44.

34. Zall, ed., *Abe Lincoln Laughing*, p. 6.

35. Basler, *Collected Works of Lincoln*, 3: 441-42.

36. F. B. Carpenter, *Six Months at the White House with Abraham Lincoln* (New York: Hurd and Houghton, 1866), p. 49.

37. Circumstances, sources, and analogues are discussed in Zall, ed., *Abe Lincoln Laughing*, pp. 108-9.

38. P. D. Gurley diary in Ervin Chapman, *Latest Light on Lincoln*, vol. 2 (New York: Revell, 1917), p. 502.

39. Ibid., p. 26, reprints Hay's reply to a newsman asking for Lincoln stories from the White House. Even the anti-Lincoln *New York Herald* recognized their power: "With the caustic wit of Diogenes he combines the best qualities of all the other celebrated jokers of the world. He is more political than Horace, more spicy than Juvenal, more anecdotal than Aesop, more juicy than Boccacio [*sic*], more mellow than rollicking Rabelais, and more often quoted than the veteran Joe Miller" (editorial, Feb. 19, 1864).

40. Joshua Fry Speed, *Reminiscences of Abraham Lincoln* (Louisville: J. P. Morton and Co., 1884), p. 30.

41. From the oft reprinted collection mistakenly attributed to Alexander K. McClure, who wrote only the preface, *"Abe" Lincoln's Yarns and Stories* (Philadelphia: Times Publishing Co., 1901), pp. 401-2; *Ladies Literary Cabinet* 6 (Sept. 21, 1822): 158.

42. Zall, ed., *Abe Lincoln Laughing*, p. 19, compares Carl Sandburg's famous version with those by Lincoln's contemporaries; *Harper's Monthly* 38 (1868): 282, has the wheat biscuit version.

43. Adapted from *Harper's New Monthly Magazine* 36 (1868): 537.

44. Adapted from *Lincolniana; or, The Humors of Uncle Abe* (New York: J. F. Feeks, 1864), p. 88.

45. Ibid., p. 75; discussed in Zall, ed., *Abe Lincoln Laughing*, p. 42.

46. "Only $2,500,000 worth of books were manufactured in this country in 1820; by 1850 the value of book publications was set at $12,500,000"; James D. Hart, *The Popular Book: A History of America's Literary Taste* (New York: Oxford University Press, 1950), p. 90. An overview of expanding technology for this period is in Bernard A. Weisberger, *The American Newspaperman* (Chicago: University of Chicago Press, 1961), pp. 88-93; e.g., railroad tracks multiplied tenfold and the telegraph, which started in 1844, extended to 50,000 miles fifteen years later. Weisberger estimates the average newspaper circulation at the time of Lincoln's election as well under 4,000 (p. 111) and shows also that country weeklies were the most common (3,173 of them to 387 dailies). Leader in daily circulation in 1860 was the *New York Herald* with 60,000; the *Tribune*'s weekly edition boasted nearly 200,000.

47. Abraham Lincoln, *Long Remembered: Facsimiles of the Five Versions of the Gettysburg Address*, ed. David C. Mearns and Lloyd A. Dunlap (Washington: Library of Congress, 1963), p. [8].

48. *Littell's Living Age*, Feb. 6, 1864, quoted in *Abraham Lincoln, a Press Portrait*, ed. Herbert Mitgang (Chicago: Quadrangle Books, 1971), p. 377.

49. *Century* 42 (July 1891): 371-82, reprinted in Horace Greeley, *Greeley on Lincoln*, ed. Joel Benton (New York: Baker and Taylor Co., 1893), pp. 72-73.

50. "CBS Evening News," KNXT (Los Angeles), June 21, 1984.

51. See Zall, ed., *Abe Lincoln Laughing*, p. 137.

52. "I have now come to the conclusion never again to think of marrying; and for this reason; I can never be satisfied with anyone who would be block-head enough to have me." Basler, *Collected Works of Lincoln*, 1: 119, collated with manuscript at the Huntington Library, HM 25119.

53. Edmund J. Murphy transcript, Lincoln Fellowship Dinner, New York, Feb. 11, 1911; Huntington Library, HM 2037.

Commentary on "Abe Lincoln Laughing"

Norman A. Graebner

Any analysis of Abraham Lincoln, the storyteller, says little about the sectional issues that gripped the nation of his day and propelled him into national prominence and ultimately the presidency. But it says much about the man, his character and personality, his qualities of mind, his tenacity, his view of himself and society. For Lincoln storytelling apparently comprised a way of life that came naturally. His endless resort to witticisms and anecdotes suggests that he was a natural comic—a man who thoroughly enjoyed amusing others and, in the process, amusing himself. George W. Julian, the Indiana congressman, once commented on Lincoln's storytelling: "When he told a particularly good story, and the time came to laugh, he would sometimes throw his left foot across his right knee, and clenching his foot with both hands and bending forward, his whole frame seemed to be convulsed with laughter." Mrs. William H. Bailhache of Springfield, wife of the owner of the *Illinois State Journal,* wrote to her mother shortly after Lincoln's election in November 1860: "Mr. L. . . . amused us nearly all the evening telling funny stories and cracking jokes."[1]

Undoubtedly Lincoln's talent for storytelling was unique; perhaps no one in American public life has equaled it. Lincoln possessed the peculiar qualities that made his mode of storytelling effective—his backwoods origin, his gangling appearance, his mobile face and comic expression, his terse, epigrammatic style, and his marvelous sense of timing. Yet even with such assets as a humorist Lincoln would not have developed the art of storytelling unless it had satisfied some deep psychological need. Lincoln's storytelling, as Professor Zall informs us, evolved in a frontier environment, but not everyone who experienced life in the wilderness had an interest in storytelling, much less a gift for it. Lincoln turned to humor to save himself. According to his law partner, William Herndon, Lincoln was sad and cheerful by turns. He often wept over the plight of the desperate; at times his sensitivity to tragedy sent him to the depths of gloom. Judge David Davis once observed that "Lincoln's stories were merely devices to whistle down sadness."[2] Lincoln admitted to friends that except for occasional flights into joking and storytelling he could not survive.

If a humorous style might come naturally, the acquisition of humorous material does not. Lincoln devoted much time and effort in acquiring the seemingly endless supply of stories and anecdotes with which he delighted his listeners. Lincoln was no gag writer, although many of his witticisms in response to immediate and unanticipated circumstances were original. Much of Lincoln's humor simply flowed from his epigrammatic style. He created few stories of his own. He once confessed to Chauncey M. Depew, the New York politician, that he had originated only two.[3] He acquired his stories from newspapers and the comic writers of the day who wrote under a variety of pen names and pseudonyms. One of his chief sources of stories was *Joe Miller's Jests; or, The Wits Vade Mecum*, first published in 1739 but reissued many times thereafter. Sometimes Lincoln merely read aloud from the book. In memorizing a story Lincoln would grasp the essence of the humor in it and then modify the story both to fit specific situations and to suggest a high degree of originality. Despite his good memory, Lincoln wrote many stories down to assure the necessary retention. Storytelling, for Lincoln as for any humorist, required unrelenting preparation.

During his four terms in the state legislature and one term in Congress, then as a successful practicing lawyer traveling from one county seat to another in east-central Illinois, Lincoln discovered the effectiveness, power, and usefulness of the well-placed anecdote. Storytelling enabled him to clarify arguments with a minimum of words, to cheer a disconsolate friend; or, when he possessed little time or no answer, a story could dispose of troublesome visitors without actually insulting them. On the political stump Lincoln often demolished an opponent by dramatizing with a story the dearth of logic in the argument and the ridiculous extremes to which the argument would lead. One-liners, Lincoln knew, could be effective, especially when they had some resemblance to reality. Lincoln was innately conservative. Many of his stories illustrated the folly of attempting too much. Let men not promise what they ought not, he once observed, lest they be called upon to perform what they cannot. Lincoln turned his awkward appearance into an asset by making fun of it. On one occasion in 1858 he declared that if he met a man homelier than himself he would shoot him. Shortly thereafter he met this imaginary man, who agreed to be killed, commenting: "Sir, all that I have got to say is, if I am any worse looking than you are, for *God's sake, shoot me,* and git me out of the way."[4] Lincoln's occasional references to his poor, lean, lank face always brought tremendous cheering and laughter from the crowd. In the paper we just heard, Lincoln justified his storytelling by noting the effect of humor on the common people. Whatever his critics might say, storytelling provided Lincoln an important means for influencing and informing his constituents.[5]

As Professor Zall has demonstrated, Lincoln embodied in his Western tales the tendency toward exaggeration that came easily in a land of open skies and vast distances. Typical of the Western mode was Lincoln's story of the little Frenchman whose legs were so short that the seat of his trousers rubbed out his footprints in the snow. That same style appears in Lincoln's story of the farmer who boasted that his hay crop was so big that at harvest time he stacked all he could outdoors and put the rest in his barn. Much of Lincoln's exaggeration possessed a fine grain of reality. He once passed judgment on a lawyer who prepared an overlong brief: "It's like the lazy preacher that used to write long sermons and the explanation was he got to writin' and was too lazy to stop." On another occasion he characterized an unusually garrulous acquaintance: "He can compress the most words in the fewest ideas of any man I ever met." He remarked on the large funeral of a vain politician: "If General X had known how big a funeral he would have, he would have died long ago."[6]

The Lincoln-Douglas debates of August-October 1858, one of the great forensic efforts of American history, comprised the ultimate measure of Lincoln's political humor. Because the issues of the debate were emotional and divisive, Lincoln's speeches were overwhelmingly filled with lengthy and serious argumentation that often eliminated any occasion for storytelling. Lincoln spent much of his time defending himself against Douglas's charges that he was an abolitionist, that he believed in equality of the races, that he opposed the slave trade between states but favored the unconditional repeal of the Fugitive Slave Act, and that he even advocated a war between North and South to free the slaves. In response Lincoln accused Douglas of falsifying his position on matters of politics and slavery. He averred

LIBRARY ST. MARY'S COLLEGE

on one occasion that Douglas warred on his ideas "as Satan does upon the Bible." Repeatedly Lincoln called Douglas a liar. At the same time Douglas spent much time in defending himself against Lincoln's accusation that he favored slavery and its extension. Both Lincoln and Douglas repeated their arguments endlessly before different Illinois audiences, often to their mutual annoyance.[7]

Still the debates revealed Lincoln's humor at its best. Most of the laughter that Lincoln produced came from his choice of words and the nature of his argument, not from anecdotes. The tone and expression can only be surmised from the printed word, but the effect was dramatic. To Douglas's criticism early in the debates of his statement that a house divided cannot stand, Lincoln retorted that if Douglas believed that a house divided *could* stand, "there is a question of veracity, not between him and me, but between the Judge and an authority of somewhat higher character."[8]

Much of Lincoln's humor in the debates lay in his rephrasing of Douglas's words in a manner designed to draw laughter as well as applause. At the opening debate at Ottawa in August Douglas asked the audience to act "conscientiously" on his principle of popular sovereignty, permitting each state and territory to do as it pleased on the subject of slavery. To the amusement of the crowd, Lincoln responded that Douglas had no doubt been "conscientious" in all his false accusations. Douglas's charges that he favored perfect political and social equality between the races, Lincoln continued, was but "a specious and fantastic arrangement of words, by which a man can prove a horse chestnut to be a chestnut horse." Also at Ottawa Lincoln thanked Douglas for calling him "kind, amiable, and intelligent," although thereafter Douglas accused him of setting the states against one another. "I was not very much accustomed to flattery," said Lincoln, "and it came the sweeter to me. I was rather like the Hoosier, with the gingerbread, when he said he reckoned he loved it better than any other man, and got less of it."[9]

At Freeport on August 27 Lincoln noted that Douglas had accused President Buchanan and the *Washington Union* of a conspiracy to deprive the states of the right to exclude slavery until Robert Toombs of Georgia told him that it was not true. To embarrass Douglas for his change of mind—for he hoped that the attacks on the administration would continue—Lincoln recalled a story told by John Phoenix, the California railroad surveyor:

LIBRARY ST. MARY'S COLLEGE

He says they started out from the Plaza to the Mission of Dolores. They had two ways of determining distances. One was by chain and pins taken over the ground. The other was a "go-it-ometer" — an invention of his own — a three-legged instrument, with which he computed a series of triangles between the points. At night he turned to the chain-man to ascertain what distance they had come, and found that by some mistake he had merely dragged the chain over the ground without keeping any record. By the "go-it-ometer" he found he had made ten miles. Being skeptical about this, he asked a drayman who was passing how far it was to the plaza. The drayman replied it was just half a mile, and the surveyor put it down in his book — just as Judge Douglas says, after he had made his calculations and computations, he took Toombs' statement.[10]

At Quincy on October 12 Lincoln sought to ridicule Douglas's central doctrine of popular sovereignty out of existence. Through the debates Douglas had defended the Dred Scott decision but insisted in his Freeport Doctrine that a territory could bar slaves through laws unfriendly to slavery. Where, asked Lincoln, did this leave the constitutional right of citizens to take slaves into the territories? Did this mean that a territory could do indirectly what it could not do directly? Lincoln proceeded to dramatize Douglas's intellectual dilemma to the uproarious laughter of the crowd:

The truth about the matter is this: Judge Douglas has sung paeans to his "popular sovereignty" doctrine until his Supreme Court cooperating with him has *squatted* his squatter sovereignty out. But he will keep up this species of humbuggery about squatter sovereignty. He has at last invented this sort of *do nothing sovereignty* that the people may exclude slavery by a sort of "sovereignty" that is exercised by doing nothing at all. Is not that running his popular sovereignty down awfully? Has it not got down as thin as the homeopathic soup that was made by boiling the shadow of a pigeon that had starved to death? But at last, when it is brought to the test of close reasoning, there is not even that decoction of it left. It is a presumption impossible in the domain of thought. It is precisely no other than the putting of that most unphilosophical proposition, that two bodies may occupy the same space at the same time. The Dred Scott decision covers

23

the whole ground, and while it occupies it, there is no room even for the shadow of a starved pigeon to occupy the same ground.[11]

Lincoln achieved the response he desired. His occasional efforts to illustrate the falsity of Douglas's arguments with a story or epigram always brought peals of laughter. Horace White of the friendly *Chicago Tribune* exclaimed after listening to Lincoln: "[I]t is no wonder Douglas refused to stand in the way of Lincoln's logic more than seven times in three months." Douglas himself complained that Lincoln was playful in his speeches, but to that, he said, he did not object. At Ottawa Douglas commented at length on Lincoln's early career in Illinois politics. "He was then," Douglas admitted, "just as good at telling an anecdote as now."[12] Douglas insisted that he did not fear Lincoln's logic or arguments in the debates but Lincoln's humorous strictures against Douglas brought diatribes from the partisan Democratic press— which termed his style inelegant.

Indeed, even many of Lincoln's closest associates believed that his storytelling was unbecoming to a national leader. A *London Times* correspondent, covering the Illinois senatorial canvass, expressed displeasure with Lincoln's campaigning. He was troubled by Lincoln's backwoods manner. "I had expected to find Mr. Lincoln much more able than he had yet shown himself to be," he reported. A Bloomington Republican reminded the correspondent that Lincoln's oratorical style "was not calculated to make much of an impression . . . in large crowds with ladies present; 'but,' he said, 'get old Abe before a town-meeting, where every once in a while he can get off a smutty joke and raise a laugh, he'll take the crowd, and there's no man can beat him.' "[13] There was truth in this observation. The subject matter of Lincoln's stories, especially when he addressed small, male gatherings, was often indelicate. Yet Lincoln was discriminating. His Springfield friends insisted that his stories were never improper. Dr. Preston H. Bailhache stated: "Mr. Lincoln was never given to promiscuous story telling as some times represented. . . . They were always clean. . . . I never heard a word from his lips that might not be repeated in the hearing of the most fastidious."[14]

With his political future at stake in his debates with Douglas, Lincoln honed his arguments, even his phraseology, with utmost care. Knowing that his audiences expected a measured quantity of merriment, he acceded to their wishes and in the process furthered his own cause. Some of his humor, especially his characterization of popular sovereignty as homeopathic soup, was devastating. It would be well to ponder, by studying the reaction, how devastating it really was. No amount of argumentation could have dramatized the conflict between popular sovereignty and the Dred Scott decision—which Douglas's entire political position was designed to overcome—more effectively than Lincoln's humor. Lincoln lived in a time of trouble. In addition to the everlasting plights in which people find themselves, his generation faced the awful prospect of civil war. That age, like any age, needed its share of humor. If Lincoln accepted the special obligation to find the political arguments that would meet the threat of slavery expansion without appearing to be unduly radical or sectional, he also accepted the challenge to rise above the tensions and troubles of the times to create endless occasions for laughter. It was a laudable purpose, a remarkable feat, one worthy of scholarly attention.

NOTES

1. In preparing this brief analysis of Lincoln's humor I have found the following essay especially useful: Mort Reis Lewis, "Abraham Lincoln: Storyteller," in *Lincoln through the Ages*, ed. Ralph G. Newman (Garden City, N.Y.: Doubleday and Company, 1960), pp. 130-34.

2. Davis quoted in Reinhard H. Luthin, *The Real Abraham Lincoln* (Englewood Cliffs, N.J.: Prentice-Hall, 1960), p. 116.

3. See Lewis, "Abraham Lincoln: Storyteller," p. 133.

4. Quoted in Luthin, *The Real Abraham Lincoln*, p. 117.

5. See, for example, Chauncey Dewey as quoted in Lewis, "Abraham Lincoln: Storyteller," p. 134.

6. These stories appear in ibid., pp. 132-33.

7. With so much at stake in the Lincoln-Douglas debates, both Lincoln and Douglas often displayed anger at the arguments and tactics of the other. Lincoln's humor came as comic relief.

8. Paul M. Angle, ed., *Created Equal? The Complete Lincoln-Douglas Debates of 1858* (Chicago: University of Chicago Press, 1958), p. 118.

9. Ibid., pp. 117, 122.

10. Ibid., p. 174.

11. Ibid., pp. 356-57.

12. Ibid., p. 107.

13. Ibid., p. 182.

14. Bailhache quoted in Luthin, *The Real Abraham Lincoln*, p. 118.

Commentary on "Abe Lincoln Laughing"

Mark E. Neely, Jr.

Professor Zall has chosen here to characterize Lincoln's humor by emphasizing its indebtedness to his Western surroundings, "the wild frontier." There is no gainsaying the accuracy of this for a man whose humor was studded—if you'll pardon the pun—with references to horse chestnuts and chestnut horses.

Yet even when choosing to explain Lincoln by his environment, always a little dangerous in the case of a man who so often transcended it, we must be careful in selecting which aspect of that environment to emphasize. Let me suggest that Professor Zall might do well to consider not only the Western culture of Abraham Lincoln but also his political culture.

The reason no one has done this heretofore is that Lincoln's political culture was Whig political culture, and no matter what stereotype of the Whigs one accepts, it is difficult to think of the funny bone as a vital part of Whig anatomy. We have difficulty escaping an image like the one M. E. Bradford conjured up in his paper of stuffy bankers and complacent members of the elite (see pages 107-15), or on another model, moralistic Protestants.

But however contrary to our preconceptions, the Whigs were apparently funny, and Lincoln was no exception in this regard. Though Lincoln hadn't much use, for example, for his Whig rival from Chicago, Justin Butterfield, the two men shared a good sense of humor. It was Butterfield, you remember, who defied the nearly universal opposition of the Whig party to the Mexican War. When asked whether he'd oppose it, Butterfield, who had been a Federalist in New England before moving west, replied: "No, indeed! I opposed one war, and it ruined me. From now on I am for war, pestilence, *and* famine!"[1]

Nor were funny bones confined to Illinois Whigs alone. There was a substantial tradition of Whig humorists from Joseph Baldwin,

26

Charles A. Davis, and George Horatio Derby to Davy Crockett. Among the few humorous books that Lincoln certainly read in the years before his presidency are Baldwin's *Flush Times of Alabama and Mississippi* and Derby's *Phoenixiana*. (Derby's most famous prank, incidentally, occurred in San Diego in the early 1850s, when he sat in as editor for the local Democratic newspaper and gave the Democratic paper's thumping endorsement for the Whig gubernatorial candidate—while the editor was out of town.)[2]

Emphasizing the role of political culture is particularly useful because it helps explain the way that Lincoln's sense of humor set him apart from other aspects of the popular culture of his day. Political culture, Whig or Democratic, was different from the rest of American culture—Americans took their politics seriously, and the nineteenth century's preoccupation with politics is often compared in intensity to religion. Politics did have the intensity of religion for many more Americans than it does today, but it never had the *solemnity* of religion. It always had about it the boisterous prankishness of sport, the rough-and-tumble humor of the fraternity on the eve of the homecoming football game. When Billy Herndon got disgruntled in 1848 because the older men in the Whig party in Springfield seemed to leave no role for the younger ones like him, Lincoln told him this was self-indulgent nonsense: "You young men get together and form a Rough & Ready club. . . . Take in every body that you can get, . . . but as you go along, gather up all the shrewd wild boys about town, whether just of age, or little under age. . . . Let every one play the part he can play best—some speak, some sing, and all hollow."[3]

Wild *boys*—all this singing and hollering and telling jokes were vital parts of nineteenth-century American political culture, but women were largely excluded from this world. Robert H. Wiebe has argued that the absence of women was a key aspect of humor among these politicians. Relying on Ann Douglas's work, Wiebe noted that American culture in the Victorian era had been "feminized" by women and Protestant ministers, so that the dominant respectable culture was far too sentimental and prudish for the lewd and lascivious jokes of Abraham Lincoln and his political cronies. In fact, Wiebe went so far as to say that misogyny was a vital aspect of Lincoln's humor.[4]

In this, I think he went too far and mistook scatalogical humor for salacious humor. Lincoln's documented off-color humor was like that of a modern schoolboy, more dependent on turds and farts (words

27

Lincoln exploited for humor in a document in his own hand) than on violence toward or exploitation of women.[5]

Nevertheless, Lincoln's political world was a man's world and made him different from the more respectable world shaped by Protestant ministers and women. This helps explain one thing about Lincoln's humor that is missing from Zall's work. Like the rest of us twentieth-century persons, men and women alike, Zall likes Lincoln's humorousness. Lincoln's own nineteenth-century contemporaries were not as nearly unanimously fond of it.

In the Victorian era people were supposed to be earnest rather than jocular, fun-loving, pleasure-seeking, or easy-going. That is one reason why their photos seem so serious. Much respectable cultural opinion saw Lincoln as a jokester too small for his office, a trifling Nero who fiddled with funny stories while the Constitution and the republic burned.

A good argument could be made, in fact, that his humor was a political liability with large segments of the populace. And it is important to keep this in mind because it points to a fallacy that underlies much of Zall's paper—the fallacy of the "instrumental" view of Lincoln's humor.

Zall tells us it was a "pose"—that Lincoln "used" stories—that humor "helped" him—that it conveyed an "illusion." The truth of the matter is what James G. Randall said it was years ago: "Humor was no mere technique but a habit of [Lincoln's] mind."[6]

The best-known humorous episode of Lincoln's life proves this. Just before Lincoln read the first draft of the Emancipation Proclamation to his cabinet, he sat down and read a funny story called "High Handed Outrage in Utica," written by a professional humorist (Artemus Ward). Lincoln laughed but the cabinet did not.[7] This was no folksy audience Lincoln had to please or reach through the technique of homely and bucolic humor. This was an entirely private meeting with his staff, men who were lawyers and statesmen. He was just funny and some of them were not.

Less well known episodes prove it, too. Lincoln reserved most of his humor for private friends, not the public hustings. When he received a complex and legalistic forty-page letter, the busy president wrote on the back of it "Profoundly laid by" before filing it.[8] No one was going to see that but a clerk. When an office-seeker boasted in a letter that he was a direct descendent of John Randolph of Roanoke,

Lincoln knew enough Washington scuttlebut about the squeaky-voiced Randolph to know he was notoriously impotent. The president wrote on the letter: "A direct descendent of one who was never a father" and filed it where no one would see it.[9] When an army officer got in trouble for looking over a transom at a lady who was undressing, Lincoln suggested to John Hay that the officer "should be elevated to the peerage."[10]

Only Hay was going to appreciate that witticism. Only Hay and Lincoln. Or perhaps I should say, only Hay and Lincoln and all of us lucky historical voyeurs.

NOTES

1. Quoted in Donald W. Riddle, *Congressman Abraham Lincoln* (Urbana: University of Illinois Press, 1957), p. 56.

2. Stanley Trachtenberg, ed., *Dictionary of Literary Biography,* vol. 11, American Humorists, 1800-1950 (Detroit: Gale Research, 1982), pt. 1, pp. 14, 91, 104-8, 117.

3. Roy P. Basler, ed., Marion Dolores Pratt and Lloyd A. Dunlap, asst. eds., *The Collected Works of Abraham Lincoln,* 9 vols. (New Brunswick, N.J.: Rutgers University Press, 1953-55), 1: 491.

4. Robert H. Wiebe, "Lincoln's Fraternal Democracy," in *Abraham Lincoln and the American Political Tradition,* ed. John L. Thomas (Amherst: University of Massachusetts Press, 1986), pp. 11-30.

5. Basler, *Collected Works of Lincoln,* 8: 420.

6. James G. Randall, *Lincoln the President: Midstream* (New York: Dodd, Mead, 1953), p. 67.

7. David Donald, ed., *Inside Lincoln's Cabinet: The Civil War Diaries of Salmon P. Chase* (New York: Longman, Greens, 1954), p. 149.

8. Benjamin F. Butler to Abraham Lincoln, Feb. 23, 1864, Abraham Lincoln Papers, Library of Congress (microfilm).

9. Basler, *Collected Works of Lincoln,* 6: 107.

10. Ibid., 6: 539n.

CHAPTER 2

A SELECTION FROM JAMES MELLON, *THE FACE OF LINCOLN*

Selection and Captions by
GABOR S. BORITT

The picture was to the man as the grain of sand to the mountain, as the dead to the living. Graphic art was powerless before a face that moved to a thousand delicate gradations of line and contour, light and shade, sparkle of the eye and curve of lip, in the long gamut of expression from grave to gay, and back again from the rollicking jollity of laughter to that serious, faraway look that with prophetic intuitions beheld the awful panorama of war, and heard the cry of oppression and suffering. There are many pictures of Lincoln; there is no portrait of him.

—John G. Nicolay, the president's
secretary, as quoted in James Mellon,
The Face of Lincoln

GABOR S. BORITT

LINCOLN ORDINARY. "The picture ... is, I think, a very true one," Lincoln wrote in 1857, "though my wife, and many others, do not. My impression is that their objection arises from the disorderly condition of the hair." Contemporary varnished albumen print from the lost original negative made by Alexander Hesler, in Chicago, February 28, 1857. Ostendorf Collection.

THE FIRST LINCOLN LIKENESS, CIRCA 1846: THREE VERSIONS. Daguerreotype type probably made by N. H. Shepherd in Springfield, Illinois. Even the ordinary printing techniques of this book illustrate the change in the quality of the photograph books on Lincoln. *Left:* Miller (1903); *Middle:* Hamilton and Ostendorf (1963); and *Right:* Mellon (1979).

THE FIRST BRADY. "My friend Brady, the photographer, insisted that his photograph of Mr. Lincoln, taken the morning of the day he made his Cooper Institute speech in New York . . . was the means of his election." Painter Francis Carpenter. Carte-de-visite printed by Matthew B. Brady's gallery in 1860 from a lost copy negative of a retouched original print. Lincoln Kirstein.

1860: THE SCULPTOR'S LINCOLN. This full-length portrait was made for sculptor Henry Kirk Brown by an unknown Springfield photographer. Contemporary albumen print from lost original negative. Library of Congress.

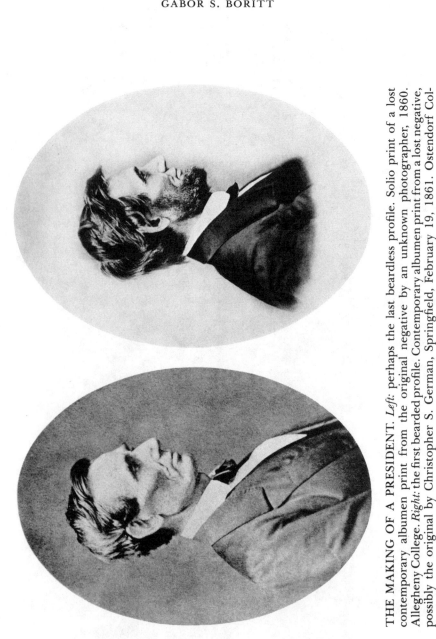

THE MAKING OF A PRESIDENT. *Left*: perhaps the last beardless profile. Solio print of a lost contemporary albumen print from the original negative by an unknown photographer, 1860. Allegheny College. *Right*: the first bearded profile. Contemporary albumen print from a lost negative, possibly the original by Christopher S. German, Springfield, February 19, 1861. Ostendorf Collection.

AND THE WAR CAME. Carte-de-visite printed from one frame of the lost original multiple-image stereographic negative by an unknown photographer at Brady's Washington gallery. c. 1862. Mellon Collection.

WITH THE ARMY. Detail from Alexander Gardner photograph taken for Brady near Antietam, October 3, 1862. Reproduced from positive on film from the original negative. Library of Congress. The general facing the president is George B. McClellan.

AT THE GARDNER STUDIO, 1863. Gelatin silver print made by M. P. Rice in 1901 from the lost original negative made by Gardner, in Washington, August 9, 1863. Mellon Collection.

AT THE BRADY STUDIO, 1864. Gelatin silver print of a lost contemporary albumen print from the lost original negative by Anthony Berger, Washington, February 9, 1864. Library of Congress.

FATHER AND SON. Contemporary albumen print of Lincoln and Tad, from lost original negative (believed to have been a multiple-image stereographic plate) made by Berger at the Brady gallery, Washington, February 9, 1864. Ostendorf Collection.

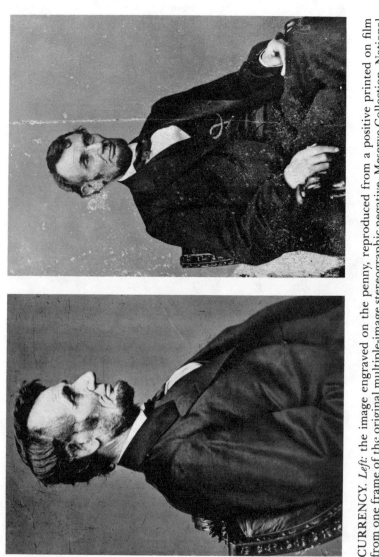

CURRENCY. *Left:* the image engraved on the penny, reproduced from a positive printed on film from one frame of the original multiple-image stereographic negative. Meserve Collection, National Portrait Gallery. *Right:* the image engraved on the $5 bill, reproduced from a positive printed on film from deteriorating original glass collodian negative. Library of Congress. Both photographs were made by Berger at the Brady gallery, Washington, February 9, 1864.

FRAGMENT. Reproduced from a positive printed on film from the original negative made for painter Francis Carpenter, by Berger at the Brady gallery, Washington, April 20, 1864. Ostendorf Collection.

H. F. WARREN, PHO.,   WALTHAM, MASS.

PRESIDENT LINCOLN.

Pho. on the Balcony at the White House, March 6, 1865.

SPRING WINDS ON THE WHITE HOUSE BALCONY. Rare, un-retouched carte-de-visite printed from the original negative by Henry F. Warren, March 6, 1865. Ostendorf Collection.

44

RECAPITULATION: THE TOLL OF WAR

1860. Reproduced from gelatin silver print of positive printed on glass, about 1900, from the original negative by Alexander Hesler, in Springfield, June 3, 1860. Mellon Collection.

1863. Reproduced from a positive printed on film from the cropped negative made by M. P. Rice, about 1890, probably from a glass positive printed from the lost original negative made by Gardner, in Washington, November 8, 1863. Ostendorf Collection.

1865. Contemporary albumen print made from the broken, and soon discarded, original negative made by Gardner, in Washington, between early February and mid-April, 1865. Meserve Collection, National Portrait Gallery.

CHAPTER 3

THE LINCOLN IMAGE:
Abraham Lincoln and the Popular Print

HAROLD HOLZER, GABOR S. BORITT,
AND MARK E. NEELY, JR.

AMERICA DISGUSTED Frances Trollope, and nothing disgusted her more than "the election fever" she found "constantly raging through the land." "It engrosses every conversation," she complained, "it irritates every temper, it substitutes party spirit for personal esteem; and, in fact, vitiates the whole system of society."[1] Mrs. Trollope was writing in 1832 after a long stay in England's former colony across the Atlantic, but had she visited some thirty years later, she might have been even more dismayed to see the evidence of election fever in the prints that now decorated the walls of American homes.

There was nothing like this election fever in Frances Trollope's native land, neither at the time of her travels to America, before the Reform Bill of 1832, nor afterward, in Lincoln's era (and the mid-Victorian governments of Derby and Palmerston and Russell). In England there were fewer voters; even after the Reform Bill of 1832 only one adult in five could vote. In America, just eight years after Mrs. Trollope's book appeared, about four out of five white males did vote in a presidential election.

Elections in England were also few, far between, and irregularly scheduled. The British custom of uncontested elections was an index of the absence of mass political parties (which came to Victoria's isle only after the Reform Bill of 1867) and of the relative unimportance of politics in the daily lives of the English.[2] Furthermore, there was no contest for national office like the American presidential race to focus countrywide attention on politics and to encourage an industry to capitalize on, advertise, or create political heroes for a mass consumer audience.

The fame of Charles Dickens's depiction of the election in Eatanswill in *The Pickwick Papers* and of Anthony Trollope's descriptions of British elections presents a classic case of the ability of literary evidence to blind historians to social reality. The fact of the matter is that by comparison with her former colony, England in the Victorian era had a none-too-rich "political culture."

Political life labored under more difficult circumstances on the Continent. France under Louis-Napoleon's Empire had a broad suffrage, but organization in mass meetings was illegal until the 1860s and the government's official candidates had overwhelming advantages that sometimes resulted in unanimous votes. In short, there was no vigorous party contention. Occasionally a rich opposition candidate, like the Comte de Chambrun, distributed to the illiterate peasants a folio of engravings illustrating his virtuous acts: giving aid in the cholera epidemic and speaking in the assembly for the first railroad in the department. But press censorship was an ultimate damper on partisanship. French printmakers constantly ran afoul of the law, from the earliest stirrings of political life through the Second Empire. In 1816 Jean-Charles Pellerin, producer of the famous Epinal prints, was sentenced to four months in prison for issuing military prints in which the soldiers sported the Napoleonic cockade forbidden by the restored Bourbon king. Daumier was condemned to six months' imprisonment for a caricature of Louis Philippe in 1832. Philipon drew his famous "pear" caricature of the bourgeois king in a law court, defending himself from indictment for inciting contempt against the king's person.[3] His defense was that the king really did look like a pear. The incident helps illustrate the sharply different political culture of mid-nineteenth century America. Its like did not evolve in any other country, or for that matter, in the United States at any other time.

Nor is the American political culture of the present day a particularly rich one, either. No one today expects to see framed portraits of Ronald Reagan anywhere save at party headquarters or in government buildings—least of all in private homes. Ask for a family's photograph album and you will not likely find pictures of the president of the United States or his cabinet alongside snapshots of the baby's christening or the Fourth of July picnic. No family sits around the piano to sing and play the "Mondale Quick Step" or the "Reagan Schottisch."

In contrast, political icons permeated the everyday environment of nineteenth-century America. Sheet music with lithographed portraits of party heroes on the covers beckoned buyers of the "Lincoln Quick Step," the "Douglas Polka," and the "McClellan Schottisch" (some were tunes without words so that the mere portrait of the party hero became a sort of endorsement for the music). And all Civil War collectors are familiar with the photograph albums of that era which contain cartes-de-visite of Lincoln and famous generals in honored places ahead of the now unrecognizable family portraits at the back.

The importance of politics in the everyday lives of nineteenth-century Americans almost calls for the approach of anthropology rather than history alone. "Dig" into a private home in the nineteenth century and one might well find some political artifacts. Dig into a modern home and one would be lucky to find even a voter registration certificate.

The political culture of nineteenth-century America was unique. In the absence of organized spectator sports and with only the most rudimentary entertainment industry, politics—with its hours of dazzling oratory, campaign songs, torchlight parades, fireworks, banners, badges, posters, and prints—offered spectacle, ritual, and time-filling amusements to an America consisting mostly of island communities locked in rural isolation. It was as though football and the process of choosing leaders had been combined into a single emotion-filled phenomenon. In an age without cinema or television, when few periodicals were illustrated (none in color) and newspapers were still unable to reproduce photographs on their pages, pictures were precious rather than, as now, contemptibly common, and Americans sought images of their political heroes as the youth of today seek posters of rock stars.

Politics in Lincoln's era had more emotion invested in it than mere entertainment or sports do today and in fact took on a nearly religious significance. "One of the functions of political prints," Robert Philippe observed in *Political Graphics: Art as a Weapon*, "has always been to decorate the walls of people's houses. . . . They testify to convictions, and provide reassurance of ways of being" as "heirs of the sacred picture."[4] Modern Americans are reluctant to "testify" to their political convictions publicly or to hang pictures of party heroes in their homes, but the peculiarities of nineteenth-century political culture demanded a public display of partisanship.

Every time Abraham Lincoln won an election before the presidential contest in 1860, he won by receiving oral votes. Kentucky, Missouri, Virginia, Arkansas, and Oregon retained oral voting into or through the Civil War, but Illinois was rather peculiar among Northern states in retaining it as late as 1848. Paper ballots had been introduced almost everywhere by 1860, but paper ballots were hardly secret ballots. All voters could and many did in fact pick up their paper ballots at the polling place at temporary sheds boldly identified by party posters. Since wooden ballot boxes could have false bottoms, clear glass bowls were favored, and in New York City, at least, there was a separate bowl inside the polling place for each party's votes. Maryland forbade the printing of ballots on colored paper in order to provide some measure of secrecy, but such was not the case in other states, and even in Maryland the ballots could feature images or devices on them identifiable from afar.[5] Newspapers were almost all identified with and supported financially by a political party, so that the paper one bought, quoted, and carried under one's arm was a public sign of partisanship as well.

Given such conditions, it would not have been surprising for political prints also to have evolved directly from political movements. What makes these pictures remarkable is that this was not the case. The political prints produced by this peculiar culture came from the bottom up, not from the politicians down, and therefore constituted genuinely popular images. Even Lincoln, who sat for more than one hundred photographs, did so, for all the sittings for which circumstances are known, at the request of someone else. This fit well with his sense of humility. Just two short months before his nomination for the presidency in 1860, he wrote to a political admirer that he did not have "a single" photograph to send him. The first mass-produced print of Lincoln was made on the very eve of the Chicago convention that nominated him and was showered on the delegates when Lincoln's name was placed in nomination. Lithographers and engravers, who made it their business to supply the political heroes' pictures to the masses, were constantly scrambling for photographs or portraits on which to base their Lincoln prints. Therefore their works were repetitiously modeled on a handful of available photographs, and piracy and fakery were common.

The rhythms of print production were dictated by business concerns and popular demand rather than by the politicians, their managers, or the parties. Nowhere is this clearer than in the case of Lincoln family prints. These sentimental images of *Abraham Lincoln as a Father, The Lincoln Family, Lincoln at Home,* or *President Lincoln and Family Circle* could have provided effective rebuttals to the Democratic party's common depiction of President Lincoln as a tyrant and despot. Yet not a single one of these many family prints appeared prior to the president's death. Lincoln seemed almost unaware of his political image in the modern sense, failing to provide a decent model for the printmakers who could have melted his detractors' hearts by showing him to be a part of the one Victorian institution that was above criticism, the family. He never sat for a photograph with his wife and was only twice photographed with his son Tad.

The industry, however, knew the market much better than the politicians of Lincoln's time did. Printmakers could recall the great and lasting success of Savage and Edwin's *Washington Family,*[6] and as soon as Lincoln was dead, they seized on the photographs of the president with his son, added the other family members from other individual photographs, drew in Victorian parlor backdrops entirely unknown to Lincoln or his family, and thus produced imaginary scenes of a domesticated Abraham Lincoln. Not a single one of these many Lincoln family prints appeared prior to the president's death.

Earlier, of course, purchasing a Lincoln print was a strictly partisan act, especially in 1860 when the first such picture appeared. But producing them was not, and lithographers like Currier and Ives simply added portraits of all the parties' candidates to their stock, hoping to attract buyers of all political persuasions. Since Lincoln was a dark-horse candidate whose physical appearance was virtually unknown outside Illinois, printmakers sought out the few existing photographic models and produced monotonous adaptations of them. It was a rare printmaker who commissioned his own artist to travel to Springfield to paint the candidate's likeness as a model for a campaign print.

All this had to be done hurriedly, as the demand for pictures, fierce as it was in July, might fall off precipitously in November if Lincoln lost. Naturally, the artist who would drop everything, take a long train ride to Illinois, and fashion a hasty portrait tended to be young, obscure, and not particularly talented. Charles Alfred Barry was typical: a Massachusetts public-school drawing master, he was commissioned by Boston lithographer John H. Bufford to travel to Springfield to capture Lincoln's likeness. It was perhaps inevitable

53

that any Massachusetts man would see something of Andrew Jackson in a Western presidential candidate, but the resemblance was especially strong in Barry's portrait and in the print based on it. The times seemed to demand a Jackson to face down this new secession threat, and a Boston newspaper critic's comment that there was plenty of "the General Jackson firmness" in Barry's portrait of Lincoln shows that some Americans wanted to hear Barry's message. Rival print-makers thought so, too. One of them pirated the Barry and reissued it in a crude copy. Loosely enforced copyright laws made such piracies possible; public interest in Lincoln pictures made them profitable.

Sometimes the urge to find more in Lincoln's face than was really there was conscious. When a Republican leader from Pennsylvania hired a miniaturist named John Henry Brown to make a portrait of Lincoln to serve as a basis for a campaign print for that state, he charged his agent "to make it good looking whether the original would justify it or not." Lincoln's ugliness was already legendary, and some of the prints aimed, for the sake of sales to the ladies if not for the sake of men's votes, to improve the candidate's looks. Judging alone from the number of surviving copies, prints of candidate Lincoln sold well enough to profit both the candidate and the publishers.

When Lincoln decided to grow a beard after his election, he made all the printmakers' works obsolete overnight. Because political prints were shaped by the marketplace and not by political managers, lithographers and engravers were forced for the first of three instances during the Civil War era to catch up frantically to events. The business motives that determined print production were nowhere more apparent than in this first episode. The public was curious and the lithographers and engravers saw an unwonted opportunity to sell political pictures at a time when demand would ordinarily have slackened. Had Lincoln not altered his visage so dramatically, extant campaign portraits might have sufficed—perhaps with only a few words eliminated from their titles—to satisfy the public appetite for pictures of the "Sixteenth President" rather than the "Republican Candidate for Sixteenth President." Since profit rather than accuracy in presidential image-making was the true motive for new picture production, printmakers behaved in the most economically conservative—that is to say, the most cost-conscious—manner. Lithographic stones and steel plates endured while politics changed constantly, and printmakers did all they could to preserve their investment in the expensive plates and rare artistic talent for the campaign. Their impulse was to add beards to already existing plates and quickly revise lithographic stones. In the rush to beat the competition, they added whiskers without waiting for the necessary photographic models which were always slow to come from the politicians—with rather comic results, to modern eyes.

In America's partisan culture, anti-Lincoln images were as much a part of the print business as prettifying portraits. Currier and Ives produced for the 1860 campaign more anti- than pro-Lincoln cartoons and as many anti-Lincoln cartoons as portraits.[7] In these poster cartoons of the day, more than in the rather straightforward and sober portraiture, one sees the importance of Lincoln's image as a railsplitter. The image represented nicely the pivotal Republican message: the American dream of the right to rise. Accordingly, the rail became a ubiquitous identifying symbol in both pro- and anti-Lincoln cartoons. Along with the rail, however, came a message threatening to many Americans, the potential for racial equality, symbolized in anti-Lincoln cartoons by a black figure and reformer Horace Greeley.

In the case of political caricature, it is difficult at first to perceive the differences among nineteenth-century cultures. English, French, and American publishers all produced a substantial body of political caricature. Most histories of caricature note that the United States had nothing to match the quality of the European tradition of Philipon, Daumier, Gillray, Rowlandson, Cruikshank, and the London *Punch*. Nor did this begin to change until the Civil War was over, Thomas Nast emerged, and *Puck* and *Judge* were established (in 1877 and 1881, respectively). Yet if the political culture of America was more vibrant than Europe's, why were these most thoroughly political of prints somehow weaker in America than elsewhere?

A partial answer lies in examining medium and subject matter and abandoning the rather subjective comparisons of caricature quality. In France, the substantial lack of press freedom shaped political cartooning toward social caricature, for the magazines in which political cartoons appeared were subject to censorship, and the artists and editors, to state trials. Therefore, the great French artists often avoided direct political statement.

In England, freedom of expression was no problem, but the appearance of *Punch* on the scene in 1841 essentially ended the production of separately published poster cartoons.[8] *Punch* was politically

In an era of primitive mass communications and widespread popular enthusiasm for politics, the torchlight parade—with its banners, fireworks,
and floats—was a spectacular community event. In this 1860 wood engraving
(20 x 14¼) from *Frank Leslie's Illustrated Newspaper,* such a parade is seen
passing before the local newspaper office as the crowd views a pro-Homestead
float: an ersatz farmhouse being pulled by a team of seven horses. This and
all subsequent photographs, unless otherwise noted, are courtesy of the Louis
A. Warren Lincoln Library and Museum.

CITIZENS
VOTING.

There was no secret ballot in mid-nineteenth-century presidential elections. This *Harper's Weekly* wood engraving from 1860 (5″ diameter) shows a figure representing an Irish Democrat, right, placing his ballot in a jar clearly marked for General McClellan. A more worthy-looking citizen, left, places his vote in the Lincoln jar. Ballots were simply dropped into clear glass bowls, and occasionally, as portrayed here, pictures of the candidates helped identify each receptacle.

Perhaps no institution was more precious to Victorian-era Americans than the family, yet these families adorned their parlor walls with political prints, which were true heirs to the religious pictures of previous centuries. Parlors frequently included pianos, too, and for these, American publishers provided campaign sheet music with lithographed covers. The *Lincoln Polka* (10½ x 14) appealed to Republican families, the *Douglas Polka* (10⁹⁄₁₆ x 13¹¹⁄₁₆), the *Douglass* [sic] *Grand March* (10⁷⁄₁₆ x 13½), and four years later, the *McClellan Schottisch* (10½ x 13¹⁵⁄₁₆) to Democrats. The *Lincoln Polka* is courtesy of the Old Print Shop, New York City.

58

Currier and Ives issued both flattering Lincoln portraiture and anti-Lincoln caricature. In this lithographed cartoon, *Political "Blondins" Crossing Salt River* (17 11/16 x 13 9/16), presidential rivals Lincoln, Douglas, and John C. Breckinridge were all depicted as daredevils teetering as they tried to bridge the chasm between North and South (Lincoln balanced on one of his ubiquitous log rails). Only Constitutional Union nominee John Bell uses the bridge "built by Washington, Jefferson, and the Patriots of '76" to keep the nation united.

The political managers of 1860 left it to the printmakers, who wanted to sell prints, to beautify the Republican presidential candidate. In the crucial swing state of Pennsylvania, however, a renowned miniaturist, John Henry Brown, was hired by a Republican leader to make a "good looking" painting of Lincoln "whether the original . . . justify it or not." When the handsome portrait was done, wife Mary, secretary John G. Nicolay, and humble Mr. Lincoln himself pronounced the likeness perfect. One of America's premier printmakers, Samuel Sartain, was engaged to create a mezzotint (4 x 5⅝) from the painting for wide distribution. Courtesy of Mr. and Mrs. Gabor S. Boritt.

From the perspective of 1865 a history of the rebellion could be neatly summed up in this lithograph (24½ x 16⅞). The Union cracked, mothers grieved, but broken shackles lay at triumphant Columbia's feet. Justice, sword in hand, faced traitors and thieves, while Lincoln presided over a selfless and patriotic people.

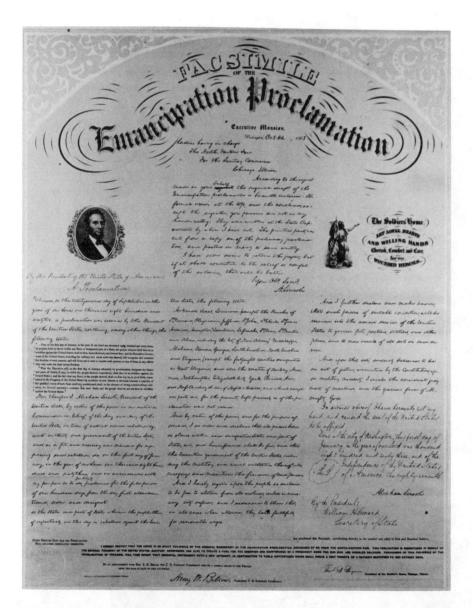

Chicago lithographer Edward Mendel was one of many printmakers who issued facsimiles of the mundane text of the Emancipation Proclamation in 1863 and 1864. After an initial outpouring of engravings and lithographs of the words alone, some, like Mendel, added emblematic portraits (29 x 23). This likeness was modeled after an 1864 photograph by Wenderoth and Taylor of Philadelphia.

The COMMANDER-IN-CHIEF conciliating the **SOLDIER'S VOTES** on the Battle Field

"Now, Marshal, sing us 'Picayune Butler,' or something else that's funny"

Although unrelentingly attacked in caricatures and cartoons from his first campaign until his death, Lincoln raised no objections. However, he felt deeply hurt by the false rumor that inspired this vicious lithograph (10^{15}/$_{16}$ x 16^{3}/$_{8}$), which showed the president asking his friend Ward Hill Lamon to sing comic songs as they walked among the dead and wounded of Antietam. This print was probably prepared for circulation during the 1864 campaign.

Lincoln and His Generals, lithographed by Peter Kramer (19⅛ x 15⅝), and published simultaneously in New York and Boston, purported to show a pre-Appomattox field conference between Lincoln and his key commanders. While such a summit never took place, the print, with its Lincoln modeled on the familiar Brady Gallery "penny profile," undoubtedly helped etch in the American mind the enduring image of the martyred president as military mastermind, marshalling his lieutenants for the final, successful offensive to restore the Union. Courtesy of the Library of Congress.

Lincoln was portrayed infrequently in British engravings and lithographs, but so were, to a lesser degree, the leading English political leaders of the day, including Disraeli, Gladstone, and Peel. Queen Victoria (4 x 7) was the only British subject depicted as often in her country as Lincoln was in his. The British Museum collection of engravings contains 372 portraits of the queen and only a handful of Lincoln prints. Courtesy of the New York Public Library.

It is tempting to say that domestic images, like this lithograph (23¾ x 17½), were elegant testimonies that the warm family man, Lincoln, was not, as his opponents depicted him and his assassin truly believed him to be, a tyrant. But not a single one of the family prints bears a date before 1865. Their quiet power to answer political criticism was obscured for the party managers by the Victorian generation's regard for the family's privacy, and also by their own rudimentary understanding of the power of the political print. The Lincoln family portraits, however, helped create a lasting cult of the first family.

THE MARTYR OF LIBERTY.

Hath borne his faculties so meek; has been
So clear in his great office; that his virtues
Shall plead, trumpet-tongued, against
The deep damnation of his taking off."

An unknown lithographer pictures here Lincoln's murder in 1865 with mundane
accuracy—a "fault" the many assassination prints rarely suffered from (8¼ x 9⅞).
The moment of murder helped transform Lincoln into the "Martyr of Liberty"
and, in time, the greatest of Americans.

Lincoln's assassination in 1865 deprived the nation of its father figure at the time of his—and his nation's—great triumph. A vast outpouring of prints intended for the American people was supplemented by lithographed sheet music such as *President Lincoln's Funeral March* (10¼ x 13⁷⁄₁₀).

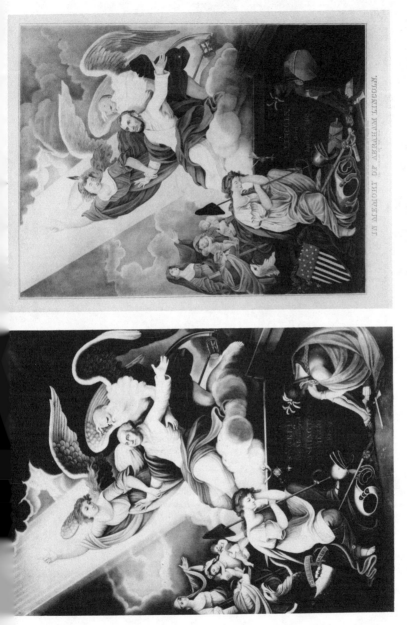

To create this apotheosis scene in 1865 lithographer D. T. Wiest took an 1802 engraving of Washington by John J. Barralet (18½ x 24), replaced the head of the first president with that of the sixteenth, and was ready to profit. Though the symbolism of the "new" print (18⅜ x 24) was now wrong—notice, for example, the fifteen stars of the American shield, the mourning Indian, and the emblem of the Society of Cincinnati in the middle—most print buyers probably did not notice. Courtesy of the Library of Congress.

Lithographed sheet music (left, 9¾ x 14, oval portrait 5 x 6) underscored the Republican manufactured image of "Honest Abe, the Rail-splitter of the West" in the 1860 campaign. Connoting integrity and the American dream of the right to rise, the image helped elect Lincoln president. Five years later, as the engraving from c.1865 suggests (12⅛ x 16⅛) his reputation for integrity continued to flourish, as it does to this day, because it was based on reality.

independent and lampooned politicians across the party spectrum; it thus captured a broad audience.⁹

Separately published political cartoons thrived in America through the Civil War, right up to the establishment of *Puck* and *Judge*.¹⁰ Americans were well aware of the success of *Punch*, and L. H. Stephens attempted to imitate it with the establishment of the magazine *Vanity Fair* in New York in 1859. It did not work. Instead of vanquishing the production of separate political cartoons, *Vanity Fair* itself went out of business on July 4, 1863.¹¹ Currier and Ives and other publishers of political cartoons continued their work through Reconstruction.

The American and European experiences were different, and the differences in political culture help explain it. *Vanity Fair's* editors followed the example of *Punch* too closely, right down to its stance of relative political independence. There were almost no independents in American politics, and readers in the United States were accustomed to getting their politics in entirely partisan form. Democrats could buy anti-Lincoln Currier and Ives cartoons (sold at the nineteenth-century equivalent of party headquarters, the newspaper office) and Republicans could buy anti-Democratic cartoons. The newspapers could stock what pleased them and their partisan readers and not what pleased the editors of *Vanity Fair. Vanity Fair's* readers were forced to see their own party heroes caricatured. *Puck* and *Judge,* the humorous serial publications that would bring real success to comic journalism in America about two decades later, were different from *Vanity Fair* in one crucial particular: *Puck* was Democratic and *Judge* was Republican. As Englishman Goldwyn Smith noted when he compared American politics to those of Britain in this period, "The power of party organizations is disproportionately strong; there is nothing to withstand them."¹²

Purchasing a Lincoln print, whether caricature or portrait, was always essentially a partisan act, but after the outbreak of the rebellion it carried with it the special weight of a vote of confidence in the outcome of the greatest war in American history. Again, however, the marketplace dictated publishing vigor, and with war spawning new military celebrities, Lincoln as a subject for portrait prints was supplanted for a time by early heroes and martyrs, including Robert Anderson and Elmer Ellsworth, the latter the first casualty of the Civil War. Then, when the president announced the preliminary Emancipation Proclamation on September 22, 1862, Lincoln ensured that the war would be the greatest revolution in America since 1776. To antislavery partisans he was no longer an ordinary president but the Great Emancipator. Once more, as with his decision to grow whiskers, he caught the printmakers, like nearly everyone else in the United States, by surprise, creating the kind of "great sensation" that correspondent Noah Brooks noted when the final draft of the proclamation was reprinted in a newspaper, inspiring "a grand rush for it."[13] The strenuous efforts of the engravers and lithographers to catch up to events yet again resulted in a rich variety of prints published over a period of two or more years. These images help us recapture the spirit of an age that found the Emancipation Proclamation genuinely fresh and liberating and not, as the modern era often does, reluctantly issued, inadequate for the problem, and lacking in humanitarian motivation. At least twenty-six different lithographs and engravings reproducing just the text of the Emancipation Proclamation, some in calligraphy, were published in 1863 and 1864, and other portraits and historical pictures celebrated the document as well. Although it is difficult to ascertain the number of copies published of any particular print, the variety of emancipation prints is suggestive of the widespread perception, among antislavery partisans at least, that this document ranked with the Declaration of Independence.

The year of 1864 was not the landmark of Lincoln print production that one might expect of a presidential election year, especially if one erroneously thinks of prints as products of political management. By then, an unusually large number of Lincoln portraits were already on the market. Prominent among them were the prints celebrating the Emancipation Proclamation, many bearing 1864 dates. Lincoln's presidential beard had also inspired relatively recent pictures that might have met the demand for portraits of the incumbent candidate. Francis B. Carpenter, an artist who lived in Lincoln's White House for six months while painting what became a model for the most famous Emancipation Proclamation print, recalled a telling Lincoln story: "A visitor, congratulating Mr. Lincoln on the prospects of his reelection, was answered with an anecdote of an Illinois farmer who undertook to blaze his own rocks. His first effort at an explosion proved a failure. He explained the cause by exclaiming, 'Pshaw, this powder has been shot before.' " Such was the case, apparently, with

President Lincoln as a subject for new popular pictures in 1864: the powder had been shot before.

Cartoons were different, however. They spoke to more immediate issues and had little life beyond political campaigns. Frank Weitenkampf's *Political Caricature in the United States in Separately Published Cartoons* notes thirty-nine different cartoons for 1860 and fifty-one for 1864, a sign that Lincoln's second campaign was probably no less hard fought than his first.[14] Cartoonists had learned more about Lincoln by 1864 and their images were different. Gone were the ubiquitous rail and Lincoln's homespun garb. Now the president was regularly portrayed in a dress suit, and there were fresh references to his fondness for Shakespeare. Cartoons frequently seized on his reputation for telling humorous stories, a political liability in the Victorian era when men were supposed to be earnest.

Generally, the humor theme dictated a depiction of Lincoln as a man too frivolous for his serious office. In one instance, this led to a bitterly memorable lithograph, *The Commander-in-Chief Conciliating the Soldier's Votes on the Battle Field,* of Lincoln in the midst of the casualty-strewn Antietam battlefield asking a grieving officer to sing " 'Picayune Butler,' or something else that's funny." The cartoon was based on a false but effective newspaper story that the president had asked an old crony to sing a comic song to cheer him up after his depressing visit to the battlefield. Lincoln, who usually claimed he ignored criticism, wrote out a long refutation of this story, deciding only at the last moment not to give it to the press. A cartoon based on this story was a potent weapon for the Democrats; but the soldier vote and the nation went Republican anyway.

Lincoln's assassination provided the final unexpected stimulus to print production, dramatically and permanently altering its guiding spirit. To be sure, it was business as usual for the lithographers and engravers, but now the demand for their prints went beyond the customary partisan boundaries of American political culture. Printmakers immediately associated the martyred president with America's first president and her original national icon, George Washington.[15] It is still doubtful that pictures of Lincoln hung in Democratic homes immediately after the Civil War, but the reasons for Republicans to want his picture after 1865 went far, far deeper than ordinary partisan identification.

Propriety suddenly dictated silence for Lincoln's critics. He quickly soared into an American heaven of reputation, portrayed with a mixture of classical, Christian, and native imagery to become a centerpiece of what some scholars describe as America's "civil religion," the mingling of vague piety with political symbols and words.[16]

Perhaps the surest sign of Lincoln's new status was D. T. Wiest's *In Memory of Abraham Lincoln: The Reward of the Just.* In 1865 Philadelphia publisher William Smith apparently hired Wiest to make a lithographic copy of John James Barralet's famed engraving of the *Apotheosis of George Washington,* substituting Lincoln's head for that of the first president and changing the name on the tomb. The hopelessly outdated and inappropriate imagery, however, remained intact, retaining a crouching Indian to do the mourning (more logically done for Lincoln by a black man) and leaving the armor (far more appropriate for General Washington than the unsoldierly Lincoln). The incongruous iconography was surely little noticed by a mass audience who would pay good money for the likes of the dwarfish figures, ridiculous perspective, and dubious reportage in period assassination and deathbed prints.

Currier and Ives alone published four different Lincoln deathbed prints, and there were many others. By contrast, the British Museum contains only one print of Palmerston published the year he died, also 1865. He was prime minister at his death—admittedly, in markedly different circumstances from Lincoln—but the contrast is still worthy of note. In fact, there are only seventeen different engraved or lithographed portraits of Palmerston in the British Museum's collections. American printmakers produced more lithographed and engraved portraits of Lincoln for the campaign of 1860 alone—at least nineteen different portraits, excluding sheet music and cartoons—before he was head of state or, indeed, anything more than a little-known prairie politician running for the presidency.

The pre-1912 prints of British statesmen that the British Museum gathered in what was "beyond all comparison the most important and extensive collection of British engraved portraits which exists" are convincing testimony to the differences in political culture between Europe and America. The Earl of Derby, three times prime minister in Lincoln's era, is represented in only ten portrait prints, Robert

Peel in twenty-seven, Benjamin Disraeli in twenty-one, and William Gladstone in thirty-six.[17] Population and other differences notwithstanding, these numbers are astonishing, especially when one considers that they include pictures removed from books and periodicals as well as separately published prints, but the numbers for Gladstone and Disraeli are especially so. These were, after all, political figures in the era of the Second Reform Bill (1867) which gave England a much broader suffrage and a real start on mass political parties, and Gladstone was a famous political campaigner by British standards.

The number of Lincoln prints by 1912 were approximated, if at all, only by those of Queen Victoria, whose sixty-four-year reign inspired the production of 372 print portraits now in the British Museum. But Great Britain's politicians are a different story. If one includes cartoons, one finds that a single American firm, Currier and Ives, published as many different pictures of Lincoln for his first campaign, twenty-one, as there are portraits of Disraeli in the entire British Museum. There are more prints of the Lincoln family, at least twenty-four, most of them published between 1865 and 1870, than there are portraits of Disraeli in the British Museum. The only available study of British sheet music, Alexander Hyatt King's "English Pictorial Music Title Pages, 1820-1885: Their Style, Evolution and Importance," published in London in 1950, fails even to mention political music as a genre; whereas a far from complete *Lincoln Sheet Music Check List* compiled in 1940 notes ten Lincoln pieces for 1860, twenty for 1864, and in 1865 a whopping sixty-eight Lincoln requiems, memorial hymns, and funeral marches.[18] In iconography, the martyred Lincoln quickly attained a status achieved only by long-reigning royalty in Europe.

Prints not only are an index of the Lincoln image, in the broadest sense, but were also creators of it, at least in part, from its partisan origins in political campaigns to its elevation to sainthood. Long ignored by professional historians, the visual record clearly deserves careful attention, but the rules of evidence are different. For the mid-nineteenth century, anyway, the historian must resist the temptation to interpret this sort of evidence by the same political assumptions applied to stump speeches and platform pronouncements. On the whole, these pictorial artifacts originated not politically but commercially, and the impulse of the businessman to protect his investment in stock plates and proven artistic designs sometimes dictated distortions of the pictorial record that signify nothing politically but which, like the crouching Indian in *The Reward of the Just,* have startling visual impact.

Those pioneers who made the earliest forays into the wilderness of political prints, the print curators and collectors, generally lacked the historian's training in historical method. They tended not to ask of the iconographic evidence the questions that historians were likely to ask—in short, how these materials were related to American politics. And their use of prints as historical evidence was skewed by the tradition of connoisseurship. We remain convinced that lithographs and engravings are significant as artifacts of American political culture—a culture different from that of Europe—and also as indices to and influences on the evolving Lincoln image. They are best seen as belonging to what Daniel Boorstin might call the lost political world of Abraham Lincoln.

Generations later, in 1936, the newspaper in Lincoln's hometown noted the change in American political life from that time in 1860 when a summer rally for Springfield's most famous citizen attracted 75,000 supporters. Most had come to the city "across the prairies in wagons or on horseback." But in 1936, the time of Franklin Delano Roosevelt, the city's newspaper observed a marked difference in political customs:

> Whatever the reason—whether the refining influence of women in politics, a more diversified interest, or whatnot—the people nowadays take their politics much more calmly than they did half a century or a century ago.
>
> In the olden days the torchlight parade was the big attraction of the political demonstration, especially in presidential campaigns. A political rally then drew a large attendance from far and near, despite difficult means of transportation and despite the then sparse population. The parade line was colorful with its torchlights, decorated floats, and banners. Farmers rode their most attractive horses, and the marchers gave vent to their enthusiasm.
>
> The torchlight parade was revived in Springfield and Sangamon county in the presidential election campaign of 1932, but the old fire was lacking. The excitement of decades ago was not in evidence.[19]

When that old world vanished, so too did the political print in the parlor, the political cartoon for sale at the party newspaper office, and the illustrated political song played on the family piano.

In *The Lincoln Image* we argued that the unique status of nineteenth-century American political prints was best explained by a contrast between the political culture of Lincoln's time and that of twentieth-century America. This paper has looked at the status of engraved and lithographed political portraits in Europe in Lincoln's time to confirm the appropriateness of an emphasis on political culture as a means to account for the very existence of such pictures. It helps explain as well—in the face of a dearth of written or printed evidence—the uses of these pictures in their day. As it is, much remains unexplained. We still have not, for example, ever seen a single reference in a letter, book, or newspaper to the actual use of an American poster cartoon. We cannot document a single case in which an American saw one in a tavern, in a shop window, in a home, or on a fence or building.

Nevertheless, what we have found thus far seems enough to encourage a wider search. These prints provide stubborn evidence that what scholars call the New Social History, by studiously avoiding politics, has ignored one of the most significant elements of nineteenth-century American social life: political culture. By leaving out politics, some historians may well have sacrificed something that was crucially distinctive about nineteenth-century American life, and by leaving out prints, others have overlooked the visual documentation that illustrated and influenced history.

NOTES

1. Frances M. Trollope, *Domestic Manners of the Americans*, 2 vols. in 1 (New York: Dodd, Mead, 1901), 2: 65.

2. Robert Worthington Smith, "Political Organization and Canvassing: Yorkshire Elections before the Reform Bill," *American Historical Review* 74 (June 1969): 1540; Asa Briggs, *The Making of Modern England, 1783-1867: The Age of Improvement* (New York: Harper and Row, 1965), p. 414. Even as late as 1865 more than 180 members of Parliament had been returned unopposed.

3. Thomas A. Sancton, "The Myth of French Worker Support for the North in the American Civil War," *French Historical Studies* 11 (Spring 1979): 60; Theodore Zeldin, *The Political System of Napoleon III* (orig. pub. 1958; New York: W. W. Norton, 1971), pp. 78, 83-85, 90-91, 93, 95; Jean Mistler, Francois Blaudey, and Andre Jacquemin, *Epinal et l'imagerie populaire* ([Paris]:

Librairie Hachete, 1961), pp. 99-100; Henry James, *Daumier: Caricaturist* ([London]: Rodale Press, 1954), p. 12; William Makepeace Thackeray, *The Paris Sketch Book of Mr. M. A. Titmarsh* (New York: Scribner's, 1911), pp. 222-27.

4. Robert Philippe, *Political Graphics: Art as a Weapon* (New York: Abbeville Press, 1980), p. 172.

5. Paul F. Bourke and Donald A. DeBats, "Individuals and Aggregates," *Social Science History* 4 (May 1980): 231; Jean H. Baker, *Affairs of Party: The Political Culture of Northern Democrats in the Mid-Nineteenth Century* (Ithaca: Cornell University Press, 1983), pp. 306-9.

6. Wendy C. Wick, *George Washington, an American Icon: The Eighteenth-Century Graphic Portraits* ([Washington]: Smithsonian Institution Traveling Exhibition Service and the National Portrait Gallery, 1982), pp. 122-24.

7. Frederic A. Conningham, *Currier and Ives Prints: An Illustrated Check List* (New York: Crown, 1949).

8. M. Dorothy George, *English Political Caricatures, 1793-1832: A Study of Opinion and Propaganda* (Oxford: Clarendon Press, 1959), pp. 258-59.

9. M. H. Spielmann, *The History of "Punch"* (New York: Cassell Publishing, 1895), pp. 99-100.

10. Arthur Bartlett Maurice and Frederic Taber Cooper, *The History of the Nineteenth Century in Caricature* (orig. pub. 1904; New York: Cooper Square Publishers, 1970), pp. 233, 277.

11. Frank Luther Mott, *History of American Magazines*, vol. 2 (Cambridge, Mass.: Harvard University Press, 1938), pp. 520-29.

12. *Vanity Fair*, Dec. 31, 1859, p. 13; Allan Nevins and Frank Weitenkampf, *A Century of Political Cartoons* (New York: Charles Scribner's Sons, 1944), p. 9; and Stephen Hess and Milton Kaplan, *The Ungentlemanly Art: A History of American Political Cartoons*, rev. ed. (New York: Macmillan, 1975), p. 74; Briggs, *Making of Modern England*, p. 518.

13. P. J. Standenraus, ed., *Mr. Lincoln's Washington: Selections from . . . Noah Brooks . . .* (New York: Thomas Yoseloff, 1967), pp. 56-57.

14. Frank Weitenkampf, *Political Caricature in the United States in Separately Published Cartoons* (New York: New York Public Library, 1953), pp. 120-25, 140-47.

15. Wick, *George Washington, an American Icon.*

16. Baker, *Affairs of Party*, pp. 269-74.

17. Freeman O'Donoghue, *Catalogue of Engraved British Portraits in the Department of Prints and Drawings in the British Museums* (London: British Museums, 1912), 3: 59-65, 434-36; 4: 340-41; 6: 128, 325, 329. As a test, on May 28, 1985, the coauthors of this paper counted the prints of Palmerston in the British Museum and found no more than counted by O'Donoghue in 1912.

18. A. Hyatt King, "English Pictorial Music Title Pages, 1820-1865: Their Style, Evolution and Importance," in *The Library* (Transactions of the

Bibliographic Society, ser. 5), 4 (Mar., 1950): 262-72; *Lincoln Sheet Music Check List* (Fort Wayne, Ind.: Lincoln National Life Foundation, 1940).

19. "Torch Parade Once Feature of Campaigns," *Illinois State Register* [1936] (imperfectly identified newspaper clipping, Louis A. Warren Lincoln Library and Museum, Fort Wayne, Ind.).

Commentary on "The Lincoln Image"

Wendy Wick Reaves

In discussing the vitality of nineteenth-century American political culture and comparing it to the political atmosphere of England and France, Holzer, Boritt, and Neely have used evidence too long ignored by the historian—the pictorial material of the period. The authors should be commended for avoiding some of the pitfalls so dangerous in a historical analysis of pictures. In their book, *The Lincoln Image*, they used a large body of pictorial material produced over a period of years. Thus basing their analysis on a wide range of objects, they avoid the temptation to extrapolate too much from individual pieces. In addition, they emphasize that print production was generally "dictated by business concerns and popular demand" rather than by political manipulation. This underlying commercial aspect is an important factor in analyzing these mid-nineteenth-century publications.

While the authors are sensitive to the nature of the materials they are using, they do tend to stretch their implications a bit far in this paper. I would like not only to comment on the limitations of the Lincoln portraits as evidence of the political culture they describe, but also to set these images into the context of American print production and suggest that the specifically partisan nature of this material can be easily exaggerated.

In assessing the importance of these objects, produced between 1860 and 1865, one must remember that Americans had been enthusiastic consumers of printed pictures for a full generation, with portraiture ranking high in the list of preferred subjects. The lithographer Louis Prang quaintly described this phenomenon when he wrote in 1868: "The American people want pictures. . . . It makes their homes cheerful, and fills their imaginations with pleasant thoughts. . . . There is not a people in Christendom who buy so many pictures as the Americans. . . . This is because we are lovers of homes, and because our homes are the coziest in the world."[1] There was another reason—besides being "lovers of homes"—that Americans bought so many pictures. Print production, particularly lithography, had reached a point in this country where material could be produced in great quantity, very cheaply. In England, the expensive Victorian engraving was far more popular than it ever became in America. In France, lithography was much more sophisticated, having attracted many great French artists from the beginning. It appears that the public in England and France was willing to pay a higher price for better quality prints. In both countries, the etching revival—which did not hit America until the 1880s—was in full swing by the 1860s. Furthermore, portraiture, while it had not disappeared, was somewhat out of fashion in the print market. Americans did not care quite so much about "fine art." They just wanted pictures. And they bought them cheaply, in quantity, often sight-unseen from a catalogue listing. Not only were there differences in political culture between America and England or France, there were differences in taste. More interested in fine art, the European public was less likely to be buying great quantities of crude and inexpensive portraiture.

The Americans, however, had become compulsive picture buyers, and portraiture had always been a popular item in the print shops and sales catalogues. The faces of the famous—and the infamous—were always in demand: ministers, murderers, singers, scientists, seducers, generals, judges, magicians, mediums, politicians, artists, and writers. All their portraits were produced, quite simply, because the public would buy them.

Were pictures precious? They certainly would seem so in comparison to the twentieth century pictorial glut. But in fact, print production in the 1860s contrasts as dramatically with the opening years of the nineteenth century as it does with the opening of the twentieth. With faster and cheaper means of production, the growth of printed imagery between 1800 and 1860 was staggering. In fact, the pictures of Lincoln's era were not always as precious as it would seem from our twentieth-century perspective. Widely available, often for mere pennies, these prints were not necessarily selected with care or subsequently treasured.

What does all this imply about printed portraits in the context of American political culture? It suggests that there may have been many motivations involved in purchasing a print of a leading politician.

81

Bumper-sticker partisanship was definitely one of them. The larger and more expensive prints of Lincoln would have been framed and hung in a place of honor. Lesser portraits would have been tacked on a wall or passed around among friends. Cartoons, especially, were likely to have a specifically partisan nature. But political support was not the only reason to buy a head of Lincoln.

The news value of inexpensive prints was well recognized by the second quarter of the nineteenth century. The successive changes in the Lincoln story—nomination, election, the growth of a beard, etc. (all well chronicled in *The Lincoln Image*)—turned the portrait into a news item. Curiosity was not partisan. After the nomination, even Lincoln's opponents would have wondered about the unknown lawyer from Illinois and may well have spent some pennies on a likeness. It would not have been hung in a place of honor, but it might have been brought home to inform the family or passed around to be mocked among friends. After all, the same public that bought portraits of Winfield Scott or Jesus Christ purchased portraits of notorious murderers and criminals. Obviously, buying the latter did not indicate admiration or support. Even during the election fever of 1860, Lincoln images—particularly the earlist, cheapest versions—were information as well as party symbols. Purchasing a Lincoln portrait was not, I submit, a "strictly partisan act."

Americans have always exhibited an intense interest in celebrity. Although Lincoln's era was a weak intimation of our celebrity-conscious society today, a fascination with the famous was, even then, part of our national character. And it was another reason for the enormous number of portraits on the market. Portrait production increased dramatically during the Civil War. The pace of events spun a great general in and out of fashion so quickly, the printmakers were hard pressed to publish a portrait before the hero was defeated or eclipsed by a more significant battle. The public was curiously nonpartisan in collecting Civil War imagery, perhaps owing to the sense of history that the conflict inspired. Existing cartes-de-visite albums show the owners' efforts to collect a few Confederate generals along with the Union heroes, or vice versa. Mary Boykin Chesnut's photo albums, for instance, contained Lincoln, Charles Sumner, and Henry Ward Beecher[2]—certainly figures she would not have admired. Northern printmakers also produced sets of Confederate as well as Union officers. Although the public enthusiastically bought pictures of their own heroes, to some degree it also bought portraiture of the famous because they were famous — even if they represented the other side. The president's most vocal critics may not have been purchasing his likeness, but many Americans, including some who weren't strong supporters in 1860, undoubtedly felt that some Lincoln heads should be included in their picture collections.

Patriotism and sentiment were other motivations for buying a Lincoln print that were distinct from political support. Lincoln was not only president, he was leader of the Union cause; and as war intensified, many Northerners saw him not as a mere politician but as the committed leader of a righteous struggle. Buying an emancipation print went far beyond showing political support for Lincoln as president. And, as the authors admit, the prints produced after Lincoln's assassination went "far deeper than ordinary partisan identification."

The political culture the authors describe is very specific and its contrast to the political atmosphere of other places and other times is very valid. The pictorial evidence, however, can be more carefully chosen than the great mass of Lincoln prints. The cartoons and some of the 1860 election prints are good evidence of America's mid-nineteenth-century political fervor. The purely partisan nature of most of the Lincoln portraits, however, must be carefully weighed against other values they would have for a nineteenth-century audience.

NOTES

1. Louis Prang, "Controversy with an Art Critic," *Prang's Chromo: A Journal of Popular Art* 1 (Apr. 1868): 2. In his rebuttal to these comments, Harold Holzer pointed out — with justification — that Prang was referring to chromolithographs in this quotation rather than the black and white prints of the early and mid-1860s. While this is undoubtedly true, the purchase of large quantities of prints was not a phenomenon that happened between 1865 and 1868. I feel that Prang's comments about quantity in this quotation were based on the experience of a dozen years of selling lithographs to the American people rather than two or three years of marketing chromos.

2. Information based on conversations with the owner of the Chesnut albums.

PART II

Ideology and Politics

☆　☆
☆

CHAPTER 4

LINCOLN AND THE ECONOMICS OF THE AMERICAN DREAM

GABOR S. BORITT

> To [secure] to each labourer the whole product of his labour, or as nearly as possible, is a most worthy object of any good government. But then the question arises, how can a government best effect this? In our own country, in its present condition. . . .
> —From fragments of a tariff discussion, c. 1847

> I hold the value of life is to improve one's condition. Whatever is calculated to advance the condition of the honest, struggling laboring man, so far as my judgment will enable me to judge of a correct thing, I am for that thing.
> —From speech to Germans at Cincinnati, Ohio, 1861

ANNO DOMINI 1865. Oak Ridge Cemetery, Springfield, Illinois. Bishop Matthew Simpson was delivering the funeral sermon. He quoted the deceased in words of deep conviction, words that spoke of a great work to be done. They conjured up the specter of an evil in the land: "Broken by it I too may be; bow to it I never will. The *probability* that we may fall in the struggle *ought not* to deter us from the support of a cause which we believe to be just; it *shall not* deter me."

The declaration was that of young Abraham Lincoln on the day after Christmas, 1839. The bishop interpreted his text in a way and with an authority that seemed wholly natural to the mourning nation: here was the testament of the beloved martyr dedicating himself in his youth to the great struggle of his life against the Slave Power.

Bishop Simpson quoted Lincoln accurately. He had unearthed a long-lost speech that would soon be lost again. But he did make one error. Lincoln's speech had said nothing about slavery. Its subject was banking.[1]

The log cabin and the bank. The combination should not surprise us.[2] In more than three decades of public life Lincoln probably talked

87

more about economics, to use the term broadly, than any other issue, slavery included.[3] The bulk of his discussions with an economic focus preceded the period of his fame and went unrecorded. But the main lines of his thinking survive, as do frequently, details. Just as significantly, Lincoln's noneconomic speeches and writings often brimmed with economic implications. For a long time historians have largely avoided this rich material—why, cannot be explained here in brief. Focusing on it, however, helps illuminate Lincoln in a clear and useful light.

The key to Lincoln's economic persuasion was an intense and continually developing commitment to the ideal that all people should receive a full, good, and ever-increasing reward for their labors so that they might have the opportunity to rise in life. For the son of an almost illiterate father and perhaps illegitimate mother, a son who in time rose to the White House, this commitment was also a personal one. And this, Lincoln's American Dream, became a central theme throughout his entire political life.

In intellectual terms the theme grew from a combination of economic orientation and sympathy for what Lincoln called "the many poor," but what we should simply label "the many," to what might be seen by the 1850s as a full-blown ideology. During the first and longer part of his public life it found profession through the support of governmental policies that primarily aimed at economic development (however rudimentarily he, and his age, understood this modern concept). Like thousands of others, Lincoln grasped the fact that such development improved the chance of the many to improve their lives.

Thus in 1830, Lincoln's first verifiable speech called for improving the transportation system of Illinois—"internal improvements" as Americans of the time spoke of it. Two years later he entered politics on a platform of such improvement. Then, in 1837, his first fully published address discussed banking in Illinois. In 1840 his first address to a national audience, too, took political economy—internal improvements again—for its subject. These "firsts" carried both symbolic and strategic meanings and reveal much about Lincoln and his age. But more important, in between these milestones, and for years after, Lincoln made economics the most substantial element of his campaigning, legislative labors, and private studies outside, and not infrequently inside, his legal practice.[4]

Illinois's brave (although often somewhat unfairly described as foolish) attempt to join the transportation revolution of the 1830s is Lincoln's best-known economic involvement. On this, as on most other economic policies, his devotion to developmental, right-to-rise economics remained essentially unchanged over a lifetime. It began with such things as the young state legislator's demand for building a bridge at New Salem on the Sangamon and ended with the federal legislation for building the Pacific Railroad.

Internal improvement, however, is one of the few Lincolnian connections with economics to receive at least some mildly focused scrutiny over the years. His often more intimate ties with hosts of related matters had been ignored, passed over lightly, or, when dealt with, generally analyzed in almost exclusively political, and thus to a degree misleading, terms. One of Lincoln's early actions toward banks provides a fine illustration of this.

Most Lincoln students are familiar with the story of his leap from the window of Springfield's Second Presbyterian Church, where the Illinois House of Representatives was meeting in 1840. Nominally the issue at stake was adjournment. The Democratic majority desired it; Lincoln and his fellow Whigs hoped to block it by boycotting sessions and preventing the presence of a quorum. Lincoln and a few followers, however, remained in attendance to keep an eye on the proceedings, which at the crucial moment included the sergeant at arms fetching delinquent solons back into the church by force. What followed was described with great relish by the press of the time and has been recited by historians since:

> Mr. Lincoln . . . who appeared to enjoy the embarrassment of the House, suddenly looked very grave after the Speaker announced that a quorum was present. The conspiracy having failed, Mr. Lincoln, came under great excitement, and having attempted and failed to get out at the door, very unceremoniously raised the window and jumped out, followed by one or two other members. This gymnastic performance of Mr. Lincoln and his flying brethren did not occur until after they had voted and consequently the House did not interfere with their extraordinary feat. We have not learned whether these flying members got hurt in the adventure, and we think it probable that at least one of them came off without damage, as it was noticed that his legs reached nearly from the window to the ground! . . . We learn

that a resolution will probably be introduced into the House this week to inquire into the expedience of raising the State House one story higher . . . so as to prevent members from jumping out windows! If such a resolution passes, Mr. Lincoln in future will have to climb down the spout.[5]

The virtue of narrating the honorable gentleman's action this way is obvious, and stressing the politicking has a certain validity. But it does in the end obscure the fundamental meaning of Lincoln's action. For he acted in such an unorthodox fashion in a desperate attempt to defend the banking system of Illinois against what he believed to be politically prejudiced and economically ignorant attacks.

Lincoln won many such battles, but the Springfield defenestration failed. The adjournment of the legislature in turn meant that the State Bank of Illinois, which like most other banks in the nation had suspended specie payment because of the depression, was forced to resume payment, that is to redeem its paper money in silver and gold. Since in the Midwest, Illinois acted alone in allowing redemption, the exaggerated demand of the whole region for specie fell upon her. In a few weeks nearly half a million dollars were drained from the state — an exceedingly large sum for that time and place. When at last the legislators came around to Lincoln's way of looking at things, the damage had been done. They thus deserve part of the blame for the collapse of the state's banking system within a year. Lincoln's hasty departure through the church window aimed at preventing that collapse.

Fighting for long years the unpopular battle for banking, Lincoln insisted that he was above all fighting for the "farmer and mechanic."[6] In part, he thus met the requirements of American politics. In part, however, he also gave voice to the prime element of a developing economic persuasion. The fact was that for those who would rise, for the nation that would rise, banks were necessary.

Lincoln's Whiggish economics (for on the whole they were such even if their underlying worldview was broadly American) went hand in hand with the hope that a wide recognition of their benefits would provide political preferment. His hopes for America and his Whig, and later Republican, attachments were firmly intertwined. Yet his willingness to uphold economic measures that were unpopular in Illinois deserves repeated emphasis. And lest we make too much of his partisan loyalties and party regularity, we should note that for more than a decade and a half he failed to champion the noneconomic policies of his Whig party—the single-term presidency, for example, or opposition to immigrants or to a tight political organizaton. In contrast he upheld his own version of the Whig economic vision even in private, whether writing to a political opponent about taxes or to his kin about the way to rise in life.

Lincoln supported banking, above all, for the same reason he supported a whole set of related economic policies. Even the skeletal records of his early career speak to us of a vision of American progress, a dream of national improvement in the fullest sense of the term. He worked to build up the nation, he said, to cultivate it, "making it a garden." The "garden," of course, would be commercial and industrial as well as agricultural, and would secure for all the opportunity for full, fair, and growing "reward of their labors."[7] I am quoting here Lincolnian words that carried the deepest meaning for him throughout his life and were at the heart of his fully formed ideology.

Lincoln's intelligent interest in the banking question began in New Salem. Three decades later as president he played a crucial— and by historians almost totally ignored—part in pushing Congress to adopt a national banking system. Fiscal matters, especially taxation, also drew his interest early. As a freshman representative in the Illinois House, for example, he demanded tax privileges for new settlers who had to start at the bottom—doing so in a minority of six against forty-one nays. A few years later he sought tax breaks for those who would plant forests on the treeless prairie. All along he groped in the direction of what our century calls progressive taxation. As president he signed such legislation into law.

On the specific issue of industrialization, and the policy most tied to it, tariff protection, not a single Lincoln speech is extant. Yet if all he had said on the subject came down to us, that alone would have occupied perhaps two volumes of his *Collected Works*. As it is, we have fragments, such as Lincoln singing of the blight of an agrarian triumph: "All is cold and still as death—no [sm]oke rises, no furnace roars, no anvil rings."[8] And on this question he became sufficiently learned— his reading included political economists—to adopt the most avant-garde argument of his time, as developed by Henry Carey.

His support of industry notwithstanding, Lincoln had a commitment to the small, independent producer that dominated his America, which those taking note of his economic views—Richard Hofstadter, for example—tend to stress. Even Daniel Walker Howe's study of the Whigs appealed to Hofstadter's memorable words about Lincoln: "Booth's bullet, indeed, saved him from something worse than embroilment with radicals over Reconstruction. It confined his life to the happier age that Lincoln understood—which unwittingly he helped destroy—the age that gave sanction to the honest compromises of his thought." What therefore needs emphasis here is that Lincoln's commitment to individualism went hand in hand with an understanding attitude toward the concentration of capital, the factory system, and, to balance these, an early, firm commitment to labor unions. In the process of promoting railroad building in Illinois, for example, Lincoln gladly predicted—in the 1840s—the movement toward giant corporations which came to characterize the industry only after the Civil War. In the same breath it should be mentioned that as president he pioneered what we call "jawboning"—he used the executive power to coerce railroads into reducing freight charges. And he declared to a delegation of striking workers that "I know that in almost every case of strikes, the men have just cause for complaint." Lincoln's attitude thus foreshadowed the one the United States would adopt, however, haltingly, over the next century.[9]

The significant point about Lincoln's commitment to the small, independent producer is that it stemmed much more from Whig-Republican economics than Jeffersonian-Democratic sociopolitical reasoning. Thus his small producer embodied both the right to rise *and* ever greater productivity and economic development. The two indeed were identified so fully in his mind that we cannot say which was more important to him. This in turn implies a substantial potential to accept economically inspired social change, leading away from the independent producer, so long as the road to opportunity remained open.

There is no need here to analyze, much less catalog, every aspect of Lincoln's economic views. But before we come to slavery and war one more topic should be touched upon: his neglect of agriculture and his indifference to the nation's rapid westward expansion. His economic outlook helped shape his lack of enthusiasm toward expansionism for it bespoke an inward-looking orientation characteristic of many Whigs: a desire for internal instead of external development. Perhaps Lincoln was not as much against territorial expansion per se, as he was in favor of concentrating the nation's energies within the country, making it a "garden." Rightly or wrongly, he refused to go along with the majority of Americans and equate geographical with social mobility.[10]

Lincoln's opposition to manifest destiny went hand in hand with his Whiggishly humane feelings toward Indians (tragically little difference though that made) and with an un-Whiglike blurred stance on public land policies. He showed little interest in agricultural subjects, above all, because advancement was so important but working the soil hardly the best road to it—whether for the individual or the nation. He had grown up in the Arcady his fellow Americans venerated, but had no illusions about it. His campaigning in 1840 gave a poignant illustration of his attitudes. While the nation sang the jolly rhyme, "But we'll have a ploughman President of the Cincinnatus line," and while many of his Whig brethren became intoxicated with log cabins and hard cider, Lincoln spoke soberly of the virtues of centralized banking. He never changed his priorities.

Party politicking aside, Lincoln could sustain such a stand with much immunity, in part because his message was attractive to many, including farmers. Country lawyer that he was, he knew, better than Emerson did, that the "Man with the Hoe" was "covetous of his dollar." He presented his Whiggish economic policies as opening the road of advancement to the farmer as well as to others. And over the long run, at least in economic terms, he was right.

Lincoln's success with his predominantly farming constituency—whether in Illinois or in the White House—stemmed also from great political ability that was reinforced by his sincerity and his appearance and ways. He seemed like a man of the soil with manure on his boots, even if the manure was not there. When accused of siding with the aristocracy, he could ward off the charge rudely. In one debate when his opponent warmed up to such a haranguing performance, Lincoln ripped open the good tribune's coat to reveal an opulent gentleman with ruffled shirt, vest, and gold chain. The people roared. Then Lincoln reminisced about the times when he had worked for eight dollars a month and about the single pair of buckskin breeches he had to his name: "Now if you know the nature of buckskin when wet and dried by the sun, it will shrink; and my breeches kept shrinking until they left several inches of my legs bare between the tops of my socks and the lower part of my breeches; and whilst I was growing taller they were becoming shorter, and so much tighter that they left

93

a blue streak around my legs that can be seen to this day. If you call this aristocracy I plead guilty to the charge."[11] There were not many who could doubt where Lincoln's allegiance lay. He was of the people, the common man whom Lincoln said God loved so and made so many of.[12]

And how does slavery fit into the picture sketched out here? The answer is—centrally. Slavery, the lethal cancer that Lincoln (blindly and perhaps to a degree self-servingly) assumed to be on its way to slow cure and dissolution through much of his political life, was proved by the passage of the Kansas-Nebraska Act to be thriving and aggressive. It became clear that no amount of improvement legislation could build the American Dream if the whole nation became a slave society. To put up an effective front against slavery, a Whig-Democratic coalition had to be created. The principal price of the new alliance was submerging the economic differences between the two old parties. Lincoln was willing to pay that price because of his sharp perception of both the moral and the practical realities of the 1850s.

In his mind the roles of slavery and economics were thus reversed. Economics provided the central motif of Lincoln's career before 1854; antislavery was pushed in the background, its triumph placed at a distant day. After 1854, antislavery became Lincoln's immediate goal, and the economic policies that he continued to esteem highly and work for when possible, he relegated to the background and to a future triumph. Political expediency had much to do with both the first and second compromises of his beliefs. His underlying assumptions, however, his moral underpinnings, remained unchanged. Indeed, when Lincoln actively embraced the antislavery cause, he raised his Dream to its highest plane. The challenge of this moral ascent, in turn, inspired him to enunciate more clearly and more beautifully than ever before the ideals he stood for.

The "central *idea*" of America was equality, Lincoln noted in 1856, taking his stand squarely on the Declaration of Independence. Whether his historical judgment was accurate is open to question. But we can be certain that the meaning he gave to Jefferson's words was scarcely identical with Jefferson's own. Whatever equality meant to the Virginian and his age, Lincoln crowned the work of the Jacksonian generation by extending its meaning to equality of opportunity to get ahead in life. This was his "central idea." One may dare to suggest that this is one of the most important metamorphoses of an idea in American history.[13]

In the 1850s, Lincoln defined again and again his central idea as "the principle that clears the path for all—gives hope to all—and, by consequence, *enterprize,* and *industry* to all." Hofstadter was therefore correct in concluding that Lincoln's most "vital test" of democracy was economic. In the absence of previous research, he could not add that this was the fruit of the Illinoisan's economic orientation and of the orientation of the age that spawned him and that eagerly accepted this new definition of equality.[14]

Slavery subverted the American Dream. It did so in myriad ways, but perhaps most important, by denying blacks the right to rise, slavery endangered that right for all. Thus Lincoln slowly found his way to the view that blacks, too, must be allowed to rise as high as their ability could take them. "I want every man to have a chance," he said as early as 1860. "And I believe a black man is entitled to it—in which he can better his condition—when he may look forward and hope to be a hired laborer this year and the next, work for himself afterward, and finally to hire men to work for him! That is the true system." This was no easy ideal to begin to point America toward. The nation has been struggling to live up to it since.[15]

In the presidency Lincoln could once again give attention to economic policies. Because he had the pleasure of signing into law much of the program he had worked for through the better part of his public life, because he presided over a revolution that changed the government's role in the economy, because under him the government for the first time began to try to face up to the problems created by industrialization, the temptation is strong to exaggerate the importance of his role. In fact, as a rule, Lincoln Whiggishly stayed in the background, letting Congress shape legislation. He benefited thus politically. And if in the 1850s the shadow of slavery helped confound his economic vision, in the 1860s the war performed a like function. His best energies had to be devoted to winning that war "upon which all else chiefly" depended.[16]

It is also true, however, that Lincoln tried—though failed—to set the tone for the revolution he presided over and made crucial contributions to it. When he was needed, as in the case of the establishment of the national banking system and a scientifically minded Department of Agriculture, he brought the full weight of the presidency to bear. He encouraged movement toward graduated income taxes (though such taxes were later declared unconstitutional); a uniform paper currency, the greenbacks; internal improvements, notably the Pacific Railroad; immigration; the Homestead Act; the Land Grant College Act; and higher tariffs. The net result, as the president reported while calling for the support of immigration, was that the nation at last "was beginning a new life."[17]

In the significant area of labor policy he and much of the leadership of the country favored different directions. The homestead, education, and tariff protection legislation constituted the Republican labor program, the American government's "first positive response to industrialism." This was a middle-class agenda, however, with labor itself increasingly opting for trade unionism for protection.[18] Lincoln supported enthusiastically his party's program but he also accepted labor's own approach. He instinctively understood that in the new economic world coming into being the right to strike was allied to the right to rise. While employers denounced the supposed illegal nature of unions, the president welcomed strikers to the White House and expressed his strong sympathy for them.

Over the years he had repeatedly warned against "the effort to place capital on an equal footing with, if not above labor." When he sent his ideas to Congress, warning that if working people surrendered their political power "it would be used to close the door of advancement" against them, it grew painfully clear that in these matters his leadership was unacceptable. The House of Representatives, laying the groundwork not only for the modern American economy but also for the abuses of the Gilded Age, snubbed the president's message. Ironmaster and radical Republican Thaddeus Stevens explained the tabling of Lincoln's message by saying that there was "no appropriate committee on metaphysics in the House." Copperhead Clement Vallandigham agreed: "I presume it will go to the Committee of Unfinished Business." And as one historian added, "Unfinished business it remained for the rest of the century."[19]

By mid-1863 there were huge riots in New York City. After mulling over their meaning, Lincoln found their "most notable feature . . . the hanging of some working people by other working people." He concluded, "It should never be so. The strongest bond of human sympathy, outside of the family relation, should be one uniting all working people, of all nations, and tongues, and kindreds." The words might have come from one of his European admirers, Karl Marx, indicating some common leanings and also this particular idea's international currency. Yet Lincoln had something quite American in mind. The workingmen hanged in 1863 were blacks. His words therefore carried the hope that black and white laborers might be awakened to their common interest.[20]

Emancipation had a huge economic ingredient. So did (but disastrously so, and Lincoln could not help but know) the cherished American hope for colonizing blacks abroad. With the aid of black people, the president effectively killed that hope during the war. As for the future, holding honest wages to be the key to advancement for the poor, he projected a fair wage relationship as the heart of his policies toward the freed slaves. He was certainly willing to go beyond fostering that relationship but how far we do not know. His commitment to black freedom fit into a larger commitment to a democratic-capitalist America. Thus Lincoln's postwar response to black needs would have depended in no small part on his response to the coming Gilded Age.

Emancipation, Lincoln believed, did not liberate merely the blacks but also the whites. It made the American Dream also a Southern Dream, with a resultant prosperity for all. In the midst of the hatreds of war, he took pleasure, in private, in creating a "word painting of what the South would be when the war was over, slavery destroyed, and she had an opportunity to develop her resources." Long after one of Lincoln's treasury officials had heard him dream thus, the official found himself listening to a new breed of Southerner advocating economic development and a "New South." The official experienced a flash of memory that came with "the vividness of an electric light," as he "recognized the word-picture of Mr. Lincoln."[21]

But first peace had to be reached and the president's search for it fully reflected his economic orientation. His best and most extensive argument for reunion ("Physically speaking, we cannot separate") was largely economic.[22] A major component of his numerous peace feelers and reconstruction schemes was an appeal to the economic interests of the Rebels. He assumed somewhat naively and in a way that can now be labeled "typically American" that the South could be seduced into peace via materialist enticement. This assumption helps explain the absurdly vast amount of time he devoted to the problems of trading with the Confederacy, especially in cotton. The same is true of his secret feelers about the federal takeover of the Confederate war debt (obliquely attacked in the Wade-Davis Manifesto), his persistent offers for large-scale compensation for slaves, his lack of enthusiasm for congressional laws of confiscation, perhaps even the unrealistic demand that the Pacific Railroad be built on the five-feet gauge used primarily in the South.

The large economic ingredient in his plans for reunification and peacemaking was quite matched in Lincoln's war making. The blockade, his emphasis on the military importance of railroads and new weapons, and, in part, his insistence on the strategic significance of the black troops, or the Mississippi Valley, provide straightforward illustrations of this ingredient. More subtle is the link between his economic persuasion and his strategic ideas that permits some historians to speak of Lincoln's military genius. Thus, the man who in the 1840s demanded from Congress a centralized and coordinated plan of national improvements, in the 1860s made like demands upon his generals for centralization of authority and coordination of plans. He thus helped create the Union's unified command system and its central, overall plan of strategy. Similarly, Lincoln's decisive championship of cordon offense (advancing on the enemy on every front, thus pitting all the Northern resources against all the Southern ones) stemmed in no small part from his view that economic might, perhaps more than anything else excepting morale, would determine the outcome of the war. This oft attested view also helped catalyze his recognition that the objective of the Union forces, at least in the East, should be not the conquest of territories but the destruction of opposing armies, the destruction of "the most important branch of . . . resources": men.[23] Many scholars agree that this recognition played a pivotal role in the Union victory.

Perhaps the most unsettling facet of Lincoln's military policy was the drastic rate at which federal commanders were replaced. On the Eastern front, for example, in a period of two years Lincoln removed the general in charge an unprecedented seven times. He was criticized harshly then, and since, for failing to support his commanders in defeat. Without engaging in the details of this controversy, we should note that Lincoln's actions reflected a core aspect of his economic outlook which under the pressure of war became extreme: he conducted a ruthless campaign of pushing the successful of the lower ranks to the fore. And his view that in the Civil War one side stood for the "open field" for all, and the other against it, thus received more than symbolic corroboration. In the Confederacy the men who held the chief commands early in the war were there when Appomattox came. Even if Jefferson Davis made a relatively fortunate initial selection of top generals, it is startling to note that the one exception to the above was the gallant Albert Sidney Johnston—and he was dead. In contrast, there was not a single general commanding a main army in the Union service of 1865 who had held high command at the beginning of the struggle. In this respect, Lincoln's American Dream had triumphed on the battlefield, too.

Recognizing the central role he assigned to the right to rise is not to diminish Lincoln's devotion to other manifestations of democracy. Indeed these tended to become interchangeable in his utterances, particularly toward the end of the war. It hardly need be said that he was devoted to the Union, liberty, political democracy, and the importance of the American example to the world. But all these concepts, vital as they were, carried a certain aura of abstraction about them by his day, excepting perhaps the last few years of his life. His more down-to-earth, deep commitment to social order, in turn, was much more contravened than upheld by his decision to "accept war" in 1861. In contrast, the right of all people to the product of their labor, the right to rise, was almost palpably real, material—something ordinary folk could fully understand and identify with. And Lincoln's devotion to this right, which he correctly linked to economic development, provides one of the strongest threads of his life, which runs from New Salem through Washington.

If one is satisfied with pointing to the occasional early Lincoln utterance about political democracy and tying this to his eloquent presidential statements on the subject, it is possible to establish a certain ideological continuity between the politician of Illinois and the later statesman of world significance. If one is satisfied with pointing to some early Lincoln utterances, even some speeches, about moderation, law, order, and community and finding this same strain in the mature man, once again a continuity can be developed. These continuities indeed were very real.

If one is satisfied with concentrating on the presidential years alone, one might find Lincoln's central message (as did such disparate men as Alexander Stephens and Walt Whitman—and most Americans since) in a religious devotion to the Union. But if we scrutinize Lincoln's life as a whole, take stock both quantitatively and qualitatively, and thus see those final crowning years of conflict in the perspective sketched out here, we should speak—awkward as this is—about Lincoln's war for the American Dream.

The Union to him was not an end but a means. It was precious because it was "the last best, hope of earth," because it tested whether "any nation so conceived and so dedicated, can long endure." It was to be upheld so long as it upheld "that thing for which the Union itself was made." The Union was the ship, he explained, and the American Dream its cargo: "the prosperity and the liberties of the people." And "so long as the ship can be saved, with the cargo," he added, "it should never be abandoned."

Without the ship the cargo would go down and therefore it was senseless to emphasize a distinction between the two. Yet this imagery implied that had there been another equally seaworthy ship available, Lincoln might have been satisfied with transferring the cargo. But there was no other ship; the idea itself was beyond the realm of his practical thought. And so there had to be a war, to save the ship, yes, but to save the ship so that the cargo could be saved.[24]

This distinction, however unimportant it might have appeared at the time, held fateful meaning. The idea of the Union is essentially national, that of the dream is universal. One view prizes the Civil War, to quote Francis Lieber, as "a war for nationality."[25] It makes Lincoln into the Great Nationalist of the modern historians, a man who had a religious faith in the Union. The other cherishes him as an American Moses or Christ, one who spoke to mankind.

At the same time, paradoxically, the first view denies the uniqueness of the United States. It values Lincoln as a New World counterpart of Cavour and Bismarck whose highest goal, to use the German expression, was *staatsbildung*. Without gainsaying the achievements of the Europeans, we must note that their degenerate twentieth-century descendants in the worship of the nation as an end in itself were Hitler and Mussolini. In contrast, Lincoln's dream helped lead America to the nationalism of Theodore Roosevelt, Woodrow Wilson, and Franklin Delano Roosevelt.

Early in 1861, on his way to Washington, Lincoln spoke in Trenton, New Jersey, about the Revolutionary War and the battle there in which Washington defeated the Hessians. His thoughts went back to his first childhood readings in history:

> You all know . . . how these early impressions last longer than any others. I recollect thinking then, boy even though I was, that there must have been *something more* than common that those men struggled for. I am exceedingly anxious that *that thing* which they struggled for; *that something* even more than National Independence; *that something* that held out a great promise to all the people of the world to all time to come; I am exceedingly anxious that this Union, the Constitution, and the liberties of the people shall be perpetuated in accordance with *the original idea* for which that struggle was made, and I shall be most happy indeed if I shall be an humble instrument in the hands of the Almighty, and of this, his almost chosen people, for perpetuating *the object* of that great struggle.

It was perhaps the emotions born out of the remembrance of his own beginnings that so possessed Lincoln's mind that he did not then explicitly define "that *something*," "*the original idea*" of America, which he believed the nation's founders had already struggled for. Or perhaps it was the fault of the *New York Tribune* reporter that the president-elect's reflections in Trenton remained incomplete. A day later, however, speaking at Philadelphia, in Independence Hall, Lincoln continued his revolutionary theme. He still spoke "with deep emotion," and now the press reported his completed thought: "It was that which gave promise that in due time the weights should be lifted from the shoulders of all men, and that *all* should have an equal chance."[26]

One suspects that remembering "way back," Lincoln exaggerated the clarity of his youthful ideas. Nevertheless, their seeds must have been there early, in the "earliest days of my being able to read," as he recalled. Indeed, for a moment, we must reach beyond these early days, to a toddler in Kentucky.

It was corn-planting time in the valley where the Lincolns made their home. Children had to be taught to work very young. Little Abe was beginning his lessons, walking behind his father, dropping pumpkin seeds into the hills made by Thomas's crude hoe. Two seeds in every second hill, in every second row. Then the Sabbath came and with it a great cloudburst up on the hills above them. It did not rain in their valley but the water came swirling down from the hills, washing away corn, pumpkin, and topsoil. The fruit of their labor was lost. This was the earliest memory, earliest pain, the grown man Lincoln could recall. Almost half a century later he told another Kentuckian, Cassius Clay: "I always thought that the man who made the corn should eat the corn."[27]

This then is a story of Lincoln. It had all begun with a poor boy's conviction — in a time and at a place that nurtured such convictions — that people should receive the full fruit of their labor so that they might get ahead in life. The conviction matured slowly, over decades. And as Lincoln stood on the threshold of the White House, his conviction had become unshakable. The United States had to be saved *with* the Dream. "If this country cannot be saved without giving up that principle," he declared, "I would rather be assassinated."[28]

As the Civil War reached its climax and end, the president's concept of the American Dream also reached its ultimate heights. In the spring of 1865 he summed up for a final time the Rebel cause, as he saw it: "It may seem strange that any men should dare to ask a just God's assistance in wringing their bread from the sweat of other men's faces." But he added now: "Let us judge not that we be not judged." Even for one of his legendary fortitude the "nation's wounds" and those of the men who had "borne the battle, and . . . his widow, and his orphan" proved too much to endure by reason alone. As his years of trial were about to end, he turned for support from a central idea that was human law, perhaps nature's law, to that same idea as God's law. Not surprisingly, for such is the way of humankind, Lincoln had found that the purposes of his Maker were like his own purposes.

"Fondly do we hope — fervently do we pray," he told his people, "that this mighty scourge of war may speedily pass away. Yet, if God wills that it continue, until all the wealth piled by the bond-man's two hundred and fifty years of unrequited toil shall be sunk, and until every drop of blood drawn with the lash, shall be paid by another drawn with the sword, as was said three thousand years ago, so still it must be said 'the judgments of the Lord, are true and righteous altogether.' "

Unrequited toil, unearned and bloodstained wealth: war as judgment. The denial of the Dream was to be expiated. The extorted labor of two and a half centuries had to be paid for. Lincoln's American Dream had become the will of God.[29]

Notes

1. Matthew Simpson, *Funeral Address Delivered at the Burial of President Lincoln, at Springfield, Illinois, May 4, 1865* (New York: Carlton and Porter, 1865), p. 17; Roy P. Basler, ed., Marion Dolores Pratt and Lloyd A. Dunlap, asst. eds., *The Collected Works of Abraham Lincoln,* 9 vols. (New Brunswick, N.J.; Rutgers University Press, 1953-55), 1: 178.

2. If today it is less surprising to associate Lincoln with banks than it was some years earlier, in some part that is the result—please forgive me—of *Lincoln and the Economics of the American Dream* (Memphis: Memphis State University Press, 1978). Though no additional studies of the subject have appeared since then, in a number of other books and articles, too, the significance of Lincoln's economic persuasion has received substantial emphasis. I wish to call attention to the most important of these: Daniel Walker Howe's *The Political Culture of the American Whigs* (Chicago: University of Chicago Press, 1979). Scrutinizing the book for *Reviews in American History* 8 (1980): 344-50, in an article titled "Whigs and Bankers," Sean Wilentz concluded that Howe's interpretation of Lincoln was "building upon the recent work of G. S. Boritt and others." In fact, Howe's book, published in 1979, could not have relied on *Lincoln and the Economics of the American Dream,* which appeared late in 1978. Howe was familiar with an article on Lincoln and the tariff that I had published as a graduate student ["Old Wine into New Bottles: Abraham Lincoln and the Tariff Reconsidered," *Historian* 28 (1966): 289-317], but he arrived at his understanding of the president, to which economics was vital, largely independently. History is not a science with reproducible results and one is grateful for even a whiff of the scent of reproducibility.

This is not to say that Howe's views of Lincoln's political economy and my own are identical. Among other things, Howe's single chapter could not probe as deeply as a book-length study could; I think it sometimes fails to fathom fully the intricacies of Lincoln's outlook. One consequence is that Howe somewhat overstates the differences between the Whig and the Republican Lincoln by finding him less forward-looking than I do.

All the same, thanks to Howe, we can now best understand Lincoln's strong attachment to Whiggery through the way he fit into "the political culture of the American Whigs." Lincoln's later Republicanism is best understood in like terms. The model of political culture indeed has strengths and increases our knowledge of Lincoln and his age.

Both Howe and I were influenced by Eric Foner, *Free Soil, Free Labor, Free Men: The Ideology of the Republican Party before the Civil War* (New York: Oxford University Press, 1970). Yet once again we have, to a degree, independent research producing similar results. Some of the main themes of my 1978 book appeared before I had read anything by Foner ("Lincoln and the Economics of the American Dream, the Whig Years, 1832-1854," Ph.D. diss., Boston University, 1968), but both Foner and I had been influenced by Richard Hofstadter.

At the risk of turning into a bore the point about historians independently arriving at like insights, the doctoral dissertation of Olivier Frayssé must be noted: "Abraham Lincoln: La terre et la travail, 1809-1860" (Paris: Service des publications du Centre National de la Recherche Scientifique, 1981), 3 cycle, to be published as a book by *Publications de la Sorbonne* (Sorbonne University Press) in 1988. Frayssé's work, too, found economics pivotal to Lincoln's outlook, with Frayssé reaching the congressional period before my book came to his attention. However, his somewhat Marxist ideological bent also led him to differing views about the middle portion of Lincoln's career. And so, I will repeat here the preface of *Lincoln and the Economics of the American Dream*, p. xii. I followed my own bent, "without too many misgivings because of the comforting knowlege that the facts presented will readily permit the able, other-minded student to follow different routes and reach different conclusions. Thus, it should be possible, for example, to depict the Lincolnian struggle for equality of opportunity as leading to inequality, and Lincoln as the politician and ideologist of the nascent industrial capitalist class, still upholding its democratic and humanitarian illusions but readying for the climb to power in America."

3. To illustrate, I was able to identify only twenty-four Lincoln speeches during the election year of 1840, although he probably made twice that number, if not more. The text of only one speech survives. (This focused on the advantage of national banking over other forms of monetary organization. So did Lincoln's other speeches—and his entire campaign.) If we multiply the length of the extant speech by twenty-four—and it would not be unreasonable to multiply by forty-eight or more—then Lincoln's speeches on banking in a single year alone, had they been recorded, could have taken up a volume of his *Collected Works*. (We should note, however, that the absence of good press coverage may have permitted Lincoln to repeat himself more routinely than he could do during the last few years of his life.) The above quantitative point can be supplemented with a qualitative one made by Howe, *The Political Culture of the American Whigs*, p. 26. Howe emphasizes the importance of oral communication for that age and criticizes the later scholarly tendency to undervalue it: "Our assumption is that important statements are written down; what is spoken is not taken with full seriousness. But antebellum Americans felt differently."

4. Paul K. Conklin states in his *Prophets of Prosperity: America's First Political Economists* (Bloomington: Indiana University Press, 1980), p. vii, that between 1820 and 1860 "economic issues dominated congressional debates."

5. *Illinois State Register,* Dec. 12, 1840.

6. Basler, *Collected Works of Lincoln,* 1: 69.

7. These expressions first appeared, respectively, in ibid., 2: 4 and 1: 69.

8. Ibid., 1: 414.

9. Richard Hofstadter, *The American Political Tradition and the Men Who Made It* (New York: Knopf, 1948), pp. 106-7; Howe, *The Political Culture of the American Whigs*, p. 297; *Fincher's Trades Review,* Mar. 12, 1864.

10. Basler, *Collected Works of Lincoln*, 1: 311; 3: 357-58.

11. The reconstruction of this episode by Ninian W. Edwards, Lincoln's brother-in-law, for Herndon is probably substantially accurate. William H. Herndon and Jesse W. Weik, *Herndon's Life of Lincoln*, introduction and notes by Paul M. Angle (Cleveland and New York: World Publishing Co., Forum Books, 1942), p. 157; cf. Basler, *Collected Works of Lincoln*, 1: 320.

12. Tyler Dennett, ed., *Lincoln and the Civil War in the Diaries and Letters of John Hay* (New York: Dodd, Mead, 1939), p. 143.

13. Basler, *Collected Works of Lincoln*, 2: 385 (4: 168-69). Garry Wills, *Inventing America: Jefferson's Declaration of Independence* (New York: Doubleday, 1978), pp. xiii-xxvi, devotes much of a long prologue to Lincoln's misreading of Jefferson.

14. Basler, *Collected Works of Lincoln*, 4: 169; Hofstadter, *The American Political Tradition*, 105.

15. Basler, *Collected Works of Lincoln*, 4: 24-25.

16. Ibid., 8: 332.

17. Ibid., 7: 40.

18. James L. Huston, "A Political Response to Industrialism: The Republican Embrace of Protectionist Labor Doctrines," *Journal of American History* 70 (1983): 54-55.

19. Basler, *Collected Works of Lincoln*, 5: 51-53 (cf. 3: 478, 7: 259); *Congressional Globe*, Dec. 5, 1861, 37th Cong., 2d sess., p. 20; Leonard P. Curry, *Blueprint for Modern America: Nonmilitary Legislation of the First Civil War Congress* (Nashville: Vanderbilt University Press, 1968), p. 246.

20. Basler, *Collected Works of Lincoln*, 7: 259, cf. 5: 534-35.

21. L. E. Chittenden, *Recollections of President Lincoln and His Administration* (New York: Harper, 1891), p. 368.

22. Often misunderstood as advancing the concept of a Union decreed by nature, in fact Lincoln thought and spoke in terms of a nature harnessed by "steam, telegraph"—in short, by economic might and intelligence. Basler, *Collected Works*, 4: 259, 269; 5: 53, 527-29.

23. Basler, *Collected Works of Lincoln*, 8: 150; cf. 1: 135-36. Dissenting from such a view, Herman Hattaway and Archer Jones, "Lincoln as Military Strategist," *Civil War History*, 26 (1980): 293-303, depict the commander in chief as "a conventional mid-nineteenth century military strategist." Their views do not vitiate the connections noted here between military strategy and socioeconomic persuasion, except the last one.

24. Basler, *Collected Works of Lincoln*, 5: 537; 7: 23; 4: 233.

25. Francis Lieber to Charles Sumner, Aug. 31, 1864, Francis Lieber Papers, Huntington Library.

26. Basler, *Collected Works of Lincoln*, 4: 235-36, 240. The italics in the Trenton speech are mine.

27. Ida M. Tarbell, *The Life of Abraham Lincoln*, 2 vols. (New York: Doubleday and McClure Co., 1900), 1: 17; Basler, *Collected Works of Lincoln*, 4: 70; Clay in *Reminiscences of Abraham Lincoln by Distinguished Men of His*

Time, ed. Allen Thorndike Rice (New York: North American Publishing Co., 1886), p. 297.

    28. Basler, *Collected Works of Lincoln,* 4: 240.

    29. Ibid., 8: 332-33.

Against Lincoln: An Address at Gettysburg
Commentary on "Lincoln and the Economics of the American Dream"

M. E. BRADFORD

To speak on this particular occasion is, for a scholar whose opinions concerning Abraham Lincoln have been so widely discussed and systematically misrepresented, a matchless opportunity. For the papers delivered here and the books from which they derive provide a proper context in which to set the record straight, to clarify just what it is that I have maintained against the Emancipator, and what I have not said. And especially this is true of Professor Boritt's remarks on the Whig tradition in American social and economic theory.[1] Beginning with these I may hope to situate myself in relation to both the best of modern Lincoln scholarship and the relentless gravity of the Lincoln myth, contribute to the larger conversation of this conference, and still stand aside from its drift in the rigor of my criticism of the sixteenth president of the United States.

For the past three years the mere rumor of my complaints against the continuing influence of Father Abraham's example on the nation's public life has seemed to have a life of its own, surviving and even growing in inverse proportion to the number of times when some deflation or correction of it has been attempted in my own work or in the writings of my friends. What I think of Lincoln has therefore become an issue wholly apart from what I really think of Lincoln — an issue for editorials, front-page reports, and passionate commentary — all to my general astonishment and painful instruction. In one sense it may thus be argued that the press caricature of my view of Lincoln is a confirmation of the case I make against the influence of the Lincoln myth, operating to the contrary of thoughtful deliberation where the great questions of our era are concerned, pushing us instead, with diction and rhetoric, in the direction of mindless obedience and quasi-religious submission to the secular religion summarized by the greatest monument in Washington City, the Lincoln Memorial.

With respect to Lincoln I have been the subject of outraged reports issuing from Keene, New Hampshire, to Los Angeles, California—and from such various sources as the *New York Times, Chicago Sun-Times, Washington Post, Wall Street Journal, Newsweek, New Republic, Chronicle of Higher Education, New York Review of Books,* and the CBS afternoon news. It would appear that my real function in all these has been like that of Goldstein in George Orwell's *Nineteen Eighty-Four,* as rhetorical icon or symbolic adversary. I have found that I "favor slavery," consider it to be a "tenuous multiracial experiment" yet to receive the final verdict of history, and that I censure Lincoln because of "what he did for racial equality." My "destructive idea" is that due process of law was violated by the Emancipation Proclamation. My reservations concerning Lincoln's epideictic, quasi-biblical rhetoric are described as "insulting to Lincoln's idea of liberty." And the very errors embodied in such wild charges, requiring (as they do) some rejoinder, "prove" that there is something wrong with my character, regardless of their implausibility. Furthermore, I have been described as "committed to the proposition that popular sovereignty defines the nature of democratic government," and accused of causing my erstwhile associate, George Will, to "smolder" by implying an admiration for the 1854 Kansas-Nebraska Act. I have "overturned the Declaration of Independence," called Lincoln a "villain" and argued that "there is no right principle of action but self-interest"— none of which can be documented from anything I have written.

Even so, despite outrage at a gratuitous, partisan caricature, the misrepresentation of my views is proof of how careful Lincoln scholars must be in specifying just how much we mean to say—especially if the possibility of reflection on the motives of our political "new messiah" is at stake: proof of the social problem of our research and analysis when it comes up against the force of a hieratic orthodoxy based on the logical fallacy of *post hoc, ergo propter hoc.* For according to the popular argument, the essential ingredients of the myth, since the Union was preserved and the bondsmen set free by the momentous series of events which had as their climax the great battle fought out on this ground and the hero then martyred after the completion of his victory, any criticism of Lincoln is a criticism of those results and a desecration of that sacrifice. Thus, if we fault Lincoln in anything it will be reported that we object to both the purposive and the incidental consequences of his career. Or that we reject even the best possible construction of these results. Or blaspheme. Moreover, goes the inference, that as Lincoln did, so should we, providing for freedom an endless series of "new births." In arranging for such a sequence, the United States may deserve to be described as "the last best, hope of earth."[2] Even now, Lincoln's place among us is no merely antiquarian concern. As current demonstration of his continuing (and irrational) influence I need only mention the habit of Paul Simon of Illinois in using his anger with my "terrible" Lincoln essays as ethical proof of his right to a seat in the United States Senate in 1984.[3] It is still important for any public figures or politicians to "get right with Lincoln," even if they are confused about what the effort will cost them and where the example of Lincoln's total career will lead.

The focus of my work in Lincoln studies is upon the language and rhetorical strategy of what Lincoln wrote and said. This emphasis brings me to examine directly Lincoln's invocation of the American dream of personal success, his announced devotion to certain "propositional" truths, and his dependence upon the authority of "those old-time men" who had accomplished the American Revolution and established the Republic where "the original idea" of our national enterprise might unfold and prosper. In the pattern of his utterance and the relation of his words to his life I have found reason to consider Lincoln as primarily a *rhetor* and to treat his speeches and other writings, in all of their opportunistic variety, not as expressions of a political philosophy, but as exercises in management and manipulation, an artful music played to lift and lower the passions and, in behalf of a "policy" never fully stated (in fact, altered as he went along), to persuade.[4] It is in the context of an essentially rhetorical identity that Lincoln invokes a version of the American dream — Professor Boritt's "right-to-rise economics." But Lincoln is no more consistent about that doctrine than he is about other questions of principle. Or any more straightforward in inclining, as he does from the beginning of his political life, toward packaging up a "black cockade" Federalist substance inside a democratic, Jacksonian wrapper: "I presume you all know who I am. I am humble Abraham Lincoln. I have been solicited by many friends to become a candidate for the Legislature. My politics are short and sweet, like the old woman's dance. I am in

109

favor of a national bank . . . in favor of the internal improvement system and a high protective tariff."[5] Add to this oxymoronic posturing related commitments to protection of the interests of property, land policies that served the advantage of speculators, and general sympathy with the business and professional classes (as opposed, for instance, to farmers, black freedmen, or immigrant laborers) to the idea that wealth, political order, and personal liberty come "down from the top," and you have the image of an orthodox Whig covered up by a Democratic persona—a potent and calculated brew, with an egalitarian touch of "poor mouth" tossed in for a soupçon. But nothing any conservative Republican of our time could endure, even from a distance.

By his remark that government should "do for a community of people, [that] which they need to have done, but cannot do, *at all,* or cannot, *so well do,* for themselves," Lincoln drew a blank check on the bank of political necessity.[6] His devotion to liberal economics was like his devotion to "mind, all conquering mind" and to "cold, calculating unimpassioned reason," and like his attachment to the moderate rhetoric of Washington, Webster, and Clay.[7] He stuck by them so long as convenient, so long as they fed fuel into that little "engine" that knew no rest, his political ambition, whose hopes for building a political party and with it reconstituting the government of the United States—as Solon had "remade" Athens and Lycurgus Sparta in olden times— depended on a certain flexibility: a policy "to have no policy." None of which is to say that Lincoln did not, other things being equal, prefer free states to slaveholding states, honest elections to stolen votes, the letter of the Constitution (read in a Hamiltonian way) to usurpation and tyranny, and the fruits of a free economy to fiat money, graft, peculation, and wealth created by the sponsorship of the state. And also peace to war. But it is not enough to put these preferences ahead of his political advantage. Lincoln perceived as primarily a rhetorician is more or less the mixed figure of Ludwell Johnson's recent analysis of the War between the States, a man political in most public things, but transformed into something very different by the bullet of John Wilkes Booth.[8]

The rhetorical analysis of Lincoln's work, of course, depends in great measure on insights and information developed by other kinds of Lincoln scholarship—some of it the handiwork of my coauthors in this book. For rhetorical criticism derives some of its authority from a well-developed sense of the context in which a specific effort at persuasion must occur. Where the framers of the Constitution are concerned, I have drawn up my own measure of the distance between "the old policy of the Fathers" and Lincoln's distortion of their teachings.[9] With respect to other facets of Lincoln's career, I have learned much from such commentators as Donald W. Riddle, John S. Wright, Edmund Wilson, Gottfried Dietze, V. Jacque Voegeli, Eugene H. Berwanger, Leon Litwack, Harry Jaffa, Willmoore Kendall, and James A. Rawley.[10] But in the text of Roy Basler's edition, I find the reason I understand Lincoln as I do: the trope of affected modesty; the *oraculum* (speaking, in the epideictic vein, the language of the gods); the *diabole* (slandering, predicting the worst); the *argumentum ad populum* (flattering the people); the false dilemma (*crocodilities*—unacceptable choices); and, especially, the argument *ad verecundiam* (an appeal to traditional values, to the prescription of the Revolution). Only the last of these strategies involves a serious pretense of rationality; and even in appealing to an imaginary history, Lincoln is being duplicitous. Contrary to the ethics of rhetoric, he is employing all of these techniques for essentially self-serving ends: to inspire fear and anger in others that they might act as they otherwise would not, if he were a less skillful rhetorician. In his mastery of the arts of persuasion, Lincoln leads all the other presidents of the United States, even when he is talking about economics, or slaves, or when he affirms the value and authority of the Union.

My favorite proofs of Lincoln's astonishing flexibility come from his statements about slavery and blacks because, as I have learned from his thoughtless admirers, the devotees of the myth are made most uncomfortable by seeing them combined in a certain way. It is probable that Lincoln disliked slavery during most of his life, just as it is obvious that most Southerners recognized slaves as human beings in that they hoped to see them accept Christianity.[11] But the evidence is clear that Lincoln was engaged in moralistic posturing when he spoke of his "hatred" for the "peculiar institution." Otherwise we have a lot of trouble explaining his action in the 1847 Matson case, in which he attempted to enforce the Fugitive Slave Law and recover runaways; and even more trouble (in view of what he had said about living off the "sweat of other men's faces") in explaining the case he filed in Lexington, Kentucky, on October 2, 1849, to recover Todd slaves from Robert Wickliff, who had married into the family of

Robert Todd.[12] Lincoln handled the interests of the older Todd children in the dispersal of their father's estate between 1849 and 1851.[13] This dispersal involved the sale of blacks—as is clear from the Fayette County Court papers. The Lincolns did not scruple to take money from these sales—as Abraham Lincoln's public rectitude about such profits after 1854 would lead us to expect. When the Rail-splitter got too intense about this question, he verged toward the hypocritical. Hence the measuring of distance between Lincoln's words and deeds.

The record of his rhetoric does indeed turn on October 16, 1854, with his speech against Sen. Stephen Douglas and the Kansas-Nebraska Act in Peoria, Illinois, and then intensifies further in the June 16, 1858, speech at Springfield, Illinois, "A House Divided."[14] For in his August 1852 speeches to the Springfield Scott Club, Lincoln praised the Whigs for pacifying Southern fears of abolitionist excesses, for refusing to claim a special understanding of the Divine Will, and for avoiding all arguments from definition or original uses of the presidential power. His villain in these remarks is that "wicked free-soldier," Franklin Pierce of New Hampshire, who is satirized as "darker" than the mulatto girl of an old song. This is the Lincoln who told racial jokes and who attacked Martin Van Buren for entertaining too advanced a view of blacks' rights, not the Lincoln who spoke of "two universal armed camps engaged in a death struggle against each other."[15] This is the Lincoln who urged his friends to be quiet about "white only" clauses in Western state constitutions; who allowed for serfdom on "loyal" plantations and spoke of emancipation as a "root, hog, or die" opportunity; and who, in his First Inaugural, agreed to accept a Thirteenth Amendment to the Constitution which would have precluded any effort at the federal level (including any later Constitutional amendment) to make this country "*all* one thing, or *all* the other" in the matter of slavery. We may set over against this Lincoln all of the familiar passages which more recent Lincoln scholars (who are determined to save him from his record) delight in quoting, and then add to them recent arguments on how he was about to transcend his "own feelings," as described in Illinois in 1858, and move toward the radical Republican camp on the question of the rights of the freed slaves. This is the Lincoln who, had he lived, would have come out for fair housing in Chicago and the 1964 Civil Rights Act—a product of wishful thinking. That is, unless Republican politics had required that he move in such a direction—in both North and South, which even Professor Oates is not likely to argue.[16]

I have here briefly emphasized the contradictions of Lincoln on slavery and race. But the focus could be turned as well to many other elements in Lincoln's career—his relations to persons, his view of power, his religion—or his attachment to the dreams of economic opportunity for all. In the latter instance we need think only of his suggestion that "the foreman" of his "green printing office," Salmon P. Chase, "give his paper mill another turn" and create a little money whenever funds ran short. Even on the subjects of millenarian hope and chiliastic rhetoric he "teaches it both ways," complaining quickly when someone uses the *ipse dixit* on him.

But all of his arguments *ad hominem* in behalf of his own moral refinement aside, the case against a generous enthusiasm for the political prescription left to us by Abraham Lincoln turns on whether or not his was the best way to save the Union and free the slaves. Yet Lincoln did not save "the Union as it was." Rather, as the scholarship tends to agree, he played the central role in transforming it forever into a unitary structure based on a claim to power in its own right, a teleocratic instrument which, in the name of any cause that attracts a following, might easily threaten the liberties of those for whose sake it existed. By his success in getting elected on the basis of his rectitude concerning slavery, limited as that morality was by its anti-black base of support, Lincoln was the central agent in precipitating war. And his way of freeing the slaves—at bayonet point, in the midst of war, confined in a South angry and without means, with no federal plan for an intermediate period of apprenticeship in freedom—in some respects is to blame for the nation's continuing racial problems, which even today have not been resolved. Therefore, I refuse on principle to share in that enthusiasm, because I honor those original "political institutions" praised by Lincoln in his first important speech, to the Springfield Young Men's Lyceum in January of 1838.

There is another view of Lincoln's career and the events that surround it not suggested by the fallacy of *post hoc, ergo propter hoc*, a reading that carries a very different political lesson.[17] Our labor is to assure that the sacrifice made at Gettysburg and on other ground hallowed since shall not be dishonored by the apostate vanity and intellectual arrogance of those beneficiaries of remembered courage who would, even now, distort its meaning to serve lesser causes of their own and would use Lincoln to accomplish their distortion. In all of his protean complexity, the sad man from Illinois deserves a better fate.

NOTES

1. Evidence developed in Gabor S. Boritt, *Lincoln and the Economics of the American Dream* (Memphis: Memphis State University Press, 1978), which I find to be generally persuasive.

2. Roy P. Basler, ed., Marion Dolores Pratt and Lloyd A. Dunlap, asst. eds., *The Collected Works of Abraham Lincoln*, 9 vols. (New Brunswick, N.J.: Rutgers University Press, 1953-55), 5: 537.

3. Demonstrated on p. 34 of the *Wall Street Journal* of Mar. 6, 1984.

4. My comments on Lincoln's rhetoric appear in M. E. Bradford, *A Better Guide Than Reason: Studies in the American Revolution* (La Salle, Ill.: Sherwood Sugden and Co., 1979), pp. 29-57 and 185-203; in "Dividing the House: The Gnosticism of Lincoln's Political Rhetoric," *Modern Age* 23 (1979): 10-24; and in "The Lincoln Legacy: A Long View," *Modern Age* 24 (1980): 355-63.

5. Quoted in Lord Charnwood, *Abraham Lincoln* (New York: Henry Holt and Co., 1917), pp. 65-66.

6. Basler, *Collected Works of Lincoln*, 2: 220.

7. Ibid., 1: 279. On the Whig disposition to favor a moderate rhetoric on divisive questions, see Irving H. Bartlett, *Daniel Webster* (New York: W. W. Norton and Co., 1978), p. 252; Clement Eaton, *Henry Clay and the Art of American Politics* (Boston: Little, Brown and Co., 1957), pp. 129-31; and *U.S. Annals of Congress*, 15th Cong., 2d sess., 9/15/1819, pp. 1174-75.

8. I refer to Ludwell H. Johnson, *Division and Reunion: America, 1848-1877* (New York: John Wiley and Sons, 1978).

9. Basler, *Collected Works of Lincoln*, 3: 538.

10. Donald W. Riddle, *Congressman Abraham Lincoln* (Urbana: University of Illinois Press, 1957); John S. Wright, *Lincoln and the Politics of Slavery* (Reno: University of Nevada Press, 1970); Edmund Wilson, *Patriotic Gore: Studies in the Literature of the American Civil War* (New York: Oxford University Press, 1962), pp. 99-130; Gottfried Dietze, *America's Political Dilemma: From Limited to Unlimited Democracy* (Baltimore: Johns Hopkins Press, 1968); V. Jacque Voegeli, *Free But Not Equal: The Midwest and the Negro during the Civil War* (Chicago: University of Chicago Press, 1967); Eugene H. Berwanger, *The Frontier against Slavery: Western Anti-Negro Prejudice and the Slavery Extension Controversy* (Urbana: University of Illinois Press, 1967); Leon F. Litwack, *North of Slavery: The Negro in the Free States, 1790-1860* (Chicago: University of Chicago Press, 1961); Harry V. Jaffa, *Crisis of the House Divided* (Seattle: University of Washington Press, 1973); Willmoore Kendall, "Equality: Commitment or Ideal," *Phalanx* 1 (1967), and Kendall (with George

Carey), *Basic Symbols of the American Political Tradition* (Baton Rouge: Louisiana State University Press, 1970); and James A. Rawley, *Race and Politics: "Bleeding Kansas" and the Coming of the Civil War* (Philadelphia: J. B. Lippincott Co., 1969).

11. This is my answer to Harry Jaffa's claim (in "Equality, Justice, and the American Revolution: In Reply to Bradford's 'The Heresy of Equality,' " *Modern Age* 21 [1977]: 114-26) that the "authentic" representation of the Old South appears in Alexander Stephens's Corner Stone speech of March 1861, an appeal to racial theory. There is no purpose in extending the Divine Grace made available through the death of God's Son to creatures less than human. Differences in race pale into insignificance in the context of such connections.

12. Basler, *Collected Works of Lincoln*, 9: 333. See Kentucky, *Reports* 51, 289.

13. See Fayette County Court Papers File, 1849-51.

14. Basler, *Collected Works of Lincoln*, 2: 247-83, 461-69.

15. Ibid., 2: 248.

16. I refer specifically to Stephen B. Oates, *Abraham Lincoln: The Man behind the Myths* (New York: Harper and Row, 1984), which exaggerates outrageously the connection between Lincoln and the cause of civil rights in our day.

17. To find it we should apply to Lincoln's career the machinery of modern political theory as it applies to the English Puritans—especially pp. 110-13 and 124-32 of Eric Voegelin's *The New Science of Politics* (Chicago: University of Chicago Press, 1952).

Commentary on "Lincoln and the Economics of the American Dream"

PHILLIP S. PALUDAN

Professor Boritt's paper builds on his fine book to produce a picture of Lincoln that adds important insights into the fundamental ideas of the sixteenth president. The most complete study of the economic vision of Lincoln, *Lincoln and the Economics of the American Dream* is a profoundly admiring portrait written with a beguiling personal style that persuades. Does Boritt, immigrant from Hungary, sibling of doctors, successful academician, identify with Lincoln's parallel rise? If he does, it illuminates more than it hides.

Boritt's work is part of a trend of taking seriously the political economy of the nineteenth century. At the same time that Boritt was studying Lincoln's economic ideals, Eric Foner was analyzing the cultural visions implicit in Republican economic thought and Daniel Walker Howe was connecting Lincoln to the economic visions of American Whigs. And all three gained insight from Hofstadter's 1948 essay in *The American Political Tradition.*

In uncovering the economic ideology of Lincoln and his party all these authors however faced a troubling issue. They were part of a historiography that admired Lincoln, yet they knew that the ideas he and his party espoused would find an ugly and inequitable fruition in the postwar nation. Foner could escape the dilemma most easily. His book ended as war began. The nation might yet be envisioned as living in an age of wood and not iron. Howe was similarly lucky: his discussion of Lincoln took the Whigs beyond their political lifetime. Still he was troubled by what Lincoln's whiggery would spawn. But Howe escaped by saying that events had controlled Lincoln and that presumably he could not foresee what was being wrought. Hofstadter had pointed the escape route earlier—Booth's bullet saved Lincoln

116

from confronting the corruptions of the iron dome. Boritt understands more clearly what Lincoln's future would have been, but his admiration for the president keeps him, I believe, from seriously considering Lincoln's part in forging the postwar world. Boritt finds in the confrontation with slavery a subject that obscured the more troubling picture of Lincoln.[1]

But once American economic issues are unleashed it is impossible to restrain where they roam, and another stream of economic history insures that they will raise questions about Lincoln and his world.

Concurrent with studies by Boritt, Foner, and Howe, the new social and economic history of the nineteenth-century United States began to make its appearance. Interested in grand economic forces, in the applicability of Marxist insights to the United States, the new social history provides a dark picture. It is one of workers alienated from their work, long hours in often dangerous conditions, and worker protest against low wages and dehumanizing work. Also part of the picture is a story of incremental or glacial improvement in the socioeconomic status of people on the bottom and of fortunes made and kept by people already well placed. The poor had to scratch to get ahead and the rich stayed well ahead.[2]

Even studies of rural America—home to the vast majority of the population—describe a world of inequity. The cost of starting a farm was too high for most Americans and was increasing. In 1864 one guidebook to farm acquisitions declared, "A young man will have to work out a great deal more than seven years, in most cases from twice to three times that length of time before he can even pay half down for a good farm, to say nothing of the money that will be needed to begin farming with." Paul Gates describes a nation by 1860 in which farm tenancy was increasing and permanent tenancy growing. He notes that one of the reasons for the scarcity of land was the land grants that states gave to railroads, among them the Illinois Central. Meanwhile, Horace Greeley was publicly decrying the influence of land speculation on homesteaders' dreams.[3]

Summarizing the economic conditions of the nation in which Lincoln extolled the open race, Williamson and Lindert note that 1860 along with 1929 and 1914 share the dubious distinction of being the years in which economic inequality was at its peak in the United States. This conclusion endorses work by both Lee Soltow and Robert Gallman demonstrating that 30 percent of the population owned between 93-95 percent of the wealth both in the nation and in the North alone. By 1870 two-thirds of the working population in farm, shop, and industry were not masters of their own economic destiny. They worked for someone else. It is possible that these figures are skewed by the factors of a young population, but the figures are there. How open was the race?[4]

Lincoln, of course did not do community studies of Newburyport and Lynn, and the statistical techniques of the macro studies of Gallman, Soltow, Williamson, and Lindert had yet to emerge. Lincoln, the man of the West, might have seen America as the West, where opportunities were comparably better than in the East.

Furthermore the story was mixed and hard to read. The burgeoning economy was increasing its output as the nation continued its takeoff. Per capita income was increasing and fortunes were being made. The young Lincolns and young Henry Wilsons were abroad in the land. The young Ulysses Grants, however, were also there selling firewood in St. Louis. The young William Shermans were also there, failing in law and banking, describing themselves as "a dead cock in the pit." Both men were waiting, looking, for something, maybe a war, which might save their lives.[5]

Still, the Gilded Age was just peeking over the horizon. As David Montgomery shows, even the terminology of the period hid the economic dislocations. The phrase "middle class" was still being put in quotation marks when it was used, and when people spoke of the economic system as a whole they did not call it capitalism, they called it "the free labor system." American workers were still not clearly settled into obvious class patterns. As a recent paper on labor history notes, describing the workers' culture in stark class lines "involves a sacrifice of historical complexity for descriptive clarity." The workplaces of even industrial workers averaged about eight to nine workers per establishment, and strikers even in Lynn, in the largest strike to that time in our history, could cheer some of the factory owners and assail others. Despite the low *average* number in the nation's workplaces, every city had factories housing hundreds who worked in conditions described by American Iron Molders leader William Sylvis as producing "thousands sunk to a degree of mental, moral, and physical wretchedness horrible to contemplate, whose very souls are crushed within their living bodies." The cause? "Capitalists . . . the worst enemies of our race [who] make commerce of the blood and tears of helpless women and merchandize souls."

And the fiction of the age offered a critique of the expanding influence of industrial power and its impact on frail humanity. The most popular author of the 1850s was Charles Dickens, whose novels explored the evils of English industrialization. Hawthorne had looked into industrial furnaces and seen the fires of hell. Melville's short fiction of the 1850s included several tales of the evils of industrialization—the most telling "Paradise of Bachelors and Tartarus of Maids." Emerson was decrying a world in which "things are in the saddle and ride mankind." And Thoreau saw a world where "we do not ride on the railroad. It rides on us."[6]

The law of the period, if Morton Horwitz is right, was being transformed to protect the exploiting capitalist and merchants at the expense of buyers, who had to learn to beware, and at the expense of laborers, who had to look for redress for mutilation from railroad accidents to impecunious "fellow servants" rather than railroad corporations. Citizens mangled by trains lost the benefits of strict liability and had to hope that a judge would find a railroad negligent. Did the former lawyer for the Illinois Central Railroad know nothing about all this? Lincoln liked *Commonwealth* v. *Hunt* but how did he feel about *Farwell* v. *Boston and Worcester R.R.?*[7]

Slavery distracted him, as it distracted the nation. Slavery crystallized so many evils: threats to political, constitutional system, corruption of the founders' ideals. Slavery epitomized evil to a man who saw the right to rise as the basic American dream. Slavery thus was clearly the antithesis of this dream. Yet slavery might also have been the scapegoat for other Northern troubles. For example, look at *Uncle Tom's Cabin* as a reflection of Northern anxieties.

Even in his wrestling with slavery Lincoln would have found the evils of free labor laid before him. George Fitzhugh in *Sociology for the South* and *Cannibals All* had offered spirited and sophisticated indictments of ideas that Republicans of the North lionized. "Equality where are thy monuments?" Fitzhugh asked, and answered, "Deep in the bowels of the earth where women and children drag out their lives in darkness harnessed like horses to heavy cars loaded with ore. Or in some gloomy and monotonous factory, where pallid children work fourteen hours a day and go home at night to sleep in damp cellars. It may be, too, that this cellar contains aged parents too old to work, and cast off by their employer to die." Republican politicians and abolitionists were stung by this critique and as Lincoln's partner William Herndon recalled, "Sociology for the South aroused the ire of Mr. Lincoln more than most pro-slavery books." One can well imagine that it did.[8]

Lincoln did give speeches defending the free labor system. He applauded the free laborers of the North and asserted that he believed that labor was the basis of all economic value. He told workers that he was happy to live in a country where workers had the right to strike. He called the conflict a people's contest in which the North stood for the idea "of lifting artificial weights from all shoulders to clear the paths of laudable pursuit for all—to afford all an unfettered start and a fair chance in the race of life." During the war he exchanged letters with workers in Manchester, England, agreeing with them that the Civil War would, if the North were victorious, be a bold step for workers everywhere.

Yet when the rhetoric (and beautiful, eloquent rhetoric it is) is transcended, what do we see Lincoln doing during the war? Lincoln supported legislation that undercut the position of the working class of the war years. At the same time that real wages were declining, he signed bills that increased the prices that average citizens paid for practically every item they purchased, in the form of excise taxes and higher tariffs. He approved an immigrant aid bill which William Sylvis called "the most infamous in America" and which the mayor of New York deplored at a time when "nearly 50,000 operatives in this city alone are contending against the oppression of capital and the wages paid are inadequate for their support."[9] He did something perhaps, but not much, to limit the supression of strikes by the military in one case in St. Louis. What he did do most often was to give speeches and send letters to workers' meetings assuring them of his sympathies. He also signed a draft bill that allowed men with $300 to stay home while those poorer had to go off to war. His vigorous support for the National Banking Bill led to a measure that consolidated the economic power of the Northeastern bankers to such an extent that even Henry Carey protested against "the Money monopolists" of New York. By 1866 this new banking system would provide a per capita circulation of money in the Northeast of $33.30 while it stood at $6.36 in the seven Midwestern states. Lincoln's tariff policy did have some labor support and the Homestead Act did provide more farms even amidst "an incongruous land system." But the dark side of the ledger as well as the light must be considered.[10]

For all his speeches and his undoubtedly admirable and advanced equalitarian ideals, Lincoln's behavior needs to be examined in light of the new social-economic history. I think that Boritt played a vital role in pushing inquiry to a troubling point. We have known for years of "the Tycoon's" political talent, and his extraordinary ability to sense the currents of the time. LaWanda Cox, building on the insights of Richard Current and David Donald, has clarified these capacities in the emancipation area. Surely this sensibility and this ability might be used in the economic realm.

But we have had an escape clause that kept the insight from being explored. The Whig theory of the presidency, which Lincoln allegedly adopted, allowed him to be the master of war making but not responsible for forging the foundations of the Gilded Age. But Boritt and colleagues have demonstrated that Lincoln's whiggery was an active one in the economic arena as well. He promoted banking and supported other elements of what we might call the Second American System. Can we still keep Lincoln unsoiled by the age of Grant?[11]

The time may be right for a serious inquiry. The economic ideas of contemporary America correspond to many of those in Lincoln's day. Economic history is being woven into the mainstream. We are beginning to understand and respect the economic beliefs of political leaders. We are beginning to evaluate the economic experience of the "many poor" or "the many." Because of the work of Boritt, Foner, and Howe and that of the new social-economic history, we are approaching the point where we can look more carefully at Lincoln's relationship to the world that Thernstrom, Knights, Dawley, Dublin, and Williamson have found.[12] We may be ready to ask more profitably the question we asked before of another Republican president, "What did the president know, and when did he know it?"

Do not mistake me. I do not look forward to tarring Lincoln with a Nixonesque result. I love the man too. Like Stephen Oates and probably everyone here, Lincoln's death can make me almost weep, every time it happens. But still I would like to know him as a man of his age, not as a man too good for it.

NOTES

1. Eric Foner, *Free Soil, Free Labor, Free Men: The Ideology of the Republican Party before the Civil War* (New York: Oxford University Press, 1970); Daniel Walker Howe, *The Political Culture of the American Whigs* (Chicago: University of Chicago Press, 1979); Gabor Boritt, *Lincoln and the Economics of the American Dream* (Memphis: Memphis State University Press, 1978); Richard Hofstadter, *The American Political Tradition and the Men Who Made It* (New York: Alfred A. Knopf, 1948), ch. 5.

2. The extensive literature in the new social and economic history is summarized in Michael Kammen, ed., *The Past before Us: Contemporary Historical Writing in the United States* (Ithaca: Cornell University Press, 1980); and in vol. 20 of *Reviews in American History*.

3. Paul Gates, *Agriculture and the Civil War* (New York: Alfred Knopf, 1965); David Schob, *Hired Hands and Plowboys: Farm Labor in the Midwest, 1815-60* (Urbana: University of Illinois Press, 1975); *New York Tribune*, Jan. 26, 1860; Fred Bateman and Jeremy Atack, "The Profitability of Northern Agriculture in 1860," *Research in Economic History* 4 (1979): 87-125; Jeremy Atack, "Farming and Farm Making Costs Revisited," *Agricultural History* 56 (Oct. 1982): 661-76.

4. Lee Soltow, *Men and Wealth in the United States* (New Haven: Yale University Press, 1975); Robert Gallman, "Professor Pessen and the Egalitarian Myth," *Social Science History* 2 (Winter 1978): 194-95; Jeffrey Williamson and Peter Lindert, *American Inequality: A Macroeconomic History* (New York: Academic Press, 1980).

5. Lloyd Lewis, *Sherman: Fighting Prophet* (New York: Harcourt Brace and Co., 1932); William S. McFeely, *Grant: A Biography* (New York: Norton, 1981).

6. Frank Luther Mott, *Golden Multitudes: The Story of Best Sellers in the United States* (New York: Macmillan Co., 1947); James David Hart, *The Popular Book: A History of America's Literary Taste* (New York: Oxford University Press, 1950); William B. Dillingham, *Melville's Short Fiction 1853-56* (Athens: University of Georgia Press, 1977); Marvin Fisher, *Going Under: Melville's Short Fiction and the American 1850s* (Baton Rouge: Louisiana State University Press, 1977); Carolyn L. Karcher, *Shadow over the Promised Land: Slavery, Race and Violence in Melville's America* (Baton Rouge: Louisiana State University Press, 1980); Beryl Bowland, "Melville's Bachelors and Maids," *American Literature* 41 (1969): 389-405; David Montgomery, *Beyond Equality* (New York: Knopf, 1967), p. 40; Leonard Wallock, "Limits of Solidarity: Philadelphia's Journeymen Printers in the Mid Nineteenth Century," paper, Organization of American Historians Meeting, Los Angeles, 1984, p. 21.

7. Morton J. Horwitz, *The Transformation of American Law, 1780-1860* (Cambridge, Mass.: Harvard University Press, 1977); Wex Malone, "The Formative Era of Contributory Negligence," *Illinois Law Review* 41 (July 1946): 151-82; Leonard Levy, *The Law of the Commonwealth and Chief Justice Shaw* (Cambridge, Mass.: Harvard University Press, 1957), pp. 166-82.

Commentary on "Lincoln's Economics"

8. Harvey Wish, *George Fitzhugh* (Baton Rouge, 1943), pp. 174-88; Stephen B. Oates, *With Malice toward None: The Life of Abraham Lincoln* (New York: Harper and Row, 1977), pp. 137-38, 179; Boritt, *Lincoln and the Economics of the American Dream*.

9. *Fincher's Trades Review*, Mar. 19, 1865; Apr. 9, 1864; Lawrence Costello, "The New York City Labor Movement, 1861-1873" (Ph.D. diss., Columbia University, 1967); Susan P. Lee and Peter Passell, *A New Economic View of American History* (New York: Norton, 1979); Jeffrey Williamson, "Watersheds and Turning Points: Conjectures on the Long Term Impact of Civil War Financing," *Journal of Economic History* 34 (Sept. 1974): 652-61.

10. Richard Sylla, "Federal Policy, Banking, Market Structure and Capital Formation in the United States," *Journal of Economic History* 29 (1969), 657-86; Robert Sharkey, "Commercial Banking," in *Economic Change in the Civil War Era*, ed. David T. Gilchrist and W. David Lewis (Greenville, Del.: Eleutherian Mills-Hagley Foundation, 1964), pp. 27-30; David Gische, "The New York City Banks and the Development of the National Banking System," *American Journal of Legal History*, 23 (Jan. 1979): 33-55.

11. LaWanda Cox, *Lincoln and Black Freedom: A Study in Presidential Leadership* (Columbia: University of South Carolina Press, 1981); Richard N. Current, *The Lincoln Nobody Knows* (New York: McGraw-Hill, 1958), pp. 187-213; David H. Donald, *Lincoln Reconsidered: Essays on the Civil War Era* (New York: Knopf, 1956).

12. Stephan Thernstrom, *Poverty and Progress* (Cambridge, Mass.: Harvard University, 1964); Peter R. Knights, *The Plain People of Boston, 1830-1860: A Study in City Growth* (New York: Oxford University Press, 1971); Alan Dawley, *Class and Community: The Industrial Revolution in Lynn* (Cambridge, Mass.: Harvard University Press, 1976); Thomas Dublin, *Women at Work: The Transformation of Work and Community in Lowell, Massachusetts, 1826-1860* (New York: Columbia University Press, 1981); Williamson and Lindert, *American Inequality*. Boritt does make reference to Thernstrom and Knights in one footnote and in his bibliography.

CHAPTER 5

ABRAHAM LINCOLN AND AMERICAN POLITICAL RELIGION

Glen E. Thurow

"POLITICAL RELIGION" seems to combine two things that ought to be separated—politics and religion. On the one hand it suggests the danger that politics will be inflamed with passions of religious intensity or made subservient to the designs of a clergy claiming special dispensation. On the other, it offers the specter of religion debased by the arts of worldly politics or threatened by the irreligion of partisan politicians. A proper concern both for our salvation and for our political liberty and peace seems to demand that a "wall of separation" be erected between politics and religion.

Indeed, this opinion seems to be enshrined in the American Constitution. The First Amendment to the Constitution provides that "Congress shall make no law respecting an establishment of religion, or prohibiting the free exercise thereof," thus guaranteeing that no religion shall have a position of national authority from which it may claim the power of the state to impose its own ends, and also assuring that Americans may have the liberty to worship as they please without the danger of political corruption of religion. That we are a liberal democracy, not a pure democracy, means, among other things, that politics is free of ecclesiastical authority and religion free of political authority.

Yet, of course, the United States has never seen the complete separation of church and state. Not only is there vast governmental encouragement of religion through indirect means—one need only think of the tax exemptions given religious institutions—but there is also much direct governmental encouragement. As Robert Bellah and others have noted, nearly all of the most solemn state papers and speeches in American history have referred to God.[1] Every presidential inaugural address, with the exception of the perfunctory Second Inaugural of George Washington, has referred to God. The motto "In God We Trust," found on our coins, the pledge to the flag ("one nation, under God"), and perhaps such a national holiday as Thanksgiving give religion a conspicuous public place in our political life.

For all their pervasiveness, these manifestations of religion by themselves do not necessarily raise any doubts about our common understanding of the relation of religion and politics. Some of them may be required or permitted by the Constitution in order to assure religious liberty (as the Supreme Court has suggested tax exemption may be). Others may be necessary concessions to the religious sensibilities of the people, but in no substantial way aid or inhibit religion or give the government religious ends. Some may simply be violations of the Constitution that the courts or other branches of government have not yet got around to rooting out for one reason or another.

What requires closer attention is that many of the greatest American statesmen have thought that the kind of government the Constitution erected involved a connection between politics and religion. Among the founders even those who were most adamant that the new government require separation of church and state thought that politics required religion. Thomas Jefferson, more than any other, has been given credit for establishing religious liberty in America. Unlike many of the signers of the Declaration of Independence, Jefferson thought one of its central purposes was to free us from "monkish ignorance and superstition." He regarded his Bill for Establishing Religious Freedom in Virginia as one of the three most notable works of his life, and rejected most of the traditional theological doctrines of Christianity.[2] Yet in discussing the threat to liberty posed by slavery, Jefferson wrote: "And can the liberties of a nation be thought secure when we have removed their only firm basis, a conviction in the minds of the people that these liberties are the gift of God? That they are not to be violated but with his wrath? Indeed I tremble for my country when I reflect that God is just; that his justice cannot sleep forever."[3] In the face of the mighty passions aroused by slavery, Jefferson wondered whether human liberties need the support they find in the conviction that these liberties are from God. While he thought that the state cannot establish religion or use its laws to enforce belief or worship, the state apparently can use the means of persuasion at its disposal to help establish this conviction—even as he had earlier taught that "nature's God" entitled Americans to independence.

Perhaps the most impressive statements about the connection between religion and politics made by the founders are to be found in George Washington. In his "Farewell Address" he wrote: "Of all the dispositions and habits which lead to political prosperity, religion and morality are indispensable supports. In vain would that man claim the tribute of patriotism who should labor to subvert these great pillars of human happiness, these firmest props of the duties of men and citizens. The mere politician, equally with the pious man, ought to respect and to cherish them. . . . [L]et us with caution indulge the supposition that morality can be maintained without religion."[4] Washington, like Jefferson, not only invokes God, but also argues that sound politics requires the cultivation of certain religious beliefs and opinions.

In no American statesman does the union of political and religious sentiments reach more sublime heights than in Abraham Lincoln. Lincoln is the central figure of American political religion, not only because of the way in which Americans have venerated him, but chiefly because of what he himself said.[5] His most famous speeches, the Gettysburg Address and the Second Inaugural, are the poems of his political religion. Lord Charnwood commented on the Second Inaugural: "Probably no other speech of a modern statesman uses so unreservedly the language of intense religious feeling."[6] Said Lincoln:

> The Almighty has His own purposes. "Woe unto the world because of offences! for it must needs be that offences come; but woe to that man by whom the offence cometh!" If we shall suppose that American Slavery is one of those offences which, in the providence of God, must needs come, but which, having continued through His appointed time, He now wills to remove, and that He gives to both North and South, this terrible war, as the woe due to those by whom the offence came, shall we discern therein any departure from those divine attributes which the believers in a Living God always ascribe to Him? Fondly do we hope—fervently do we pray—that this mighty scourge of war may speedily pass away. Yet, if God wills that it continue, until all the wealth piled up by the bond-man's two hundred and fifty

years of unrequited toil shall be sunk, and until every drop of blood drawn with the lash, shall be paid by another drawn with the sword, as was said three thousand years ago, so still it must be said "the judgments of the Lord, are true and righteous altogether."[7]

The language of the Gettysburg Address, on the other hand, is not so explicitly theological. Apart from the phrase "under God," the speech contains nothing explicitly religious. Yet religion seems somehow evoked. The biblical cadences of the language; the theme of birth, death, and rebirth; the overtones in the dedication of the nation to equality that suggest the dedication of a child to God in baptism; and in the testing of that nation that suggests the test of religious faith all endow the speech with the seriousness and solemnity of religion. The Second Inaugural sees the nation under the providence and judgment of God; the Gettysburg Address appropriates for the nation the language and dignity of religion.

A host of books were written in the late nineteenth and early twentieth centuries seeking to show that Lincoln was a conventional believer of one sort or another. Yet the beauty and power of Lincoln's words compel us to wonder whether they do not reflect an understanding equally beautiful and powerful. Lord Charnwood again catches the problem in speaking of the Second Inaugural: "Neither the thought nor the words are in any way conventional; no sensible reader now could entertain a suspicion that the orator spoke to the heart of the people but did not speak from his own heart. But an old Illinois attorney, who thought he knew the real Lincoln behind the President, might have wondered whether the real Lincoln spoke here."[8] The old Illinois attorney to whom Charnwood refers was Lincoln's law partner, William H. Herndon, who, with other of Lincoln's close associates, claimed after his death that Lincoln was not a believer in Christianity; some even testified that he was an atheist.

Herndon tells us that as a young man Lincoln was a skeptic and associated with fellow skeptics in New Salem. In 1834 he supposedly wrote an essay showing that the Bible was not God's inspired word, nor Jesus God's divine son. An employer, either scandalized or fearing its effects on Lincoln's future, threw it into the stove. Lincoln's first law partner told Herndon that Lincoln was "an avowed and open infidel, and sometimes bordered on atheism."[9] Herndon did not believe that Lincoln's skeptical opinions ever changed. As he put it:

128

"Lincoln was very politic, and a very shrewd man in some particulars. When he was talking to a Christian, he adapted himself to the Christian . . . he was at moments, as it were, a Christian, through politeness, courtesy, or good breeding toward the delicate, tender-nerved man, the Christian, and in two minutes after, in the absence of such men, and among his own kind, the same old unbeliever."[10] (Of course, Lincoln may have been tender with atheists.) Lincoln never belonged to a church, although he sometimes attended with his wife.

Various explanations have been given for the apparent dichotomy between the private and the public Lincoln, beginning with Herndon's explanation that Lincoln merely used conventional religious language because he was president of a religious people. A reading of the Second Inaugural and Gettysburg Address should convince one, however, that this explanation is hardly sufficient. The typical presidential inaugural tenders a general thanks to the Almighty. Lincoln sees the providence of God exacting punishment through war while directing Americans to their sins. As Lincoln himself noted, such a message is not calculated to be immediately popular or to simply sooth prejudices.

The other major explanation is that Lincoln experienced a conversion, or, since there does not seem to be one point at which Lincoln changed, several crises of the spirit. This explanation gains some plausibility from the fact that the testimony regarding Lincoln's freethinking comes mostly from his younger days. Herndon was not closely associated with Lincoln during his presidential years. However, when one considers that the testimony about Lincoln's beliefs comes not only from his earlier career but from men like Herndon, whose interests make their testimony suspect, one doubts the need for this explanation. Furthermore, evidence for the opinion is scanty, and largely rests upon presumed effects of years of personal misfortunes and heavy public burdens. What is not debatable, however, is what Lincoln himself said.

It must be stressed that Lincoln's speeches were political speeches, not personal confessions. Religion is present in Lincoln's speeches because of its relevance to political problems. Much of the confusion surrounding Lincoln's religion stems from the fact that commentators have tried to see whether he belonged to the religion of the churches, neglecting the possibility that his speeches were political, not religious; or were religious because they were political. In Lincoln's speeches one cannot find personal piety divorced from politics. Lincoln leads us not to religion, but to political religion. The Gettysburg Address and the Second Inaugural are the speeches of Lincoln in which religious language is most apparent and pervasive; they are also the speeches that contain or point to Lincoln's most enduring reflections on American politics.

Lincoln's political religion must be understood in the context of his view of the central political problem facing the American people. For Lincoln the central task of statesmanship was to maintain the loyalty of Americans to the principle that all men are created equal. "He who molds public sentiment goes deeper than he who enacts statutes and pronounces decisions. He makes statutes or decisions possible or impossible to execute."[11] America *is* the public belief in equality:

> Our government rests in public opinion. Whoever can change public opinion, can change the government, practically just so much. Public opinion, on any subject, always has a *"central idea,"* from which all its minor thoughts radiate. That "central idea" in our political public opinion, at the beginning was, and until recently has continued to be, "the equality of men." And although it was always submitted patiently to whatever of inequality there seemed to be as matter of actual necessity, its constant working has been a steady progress towards the practical equality of all men.[12]

The principle of equality, in Lincoln's view, was the foundation of popular justice. In a speech delivered in Chicago on July 10, 1858, Lincoln attempted to explain the tie between the Union and equality. In explaining why we celebrate the Fourth of July, he said we try to account for our present prosperity by looking back to

> a race of men living in that day whom we claim as our fathers and grandfathers; they were iron men, they fought for the principle that they were contending for; and we understood that by what they then did it has followed that the degree of prosperity that we now enjoy has come to us. We hold this annual celebration to remind ourselves of all the good done in this process of time, of how it was done and who did it, and how we are historically connected with it; and we go from these meetings in better humor with ourselves — we feel more attached the one to the other, and more firmly bound to the country we inhabit.[13]

But, Lincoln goes on to say, to look back to "a race of men living in that day whom we claim as our fathers and grandfathers" would not necessarily unite us the one to the other. "We have not yet reached the whole." After all, he continues, we have many citizens who cannot look back to those men as their fathers and grandfathers. They, or their ancestors, have come from Europe since the Revolution. They have no common ties of blood to that earlier race that would connect them to us: "but when they look through that old Declaration of Independence they find that those old men say that 'We hold these truths to be self-evident, that all men are created equal,' and then they feel that that moral sentiment taught in that day evidences their relation to those men, that it is the father of all moral principle in them, and that they have a right to claim it as though they were blood of the blood, and flesh of the flesh of the men who wrote the Declaration, and so they are."[14]

The Union can assimilate newcomers because it is based on a principle that is the father of morality in us; we do not have a union because of a common history, according to Lincoln, but we have a common history because the Union is the triumph of moral principle within ourselves. Lincoln always made it clear that in working for the preservation of the Union, he was not so much working for the mere adherence of one state to another as he was working for the principle upon which the Union was based: the "Union *must be preserved in the purity of its principles as well as in the integrity of its territorial parts.*" If the territorial union could be saved only by giving up the principles of the Declaration, Lincoln once said, "I would rather be assassinated on this spot than to surrender it."[15]

The Union was so important for Lincoln because it was the necessary means to the preservation of the belief in equality. Although Lincoln thought the proposition that all men are created equal to be the foundation of popular morality, people did not automatically follow this principle. To be effective it had to be embodied in a nation and gain the weight of public opinion. Our moral good, in Lincoln's view, was dependent upon a sound political order.

The greatest threat, as Lincoln saw it, in the political events leading up to the Civil War was the threatened erosion of the principle of equality. As he once explained:

> But soberly, it is now no child's play to save the principles of Jefferson from total overthrow in this nation.

One would start with great confidence that he could convince any sane child that the simpler propositions of Euclid
are true; but, nevertheless, he would fail, utterly, with one
who should deny the definitions and axioms. The principles
of Jefferson are the definitions and axioms of free society.
And yet they are denied and evaded, with no small show of
success.[16]

In his Lyceum Speech Lincoln described and analyzed the erosion of
revolutionary sentiments taking place as early as the 1830s: This
erosion was due not only to the mere passage of time, but also to the
fact that the revolutionary fervor had never been firmly attached to
the Constitution and laws of the United States.[17] And this was in part
due to the very nature of those revolutionary principles.

The Declaration of Independence asserts its principles to be self-
evident truths, applicable to all men everywhere. No particular circumstances can add or detract from them. According to the declaration, we hold to these principles because they are true, not because
they are ours. It does not look back to our peculiar customs to justify
its principles, but appeals only to the "laws of Nature and of Nature's
God." The universal character of the principle of human equality
points away from, not toward, the nation.

Yet a self-evident truth, for all its rationality, is not teachable. As
Lincoln notes, if some deny the axioms of the declaration, there is
no way to teach them by reasoning that they are indeed true. The
maintenance of those truths requires the support of public opinion,
the support of a nation, yet those truths as stated by the declaration
do not suggest the way in which that support can be achieved.

In the poetry of the Gettysburg Address, Lincoln unites the
universal principle of the declaration with the life of this one particular
nation. In so doing he subtly changes the status of the principle of
equality and ennobles and impassions political life. I cannot here fully
describe Lincoln's masterful weaving, but consider simply the opening
sentence: "Four score and seven years ago our fathers brought forth
on this continent, a new nation, conceived in liberty, and dedicated
to the proposition that all men are created equal." Lincoln both tells
the story of the nation's founding and reasserts the principles of its
founders, suggesting either that we hold to the principles because
they were held by our fathers, or that the truth itself is in question
because it rests only upon the customary authority of our fathers, or

both. Although Lincoln believes that equality applies to all people everywhere, he points not to a natural but to a customary origin of the principle. This implication is strengthened by Lincoln's terming the self-evident truth of the declaration a proposition. A self-evident truth is necessarily true and does not need to be proven; a proposition may be either true or false and must be proven to be one or the other. A proposition, unlike an axiom, may be teachable.

In assessing these changes from the declaration, it is important to remember that the Gettysburg Address was part of Lincoln's effort to win the Civil War. The issue involved in that war, according to the address itself, was not whether it is true that all men are created equal, but whether a nation dedicated to that proposition could long endure. The perpetuation of such a nation requires, in Lincoln's view, that the axiom of equality become teachable.

To be dedicated to a proposition is to be dedicated to proving it. What for Jefferson was a truth upon which all else is to be built becomes for Lincoln a proposition that one must prove. Because the truth of human equality requires the support of public opinion to be the effective basis of a nation, to prove the proposition politically means to make it the animating heart of the nation. The viewpoint of the Gettysburg Address is the viewpoint of a nation seeking to endure. It is from that viewpoint that the principle of human equality is but a proposition. For the nation it is a principle of faith and it is yet to be shown that it can be the enduring basis of its own order.

But matters of faith require testimony to be believed. It is for this reason that the principles of the Declaration of Independence are entwined in the story of the nation in the Gettysburg Address. The way in which Lincoln tries to solve the problem posed by the erosion of the belief in equality can now be seen. How does one maintain the principle of equality when public opinion slips away from it? The answer is that one forces attention away from the public opinion of the moment to the public opinion of the founders. The authority of the founders may recall the public opinion of the moment to its moral principle.

Lincoln's view of the relationship of past and present in the American nation can be clarified by comparing it with that of John Dewey, who writes: "The things in civilization we most prize are not of ourselves. They exist by the grace of the doings and sufferings of the continuous human community in which we are a link. Ours is the

LIBRARY ST. MARY'S COLLEGE

responsibility of conserving, rectifying and expanding the heritage of values we have received that those who come after us may receive it more solid and secure, more widely accessible and more generously shared than we have received it."[18] This is not the relationship of past and present suggested by Lincoln's analysis of public opinion. Lincoln cannot be understood unless we see that the past does not pass on a set of values, as a father might pass his estate to his heir. A later generation does not simply receive the past as though it were a material object. For the founders to have their proper authority, the present generation must also see the truth of the principles that moved those earlier men. Lincoln's interpretation of the Civil War can be experienced as the correct interpretation because the citizens can understand themselves as the result of the past which Lincoln draws for them.

By tying present events to the story of the nation's founding in the Gettysburg Address, Lincoln seeks to use the Civil War to point to the principles of the founding. In Lincoln's view the war had universal significance because it did not stem from causes peculiar to the United States. The cause of the war was not simply the accidental fact that America happened to have slavery, but was to be found in the erosion of the belief in human equality. This erosion was due to causes endemic to free governments. However, it was by tying the belief in human equality to the particular experiences of Americans that those beliefs could be saved.

Lincoln portrays the possibility of a government founded on human equality as being absolutely dependent on the actions of Americans. Americans will determine for all mankind whether such a government is possible. In the Gettysburg Address the universal principles of the Declaration of Independence are portrayed as embodied in this country, and as dependent upon its perpetuation for their political efficacy. It is not an exaggeration to say that the Gettysburg Address pictures everything of importance, including the meaning of life and death itself, as being dependent upon the continued existence of an American nation dedicated to human equality. The Union becomes a sacred union.

Yet it would be a mistake to conclude that Lincoln is simply a complete nationalist, one who finds all meaning to reside in the nation. The great importance attached to the political action of Americans in the Gettysburg Address must be counterbalanced in Lincoln's

134

thought by the Second Inaugural, which seems to draw limits to the possibilities of political action.

The subject of Lincoln's Second Inaugural Address, delivered as the war neared its close, is the ground on which the two sections might be rejoined. Its intent is to point away from war toward reunion. The heart of the speech, its second and third paragraphs, is a compact piece of rhetoric. These paragraphs conclude that neither the intentions nor the prayers of the people have been fulfilled in the course of the war, and that the judgment of God must be said to be just if the war is a punishment for the sin of slavery. The speech attempts to end the war in people's minds (even as it would soon be ended on the battlefield) by convincing them that the war is a completed action and that justice has been done. They need no longer be the warriors of justice. Charity may rule their actions.

It is in Lincoln's speculations on the meaning of the Civil War that his political religion becomes fully revealed. To see its character let us follow Lincoln's argument with some care.

In searching for the meaning of the war, Lincoln first concludes that it has not been determined by intentions or prayers. Both North and South "looked for an easier triumph, and a result less fundamental and astounding. . . . The prayers of both could not be answered; that of neither has been answered fully." A third possibility remains — that people are not the source of the meaning of the war. "The Almighty has His own purposes."

The Almighty's purposes are expressed in the words of Matthew 18:7: "Woe unto the world because of offences for it must needs be that offences come; but woe to that man by whom the offence cometh." Lincoln applies this quotation to the Civil War by asking and answering a question. The question is unexpected. It is neither "What are the purposes of God in the present situation?" nor "What is the relationship between God's purposes and ours in the present situation?" but, "Assuming God's purposes, what are we to say about His qualities?": "If we shall suppose that American Slavery is one of those offences which, in the providence of God, must needs come, but which, having continued through His appointed time, He now wills to remove, and that He gives to both North and South, this terrible war, as the woe due to those by whom the offence came, shall we discern

135

therein any departure from those divine attributes which the believers in a living God always ascribe to Him?"

The answer has nothing to do with whether one likes the war, or whether the war is terrible. "Fondly do we hope—fervently do we pray—that this mighty scourge of war may speedily pass away.[19] Yet, if God wills that it continue, until all the wealth piled up by the bond-man's two hundred and fifty years of unrequited toil shall be sunk, and until every drop of blood drawn with the lash, shall be paid by another drawn with the sword, as was said three thousand years ago, so still it must be said 'the judgments of the Lord, are true and righteous altogether.' " Thus, in the words of Psalm 19:9 Lincoln finds the order in God that he found wanting in human intentions and prayers.

Now the character of Lincoln's argument needs to be precisely understood. Lincoln does not assert that God was the author of the Civil War, as a playwright is the author of a play. The only statements made about the relationship of the Civil War to God are conditional, and the only affirmation made concerns not the cause of the war but the justice of God's judgment under assumed conditions. Furthermore, the hypothetical conditions under which Lincoln affirms that the judgments of God could be declared just are not restricted to the actual circumstances of the war. The judgments of God would be just even if the war continued until all the bondman's wealth should be destroyed and the blood drawn with the lash paid for with the sword.

In understanding what Lincoln does claim to know about the purposes of God, we have the testimony of Lincoln upon the precise point in a letter to Thurlow Weed written shortly after the inaugural. Lincoln wrote that he expected the Second Inaugural to wear as well as and perhaps better than anything he had written. However, it was not immediately popular: "Men are not flattered by being shown that there has been a difference of purpose between the Almighty and them. To deny it, however, in this case, is to deny that there is a God governing the world. It is a truth which I thought needed to be told; and as whatever of humiliation there is in it, falls most directly on myself, I thought others might afford for me to tell it."[20]

Lincoln perceives a gulf between human purposes and God's and comes to this perception by seeing the imperfection of human purposes. What becomes clear is not the content of God's purposes, but that they differ from ours. This central truth is placed in the inaugural immediately following Lincoln's discussion of prayer, and reveals the importance of prayer. We may note that although prayer may be rational in content, it is folly to believe that God can be given directions even through our prayers. To ask God for something assumes that human reason may govern the world. But "the Almighty has His own Purposes." Prayer shares the limits of human reason, but does not confess them. Because Lincoln sees the limits of our purposes and prayers, he is able to see that they are not God's.

One can see the kinship of the Second Inaugural to that skepticism for which Lincoln was noted among his friends. The faith that regards providence as essentially unknowable and the skepticism of all providence agree that the pattern of future events cannot be known and hence that our capacity to manage the future is limited.

In a perceptive and well-known essay, Edmund Wilson attempts to identify Lincoln's discussion of providence with the Marxist conception of history — that of "a power which somehow takes possession of men and works out its intentions through them. . . . [It is] a kind of superhuman force that vindicates and overrides and that manipulates mankind as its instruments."[21] The difficulty in making this identification is well illustrated by the quotation Wilson brings forward to prove it. In one of the debates with Douglas, Lincoln said: "Accustomed to trample on the rights of others, you have lost the genius of your own independence, and become the fit subjects of the first cunning tyrant who rises among you. And let me tell you that all these things are prepared for you with the logic of history, if the elections shall promise that the next Dred Scott decision and all future decisions will be quietly acquiesced in by the people."[22] It is a strange sort of superhuman historical force that depends on the results of an election whose outcome Lincoln clearly regards as within human choice! Rather, as the Second Inaugural shows, Lincoln does not claim to know anything about the workings of history except that it has not been governed by human intentions and prayers. Nor is Lincoln skeptical of the possibility of ethical judgments. He does not deny, indeed he affirms, that the South is the aggressor, the North the aggressed upon, and that slavery is unjust.

What, then, does Lincoln claim to know about the war? Lincoln affirms that it must be said that "the judgments of the Lord are true and righteous altogether" even if the misery wrought by slavery is paid for with great destruction and bloodshed. It is not the war, considered as a human action, but punishment for the sin of slavery which Lincoln affirms to be just. Only if we suppose the war to be the will of God can it be seen as punishment.

Lincoln finds meaning in the war only by diverting his glance from the war and fixing it on slavery. The injustice of slavery means that punishment is deserved. Lincoln's position on the sin of slavery and the justice of punishment would remain whether there was a war or not. The easy misinterpretation of the Second Inaugural—that Lincoln says that the Civil War is a punishment of God—is allowed by Lincoln in order to teach the crucial truth that slavery is unjust. The horror of war was easier for most people to see than was the sin of slavery.

Lincoln seeks to use belief to make his listeners aware of the limits of their reason. As their prayers reveal, people are not aware of the limits of their own governing, and hence are not perfectly rational animals. Their feelings and sentiments must come to the support of reason. At the end of the penultimate paragraph of the address Lincoln asks his audience to testify to the justice of God's punishment. In so doing, Lincoln seeks to create a public opinion that is neither fully rational nor merely imposed belief, but partly rational and partly self-imposed belief.

Lincoln's practical aim in the Second Inaugural is to instill a spirit in the people that would lead them to support his policies for reunion. Reunion could not be built upon the hatreds of the war, or by giving up justice. One had to combine justice with charity. The Second Inaugural ends with the enduring words: "With malice towards none; with charity for all; with firmness in the right, as God gives us to see the right, let us strive on to finish the work we are in; to bind up the nation's wounds; to care for him who shall have borne the battle, and for his widow, and his orphan—to do all which may achieve and cherish a just, and a lasting peace, among ourselves, and with all nations."

This counsel of charity becomes possible insofar as Lincoln succeeds in teaching an opinion about the war. If people acknowledge that the war is a just punishment of God for the sin of slavery, it is possible to be charitable to the South, for both North and South are then equals in the eyes of God. Human charity requires divine vengeance. In punishment and confession North and South become equal and are restored to justice. All are equally under God's judgment.

Lincoln thus leads the people to acknowledge limits to their government. Their actions must be bounded by an order they did not create. Lincoln teaches the people to be reasonable or moderate by teaching that an exact justice is to be left to God alone. It can be left to Him alone because the war demonstrates the justice of His providence. That passion for a cold or inhuman justice that would demand an eye for an eye is moderated by a human charity that rests upon divine retribution.

In the Second Inaugural Lincoln teaches by example that the passions of the people can be controlled only by counterpassions, not by a mere statement of the truth. It is necessary for the passions to be controlled because even the government of the people is not unlimited. It must adhere in thought and action to certain principles. But the people must impose these limits on themselves if self-government is not to be abandoned. Lincoln found the possibility of such self-limitation in belief in a God whose purposes were not those of the people, whose purposes could not be known, but could nevertheless be recognized to be just.

But if we compare the Second Inaugural with the Gettysburg Address, we are faced with another problem. The universal purposes to which Lincoln dedicated the nation anew in the earlier address are now gone from view. There the nation was dedicated to the proposition that all men are created equal and upon its fate rested the great question of whether government of, by, and for the people would perish from the earth. But if we do not govern the course of history, if the Almighty has His own purposes, then human action cannot prove or disprove a proposition. One cannot know the experience of one nation to be decisive because God's purposes are not ours. In endowing human actions with decisive historical significance, the Gettysburg Address seems to deny chance or God's providence. In the Second Inaugural human purposes and actions seem neither theoretically nor historically decisive.

The Gettysburg Address is not rejected, but transcended, by the Second Inaugural. It is transcended by transcending the viewpoint of a nation which the Gettysburg Address has been held to express so supremely. "Fourscore and seven years ago." The horizon of the Gettysburg Address is clearly indicated by its opening words. It tells the story of the nation in such a compelling manner that popular opinion has considered the address to be the supreme expression of American democracy. It may well be that Lincoln was recreating the nation in giving the speech. As Edmund Wilson has noted: "When we put ourselves back into the period, we realize that it was not at all inevitable to think of it as Lincoln thought, and we come to see that Lincoln's conception of the course and the meaning of the Civil War was indeed an interpretation that he partly took over from others but that he partly made others accept, and in the teeth of a good deal of resistance on the part of the North itself."[23] But it remains true that Lincoln spoke from the viewpoint of the nation—with the qualification that it was the viewpoint of the nation he was helping to create.

The Second Inaugural, however, does not speak from the viewpoint of the nation: "As was said three thousand years ago, so still it must be said, the judgments of the Lord are true and righteous altogether."[24] It ties the present not to our forebears, but to those who have acknowledged the justice of God at whatever time and place, and specifically to ancient Israel. The Second Inaugural speaks standing under God's judgment. On the nation's part, our responsibility is for the living and the dead, for our forebears and for the soldiers on the battlefield, and for the principles upon which the nation is founded; from the viewpoint of judgment, our responsibility is to God for our injustices.

These perspectives do not abolish each other; neither expresses the whole truth. They are both addressed to the nation. If we did not notice their different perspectives, we would conclude that they are contradictory. But to speak to the nation means to use rhetoric. It is not possible to unite the perspectives or to find a unifying perspective because of the need for rhetoric. The perspective of the nation is necessary because it both reveals and hides: it reveals the fundamental principle of popular morality which is not seen without being embodied in a nation; it hides that which could only be misinterpreted.

The Second Inaugural Address suggests that it is also necessary for the citizens of democracy to have a perspective transcending the nation. Only by seeing themselves as standing under the judgment of God will the intoxication of their own sovereignty be sobered by awareness of human limits. According to Lincoln in his Lyceum Speech

140

a democratic people is either too complacent or too aroused: it either denies human responsibility by trusting the inevitable course of events, or it denies human limitations by trusting to human experiments. The principles of the founders helped to create and exacerbate these tendencies by too great a reliance on the temporary spirit of the Revolution and by praise of novelty. The result was moral indifference or a morality without prudence and compassion. Reason alone could not bring about reform of the founder's work, but passions had to be brought to the aid of reason. Yet to do this by dangling before the people the image of a perfected society, freed of all human weakness as well as all human evil, is to neglect the permanence of the passions and the roots of popular morality in public opinion. The essential support of the Union to the moral well-being of the citizens was thus overlooked. The habits and prudence that were necessary to preserve such a society were in turn neglected.

Lincoln's solution to this problem in the Gettysburg Address and the Second Inaugural is a political religion that teaches responsibility while allowing prudence and sets limits that allow justice while teaching compassion. The contrasting tendencies of democracy must be brought to moderation by a political religion with a dual viewpoint: one, that of the nation; the other, transcending it. The first would arouse us to our duties and to the nobility of our task; the second would teach us the limits of that task and the humility from which compassion might spring.

The two viewpoints of Lincoln's speeches stand in tension in American political religion, and that tension is not resolvable unless reason were to replace the need for political religion, or democratic principles were found to be inferior — the very things Lincoln denied. One needs both, perhaps more at some times than at others. The political religion can ultimately be held in proper tension only by a statesman, such as Lincoln.

The Second Inaugural suggests that people must participate in God's order by acknowledging the justice of God. But we may note that they cannot transcend the nation in this sense unassisted. They need someone who will point out to them what God's judgment is. All too often people they will think that God's judgment is the same as the nation's judgment, or, conversely, they will substitute their private judgment for the nation's judgment. They do not see by themselves that "the Almighty has His own purposes." The need of democratic citizens to transcend the nation can be fulfilled only if they have a guide who stands between God and themselves.

At the beginning of this paper we noted the danger of combining religious and political passions. Lincoln's political religion has a moderation that religious-political "ideologies" frequently lack. It is not oriented toward the future. It provides no assurance concerning one's destiny. One cannot earn salvation by participating in its cause. Since it does not claim to know what is going to happen in the future, it cannot justify present actions in terms of the future. If our actions are not justified by reference to the future state of perfection, then reformers may escape the indifference to prudence that such an orientation implies. If perfection is possible, weakness is the same as evil. Lincoln's political religion, on the other hand, is formed from awareness of human weakness and from knowledge that we are not perfectly rational.

Lincoln's view also differs from such ideology in requiring great deeds. It does not present a way of acting that is universally good; it appeals to the sacrifices and deeds of the founders, not simply to their doctrines. It requires someone who can interpret the founder's advice in the light of their deeds for the present time. Political religion is made just in new circumstances by being formed in the hands of a statesman. Political religion requires prudence.

But one must also consider the difficulty of what Lincoln proposes. In making human equality the goal of the nation, Lincoln enshrines the continuing consent of the people. Freed of their aristocratic competitors, the people are granted a nobility certainly not granted them by the *Federalist* or even Jefferson. To be sure they are to be chastised and rendered noble by the apparent judgments of God, but is it so surprising that the statesmen who would make those judgments apparent have been so infrequent? Without the Second Inaugural does the Gettysburg Address not assume a rigidity it did not have in Lincoln's own thought?

NOTES

1. See Robert N. Bellah, "Civil Religion in America," *Daedalus* 96 (Winter 1967): 1-21. Bellah has pursued his ideas in several subsequent works.
2. For a good, brief discussion of Jefferson's religion, see Harvey C.

Mansfield, Jr., "Thomas Jefferson," in *American Political Thought*, ed. Morton J. Frisch and Richard G. Stevens (New York: Scribners, 1971), pp. 36-38.

3. Thomas Jefferson, *Notes on the State of Virginia* (New York: Harper and Row, 1964), p. 156.

4. John C. Fitzpatrick, ed., *The Writings of George Washington*, 39 vols. (Washington: Government Printing Office, 1931-44), 35: 229.

5. Robert Bellah notes that a major change occurred in what he calls "civil religion" with the Civil War and Lincoln. He compares this change with the change from the Old to the New Testament. While he does not say whether these changes came about through accident or design, he argues that they received their finest expression in Lincoln. Bellah, "Civil Religion in America," p. 18.

6. Lord Charnwood, *Abraham Lincoln* (Garden City, N.Y.: Doubleday, 1917), p. 439.

7. Roy P. Basler, ed., Marion Dolores Pratt and Lloyd A. Dunlap, asst. eds., *The Collected Works of Abraham Lincoln*, 9 vols. (New Brunswick, N.J.: Rutgers University Press, 1953-55), 8: 333.

8. Charnwood, *Lincoln*, p. 439.

9. Quoted from notes of Herndon in Richard N. Current, *The Lincoln Nobody Knows* (New York: McGraw Hill, 1958), p. 52.

10. William H. Herndon, *Lincoln's Religion*, supplement to the *State Register of Springfield*, 1873, reprinted in *Lincoln's Religion*, ed. Douglas C. McMurtrie (Chicago: Black Cat, 1936), pp. 17-18.

11. Basler, *Collected Works of Lincoln*, 3: 27.

12. Ibid., 2: 385.

13. Ibid., 2: 499.

14. Ibid., 2: 500.

15. Ibid., 2: 341; 4: 240

16. Ibid., 3: 375.

17. Ibid., 1: 108-15. See my analysis of the Lyceum Speech in my *Abraham Lincoln and American Political Religion* (Albany: State University of New York Press, 1976), pp. 20-37, and in Harry V. Jaffa, *Crisis of the House Divided: An Interpretation of the Lincoln-Douglas Debates* (New York: Doubleday, 1959), pp. 183-232.

18. John Dewey, *A Common Faith* (New Haven: Yale University Press, 1934), p. 87.

19. Notice that the prayers presuppose that the war is a scourge.

20. Basler, *Collected Works of Lincoln*, 8: 346.

21. Edmund Wilson, *Patriotic Gore: Studies in the Literature of the American Civil War* (New York: Oxford University Press, 1962), p. 102.

22. Quoted in Ibid., p. 103.

23. Ibid., p. 123.

24. Basler, *Collected Works of Lincoln*, 8: 333.

Lincoln's Faith:
Commentary on "Abraham Lincoln and
American Political Religion"

DAVID HEIN

Professor Thurow's work on Lincoln's political and religious beliefs is valuable because it contains a number of significant insights. Perhaps I should mention right off, though, that it happens to be the case that both he and I stand outside what has been the mainstream of those writers who have dealt at length with Lincoln's theology. Two of the chief representatives of that group—William J. Wolf, author of a book called *Lincoln's Religion,* and D. Elton Trueblood, who wrote *Abraham Lincoln: Theologian of American Anguish,* would have very different things to say about Professor Thurow's paper than I will. To give just one example of what I mean, Trueblood—I think Thurow would agree with me on this—gets off to a very problematical start with his book's title. Thirty years ago a young scholar named Kermit E. White said in a truly neglected dissertation called "Abraham Lincoln and Christianity" that "Lincoln was not a theologian"; and he was quite right to point that out.[1] One immediately starts to veer off on the wrong course if one fails to see Lincoln as a statesman whose utterances were very much in the nature of occasional pieces and not the systematic reflections of a Christian theologian. Thurow's effort is to take seriously the actual historical and political context in which Lincoln spoke. And it should be noted as well that the statements of Lincoln he examines are all well-known items that Thurow has taken from the standard edition of Lincoln's words. It is hard enough to attain to an accurate perception of what Lincoln meant by examining those letters and speeches we know to be truly his own; it is virtually impossible if the analyst strays far beyond the corpus of authentic utterances known as the *Collected Works.*

Here's another example of a case where Thurow and I happen to stand outside the mainstream of Lincoln commentators. It also reveals the danger of relying too heavily on reported conversations and frequently apocryphal recollections. Thurow mentioned in his paper his doubts concerning Lincoln's ever having undergone a conversion experience whereby he moved from being a freethinker or even atheist to being an orthodox Christian believer. Many writers have pointed to a change in Lincoln's religious life, but the curious thing is that each seems to have pinpointed a different date for this event. Some would have us believe that a change came over Lincoln in 1839 when he was thirty years old. Others say peace came to him at his conversion several years earlier—which also happens to be about the time another writer says Lincoln turned his back on Christianity. In a recent article the author points to a decisive transformation in Lincoln's thinking about spiritual matters after a crisis in early 1841. One could go on and on with this. Conversion occurred upon Eddie's death in 1850, upon Willie's death in 1862, after the Battle of Gettysburg in 1863—depending upon whose conjectures one reads.

Now my own view—and here I go beyond Thurow and find myself paying much more attention to Lincoln's "personal piety" and "the religion of the churches" than Thurow wants to—is that Lincoln's religious beliefs did not undergo any truly decisive transformation over time—any change, as far as we can tell, that really altered the whole course of his theological outlook. Obviously, Lincoln was a reflective man whose thinking undoubtedly deepened over the years; unquestionably he arrived at fresh insights as he confronted dramatically changed and harrowing circumstances. But the central elements of Lincoln's mature religious faith were already present in the religious outlook of the young Lincoln. This continuity should not come as any great surprise to us if we recall the ecclesiastical milieus in which Lincoln worshiped. As a man and as a boy he went to churches whose theology was basically Calvinistic. It is far more likely in my view that he attended Old School Presbyterian churches in Springfield and Washington because of an appreciation he felt for their doctrine than that he did so only because he happened to be friends with their pastors. And I think it not unlikely that his theological taste was first cultivated in the religious environment of his childhood.

Consider a letter Lincoln wrote in 1842 to his closest friend, Joshua F. Speed, in which he discussed Speed's engagement to be married. He told his friend it was his belief that "God made me one of the instruments of bringing" Speed and his future wife together, and that theirs was a "union, I have no doubt He had fore-ordained." Here Lincoln clearly expressed a strong belief in God's overruling providence and a conviction that he might be employed by God as an "instrument" to bring about the specific good of reconciliation. Both would be among the wartime themes of Lincoln's faith. In this same letter he went on to state confidently: "Whatever he [God] designs, he will do for *me* yet. 'Stand *still* and see the salvation of the Lord' is my text just now."[2] This quotation from the fourteenth chapter of Exodus expresses an important feature of the faith of the Civil War president. He believed God was capable of bringing good out of difficult situations, whether that situation was Egyptian bondage, his own troubled life, or the terrible affliction of war.

In his paper Professor Thurow analyzes the Gettysburg Address and Lincoln's Second Inaugural and distinguishes sharply between them. The former he sees as focusing on human action—specifically the need to establish the principle of equality—as decisive, that is, as all-determinative to the point of excluding chance or Providence as effective causal agents in history; and he sees the latter, the Second Inaugural, as indicating the inconsequential nature of any purposes save God's. Then he tries to show how these two apparently irreconcilable perspectives may be brought together in what he refers to as "a political religion with a dual viewpoint." I find this aspect of Thurow's treatment—this sharp opposing of the two speeches to one another—to be forced and confusing and finally unnecessary.

Both speeches may be better and I think more clearly understood simply as consistent expressions of Lincoln's monotheistic faith. A shorthand description of that faith might describe it by using the familiar words "trust" and "loyalty." Faith in God means trust, confidence in the One whose power is good and whose goodness is powerful, and loyalty, responsible commitment to this One's cause of universal community. Lincoln knew that he could not, as he put it, "expect a direct revelation" from God telling him what he should do.[3] Thurow is quite right in pointing out—against many who have asserted the opposite—that in the Second Inaugural the president's intention was not to disclose his fresh realization of the divine purpose of the Civil War. But it is wrong to go on to claim, as Thurow does, that Lincoln believed God's purpose to be "essentially unknowable."

It is a mistake to conclude that Lincoln had absolutely no notion of God's intentions in history. If that were the case then there really would be a complete disjunction between Lincoln's religious beliefs and his political practice, or at least his theology could only function negatively to remind him of his limitations. In that event there would remain only the trust side of his faith, which would really be a kind of blind faith that, as Thurow says, cannot have any idea what is going to happen in the future and cannot enable one to feel any "assurance concerning one's destiny." In fact, though, Lincoln did have some idea of what the will of God was for the United States. It is true that he did not derive this understanding from any perception of the intentions of God revealed to him in discrete epiphanic moments. No special knowledge was vouchsafed to him. But Lincoln felt that God's will regarding such matters as slavery was pretty clear. Slavery, he said, violated rights God had given "to *all* His creatures, to the whole great family of man," and "nothing stamped with the Divine image and likeness was sent into the world to be trodden on, and degraded, and imbruted by its fellows."[4] Proof that "slavery is morally wrong" could be found in what he called "natural theology, apart from revelation." "God," he said, "gave man a mouth to receive bread, hands to feed it, and his hand has a right to carry bread to his mouth without controversy."[5] Lincoln proclaimed and sought to establish the principles enunciated in the speech he gave at Gettysburg precisely because of his loyalty to what he took to be God's will for the human community.

The sixteenth president knew much better than most how partial is our knowledge, how deficient our basis for self-congratulation. But he also knew the depth of our responsibility to seek to make our own efforts conform to the divine intentions in history. As he told Mrs. Gurney in 1864, "We must work earnestly in the best light He gives us, trusting that so working still conduces to the great ends He ordains." And he went on immediately to express a faith—and I do prefer this straightforward term to "political religion"—that was, in fact, future-oriented and capable of some measure of assurance because it was bound up with a hope that was rooted in God and not in human beings: "Surely," Lincoln said, God "intends some great good to follow this mighty convulsion, which no mortal could make, and no mortal could stay."[6]

NOTES

1. Kermit E. White, "Abraham Lincoln and Christianity" (Ph.D. diss., Boston University, 1954), p. 82.

2. Roy P. Basler, ed., Marion Dolores Pratt and Lloyd A. Dunlap, asst. eds., *The Collected Works of Abraham Lincoln*, 9 vols. (New Brunswick, N.J.: Rutgers University Press, 1953-55), 1: 289.

3. Ibid., 5: 420.

4. Ibid., 2: 546.

5. Ibid., 4: 3, 9.

6. Ibid., 7: 535. For a much fuller treatment of the main themes of this paper, see David Hein, "Lincoln's Theology and Political Ethics," in *Essays on Lincoln's Faith and Politics*, ed. Kenneth W. Thompson (Lanham, Md.: University Press of America, 1983), pp. 105-79.

CHAPTER 6

LINCOLN AND THE INDIANS

DAVID A. NICHOLS

THE DATE WAS AUGUST 21, 1862. The news came at the worst possible moment in the war for the Union. Abraham Lincoln's armies were desperate for manpower and it appeared that Lincoln might even have difficulty defending Washington against Confederate attack. The telegram from the governor of Minnesota read: "The Sioux Indians on our western border have risen and are murdering men, women and children." Possibly five hundred whites had died. When Gov. Alexander Ramsey demanded that President Lincoln extend the draft deadline for Minnesota's quota of 5,360 men, Lincoln's response was harsh: "Attend to the Indians. If the draft can *not* proceed, of course it *will* not proceed. Necessity knows no law. The government cannot extend the time."[1]

Two arenas of conflict, the Indian Territory (later Oklahoma) and Minnesota, drew Lincoln directly into Indian affairs during his first two years in office. When Lincoln entered office, he was understandably preoccupied with the showdown with the Confederacy taking place in South Carolina. There were those around him who argued that the Indian Territory, inhabited by the "five civilized tribes" was strategically important. Held by the North, it could be a base for attacks on Arkansas and Texas. Controlled by the Confederacy, it could be employed to threaten Kansas.

However, Lincoln initially chose to abandon the Indian Territory, even though his commissioner of Indian affairs, William P. Dole, dissented against the move. Indian leaders protested to Lincoln that Confederate agents were telling their people that "the Government represented by our Great Father at Washington has turned against us."[2] The success of those Southern agents, more than anything, probably persuaded Lincoln to reverse his decision. On November

149

22, 1861, the Confederacy organized the Indian Territory into a separate military department. Abandonment began to look like a blunder. On December 3, Lincoln informed the Congress, "The Indian country south of Kansas is in possession of the insurgents" and he noted press reports that the Confederates were organizing Indian troops. Lincoln communicated his new decision: "It is believed that upon repossession of the country by the federal forces the Indians will readily cease all hostile demonstrations, and resume their former relations to the government."[3]

Beyond Commissioner Dole, the man most responsible for persuading Lincoln to retake the Indian Territory was Kansas Senator James H. ("Bloody Jim") Lane. Lane was a colorful, unscrupulous character whose tricolored brigade, composed of blacks, Indians, and drifters, was alleged to have plundered Unionist civilians as readily as the Confederates. Lane's great obsession was to lead an expedition designed to shorten the war by attacking the exposed flank of the Confederacy in Arkansas and Texas via the Indian Territory. But it was a flood of Indian refugees from the Indian Territory into Kansas that appears to have pushed Lincoln into approving a Southern expedition. Kansans did not want hungry, dependent Indians in their midst. The refugee problem dovetailed with the need for troops to retake the Indian country from the Confederacy. In early December, the decision was made to receive 4,000 Indians into the army. They would receive pay and benefits equal to that of white troops.

Lincoln, with Dole's help, negotiated a bargain concerning the command of the so-called Lane Expedition. Lane would command the troops but be subject to the overall authority of Gen. David Hunter. Lincoln may have thought he could appease the politically popular senator, make military gains in the West, and still keep Lane's excesses under control. Hunter had no liking for Lincoln's arrangement, however. With Lane commanding the expedition, the general believed he would become a mere figurehead. Hunter angrily wrote Lincoln that he was "very deeply mortified, humiliated, insulted and disgraced." Lincoln replied that it was difficult to answer "so ugly a letter in good temper" and warned his old friend, "You are adopting the best possible way to ruin yourself."[4] However, the adjutant general confirmed Hunter's authority and that Lane would be subordinate to him: "If you deem it proper you may yourself command the expedition."[5]

Lincoln's bargain began to unravel. Commissioner Dole, on the scene, had assumed that Hunter would be content with a superior command but let Lane command the expedition. When Lane arrived in Kansas, he was shocked to read newspaper stories proclaiming that Hunter, not Lane, would command the "Lane Expedition." Accordingly, Jim Lane decided to sabotage the expedition project unless he could command it with a force of 30,000 men.

On January 31, Lincoln tried to break the Hunter-Lane deadlock and instructed the secretary of war:

> It is my wish that the expedition commonly called the "Lane Expedition" shall be as much as had been promised at the Adjutant-General's Office under the supervision of General McClellan and not any more. I have not intended and do not now intend that it shall be a great exhausting affair, but a snug, sober column of 10,000 or 15,000. General Lane has been told by me many times that he is under the command of General Hunter, and assented to it as often as told. It was the distinct agreement between him and me when I appointed him that he was to be under Hunter.[6]

Instead, the pressure increased. On February 6, the House of Representatives passed a resolution urging Lincoln to appoint Lane to head the expedition. Joseph Medill of the *Chicago Tribune* reminded Lincoln that 850,000 men in the West had voted for him in 1860 and they would not want Lane's expedition to fall through: "Mr. Lincoln, for God's sake and your country's sake rise to the realization of our awful national peril."[7] Furthermore, Lincoln's new secretary of war, Edwin Stanton, was reluctant to put Indians in the army. Caleb Smith informed Commissioner Dole on February 6 that Lincoln was going to see Stanton "and settle it today."[8]

Weary of the whole business, on February 10 Lincoln told Hunter and Lane that he would give them one more chance to work things out: "My wish has been and is to avail the Government of the services of both General Hunter and General Lane, and, so far as possible, to personally oblige both. General Hunter is the senior officer and must command when they serve together; though in so far as he can, consistently with the public service and his own honor, oblige General Lane, he will also oblige me. If they cannot come to an amicable understanding, General Lane must report to General Hunter for duty, according to the rules, or decline the service."[9]

151

Lane tried again to persuade Hunter to let him command but Hunter refused. An angry Lane left Kansas for Washington to resume his Senate seat. He is reported to have muttered all the way about the man in the White House being a "d——d liar, a demagogue, and a scoundrel." Lane believed that Lincoln was guilty of "leaving him before the public in the light of a braggart, a fool and a humbug."[10] However, Lincoln had also decided to transfer David Hunter to the East. He ordered a reorganization that placed the Department of Mississippi, including Kansas, under Henry Halleck. The Indian expedition was canceled.

That "persistent fellow" Jim Lane then managed to convince Lincoln to restore the Department of Kansas and place Lane's man, Gen. James G. Blunt, in command. Once again, Lincoln reversed himself on the Indian expedition. One factor explaining the reversal was that Confederates demonstrated the utility of Indian troops against the Union during the Battle of Pea Ridge (Elkhorn Tavern) in Arkansas, March 6-8. A second factor was that the number of Indian refugees in Kansas had increased to 7,600 starving people.

The president ordered the commander of the Department of Mississippi to "detail two regiments to act in Indian country, with a view to open the way for friendly Indians who are not refugees in Southern Kansas to return to their homes." Five thousand Indians were to be armed and were to be "used only against Indians or in defense of their own territory and homes."[11] The new expedition was to be considerably less grand than Jim Lane's original scheme to turn the tide for the war for the Union and he no longer wanted to command this meager force.

The expedition was launched on June 28, 1862, under the command of Col. William Weer. It included 2,000 whites and 3,000 Indians. Initially, the troops encountered little opposition. Unionist Indians, including Cherokee leader John Ross, welcomed Weer's forces. However, on July 18, white soldiers mutinied against Weer and the expedition retreated to Kansas. A major reason for the mutiny seems to have been the resistance of white soldiers to serving with Indians.

Once again the expedition was canceled. The situation of the refugees was worse than ever and John Ross traveled to Washington in September 1862 to petition Lincoln for assistance. Two weeks after their first meeting, Lincoln wrote Ross that "a multitude of cares" had prevented him from a promised examination of the relationship of the government to the Cherokees. In October, Lincoln joined with Ross to inquire about the possibility of utilizing Indian troops already fighting the Confederacy to return the refugees to Indian country, but nothing was done.

It was indeed a time of "a multitude of cares." In late 1862 Lincoln's army seemed in peril of losing the contest with the Confederacy. He had not yet identified competent military leadership for the Union army. Indian Office officials warned Lincoln that to return the Indian refugees to the Indian Territory without military protection would only expose them to harm. For Lincoln, soldiers were scarce and General Blunt's white troops were still reluctant to fight alongside Indians.

Lincoln eventually capitulated. John Ross went to see him again in the autumn of 1863. In May 1864, Jim Lane pushed a bill through Congress to remove the Indians from Kansas and in the process extinguished the title to lands belonging to native Kansas tribes which, the Kansas congressman openly admitted, "occupy central positions, holding large tracts of productive country in the very heart of our state." They called the removal "an act of justice to the Indians and the people of Kansas."[12]

In June 1864, 5,000 Indians were taken from Kansas to the Indian Territory where, because they arrived too late to plant crops, they endured even greater deprivation. Lincoln recognized their need as "so great and urgent" that he stretched the Constitution by authorizing $200,000 worth of clothing and food on credit and asked Congress to appropriate the money after the fact. Lincoln's indecisive policies toward the Southern tribes were, by any measurement, unsuccessful. He failed to exploit any potential military advantage in the region and the results for the Indian refugees were disastrous.

The Indian war in Minnesota broke out on August 17, 1862. Several white settlers were killed in an incident near Acton. The Sioux, fearing reprisal, launched a preventive war. This came at a time when the war with the South was going badly. Lincoln's army was short of manpower. He was discouraged with the bickering and ineptness of his generals. On August 29-30, the Union forces under Gen. John Pope were defeated at Second Bull Run. An outraged Pope was blaming his defeat on General McClellan.

In this context, the news of the Indian war had an electric effect.

Governor Ramsey's insistence on delaying the draft linked together the two theaters of war. One report claimed "Indians, from Minnesota to Pike's Peak, from Salt Lake to near Fort Kearney, committing many depredations." Lincoln's own secretary, John G. Nicolay, was in Minnesota and he reported: "We are in the midst of a most terrible exciting Indian war. Thus far the massacre of innocent white settlers has been fearful. A wild panic prevails in nearly one-half the state."[13]

Especially ominous was the possibility that the Indian attacks were part of a "deep-laid plan," a Confederate conspiracy to open a new front in the war for the Union. Interior Secretary Caleb Smith insisted months later, "I am satisfied the chief cause is to be found in the insurrection of the southern states." Lincoln himself spoke of his "suspicions" and reported to the Congress, "Information was received . . . that a simultaneous attack was to be made upon white settlements by all the tribes between the Mississippi River and the Rocky Mountains."[14]

It is in this context that Lincoln ordered Governor Ramsey to "attend to the Indians." At about that same time Lincoln authorized the first official enlistment of blacks into the Union army. While the Indian war was not the central element in this decision, it may have influenced the timing of the orders to Gen. Rufus Saxton on August 25 to organize black soldiers. This came only three weeks after Lincoln had publicly declined to do so and two days after Senator Lane had been denied the same authority.

Governor Ramsey demanded a new military department in the Northwest. Halleck at first denied the request, but Lincoln overruled Halleck. The president intended to solve two problems with one stroke. Gen. John Pope was threatening McClellan over his failure to support Pope adequately at Second Bull Run. Lincoln needed to separate his quarrelsome generals and the Indian war gave him some place to send Pope. Pope thought himself banished, but Stanton called the Indian war an "emergency" and assured Pope, "You cannot too highly estimate the importance of the duty now entrusted to you."[15]

By mid-September, General Pope arrived in Minnesota to join forces with Col. Henry Sibley. He immediately launched a campaign that would "utterly exterminate the Sioux." Pope claimed that 50,000 people were refugees and predicted that "the whole of Minnesota west of the Mississippi and the Territories of Dakota and Nebraska will be entirely depopulated." It would require "a large force and much time to prevent everybody leaving the country, such is the condition of things."[16]

Then in early October, General Pope informed the government that "the Sioux War may be considered at an end." The extent of the Indian war had been grossly overestimated. However, the war was not over for Lincoln. Pope's communications revealed a new problem: "We have about 1,500 prisoners—men, women, and children—and many are coming each day to deliver themselves up." Pope continued: "Many are being tried by military commission for being connected in late horrible outrages and will be executed." That phrase, "will be executed," meant that Abraham Lincoln would be confronted with a wrenching decision about whether to sanction the largest mass execution in American history.[17]

On October 14, Stanton read Pope's report aloud to Lincoln and an uncomfortable cabinet. Gideon Welles called the report "discreditable" and perceived ulterior motives: "The Winnebagoes have good land which white men want and mean to have." Lincoln moved immediately to prevent any wanton slaughter. He dispatched John P. Usher to the scene and asked Episcopal Bishop Henry Whipple to assist him. On October 17 Pope informed Sibley that "the President directs that no executions be made without his sanction."[18]

On November 8, Sibley transmitted to the government a list of 303 Sioux men whom he had sentenced to death. Two days later Lincoln wired Pope: "Please forward, as soon as possible, the full and complete record of these convictions." He instructed Pope to include any materials that might discriminate as to the most guilty and "a careful statement" concerning the verdicts.

Pope's response was anything but "careful." "The only distinction between the culprits is to which of them murdered most people or violated most young girls," the general replied, and he warned Lincoln of mob action: "The people of this State . . . are exasperated to the last degree, and if the guilty are not all executed I think it nearly impossible to prevent the indiscriminate massacre of all the Indians— old men, women and children."[19]

Despite this testimony, Lincoln and his lawyers were disturbed at what they found in the trial records. The trials had become progressively shorter as they went forward, averaging only ten to fifteen minutes per case. The lack of evidence was alarming. Lawyers labored over the records for a month, trying to make distinctions. Even then, the lack of solid evidence of guilt haunted Lincoln.

Meanwhile the advocates for and against the executions crowded into the White House. Governor Ramsey offered Lincoln a way to evade responsibility: "If you prefer it turn them over to me & I will order their execution." In Lincoln's annual message, he sidestepped the issue. "The State of Minnesota has suffered great injury from this Indian War," he reported, mentioning the number killed and the alleged atrocities. Lincoln took note of the desire of Minnesotans to remove the Indians from the state, although he made no clear recommendation. Lincoln even raised "for your especial consideration" the idea of remodeling the Indian system. But he said not one word about the proposed executions.[20]

Lincoln was apparently still trying to decide what to do. On December 1, the date of his annual message, he sought advice from the judge advocate: "I wish your legal opinion whether if I should conclude to execute only a part of them, I must myself designate which or could I leave the designation to some officer on the ground." Lincoln's use of the word "designate" is significant. After a month of studying the trial records, Lincoln's lawyers apparently could not decide who merited execution. Perhaps Lincoln was tempted by Ramsey's proposal to shift the responsibility. However, Judge Joseph Holt gave him no option: "The power cannot be delegated."[21]

Lincoln, despite the lack of clear evidence, had concluded that a blood sacrifice was imperative but not on the scale sought by the Minnesotans. Welles noted in his diary: "The members of Congress from Minnesota are urging the President vehemently to give his assent to the execution of three hundred Indian captives, but they will not succeed." Lincoln had decided to execute only thirty-nine of the prisoners.[22]

The Minnesotans desperately tried to reverse the decision. Sen. Morton Wilkinson recited the details of rape and murder to the Senate. Sibley reported that citizens had attempted to attack the prisoners being held at Mankato. Lincoln was bombarded with warnings of mob action. However, once decided, Lincoln never wavered. When the Senate, at Wilkinson's instigation, demanded an explanation, Lincoln responded that he had listened to various opinions, sent for the trial records, and had them studied carefully. The president had walked a careful line between the poles of opinion: "Anxious to not act with so much clemency as to encourage another outbreak on one hand, nor with so much severity as to be real cruelty on the other, I ordered a careful examination of the records of the trials to be made, in view of first ordering the execution of such as had been proved guilty of violating females." In that statement, Lincoln tried to appease almost everyone. He had found only two Indians guilty of rape and had further attempted to distinguish those who had participated in "massacres" from those who had taken part in "battles."[23]

Lincoln remained personally involved. He had Nicolay caution General Sibley concerning one prisoner whose name was similar to another: "The President desires to guard against his being executed by mistake before his case shall be finally determined."[24] Before the year ended, thirty-eight men were hanged. A large crowd was present but there was no violence. Evidence later indicated that, despite Lincoln's cautions, one prisoner was executed by mistake.

Lincoln's actions had a price. He reduced the execution list but he struck a bargain with the Minnesotans that gave them much of what they wanted otherwise. Lincoln agreed to continued incarceration for the Indians not executed. The government paid the cost of the war, around $350,000, and compensated Minnesotans for damages, claims for which eventually exceeded $1.3 million. Lincoln appointed John P. Usher as his new secretary of the interior, an appointment sought by the Minnesotans because they believed that Usher sympathized with their plans for Indians. Finally, Lincoln acquiesced in the removal of both the Sioux and the Winnebagoes, the latter of which had nothing to do with the Indian war.

Lincoln traded lives for land and money. He also permitted a series of military missions during 1863-66 throughout the region. The military claimed that 8-10,000 Indians were driven out of Minnesota. Sibley boasted that "the Indians have been badly beaten, demoralized, and have sent me messages desiring peace on any terms." Lincoln, with his enormous burdens in the conflict with the South, wanted to forget the whole Minnesota affair, just as he had tended to do with the refugees in Kansas. In March 1863 Alexander Ramsey asked Lincoln about the Indian prisoners he had not hanged and reported that Lincoln "said it was a disagreeable subject but he would take it up and dispose of it."[25]

157

There were still 329 prisoners at Mankato, including forty-nine who had been acquitted in the trials but for unknown reasons had never been released. Sibley pressured Lincoln to execute fifty more but Lincoln refused. However, he agreed to move the prisoners to Davenport, Iowa. Eventually, in response to pleas from missionaries, Lincoln pardoned twenty-six more men. Symptomatic of his problems with subordinates, Lincoln ordered the release of one prisoner, Big Eagle, and discovered weeks later that his order had been ignored: "Let the Indian Big Eagle be discharged. I ordered this some time ago."[26]

Lincoln never released the rest of the prisoners. The prison conditions were so unhealthy that between the executions in December 1862 and April 1864, an estimated sixty-seven additional men died—nearly twice the number who perished on the gallows. And the prisoners were only part of the residual problem. Sibley still had 1,600 Indians, mostly women and children, in custody. Disease and starvation afflicted them. In 1863, the Sioux and Winnebagoes were removed to the Dakota Territory. Both tribes arrived too late to plant crops and found themselves in miserable conditions. Meanwhile, in Minnesota, Commissioner Dole granted Sen. Morton Wilkinson's request that the Sioux reservation be opened for settlement.

Following the 1864 election, Sen. Alexander Ramsey visited the White House and talked politics with Lincoln. The president noted that he carried Minnesota by only 7,000 votes compared to 10,000 in 1860. Ramsey responded "that if he had hung more Indians, we should have given him his old majority." Lincoln failed to appreciate the humor of the remark. "I could not afford to hang men for votes," he said.[27]

The events in the Indian Territory and Minnesota converged in late 1862. The Indian expedition fell apart in July and John Ross visited Lincoln in September. The Minnesota war began in late August and by mid-October the executions were an explosive issue. Meanwhile, Lincoln had to both wrestle with the lack of success of the Union armies and find a way to emancipate the slaves.

The times pushed Lincoln more toward reformers of all kinds, both the abolitionists and those who sought to reform the "Indian system." Indeed, some of them were the same people. The reformers argued that crises like the Minnesota Indian war derived directly from the abuses of the Indian system. By the time Lincoln reached office, this structure had become a system of institutionalized corruption, deeply entrenched in the political and economic interests of ambitious men in the West. The system originated in the practice of making treaties with the tribes. Treaties were almost always negotiated as a means of removing Indians from lands that whites wished to occupy, usually following armed conflict. Removal opened valuable land for speculation and settlement.

Beyond that, the treaties usually provided government annuities for the tribes, in compensation for the land. The Indian system then revolved around the strategies that whites developed for tapping these government monies. Citizens could file claims for alleged Indian depredations. Contractors provided goods and services for newly removed, heavily dependent Indian tribes. Licensed traders on the reservations provided retail outlets for the goods, the costs of which were charged to annuities.

At the center of all this was the Indian agent. All Indian officials, including agents, were political appointees. Claims, contracts, and traders' licenses needed the agent's approval. As one Minnesotan claimed, "It is believed that the trader is, in all cases, a partner of the Agent. He is usually a near relative."[28] Agents could, through kickbacks and partnerships, become wealthy men themselves.

Corruption stories abounded. In Oregon, an 1859 report charged that one agent, on a $1,000 per year salary, retired after two years with $17,000. Another accumulated $41,000 in three years. An investigator in Minnesota charged that a superintendent had spent $100,000 to $200,000 on a $2,000 salary. Agent Walter Burleigh in Dakota Territory was accused of using government funds to transport his own goods, hiring his daughter to teach at a nonexistent school, buying farm implements that no one could locate, and hiring men to work at half the price he reported to the government. Another agent allegedly stole $870,000 in bonds out of a safe in the Interior Department.

Men like Ramsey and Sibley made the Indian system a pathway to political power. Sibley represented the traders at the Sioux treaty negotiations in 1851. That treaty granted the Santee Sioux $475,000, but Sibley put in a claim for $145,000 for *overpayments* to the Sioux for furs. That claim was approved by Indian agent Ramsey. Sibley became Minnesota's first governor in 1858. His successor was Ramsey.

Congress was central to the system. While the president appointed Indian officials, these appointments were nearly always made on the recommendation of congressmen, who themselves often got in on the spoils. Sen. Samuel C. Pomeroy of Kansas obtained 90,000 acres of Pottawatomie land after helping to negotiate a treaty with those Indians. He got 50,000 acres of Kickapoo land in similar fashion.

Sometimes the charges of corruption went high in the Lincoln administration. Commissioner Dole was frequently accused of profiting from his post. The insensitivity of the system to conflicts of interest was symbolized by the sale of Sac and Fox trust lands in 1864. Tracts of land were purchased by Commissioner Dole, Secretary of the Interior Usher, Comptroller of the Currency Hugh McCulloch, and John G. Nicolay, Lincoln's personal secretary.

The corruption reached into the presidential office in other ways, although Lincoln himself had not profited. John Hay jokingly wrote Nicolay in Minnesota, just prior to the Indian war, to steal some moccasins for him from a vulnerable Indian maiden: "The Tycoon [Lincoln] has just received a pair gorgeously quilled, from an Indian agent who is accused of stealing. He put them on and grinned. Will he remember them on the day when Caleb [Smith] proposes another to fill the peculating donor's office? I fear not, my boy, I fear not."[29] Clear Sky, an aged Chippewa chief, succinctly characterized what the Indian system did to his people: "Dam rascal plenty here. He steal him horse. He steal him timber. He steal him every thing. He make him good business. Many agents come here. Sometimes good. Sometimes bad. Most bad. The agent say, you must not do so. The next one come, he say you do very foolish. The Government not want you to do so. Agent much dam rascal. Indian much dam fool." Bishop Henry Whipple of Minnesota described the system's impact more starkly: "It commences in discontent and ends in blood."[30]

It ended "in blood" in Minnesota in 1862. That war and the projected executions gave reformers a platform on which to push for reform of the Indian system. Lincoln's subordinates preferred the policy of concentration which had begun in the 1850s. Commissioner Dole enthusiastically coupled his desire "to foster and protect our own settlements" with "the concentration of the Indians upon ample reservations."[31] Concentration was an updated removal policy, the logical next step when the continent no longer had uninhabited regions in the West. Concentration was really a form of racial segregation, justified to protect the Indians and make way for the advance of civilization. Concentration also, like earlier forms of removal, was the activator of the Indian system's money machine. Many reformers accepted concentration as inevitable but they viewed it as an intermediate step toward the assimilation of the Indian into American life. Indian haters tended to view concentration as a step toward extinction.

Henry Benjamin Whipple, Episcopal bishop for Minnesota, was the man with the most coherent reform program and the reformer who most influenced Lincoln. During Lincoln's first two years in office, Whipple made several attempts to move Indian officials toward reform, all without success. On March 6, 1862, Whipple wrote directly to Lincoln. Whipple avoided blaming Indian problems on persons with evil intent. He identified the Indian system, with its "dishonest servants, ill conceived plans, and defective instructions," as the primary cause of the degradation of the natives. Indians were degraded because the treaty system destroyed tribal governments and left their people without protection.

The root of the problem was the patronage system for selecting agents and other officials. "The first thing needed is honesty," the bishop told the president. Select agents on merit and not politics. Make Indians wards of the government and help them build homes, begin farming, and adopt "civilized" life. "The Indian must have a home," the bishop contended. "He must be furnished with seed, implements of husbandry and taught to live by the sweat of his brow. The government now gives him beads, paint, blankets and scalping-knives, teaching him to idle away his time, waiting for an annuity of money he does not know how to spend." Whipple proposed paying annuities in goods, not cash, thereby cutting traders out of the money flow.

Bishop Whipple urged Lincoln to appoint a special commission to investigate and recommend further reforms. These commissioners should be "men of inflexible integrity, of large heart, of clear head, of strong will, who fear God and love man." In short, they should be "above the reach of political demagogues." Whipple's proposal to depoliticize the system was made to a lifelong politician who, in perfunctory manner, referred the bishop's letter to the "special attention of the Secretary of the Interior," one of the system's political appointees. Caleb Smith wrote Whipple a long letter but Lincoln said nothing more.[32]

Whipple went to see Lincoln, just after the Minnesota war had begun, taking his cousin, General-in-Chief Henry Halleck, along for support. Whipple made his whole case to the president—the corruption of agents and the traders, the lack of governmental protection, and examples of how corruption had led directly to bloody war. Whipple believed that Lincoln "was deeply moved." Lincoln later told a friend that Bishop Whipple "came here the other day and talked with me about the rascality of this Indian business until I felt it down to my boots."

The president's response to Whipple was one of those famous Lincoln stories: "Bishop, a man thought that monkeys could pick cotton better than negroes could because they were quicker and their fingers smaller. He turned a lot of them into his cotton field, but he found that it took two overseers to watch one monkey. It needs more than one honest man to watch one Indian agent." The story was a curious one. Did it imply agreement with Whipple or was it a way of putting him off? Whipple obviously believed that Lincoln made a commitment, hedged with two significant "ifs." Lincoln said, "If we get through this war, and I live, *this Indian system shall be reformed.*"[33]

In his 1862 annual message, even as Lincoln struggled with the issue of the executions, he asked Congress to reform the Indian system. "Many wise and good men have impressed me with the belief that this can be profitably done," he said. Lincoln urged the Congress to give the matter its "especial consideration." It appeared that Bishop Whipple had achieved a great triumph. However, the ambiguity of Lincoln's proposal was troubling. It failed even to mention the cornerstone of Whipple's program, the depoliticization of the system. Lincoln did not risk offending the congressmen who controlled the patronage. Both Secretary Smith and Commissioner Dole joined in the reform chorus but they, like Lincoln, said nothing about changing the mode of selecting Indian officials.[34]

While the reformers rejoiced, the omission in Lincoln's recommendation had not escaped Bishop Whipple's scrutiny. Whipple wrote the politician in the White House: "Will you not see that the commission is made up of better stuff than politicians." Whipple again enlisted Halleck's aid. "You have his ear," he wrote, referring to the president. "Do, for the sake of the poor victims of a nation's wrong, ask him to put on it something better than politicians."[35]

The euphoria did not last long. The executions were over and the Minnesota crisis faded from Lincoln's attention. Sen. Henry Rice summarized the situation: "The do nothing policy here is complete." As the months passed, Bishop Whipple's despair grew. "I tremble for my country," he wrote Commissioner Dole, "when I remember that God will compel us to reap what we sow. There is a reason why every advance of civilization is marked with blood."[36]

Lincoln maintained a verbal commitment to reform. In his 1863 annual message, he again called on Congress to reform the Indian system, proclaiming the "urgent need for immediate legislative action." Lincoln's outlook was paternalistic: "Sound policy and our imperative duty to these wards of the Government demand our anxious and constant attention to their material well-being, to their progress in the arts of civilization, and, above all, to that moral training which, under the blessing of divine Providence, will confer upon them the elevated and sanctifying influences, the hopes and consolations of the Christian faith."

These words were the skeleton at the feast. More significant, Lincoln's kind words for Indians directly followed sentences expressing his pride concerning the removal of many tribes, "sundry treaties," and "extinguishing the possessory rights of the Indians to large and valuable tracts of land." Lincoln's administration had settled on an Indian policy. Commissioner Dole stated it plainly: "The plan of concentrating Indians and confining them to reservations may now be regarded as the fixed policy of the government."[37]

Bishop Whipple tried once again with Lincoln. He went to see the president in March of 1864 but Lincoln merely referred him to the chairman of the House Indian committee. John Beeson, an even more radical reformer, discussed Indian reform with Lincoln in late 1864 and the president told him "to rest assured that as soon as the pressing matters of this war is settled the Indians shall have my first care and I will not rest until Justice is done their and your Sattisfaction [*sic*]." Whipple could not wait. In 1864 he supported George B. McClellan for president.[38]

Meanwhile, in the wake of military success in the war against the South, Lincoln's Indian concentration policy drifted toward militarism. Secretary Usher was clear in his statement: "This department will make provision for such Indians as will submit to its authority and locate upon the reservation. Those who resist should be pursued by the military and punished." This was the harsh policy of a government at war.

Abraham Lincoln was the indirect author of this policy. His determination to develop the resources of the West was linked in his mind to winning the war for the Union. Therefore, he was exultant that "the steady expansion of population, improvement, and governmental institutions over the new and unoccupied portions of the country has scarcely been checked, much less impeded or destroyed by our great civil war." Lincoln noted that "Indian hostilities" had only temporarily obstructed the formation of new governments in the West.

The very order of topics in Lincoln's annual message of 1864 reflected his priorities — new territories, railroads, minerals, and finally Indians. While he spoke of "the welfare of the Indians," his first concern for the West was "to render it secure for the advancing settler." For Lincoln, that expansion was connected with the resources for winning the Civil War because "the national resources . . . are unexhausted, and as we believe, inexhaustible."[39] In this context, Indians were increasingly treated as a military problem.

Indian Office officials became increasingly uneasy about military control of the Indians. Their worst fears were realized when the operations in New Mexico and Colorado generated public scandal even as the Civil War was coming to a close. In New Mexico, Gen. James Carleton's concentration operations resulted in 7,500 starving captives and excessive costs. In Colorado, Gov. John Evans and Col. John M. Chivington launched a campaign that culminated in the Sand Creek Massacre, which killed 150 Indians, mostly women and children. The scandal over Sand Creek resulted in a congressional investigation which produced a report in 1867 outlining a "peace policy" which was implemented in the Grant administration.

Was Lincoln's proposal in 1862 to reform the Indian system genuine or mere rhetoric? Was Lincoln a reformer? It is significant that Lincoln never directly endorsed the reformers' proposal to depoliticize the system. On the other hand, he could have chosen to say nothing about reform. His proposal gave legitimacy and exposure to reform ideas that eventually culminated in the "peace policy." As in his relationship with the abolitionists, Lincoln was more cautious than the reformers, but he was pushed in their direction by events and his own sympathies. If he was not a radical on Indian policy, he was clearly more reformist than most of the congressmen who, in reality, controlled the Indian system through their committees. Without their help, there was little he could do.

The reform movement was doomed. The national commitment to economic development of the West, which Lincoln certainly shared, bound economic self-interest to the war effort and made Indian welfare a low priority. The war for the Union consumed too much of everyone's energies, including Lincoln's. Nevertheless, if Lincoln had lived, there is reason to believe that he would have supported the reform proposals of 1867 and tried to fulfill his pledge to Bishop Whipple: *"This Indian system shall be reformed."*

While Lincoln was a cautious reformer, that does not completely answer the question as to whether his Indian policies support his traditional image as a humanitarian. One might point to what happened to Indian people following Lincoln's interventions in both Kansas and Minnesota. While his attention was elsewhere the Kansas refugees suffered. Lincoln's armies killed more Indians than he pardoned in Minnesota. While he pardoned a large number, he still executed thirty-eight men on superficial evidence and permitted even more to die in miserable prison conditions and under forced removal.

Nevertheless, Bishop Whipple's humanitarian pleas struck a responsive chord with Lincoln, leading to his reform proposal. The executions commanded his attention during one of the most burdensome times of his presidency. Considering his other responsibilities, it is remarkable how involved he became. Lincoln could have chosen to do nothing. There is little question that all 303 Sioux men would have died without his intervention. The remaining Indians would have fared no better. Given the circumstances, it is difficult to imagine any other president doing more.

Lincoln was clearly more humanitarian toward Indians than most of the main military and political figures of his time. Lincoln could not do it all himself. He could not reform a chaotic and brutal system without help from Congress. He could not single-handedly enforce humane treatment in Kansas or Minnesota. He could not, given the burdens of the Civil War, give these matters his attention all of the time.

Despite his humanitarian inclinations, Lincoln's basic attitudes should be viewed in context. Most Americans of the Lincoln era, including the reformers, viewed Indians as degraded savages. Reformers blamed the degradation on the Indian system, whereas the anti-Indian forces ascribed the degradation to the Indian race itself.

However, they shared many assumptions. Both believed that Indians must assimilate and learn to farm like white people or perish. Sen. James Doolittle, chairman of the Senate Indian Committee, argued that Indians were "a dying race . . . giving place to another race with a higher civilization. It is dying through natural causes growing out of its contact with a superior race inhabiting the same country. . . . And the warfare when once begun between civilized and savage life becomes an eternal and irrepressible conflict which, in the very nature of things, will only cease when the savage life ceases." This was the "irrepressible conflict" of the Indian civil war, sanctioned by God, who "in his providence is giving this continent to a hundred millions of human beings of higher civilization, of greater energies, capable of developing themselves, and doing good to themselves and the world, and leading the advance guard of human and Christian civilization."[40]

Abraham Lincoln shared most of these attitudes. In the spring of 1863, Lincoln met leaders from several tribes in the East Room of the White House. He spoke to them of the "great difference between this pale-faced people and their red brethren both as to numbers and the way in which they live. The pale-faced people are numerous and prosperous because they cultivate the earth, produce bread, and depend upon the products of the earth rather than wild game for a subsistence. This is the chief reason of the difference; but there is another. Although we are now engaged in a great war between one another, we are not, as a race, so much disposed to fight and kill one another as our red brethren."[41] In three sentences, Lincoln linked the nonfarming hunter-savage with the innately violent barbarian. Considering the bloodiness of the white Civil War in 1863, this was a remarkably ethnocentric statement.

If Lincoln's prejudices were never as virulent as was common to America, he was not a social equalitarian either. He always remained a politician, forever in the middle of public opinion. Even his proposal to reform the Indian system avoided the delicate question of ending political appointments, knowing how that would upset congressmen who profited from the patronage. Lincoln managed to keep the Minnesota Republican leaders on his reelection team, despite refusing to do all they wished. If good politics is leadership toward the possible, Lincoln measures up rather well. Not much was possible, given the circumstances. Nevertheless, Lincoln recommended reform, saved lives, *and* got reelected. A man who would not "hang men for votes," he still corralled the votes he needed to govern.

Indian affairs also show up the hard side of Lincoln's nature, a side that bordered on militarism. This toughness was evident in his adamant refusal to let the South go, even if he had to use force to make his view prevail. It also surfaced in his message to Governor Ramsey in Minnesota to "attend to the Indians." The Lincoln who believed that "necessity knows no law" was the same man who, in the war with the South, threw out one general after another until he found one, in Ulysses S. Grant, willing to shed enough blood to get the job done. This Lincoln, for all his caution and political manipulations, was obsessed with a goal and would use violence to resolve problems when Indians, or anyone else, forcibly got in the way of his highest priorities.

NOTES

1. Roy P. Basler, ed., Marion Dolores Pratt and Lloyd A. Dunlap, asst. eds., *The Collected Works of Abraham Lincoln*, 9 vols. (New Brunswick, N.J.: Rutgers University Press, 1953-55), 5: 396.

2. "Report of the Commissioner of Indian Affairs [1861]," *Senate Executive Document* no. 1, 37th Cong., 1st sess., 1861-62, serial 1117, p. 651; in roll 59, microcopy 574, special file 201, Office of Indian Affairs, record group 75 (hereafter cited as RG 75), National Archives.

3. Basler, *Collected Works of Lincoln*, 5: 46.

4. Hunter to Lincoln, Dec. 23, 1861, roll 30, Lincoln Papers, Library of Congress; Basler, *Collected Works of Lincoln*, 5: 84-85.

5. *The War of the Rebellion: A Compilation of the Official Records of the Union and Confederate Armies*, vol. 1, pt. 8, p. 525.

6. Basler, *Collected Works of Lincoln*, 5: 115-16.

7. Resolution of the House of Representatives, Feb. 6, 1862, Joseph Medill to Lincoln, Feb. 9, 1862, roll 32, Lincoln Papers.

8. Caleb B. Smith to Dole, Feb. 6, 1862, roll 4, microcopy 606, Letters Sent, Indian Division, Office of Indian Affairs, RG 48, National Archives.

9. Basler, *Collected Works of Lincoln*, 5: 131.

10. Albert Castel, *A Frontier State at War: Kansas, 1861-1865* (Ithaca, N.Y.: Cornell University Press, 1958), pp. 80-81.

11. Thomas to Halleck, Mar. 19, 1862, and Halleck to J. W. Denver, Apr. 5, 1862, *Official Records,* 1: 8, pp. 624, 665.

12. *Congressional Globe,* 38th Cong., 1st sess., Mar. 3, 1864, p. 921.

13. *Official Records,* 1: 13, p. 592.

14. Ibid., 1: 13, p. 590; roll 4, microcopy 606, Letters Sent, Indian Division, Office of the Secretary of the Interior, RG 48, National Archives; Basler, *Collected Works of Lincoln,* 5: 526ff.

15. *Official Records,* 1: 13, p. 617.

16. Ibid., 1: 13, pp. 648-49, 685-86.

17. Ibid., 1: 13, pp. 722, 724.

18. Gideon Welles, *The Diary of Gideon Welles,* ed. Howard K. Beale, 3 vols. (New York: W. W. Norton, 1960), Oct. 14, 1862, 1: 171. Pope to Sibley, Oct. 17, 1862, roll 483, microcopy 619, Letters Received, Adjutant General's Office, RG 109, National Archives.

19. Basler, *Collected Works of Lincoln,* 5: 493; *Official Records,* 1: 13, p. 788.

20. Ramsey to Lincoln, Nov. 28, 1862, roll 44, Lincoln Papers; Basler, *Collected Works of Lincoln,* 5: 525-26.

21. Basler, *Collected Works of Lincoln,* 5: 537-38; Holt to Lincoln, Dec. 1, 1862, roll 44, Lincoln Papers.

22. Welles, *Diary,* 1: 186.

23. Basler, *Collected Works of Lincoln,* 5: 550-51.

24. John G. Nicolay to Sibley, Dec. 9, 1862, roll 96, Lincoln Papers.

25. Ramsey Diary, Mar. 25, 1863, roll 39, vol. 36, Ramsey Papers, Minnesota Historical Society, St. Paul.

26. Basler, *Collected Works of Lincoln,* 8: 116.

27. Ramsey Diary, Nov. 23, 1864, roll 39, vol. 36, Ramsey Papers.

28. John J. Porter to Alexander Ramsey, Oct. 3, 1862, roll 20, M825, Letters Received, Indian Division, Office of the Secretary of the Interior, RG 48, National Archives.

29. David A. Nichols, *Lincoln and the Indians: Civil War Policy and Politics* (Columbia: University of Missouri Press, 1978), p. 78.

30. Wattles to Dole, June 26, 1861, roll 59, microcopy 574, special file 201, RG 75, National Archives; Whipple to [Dole], Nov. 2, 1863, box 40, letterbook 4, Whipple Papers, Minnesota Historical Society, St. Paul.

31. "Report of the Commissioner of Indian Affairs [1861]," *Senate Executive Document* no. 1, 37th Cong., 1st sess., 1861-62, serial 1117, p. 647.

32. Basler, *Collected Works of Lincoln,* 5: 173.

33. Henry B. Whipple, *Lights and Shadows of a Long Episcopate* (New York: Macmillan Co., 1899), pp. 136-37.

34. Basler, *Collected Works of Lincoln,* 5: 526-27.

35. Whipple to Lincoln, Whipple to Henry Halleck, Dec. 4, 1862, box 40, letterbook 3, Whipple Papers.

36. Henry M. Rice to Whipple, Dec. 27, 1862, box 3; Whipple to Dole, Nov. 16, 1863, letterbook 3, Whipple Papers.

37. Basler, *Collected Works of Lincoln,* 7: 47-48; *House Executive Document no.* 1, vol. 3, serial 1182, pp. 129-230.

38. Basler, *Collected Works of Lincoln,* 7: 275; Robert Mardock, *The Reformers and the American Indian* (Columbia: University of Missouri Press, 1971), p. 13; Whipple to George B. McClellan, Sept. 30, 1864, box 40, letterbook 5, Whipple Papers.

39. Basler, *Collected Works of Lincoln,* 8: 136-53.

40. *Congressional Globe,* June 10, 1864, pt. 3, p. 2873.

41. Basler, *Collected Works of Lincoln,* 6: 151-52.

Commentary on "Lincoln and the Indians"

HANS L. TREFOUSSE

Professor Nichols is to be highly commended for so neatly summing up for us in this paper the main outlines of his important book, *Lincoln and the Indians: Civil War Policy and Politics.* If he has somewhat softened his strictures on the Civil War president, he has added a necessary corrective which does him credit.

To my mind, the most challenging aspect of this paper is the author's consideration of Lincoln as a reformer, Lincoln as a humanitarian, and Lincoln as a child of his age. Correctly emphasizing the importance of goal orientation for any executive, Professor Nichols recognizes the president's primary goal of saving the Union. That was his objective, and to paraphrase the famous reply to Horace Greeley's "Prayer of the Twenty Millions," Lincoln would do less whenever he believed what he was doing hurt the cause and would do more whenever he believed doing more would help the cause. If this was true of his official attitude toward emancipation, it was even more true of his policies toward native Americans. It is therefore with considerable justification that Professor Nichols, otherwise not always favorably disposed toward the Great Emancipator, states that this picture of Lincoln as a goal-obsessed executive casts a more favorable light on some of the less successful aspects of his Indian policies.

In fact, all of the president's actions concerning the Indians must be seen within this context. The author correctly gives Lincoln credit for advocating reform of the corrupt and inefficient Indian service but tends to criticize him for doing nothing much about it. It is sufficient to note here that at least he endorsed reform, and did so in spite of the burden of carrying on the most costly war fought in the West between Waterloo and Sarajevo.

Professor Nichols's consideration of the question of Lincoln's humanitarianism is thought-provoking. Conceding that the president

170

refused to trade lives for votes and commuted the sentences of all but thirty-eight of the 303 condemned Sioux in Minnesota, he faults him for not interfering with the reprieved Indians' subsequent imprisonment and for buying their escape from the executioner at a high price—the expulsion of the Sioux and of the wholly innocent Winnebagos from the state. Yet Nichols admits that these actions must again be considered in line with Lincoln's insistence on first things first. In order to save the Union, he had to keep the Republican party in Minnesota strong. And local party members were as hostile to the Indians as were the Democrats.

How much Lincoln was a child of his time becomes clear with Professor Nichols's consideration of the Emancipator's racial views. Yet although Lincoln shared, to some degree, the prevailing notion of the Indians' innate savagery, he also wanted them treated more humanely. He believed that they ought to adopt the white people's ways, a notion that despite its present-day unpopularity, was then the most forward-looking approach, and according to tradition he saved an old Indian during the Black Hawk War. To be sure, the president was a child of his times, but a very unusual and progressive one.

The succinct stories of the failed expedition into the Indian Territory and the Indian wars of Minnesota also constitute interesting portions of the paper. Lucidly written, well presented, and lively, Professor Nichols's contribution certainly merits close attention.

Balanced as the treatment tends to be, certain problems remain. Despite all the caveats that Professor Nichols has included, it would appear that the overall impression of Lincoln's Indian policies as presented here is still a negative one. But it must be remembered that the federal system of dealing with the Indians did not originate with the Lincoln administration; that the corruption to which it was prone predated the Republicans' assumption of power and continued afterward, and that at least the Civil War president attempted to call attention to its shortcomings. If the expedition into the Indian Territory did not engage his full attention, it must be viewed against the background of the campaigns in Virginia in the East, and in Tennessee, Kentucky, and neighboring states in the West. All these were infinitely more important than James H. Lane's abortive plans, and all in all, Lincoln seems to have shown considerable skill in keeping both Lane and David Hunter on his side. If in Minnesota the chief executive used military force to suppress the Sioux uprising, he really had little choice, sworn as he was to protect states from domestic violence. His commutation of the sentences of the Indian prisoners, no matter what their fate afterward, was an act of courage and compassion as well as of justice. The political risks were great; yet Lincoln did not really hesitate.

The deal whereby Lincoln reprieved the prisoners in return for the expulsion of most of the remaining Indians from Minnesota does look wholly unwarranted today. At the time, however, it was probably the best and shrewdest bargain that could be made. Indians were considered savages; their lands were attractive to settlers, so it is not surprising that given the provocation of the Sioux uprising, the native Americans had to leave. But for Lincoln, their fate would probably have been infinitely worse.

The president's racial views as described by the author were at times indeed not up to the mark of modern anthropological knowledge. But as Richard N. Current pointed out long ago in connection with Lincoln's views on the blacks, the Emancipator showed a remarkable capacity for growth. When it came to dealing with nonwhites, he was far ahead of most of his contemporaries. As Nichols himself correctly remarks, Lincoln was constantly moving toward the abolitionists. He was the first president to receive delegations of blacks at the White House; for years he fought the Democrats' constant racial slurs; he published the Emancipation Proclamation, made possible the passage of the Thirteenth Amendment, and in his last speech advocated limited black suffrage in Louisiana. What he might have done with the Indians had he ever been given time to consider the subject calmly in times of peace is hard to say. But it is quite possible that had he lived he would have softened prevailing policies toward the Indians. He was a humanitarian and much less race-conscious than most of his contemporaries.

Again, Lincoln's failure to institute far-reaching Indian Bureau reforms during his administration should not really be held against him. In the midst of the war for the Union it was decidedly too much to expect that the president would undertake other ambitious projects, especially in areas so remote from most people's everyday concerns as Indian policy. And had Lincoln truly initiated reform, it would probably have been of the type that came with the Dawes Act in 1887, a change tending toward landholding in severalty, including measures having as their goal the extinction of native American culture through the full integration and assimilation of the various Indian nations into the general American pattern. All these objectives are today considered questionable. Had Lincoln instituted them, he would now probably be criticized on anthropological and scientific grounds. As Nichols demonstrates, the policy of concentrating Indians in a few major areas, which the president did endorse, involved cruel acts of displacement of entire tribes and was found wanting by 1880, when Carl Schurz ended it.

Professor Nichols's favorable view of Bishop Henry B. Whipple, while justified in general, also needs some correction. The bishop did not have to worry about holding the Union together, and his support in 1864 of General McClellan for president may well be faulted for racial reasons. Would not the general's election have brought about the end of the war on terms far short of the final suppression of slavery? Would it not have rendered impossible the passage of the Civil War amendments to the Constitution? And would not nonwhites, including Indians, probably have been far worse off than they actually were? Lincoln's actions, as the the author himself concedes, must be seen within the context of their time, the president's preoccupation with the war, and the impossibility in a nineteenth-century climate of racial prejudice and enthnocentrism of enforcing twentieth-century notions of racial equality.

Perhaps it is impossible within the confines of so short a paper to mention all the aspects of Civil War Indian policy, but the brevity of Professor Nichols's description of the Chivington massacre is regrettable. After all, it was not only an example of the worst tendencies of the frontier and the difficulties with which Lincoln had to contend but also led to a congressional investigation that as early as 1865 concluded that the Governor of Colorado and his helpers were guilty of atrocious crimes. It is peculiar that Professor Nichols has not dealt in more detail with a subject that he has treated so well in his book.

All in all, Professor Nichols has given us a most interesting account of Lincoln's actions in connection with a topic often neglected. If he has been critical of the president's handling of the Indian problem, he has nevertheless arrestingly delineated his enigmatic character. A humanitarian who did not shy away from tough military measures, a reformer who was still able to satisfy politicians opposed to change, a person comparatively well disposed toward Indians who yet shared many of the ethnocentric attitudes of his time—Lincoln was all of these. Above all, as Professor Nichols has shown us so well, the Great Emancipator was a goal-oriented executive. It is doubtful that without him the goal would have been reached.

CHAPTER 7

LINCOLN AND BLACK FREEDOM

LaWanda Cox

A CENTRAL CHALLENGE of Reconstruction history can be defined by two questions: first, how did it happen that a racist, white North freed black slaves and made all blacks the equal of whites before the law and at the ballot box? Second, what went wrong? *Lincoln and Black Freedom* focuses on pieces of the puzzle: the actual and potential roles of the presidency, specifically of Lincoln as president; and then, on the limits of the possible—the opportunity, if any, for Republican leaders in the 1860s to have established firmly in practice the equality that they made the law of the land. The focus required a reexamination of Lincoln's presidential record in respect to the status of Southern blacks. Lincoln emerged as a consistent, determined friend of black freedom, but a friend whose style of leadership obscured the strength of his commitment—and still does.[1]

In the popular mind the image of Lincoln as Emancipator may endure. Scholarship, though divided on the issue, has cast serious doubt upon its historical validity. More than that of any other historian the work of J. G. Randall, for two decades the leading academic authority on Lincoln, in stripping emancipation of its "crust of misconception" (Randall's phrase) discredited the Emancipation Proclamation and Lincoln as Emancipator. His Lincoln acted against slavery without enthusiasm, forced by political and military necessity to issue a paper pronouncement that set no slave free. Though recognizing Lincoln's strong moral judgment against slavery, Randall portrayed Lincoln as more deeply committed to gradualism, compensation, and colonization than to emancipation itself. Randall's views reverberated across college campuses in the arresting prose of two distinguished historians, Richard Hofstadter and Kenneth M. Stampp. According to Hofstadter, the proclamation "had all the moral grandeur of a bill of lading." In Stampp's words, "If it was Lincoln's destiny to go down

175

in history as the Great Emancipator, rarely has a man embraced his destiny with greater reluctance than he." Richard N. Current, who completed Randall's *Lincoln the President* after Randall's death and became a leading authority in his own right, found justification for the title of Emancipator in Lincoln's support for the Thirteenth Amendment, but he let stand Randall's view that expediency had pushed Lincoln the president into an actively antislavery policy. As more recent historical writing increasingly, and validly, presents blacks as active participants in achieving emancipation, Randall's interpretation is implicitly accepted, Lincoln's role diminished, and the popular image of the Emancipator overtly attacked as robbing blacks of credit "for setting themselves free."[2]

The term *freedom* as I have used it encompasses more than the absence of property rights in men. It includes as well release from the bondage of discrimination imposed by white prejudice through law. More than the reassertion of Lincoln's claim to the title of Emancipator, the conclusion that Lincoln was a friend of black civil and political rights is controversial. Here again the persistence of Randall's influence has been significant. Hostile to abolitionists and Radicals, Randall found and commended contrasting qualities in Lincoln: pro-Southern empathy, generosity toward the vanquished, an unqualified priority for speedy restoration of the Union, respect for state rights, willingness to let the Southern people (i.e., white Southerners) "solve their own race problem."[3]

Historians writing in the spirit of the civil rights revolution of our time repudiated Randall's pro-Southern, anti-Radical bias but generally accepted his characterization of Lincoln's policy. One wrote regretfully that it was difficult to reconcile Lincoln's role "with our own consciences."[4] Current found a way. He enlisted Lincoln on the side of civil rights by holding him up as an example of "man's ability to outgrow his prejudices," citing as evidence the respect with which Lincoln as president treated blacks, notably Frederick Douglass.[5] This was limited reassurance. Other historians discovered a bond between Lincoln and the Radicals, in goal if not in method. A few went so far as to hold that at the time of his death Lincoln was about to align himself with the Radical policy of a broad enfranchisement of Southern blacks. That view has not been generally accepted. Indeed, Lincoln's racial attitudes have attracted closer scrutiny than his racial policy.

Bennett's / King

NO!
See
letters

For a time in the 1960s and 1970s, particularly after Lerone Bennett's charge in *Ebony* that Lincoln was a white supremacist, the Lincoln image seemed in danger of being transformed into a symbol of white America's injustice to black America. Even sympathetic scholarly replies left Lincoln sadly wanting in moral indignation at the racial discrimination that permeated American society, North and South. He was also faulted for lack of thoughtful concern for the future of the freed slaves. By the 1970s another development compromised the Emancipator. Writings on Reconstruction had become sharply critical of federal policy toward Southern blacks and traced back to the war years what were seen as its fatal flaws in the postwar era. Lincoln was not the focus of these studies but by implication, and at times by direct accusation, he was held responsible.

The vulnerability of Lincoln's reputation as friend of black freedom in his day, and in the historiography of ours, derives in considerable part from his style of presidential leadership. In dealing with matters affecting the status of blacks it left his purpose and his resolve open to understandable doubt. On occasion he acted boldly. More often, however, Lincoln was cautious, advancing one step at a time, and indirect, exerting influence behind the scenes. He could give a directive without appearing to do so, or even while disavowing it as such. Seeking to persuade, he would fashion an argument to fit the listener. Some statements were disingenuous, evasive, or deliberately ambiguous.

Examples of Lincoln's less than forthright style are familiar, though not always recognized as such. Best known is his response to those urging emancipation during the weeks when he had decided to issue the proclamation but was awaiting a propitious moment. He gave no public indication of his intent, he questioned the efficacy of an executive order, and he wrote the famous reply to Horace Greeley. That letter was skillfully fashioned to deflect criticism from both Radicals and their opponents, but principally the latter. Lincoln stated that what he did, or did not do, about slavery and "the colored race" was determined by what he believed would help save the Union. Later he acknowledged that even as he issued the proclamation he had been uncertain whether it would do more good than harm. The same action might not have been taken by another president, equally committed to saving the Union but of lesser moral conviction that all men everywhere should be free.

Lincoln's decision on the proclamation was not his first decision as president to move against slavery. His earlier offensive also is illustrative of his presidential style. It was behind the scenes in late 1861 that he pressed Delaware to enact a plan of emancipation, drafting alternative bills to guide the state legislature. More open was the initiative that followed in March 1862 when he sent Congress a special message asking passage of a joint resolution promising financial aid to any state that would adopt gradual abolishment of slavery. More open, but not altogether open. He had worked three months on the message—"all by himself, no conference with his cabinet." Shortly thereafter he confided to Wendell Phillips that he meant slavery "should die," that the message, like the drink slyly requested by the Irishman in legally dry Maine, contained "a drop of the crathur. . . *unbeknown to myself*"; that is, the message was stronger than it appeared to be.[6] A passage therein characterizing the resolution requested of Congress as "merely initiatory" and expressing hope that it "would soon lead to important practical results" had suggested as much but ambiguously.[7] Seeking implementation of the proposal, Lincoln attempted to persuade border-state representatives with assurances and arguments that strain credulity. His basic argument, though fervent, was unrealistic: compensated emancipation by Union slave states would discourage the enemy and shorten the war. If such action were taken, Lincoln told their congressmen, he would countenance no coercive measure against slavery by the federal government. This assurance must not be made public lest it force a quarrel with the Greeley Radicals.

Lincoln followed his initial request with two additional ones to Congress. A special message in July presented the draft of a bill to compensate any state that abolished slavery "either immediately or gradually." In December his annual message included the text of a constitutional amendment to the same end—giving the states until 1900 to act. Ostensibly conservative and deferential to the rights of the states, the proposed amendment held more than a single "drop of the crathur." One provision stated that all slaves "who shall enjoy actual freedom by the chances of war" would be "forever free." Note that for a not inconsiderable number (many slaves were already fleeing to Union lines), freedom would be legalized not by state action but by constitutional amendment. Only loyal owners would be compensated. Although Lincoln expressed, and would continue to express, the judgment that gradual rather than sudden emancipation would be better for all, the amendment he drafted would have sanctioned immediate emancipation. Here was antislavery medicine of stronger proof than its label. A comparable stratagem was embodied in the preliminary Emancipation Proclamation. It offered, or seemed to offer, protective immunity to slavery in the Confederate states if they returned to the Union. The likelihood that any would do so within the 100-day grace period between the two proclamations was practically nil. This was not the only product of Lincoln's pen that appeared to offer more protection to slavery than he was prepared to give.

With the final Emancipation Proclamation issued, Lincoln in early 1863 turned his antislavery effort to occupied Louisiana, again acting indirectly and discreetly. An earlier effort at restoration had led to the election of two Unionists as congressmen, and they were briefly seated during the last days of the Thirty-Seventh Congress. Lincoln made it a point to cultivate them. As Benjamin F. Flanders, one of the two, later reminded Lincoln: "You took me by the hand and said there was a strong effort to break down your administration and asked me to support you. . . . I did it then to the extent of my influence and have ever since."[8] Lincoln used Flanders and his colleague Michael Hahn as conduits to encourage local Union leaders to take an antislavery stance. He dispensed patronage as Flanders, Hahn, and the local Free State leader, Thomas J. Durant, considered necessary in order to carry the state for freedom. Through Secretary Salmon P. Chase, Lincoln not only dispensed such patronage but sought to neutralize the influence of proslavery Unionists. One of their number was appointed to the important post of collector of the New Orleans customhouse with the understanding that his brother-in-law, the owner and editor of an influential proslavery newspaper, would change its editorial policy to one of support for emancipation.

All this, and more, Lincoln did in such a way as to keep an appearance of neutrality and of respect for the right of Louisianians (white) to decide freely the slavery issue. He so adroitly rejected an overture from proslavery Unionists to return Louisiana to the Union with the old slave constitution that their first reaction was disbelief — surely, Lincoln would not refuse readmission to a state because of slavery! They continued to expect that he would make proslavery concessions; so did some Free State leaders. Even to Gen. Nathaniel P. Banks, who had taken over command from Benjamin F. Butler,

179

Lincoln expressed his objective—i.e., to end slavery by state action before readmission—as only a wish, something he would be "glad" for Louisiana to do. He admonished, however, that reorganization as a free state be "pushed forward," completed by the time Congress met in December 1863.[9]

Lincoln acted directly to obtain his goal only when the leader of the Free State movement, and registrar, wrote him in the fall of 1863 that it would not be possible to complete the work of reorganization before Congress met, that public sentiment in occupied Louisiana could not by then be brought to support emancipation. Durant gratuitously added that no harm would come of delay, a conclusion incompatible with Lincoln's fear of political defeat in 1864 with incalculable consequences for the advancement of emancipation. Thereupon Lincoln turned to Banks as commanding general, making him "master of all."

Lincoln's Proclamation of Amnesty and Reconstruction was similarly precipitated by the situation in Louisiana. Its purpose was to hasten the return of Louisiana and other occupied territory as *free* states by removing the condition Lincoln had been understood as desiring, namely a broad geographic and electoral base for reorganization. Now, in order to obtain emancipation, he would accept reconstruction by a small minority, a mere one-tenth of prewar voters. Yet the requirement that slavery be abolished, instead of being explicitly stated in the proclamation, was so worded that Richard Current has recently concluded that "it did no such thing."[10] Lincoln had obfuscated his purpose even while pushing it forward. Yet there is no question but that he was determined to insist on the destruction of the institution of slavery as a prerequisite to readmission. His approval of General Banks's plan to destroy slavery by using military authority to set aside the slavery provisions of the old state constitution and *then* obtaining the consent of voters for the fait accompli—a policy of "consent *and* force"—makes Lincoln's purpose unmistakable.

There is even evidence strongly suggesting that General Banks, with the president's approval, was prepared to set aside the confirming election if won by candidates identified as proslavery. Lincoln's approval of high-handed military action to obtain state sanction of slavery's demise was not limited to Louisiana. He directed Gen. Frederick Steele to follow a similarly manipulative procedure in Arkansas, but there the plan was overtaken by the course of local events.

My favorite example of Lincoln's elusive style is the note he wrote that ensured passage of the Thirteenth Amendment through the House of Representatives on January 31, 1865. The Democratic opposition had been assiduously and secretly undermined by Lincoln's promises of patronage and by Secretary of State William H. Seward's mobilization of an extraordinary lobby, but opposition to the amendment gained last-minute strength from rumors that Southern commissioners were on their way to Washington for peace talks. When James Ashley, in charge of the measure on the floor of the House, feared the vote would be lost without a denial of the rumor direct from the president, Lincoln sent a one-sentence response: "So far as I know, there are no peace commissioners in the city, or likely to be in it."[11] Peace commissioners, as he well knew, were on their way — not to "the city" but to Fortress Monroe.

The style of presidential leadership that characterized Lincoln's effort on behalf of freedom is only partially explained by his skill as pragmatic politician. It derived as well from the nature of the man, the goal he sought, and the obstacles to its attainment. The goal and the man were integrally related. Holding to the principle that all men are created equal and entitled to certain inalienable rights, Lincoln's goal was to realize that principle, to use his own words, "as nearly . . . as we can." The qualification is as critical to an understanding of Lincoln's role as is the objective: "So I say in relation to the principle that all men are created equal, let it be as nearly reached as we can."[12] The words carry no expectation for perfection, no demand for immediate fulfillment. By temperament Lincoln was neither an optimist nor a crusader. Human fallibility, of which he was keenly aware, did not lessen his conviction that in a self-governing society a generally held feeling, though unjust, "can not be safely disregarded."[13] Lincoln would accept what he saw as "necessity," i.e., a limitation imposed by realities. He did not, however, submit to necessity with complacency. Characteristic was his query: "Can we all do better?"[14] He stood ready to do more when more could be accomplished.

As Lincoln advanced the nation toward freedom for all, the direction he set was steady; the pace was determined by his political judgment, his sense of timing, and his acute awareness of the constraints under which he labored. Those constraints were formidable. There was the need to preserve the Union and the duty to uphold the Constitution, a constitution that recognized and protected slavery.

181

Both obligations were those of solemn oath and of deep conviction. There was the practical imperative of keeping power out of the hands of an opposition party that would sustain slavery and the political hazard of any step toward equality for blacks in view of the intractable racism pervasive among whites. Fully alert to the force of racial prejudice, Lincoln met it by maneuver and sapping rather than by frontal attack.

War, and the participation of blacks as soldiers, made it possible to "do better." And Lincoln did. Keeping political support intact, he moved from his prewar advocacy of restricting slavery's spread to a foremost responsibility for slavery's total, immediate, uncompensated destruction by constitutional amendment. To borrow the terms used by George MacGregor Burns, Lincoln's presidential leadership was both "transactional" (i.e., a matter of exchange, compromise, deference to majority sentiment) and "transforming" (i.e., a moral leadership that helps achieve needed social change). The title of Emancipator is validated by the consistency of direction evident throughout his presidency, not alone by the Emancipation Proclamation and/or the Thirteenth Amendment, and validated by his skill in seizing the opportunities war opened. Lincoln was not pushed into antislavery action by military and political expediency. He was no reluctant emancipator.

To recognize Lincoln's role as "transforming" leader in no way diminishes that of others—of the forthright abolitionist, the outspoken Radical in Congress, the slave fleeing to precarious freedom, the black soldier fighting with spade and arms (with arms less often than he wished). All were essential participants in the process that led to slavery's destruction. To credit Lincoln is a reminder, however, that presidential leadership can be critically important in effecting social change. It also constitutes recognition of "transactional" skill added to moral purpose as an essential of effective presidential statesmanship. The demise of an entrenched, evil social institution, even after it has become an anachronism, does not automatically follow upon an appeal to conscience; nor did death for the South's peculiar institution follow with inevitability the outbreak of civil conflict.

There is less evidence of Lincoln as friend of black rights than of Lincoln as Emancipator. That evidence, however, conforms to the pattern of Lincoln's style and purpose in dealing with emancipation, and thereby carries weight. Its significance is further enhanced by recognition that Lincoln's first priority was the destruction of slavery, an objective that could be jeopardized by open support for the rights of free blacks. From the distant perspective of a century, victory over slavery may appear to have been inevitable and Lincoln's priority misplaced. To contemporary antislavery spokesmen the outcome as late as mid-1864 was frighteningly uncertain, contingent upon the success of Union forces on the battlefield and of the Republican party in the political arena. Frederick Douglass held that a victory for the Democratic party in 1864 would have been "a fatal calamity," leaving slavery "only wounded and crippled not disabled and killed."[15] Lincoln's concern that slavery be "killed" continued even after passage of the abolition amendment through Congress. His apprehension that the amendment might not be ratified is evident in his very last public address.

Once Lincoln's style and the priority he gave emancipation are recognized, there is no mistaking the fact that he considered the unequal treatment of free blacks an injustice. "Not a single man of your race is made the equal of a single man of ours," he bluntly stated to a group of black leaders upon whom he was urging colonization. He added: "It is a fact, about which we all think and feel alike, I and you."[16] The interpolation has been generally overlooked, for which Lincoln may have been as responsible as the historians who have deleted it. Whether or not he had arranged the interview in order to use colonization as a means of diffusing opposition to emancipation, as many historians now believe, Lincoln's purpose certainly was not the disclosure of his racial attitude. Yet as he indicated to his black audience, Lincoln's emotions as well as his sense of justice were stirred by the inequality to which white prejudice subjected blacks. His feelings are evident in the sardonic response he ordered sent to the man who wrote him that "white men is in class number one and black men is in class number two & must be governed by white men forever." The reply asked whether the writer was a white man or a black one "because in either case you can not be regarded as an entirely impartial judge. It may be that you belong to a third or fourth class of yellow or red men, in which case the impartiality of your judgment would be more apparent."[17] Similarly, Lincoln responded with indignation on learning of the exploitation of freed slaves by lessees of abandoned plantations in the Mississippi Valley. Only matters of utmost import loosened the tight rein Lincoln kept on a display of emotional reaction.

183

Although the uncertainty of slavery's destruction, the political hazard posed by white racism, and the multitude of wartime demands necessarily left decisive action to the future, Lincoln took steps toward equal status for blacks where he felt it possible to do so. His initiative brought the official diplomatic recognition of two black nations, Haiti and Liberia. In urging colonization upon black Americans, and in directing efforts to find suitable places, he sought assurance from governments that black colonists would be made citizens, legal "equals of the best." Through an official opinion of the attorney general, the Lincoln administration quietly repudiated the Dred Scott dictum that blacks were not citizens and had no rights as such under the Constitution. That opinion was made available to the military governor of Louisiana in August 1863 when, on the president's instruction, he was authorized to register all loyal citizens, an encouragement, though not a directive, to enroll as voters the free blacks of New Orleans. With issuance of the Reconstruction Proclamation in December 1863 Lincoln appeared to rule out black voting in the reorganization of seceded states; in fact, he did not. Publicly he indicated only in general terms that variants from the procedure outlined would be accepted; privately through Secretary Chase he again gave approval for the registration of blacks. Lincoln's actions were generally unknown, discreet, and indirect. Until a free state was established, he left to others the initiative in respect to black enfranchisement.

Louisiana was the one state that provided Lincoln relative freedom to push for more than emancipation. The plan General Banks put into effect was highly irregular and rested upon the military to an extent Lincoln had hoped to avoid, but it gave Louisiana a reorganized, elected government that Lincoln could and did recognize as a free state—i.e., one with slavery abolished—*before* a state convention met to rewrite the prewar constitution. This was not the case in Arkansas or Tennessee. Nine days after the inaugural of Michael Hahn as free state governor, Lincoln sent him a mere "suggestion"— that the upcoming Louisiana constitutional convention admit some blacks to the franchise, mentioning specifically "the very intelligent," and "those who have fought gallantly in our ranks." Marked "private," the letter was not made generally public, though Governor Hahn used it behind the scenes. Both he and General Banks recognized Lincoln's "mild and graceful" suggestion (Hahn's phrase) for what it was, a directive.[18] Neither man had previously looked with favor on black

184

enfranchisement, at least so soon, yet they pressured members of the convention. Their effort did not succeed in fulfilling Lincoln's wish, but by changing at least twenty votes it reversed a majority decision to forbid ever giving the vote to blacks and in its place obtained a constitutional provision authorizing black enfranchisement on the basis of military service, taxation, or intellectual fitness (the latter an extremely elastic qualification) by simple act of the Louisiana legislature. This limited but not insignificant advance unmistakably was due to Lincoln. Governor Hahn after Lincoln's death (and B. Gratz Brown while Lincoln still lived) attributed the provision to the president. Hahn also credited to Lincoln's influence other constitutional provisions favorable to blacks, the education of all children without distinction of color and the enrollment of all men, black and white, in the state militia. Lincoln's desire that blacks share public education is well documented.

The framing of the Louisiana constitution did not mark the end of Lincoln's interest and influence. He helped mobilize support for ratification of the document by letting "the civil officers in Louisiana, holding under me, know this is my wish," and implied discipline for those who did not "openly declare for the constitution."[19] When Louisiana's representatives came knocking at the doors of Congress, Lincoln privately assured Radicals reluctant to seat them that the administration's influence was being exerted for enfranchisement. William D. Kelley, the Pennsylvania Radical, was among those convinced. Extension of suffrage to blacks "was not a mere sentiment with Mr. Lincoln. He regarded it as an act of justice to the citizens, and a measure of sound policy for the States."[20] Working with Lincoln for Louisiana's admission in the fall and winter of 1864, Banks too gave private assurances. And in his public speeches in New England, the general interpreted the authorization in the Louisiana constitution as "under the circumstances . . . a command."[21] Back in New Orleans, Republican leaders of the Lincoln-Banks faction, both white and black, openly supported black enfranchisement.

Of utmost significance was Lincoln's insistence that Banks return to New Orleans for the express purpose of "advancing the new State government." His return was with "plenary power," to use Secretary of War Edwin M. Stanton's phrase. Lincoln further strengthened Banks's hand by stating publicly in his last address his own desire for qualified suffrage, and did so in such a way as to leave open the

185

possibility of a broad enfranchisement. By the time Banks reached New Orleans Lincoln had been assassinated. At a memorial mass meeting Banks directly assured blacks in the audience that "Abraham Lincoln gave his word that you will be free, and enjoy all the rights invested to all citizens," and that the last day of fulfillment "was not far distant."[22] Listeners recognized that the general was promising enfranchisement. Apparently he expected to succeed by ruthless removals of Conservatives from office (which he began) and by influencing the next elections. He informed Lincoln's successor, Andrew Johnson, that "we can carry an election triumphantly at any time if we are not disturbed [i.e., not disturbed in ousting hostile officeholders]." Even the question of Negro suffrage, he stated, would then be settled "without involving the Administration in any trouble, and satisfactorily to the country."[23] President Johnson did not leave General Banks undisturbed. Instead of sustaining the general, Johnson dismissed him from command.

Lincoln's support for black suffrage is sometimes minimized as limited to suffrage for only the black elite. This was not the case. Lincoln recognized, and used, military service as the most persuasive argument for extending the franchise. Most black privates could not sign their names. Nor did Lincoln restrict his encouragement for black suffrage to Louisiana. Chase did not understand as limited to that state the presidential approval for black voting during the process of reorganization. Banks believed Lincoln meant enfranchisement in Louisiana to be a model for other states. B. Gratz Brown cited Lincoln's pressure on Louisiana as an argument for extending suffrage to blacks in Missouri. Moreover, we now know that in December 1864 Lincoln was ready to accept Reconstruction legislation that would admit Louisiana with its 1864 constitution but require other returning states to include black suffrage in theirs. Although the extent of enfranchisement Lincoln desired is a matter of some uncertainty, my conclusion is that he was ready to go at least as far as the majority in Congress. With the Radicals unable to obtain any such legislation by the time Congress adjourned in March 1865, Banks's mission indicates Lincoln's intent to use executive power to obtain whatever was possible at the state level. In short, Lincoln was still looking to realize the principle of equality "as nearly . . . as we can."

No student of history can with confidence fault Lincoln's political judgment of what was attainable in the 1860s, or how best he could

186

achieve the maximum possible. The distance between the dominant racial sentiment of Lincoln's day and that of our own is too great. As late as October 1864 the electorate of Maryland, except for the soldier vote, would have rejected emancipation and celebrated not the end of slavery but the "Death Knell of Abolitionism."[24] The best that could be obtained from Unionist Missouri in 1863 was emancipation as of July 4, 1870, with continuing servitude for those over forty during their entire lifetime and for those over twelve until they reached twenty-three. Immediate and unconditional emancipation was established in Missouri only after Lincoln's death, in June 1865. In the free North white opposition to equal status for blacks suffered erosion during the course of the war, but remained tenacious. In August 1862 Illinois voters rejected a new constitution as a whole but overwhelmingly approved provisions that would have enshrined in the state's constitution prohibitions against any Negro migrating into the state and against any resident Negro voting or holding office. Before the war only four states, all in New England, provided equal suffrage. No others extended this right to blacks during the war years. In the fall of 1865 Republican attempts to do so in Connecticut, Wisconsin, and Minnesota failed in referendum voting.

The time has come to disengage Lincoln from the present and let the historic record speak for itself. To do so will diminish neither the man nor the tasks that remain before us to attain racial justice. Without hazard we can relinquish Lincoln as a mirror of the present and beacon to the future, whether of guidance or of warning. Grant that his circumspect style of presidential leadership as an instrument to reach equality irrespective of race offers no acceptable model for the present, since forthright advocacy from the oval office can now mobilize a national consensus to this end. Grant that the achievements beyond abolition that Lincoln nurtured, though essential, are insufficient for the 1980s. But let us take care to recognize that Lincoln's record as friend of freedom is impressive—that it was no reluctant concession to the pressures of a grim war, or the expediency of politics.

To summarize: Lincoln let war come rather than retreat on the expansion of servitude. Within a year of the war's beginning he determined that slavery "should die." Nine months later he boldly proclaimed as a war measure emancipation for the slaves of loyal and disloyal alike in areas of rebellion. He did so though uncertain whether the Emancipation Proclamation would strengthen, or weaken, the

Union war effort. By mid-1863 he was ready to deny readmission to any state unwilling to abolish the institution. In order to force state action in occupied territory he boldly employed the power of patronage plus that of military authority — the latter without the covering justification of military necessity. Refusing to let freedom rest solely upon the precarious authority of presidential proclamation and congressional legislation, or upon the uncertainty of state action, Lincoln succeeded in obtaining passage of the abolition amendment. Meanwhile he had officially recognized blacks as citizens and used the weight of his high office in an effort to set former slaves on the road to equality through access to the ballot box.

On the most divisive issue this nation has ever faced, the status of black Americans, Lincoln's presidential record stands without need of myth, apology, or transformation into symbolism. The preeminent meaning of Lincoln the president lies in the historic substance of his role as friend of black freedom. It is a meaning sufficient for all time.

During the years immediately following Lincoln's death his party established an impressive record on black rights. Republicans passed the first civil rights legislation in the nation's history, and passed it over President Andrew Johnson's veto. In the face of unrelenting opposition from Democratic opponents, the party also succeeded in making the Fourteenth and Fifteenth Amendments the supreme law of the land. They followed the amendments with federal enforcement acts of broad scope. Yet the Republican record has suffered harsh censure from historians of our day, criticism prompted in large measure by the failure to realize equal citizenship in practice. That the promise of legislation and constitutional amendment was fulfilled in the South only briefly and partially is a fact beyond dispute. Subjected to white violence and soon deprived of the potential for political power granted in 1867, the vast majority of freed slaves remained for decades an impoverished agrarian underclass, economically dependent upon white landowners and merchant creditors, socially subordinated as a caste to whites of all ranks. It does not necessarily follow, however, that Northern Republicans were responsible for what went wrong. The last section of *Lincoln and Black Freedom* examines an assumption and a related accusation often accepted as fact: namely, the assumption that the political leaders of the 1860s had the power to insure a

188

democratic, racially equalitarian outcome and the accusation that they promised racial equality, then wantonly betrayed the promise.

To examine the indictment it is necessary first of all to make clear what it was Republicans in the immediate post–Civil War years sought to realize through the courts and the ballot box. It was not racial equality. What they sought for the freed slaves was equality of citizenship. Strictly speaking, racial equality is a biological condition rather than a consequence of political or societal action. In our day race itself is a challenged concept. That no inferiority or superiority is biologically inherent in a people because of color or ethnicity is now generally accepted. Discrimination or enforced segregation based upon either is regarded as morally insupportable. These perceptions were not commonly held in the mid-nineteenth century, at least not among white Americans. Republican leaders sought and obtained equal citizenship in law while lacking scientific assurance or personal conviction of racial equality. It might be argued that this should enhance rather than diminish their achievement. However that may be, what was sought through public policy in the 1860s was more limited than the goals of the 1960s but as fundamental to the broader objectives of the Second Reconstruction as the destruction of slavery had been essential to the establishment of nationwide equality of legal status. To indict Republicans for betraying a promise of racial equality comports neither with logic nor with historic reality.

To recognize the indictment as faulty does not dispose of the charge that the seed of failure lay in the racial prejudice of Northern Republicans, a view widely held. Although it was their Democratic opponents who flagrantly exploited racial prejudice in the interest of party there is no gainsaying the fact that racism in one degree or another permeated the ranks of Republicans. Racial prejudice did not, however, prevent the growth of a majority consensus within the Republican party first for the recognition of black citizenship, that is of basic human rights and equality before the law, and more tardily for equality at the ballot box. If the commitments were not effectively enforced in the South during the 1870s and 1880s, the explanation does not lie primarily in Republican racism. It is true that opposition to what was viewed as an attempt to legislate social equality helped weaken Republican political power in the election of 1874 and that racist assumptions made some political equalitarians susceptible to

189

Southern white propaganda that attributed political corruption and chaos to the enfranchisement of blacks. However, Republican racism was only one of the many factors in the Northern retreat from enforcement of black civil and political rights in the South. No historian has established its effect as more than incidental.

Another explanation of Reconstruction's failure, so widely held as to have been identified in 1973 as the "New Orthodoxy in Reconstruction Historiography," is that Republicans had too tender a regard for property rights to confiscate plantation lands and redistribute them to the freedmen. The assumption behind the contention is that a land program would have provided the former slaves with power to safeguard their freedom and with insurance against poverty. The difficulty with this counterfactual projection is that small landownership in the South during the postwar decades could not protect blacks against either white violence or poverty, though it would have lightened their economic burden and immensely heightened their sense of personal freedom from white dominance. White terror struck black landowner and tenant alike. The cotton economy perpetuated poverty for both, alternative agrarian markets were scarce, and a nonmarket homestead offered little beyond subsistence. The escape hatch of industrial or commercial employment for blacks was narrow. Mid-nineteenth-century America with its optimistic assumption of economic opportunity for the individual and of prosperity for a transformed free labor South lacked awareness of impending economic realities as well as the skills requisite to meet them. A formerly dependent and deprived agrarian population is not readily lifted out of poverty. Indeed, as the present difficulties in third world nations (and the recent work of Jane Jacobs and others) remind us, no certain remedy has yet been found to assure escape from poverty. A prosperous New South, for whites as well as blacks, proved elusive; historians and cliometricians continue to pursue the reasons why.

A third major explanation for what had gone wrong was offered by constitutional historians in the 1960s: the constitutional conservatism of Republican lawmakers. A revolutionary destruction of state authority, it was argued, had been necessary. Deference to the traditional federal structure of the Union denied the national government sufficient power to protect the rights of blacks. Interestingly, this view has been substantially modified, if not abandoned, by some of the very authorities who set it forth. Others have made a strong case that the Supreme Court could have developed an expansive construction of national power to protect blacks under the Reconstruction amendments and laws.

The indictment against Republican leaders of the 1860s rests upon a counterfactual assumption that is invalid. Republicans did not possess unlimited power and opportunity. Respect for Constitution and constitutionalism, the intractable nature of postwar poverty in the South, and racial prejudice in the North placed boundaries on the possible. In the postwar years, however, the most decisive barrier to realization of the limited but essential equalitarian goals established in law was no one of these but rather the pervasiveness of Southern white resistance. That the white South resisted Republican policy is no recent discovery, but historians who reexamined Reconstruction free of the racial bias of an older generation have only belatedly recognized the full force and significance of that opposition. It is now clear that Southern whites continued the North-South conflict by determined, persistent, guerrilla-type warfare that enjoyed the overwhelming support or acquiescence of their fellows. The objective was defeat of the Northern-imposed status for Southern blacks as equal citizens and as free laborers. Recent historical writings increasingly look to internal conditions in the South for explanation rather than to Northern policy, yet more often than not, the primary role of Southern white resistance in defeating the Republican attempt to reconstruct the South is muted.

Those who attribute the failure of Reconstruction to a lack of Northern will, and influential historians still do, assume that the North could force the white South to accept blacks as equal citizens. To the contrary, without a substantial degree of consent not only from Southern white political leaders but from their white constituencies, no amount of coercion could have achieved that goal. And once Southern armies had surrendered, it was not possible for the North as a society committed to government by consent and the rule of law to sustain the prolonged use of military force and military authority necessary even to make the attempt. A very considerable amount of force and hundreds of criminal prosecutions were in fact used, far more than during the civil rights revolution of the twentieth century. Despite the limits on the possible, presidential leadership might have made a significant difference. The historic challenge of the immediate postwar years was to induce white Southerners to accept a substantial measure of freedom and equality for blacks and to institutionalize their acceptance in an effective, biracial political party. Captive to his heritage of section, class, and party, Lincoln's successor was incapable of perceiving, let alone meeting, that challenge.

Andrew Johnson identified himself as a man of the South. Until the pressures of war and politics forced him to embrace emancipation, loyalty to slavery was for Johnson a basic component of loyalty to section. As late as the spring of 1862 he assured fellow Tennesseans that he believed "slaves should be in subordination and will live and die so believing." He also assured them that Lincoln and his party had no intention of waging war to free slaves. Apparently Johnson never doubted but that, in his words, the Negro "is an inferior type of man," "not created equal in the very beginning." Unlike Lincoln, Johnson had no purpose to realize as nearly as possible the principle that all men are created equal. He held that Jefferson in writing the Declaration of Independence had meant "the white race, and not the African race." In his veto of the civil rights bill of March 1866, Johnson objected to conferring citizenship upon "the entire race designated as blacks, people of color, negroes, mulattoes, and persons of African blood."[25]

The direction indicated by Andrew Johnson's racial attitude was reinforced by his concern for state rights, his lack of loyalty to the Republican party with which he was aligned only as a Union Democrat, his desire for Southern approbation, and his ambition to be elected president in his own right. Johnson had no reason to use presidential power and persuasion, as Lincoln surely would have done, to build a Republican or predominantly Republican Union party in the South. Johnson looked with favor upon a reorganization of parties that would be a major realignment, with former Democrats at least equal partners. His break with the congressional majority in 1866 was followed by an unsuccessful attempt to create a new political party of conservative Republicans and cooperative Democrats, the former a distinct minority in their own party but the latter a powerful, perhaps predominant, influence in the Northern Democracy. For such a party, a substantial measure of equality for blacks was a condition to be avoided rather than a goal to be attained.

At war's end, party loyalties in the North were too intense to permit a major realignment, but in the South the situation was fluid. Elements existed for a broad coalition in opposition to the old planter-dominated secessionist Democracy: Unionists of varying degrees, opponents of secession, critics of the Confederate leadership, old Whigs, urban dwellers including laborers, men with origins abroad or in the North, those whose class or intrasectional interests created hostility to planter domination—plus blacks to the extent that they might be enfranchised. Such a coalition at best would be an uneasy one. Conflicting economic interests and personal ambitions would require reconciliation. There would be the ever-present hazard of deeply embedded mores of black-white relations. These were exploitable by the opposition and within a biracial party would trigger division on issues viewed by whites as social. Despite the difficulties, in the spring of 1865 the task of building a stable Union-Republican party in the South was not beyond the limits of the possible. But it would require careful nurture and, if it were to function as an instrument of social change, a purposeful direction.

Presidential nurture and direction were precluded by Lincoln's assassination and Johnson's succession. When congressional leaders attempted the task, they were faced not only with its inherent difficulties but with added obstacles. Johnson's policies had encouraged the hope among white Southerners that they would be able to maintain control over race relations, thereby strengthening resistance to change. And warfare between president and Congress had created chaos in the process of Southern political reorganization. Some elements that would otherwise have entered a Union-Republican party remained attached to Johnson's political fortunes.

Since Republicans wished to avoid a break with the president, Johnson's policies had dammed up for a time the growing sentiment for black legal equality, citizenship, and enfranchisement. When the dam broke, the accompanying flood created its own havoc. Renewed military control, immediate universal enfranchisement of black men, and the disfranchisement of some whites, intensified the bitterness of defeat and the resolve to resist. Except within limited geographical areas, the Republican party in the South was viewed as an alien intruder. It could obtain neither the loyalty of a substantial number of white Southerners nor their acknowledgment of its legitimacy. The power that it briefly held could not be consolidated without both.

A stable two-party system in the South was not assured had Lincoln lived out his second term of office, but its successful establishment would have been much less unlikely. Bonds between Lincoln and his party were strong, too strong to allow differences to escalate into open warfare. Moreover, unlike Johnson, Lincoln had the will to nurture an essentially Republican party in the South. And he possessed the skill to build one. He was experienced in consolidating a political coalition by dispensing "justice to all [factions]." He had demonstrated ability to retain the political loyalty of Southern proslavery Unionists who disliked his policy. Politically he deftly used others but did not allow others to use him. His compassion, his Southern ties, and his style of leadership admirably fitted the postwar need to minimize bitterness and undermine resistance to change. They appeared to set him apart from the hated Radical of "Black Republicanism." Yet it was Lincoln rather than the Radicals who had inaugurated a Southern policy that used "consent *and* force" to attain a political end. His insistence that General Banks return to Louisiana signaled that Lincoln would when necessary continue to supplement persuasion with coercion.

Lincoln would also bind up the nation's wounds. Too often the eloquent closing paragraph of his Second Inaugural has been read as concern only for white America. His words need not be so narrowly construed. He enjoined the nation "to finish the work we are in" "with firmness in the right, as God gives us to see the right." "The right" as God gave him to "see it" was for Lincoln color-blind. There is no reason to believe that he ever abandoned the goal of realizing "as nearly . . . as we can" the principle that all men (not whites alone) are created equal. The performance of blacks during the war and the outpouring of trust and gratitude from those freed of their bondage could only have deepened his commitment to that goal. How nearly it could have been reached in the lifetime of his generation Lincoln did not know, nor can we. To achieve a moral objective not universally held, it is necessary to make change "acceptable to those who must support it, tolerable to those who must put up with it."[26] If any man could have met that challenge in respect to the rights of blacks in freedom, the man was Lincoln. His untimely death changed the course, and perhaps the outcome, of the Republican effort to reconstruct Southern society in the interest of free labor and racial justice.

NOTES

1. This essay is based upon my *Lincoln and Black Freedom: A Study in Presidential Leadership* (Columbia: University of South Carolina Press, 1981)

and my essay "From Emancipation to Segregation: National Policy and Southern Blacks," in *Interpreting Southern History: Essays on the Recent Historical Literature in Honor of S. W. Higginbotham*, ed. John B. Boles and Evelyn T. Nolen (Baton Rouge: Louisiana State University Press, 1986).

2. For citations to the quotations from Randall, Hofstadter, Stampp, and Current, and their views generally, see "From Emancipation to Segregation," notes 42, 43, 44. The last quotation is from Vincent Harding, *There Is a River: The Black Struggle for Freedom in America* (New York: Harcourt Brace Jovanovich, 1981), p. 236.

3. Benjamin P. Thomas, *Abraham Lincoln: A Biography* (New York: Alfred A. Knopf, 1952), p. 407.

4. Robert W. Johannsen, "In Search of the Real Lincoln, or Lincoln at the Crossroads," *Journal of the Illinois State Historical Society* 61 (1968): 237.

5. Richard N. Current, *The Lincoln Nobody Knows* (New York: McGraw Hill, 1958), p. 236.

6. Wendell Phillips to Ann Phillips, Mar. 31, 1862, Blagden Papers, Houghton Library, Harvard University, printed in part in Irving H. Bartlett, *Wendell and Ann Phillips: The Community of Reform, 1840-1880* (New York: W. W. Norton, 1982), pp. 52-53.

7. Roy P. Basler, ed., Marion Dolores Pratt and Lloyd A. Dunlap, asst. eds., *The Collected Works of Abraham Lincoln*, 9 vols. (New Brunswick, N.J.: Rutgers University Press, 1953-55), 5: 146. Any subsequent Lincoln quotation from the *Collected Works of Lincoln* that is readily located by date or occasion will not be noted.

8. Flanders to Lincoln, Jan. 16, 1864, Abraham Lincoln Papers, Library of Congress, Microfilm edition, 1959.

9. Basler, *Collected Works of Lincoln* 6: 364-65.

10. Richard Nelson Current, *Speaking of Abraham Lincoln: The Man and His Meaning for Our Times* (Urbana: University of Illinois Press, 1983), p. 164.

11. Basler, *Collected Works of Lincoln*, 8: 248.

12. Ibid., 2: 501.

13. Ibid., 2: 256.

14. Ibid., 5: 537.

15. Frederick Douglass, *Life and Times of Frederick Douglass Written by Himself* (reprint of 1892 rev. ed., New York: Crowell-Collier, 1962), pp. 360-61.

16. Basler, *Collected Works of Lincoln*, 5: 372.

17. Ibid., 7: 483.

18. Ibid., 7: 243; Hahn to W. D. Kelley, June 21, 1865, *New York Times*, June 23, 1865, reprinted from the *Washington Chronicle*.

19. Basler, *Collected Works of Lincoln*, 7: 486.

20. *New Orleans Tribune*, May 23, 1865.

21. Clipping of an address at Tremont Temple, Boston, in Nathaniel P. Banks Papers, Library of Congress.

22. *New Orleans Tribune*, Apr. 25, 1865.

23. Banks to Preston King, May 6, 1865, Andrew Johnson Papers, Library of Congress.

24. From a headline in the *Maryland Union*, Oct. 20, 1864, quoted in Charles Lewis Wagandt, *The Mighty Revolution: Negro Emancipation in Maryland, 1862-1864* (Baltimore: Johns Hopkins University Press, 1964), p. 260.

25. LeRoy P. Graf and Ralph W. Haskins, eds., *The Papers of Andrew Johnson*, 7 vols. to date (Knoxville: University of Tennessee Press, 1967–), 1: 136; 2: 477; 3: 319-20, 328; 5: 231, 233, 328; for the veto message, see the documentary collection LaWanda Cox and John H. Cox, eds., *Reconstruction, the Negro, and the New South* (Columbia: University of South Carolina Press, 1973), p. 59.

26. Richard E. Neustadt, *Presidential Power: The Politics of Leadership from FDR to Carter* (New York: John Wiley and Sons, 1980), p. 135.

A Momentous Decree:
Commentary on "Lincoln and Black Freedom"

Stephen B. Oates

I applaud Professor Cox for her perceptive and persuasive analysis. She has done what the historian is supposed to do: she has examined Lincoln and black freedom in the context of his own era, not according to the needs and biases of the present. The time has indeed come to "disengage Lincoln from the present" and let his historical record speak for itself.[1]

And it was an impressive record. By war's end, Lincoln had come a long distance from the harried political candidate he had been in 1858, opposed to black political rights lest his political career be jeopardized, convinced that only the distant future could remove slavery from his troubled country, certain that only colonization could solve the ensuing problem of racial adjustment. By mid-April 1865 he had crushed slavery with his armies, had crushed an institution he had always hated—as much, he said, as any abolitionist. He had enlisted black fighting men in his armed forces, endorsed black political rights in conquered Dixie, and fought the war through to a total Union triumph, a triumph for popular government and a larger concept of inalienable human rights that now included the American black.

Still, as enlightening as her argument is, Professor Cox largely ignores the Emancipation Proclamation itself. As a consequence, she omits the central act in the story she is discussing. To appreciate the full significance of that story, we need to reexamine the proclamation in light of modern scholarship, taking care to identify popular misconceptions that still obscure its meaning.

We now know that Lincoln issued his proclamation for a combination of reasons: to clarify the status of the fugitive slaves, to solve

197

the Union's manpower woes, to keep Great Britain out of the conflict, to maim and cripple the Confederacy by destroying its labor force, to remove the very thing that had caused the war, and to break the chains of several million oppressed human beings and right America at last with her own ideals. As Professor Cox points out, Lincoln was no reluctant emancipator: he struck at slavery within a year after the war had begun, and he did so for moral as well as for political and military reasons. As much as possible in his time, he wanted America to realize the promise of equality made in the Declaration of Independence, which was the foundation of his politics. Lincoln himself was fully aware of the significance of his proclamation. "If my name ever goes into history," he said, "it will be for this act."[2]

The final proclamation of January 1, 1863, did temporarily exempt occupied Tennessee and certain occupied places in Louisiana and Virginia. But later, in reconstructing those states, Lincoln withdrew the exemptions and made emancipation a mandatory part of his reconstruction program. His proclamation also excluded the loyal slave states because they were not in rebellion, and he thought he lacked the legal authority to uproot slavery there. But he kept pressuring them to remove bondage themselves—and later pushed a constitutional amendment that liberated their slaves as well. With the exception of the loyal border and certain occupied areas, the final proclamation declared that of this day, all slaves in the rebellious states were "forever free." The document also asserted that black men— Southern and Northern alike—would now be enlisted in Union military forces.

Contrary to what many historians have said, Lincoln's proclamation went farther than anything Congress had done about slavery. True, Congress had recently enacted (and Lincoln had recently signed) the Second Confiscation Act, which provided for the seizure and liberation of all slaves of people who supported or participated in the rebellion. Under this measure, most slaves would be freed only after protracted case-by-case litigation in the federal courts. Another section of the act did liberate certain categories of slaves without court action, but the bill exempted loyal slaveowners in the rebel South, allowing them to keep their slaves and other property. Lincoln's proclamation, on the other hand, was a sweeping blow against bondage as an institution in the rebel states, a blow that would free all the slaves there— those of secessionists and Unionists alike. Thus Lincoln intended to handle emancipation himself, avoid judicial red tape, and use the military to vanquish the cornerstone of the Confederacy. He justified this as a military necessity to save the Union—and with it America's cherished experiment in popular government, which guaranteed all the "right to rise."[3]

Lincoln's proclamation was not "of minor importance," as James G. Randall contended a generation ago. On the contrary, it was the most revolutionary measure ever to come from an American president up to that time. This "momentous decree," as Martin Luther King, Jr., rightly described it, was an unprecedented use of federal military power against a state institution. It was an unprecedented federal assault against the very foundation of the South's planter class and economic and social order. As Union armies drove into rebel territory, they would tear slavery out root and branch, automatically freeing all slaves in the areas and states they conquered. In this respect (as Lincoln said), the war brought on changes more fundamental and profound than either side had expected when the conflict began. Now slavery perished as the Confederacy perished, dying by degrees with every Union advance, every Union victory.

Moreover, word of the proclamation hummed across the slave grapevine in the Confederacy; and as Union armies drew near, more slaves than ever abandoned rebel farms and plantations and (as one said) "demonstrated with their feet" their desire for freedom. Slaves like these did not sit back and wait for their liberty: they went out and got it for themselves.

The proclamation was not some anemic document that in effect freed no slaves. By November 1864 the *Philadelphia North American* estimated that more than 1,300,000 blacks had been liberated by Lincoln's proclamation or "the events of the war." By war's end, all 3,500,000 slaves in the defeated Confederacy could claim freedom under Lincoln's proclamation and the victorious Union flag. In fact, the proclamation was their only claim to freedom until the ratification of the Thirteenth Amendment in December 1865.

What is more, the proclamation did something for Lincoln personally that has never been stressed enough. In truth, the story of emancipation could well be called the liberation of Abraham Lincoln. For in the process of granting freedom to the slaves, Lincoln also emancipated himself from a painful personal dilemma: his love for a political system that preserved an institution he hated. His proclamation now brought the private and the public Lincoln together: now the public statesman could vanquish a thing the private citizen had always detested, a thing that had long had "the power of making me miserable." Now the public statesman could destroy what he regarded as "a cruel wrong" that had always besmirched America's experiment in popular government, had always impeded her historic mission in the progress of human liberty in the world.

The proclamation also opened the army to black volunteers, and Northern free blacks and Southern ex-slaves enlisted as Union fighting men. As Lincoln said, "The colored population is the great *available* and yet unavailed of, force for restoring the Union." And he now availed himself of that force, on a scale unprecedented in America. In all, some 186,000 black troops—most of them emancipated slaves—served in Union forces on every major battle front, helping to liberate their brothers and sisters in bondage and to save the American experiment in popular government. As Lincoln observed, the blacks added enormous and indispensable strength to the Union war machine. Without them, it is doubtful that he could have won the war.

With blacks now fighting in his armies, Lincoln abandoned colonization as a solution to racial adjustment in Dixie. His colonization schemes had all foundered, and in any case black people adamantly refused to participate in the president's voluntary program. Across the North, free blacks denounced Lincoln's highly publicized colonization efforts—this was their country too!—and they petitioned him to deport slaveholders instead. And Lincoln seemed in sympathy with that. Later, as the war drew to a close, he told his cabinet that he would like to frighten rebel leaders out of the country. He waved his arms as though he were shooing chickens.

After he issued the Emancipation Proclamation, Lincoln never again urged colonization in public—an eloquent silence, indicating that he had concluded that Dixie's whites and liberated blacks must somehow learn to live together. Yet there is a persistent misconception that Lincoln to the end of his life was a champion of colonization. That view rests exclusively on the 1892 autobiography of Union political general Benjamin F. Butler. In it, Butler claimed that in April 1865 Lincoln feared a race war in the South and still wanted to ship the blacks abroad. Not only is Butler a highly dubious witness, but there is not a scintilla of corroborative evidence to support his story, which Mark E. Neely, Jr., has recently exploded as "entirely a fantasy." There is not a single other source that quotes the president stating, in public or in private, that he still favored colonization.[4]

In any case, such a stance would have been glaringly inconsistent with Lincoln's Gettysburg Address, which called for a new birth of freedom in America for blacks and whites alike. (Here, in fact, is the eloquent defense of liberty that critics have found lacking in the proclamation itself.) And a colonization stance would have been inconsistent, too, with Lincoln's appreciation of the indispensable role his black soldiers played in subduing the rebellion. No one of Lincoln's honesty and sense of fair play would enlist 186,000 black troops to save the Union and then advocate throwing them out of the country. He simply did not advocate that. Still, he needed some device during the war, some program that would pacify white Northerners and convince them that Southern blacks would not flock into their communities, but would remain in the South instead. What Lincoln worked out was a refugee system, installed by his adjutant general in occupied Dixie, which utilized blacks there in a variety of civilian and military pursuits. Then Republican propaganda went to work selling Northern whites on the system and the Emancipation Proclamation. See, the argument went, liberated blacks will not invade the North, but will stay in Dixie as free wage earners, learning to help themselves and our Union cause.

Even so, emancipation remained the most explosive and unpopular act of Lincoln's embattled presidency. In the Confederacy, newspapers pronounced him a "fiend" who wanted to incite a race war in Dixie; Jefferson Davis considered the proclamation "the most execrable measure recorded in the history of guilty man," and rebels everywhere vowed to fight all the harder against the monster who had issued it. In the North, thousands of Democrats revolted against the administration in 1863, denouncing Lincoln as an abolitionist dictator who had surrendered to radicalism. In the Midwest, dissident Democrats launched a peace movement to throw "the shrieking abolitionist faction" out of office and negotiate a peace with the Confederacy that would somehow restore the Union with slavery intact. With Democrats up in arms, a storm of anti-black, anti-Lincoln protest rolled over the land, whipping up race and draft riots in several cities. And there was trouble in the army as well. Correspondents who traveled with Union forces claimed that hardly one soldier in ten approved of emancipation; and some officers from the Midwest even resigned in protest.

Clearly Lincoln's generation did not regard the proclamation as a meaningless paper decree. The wonder, of course, is that Lincoln stuck by a measure that aroused such public indignation. But the president seemed intractable. He had made up his mind to smash the slave society of the rebel South and eliminate the moral wrong of black bondage, and no amount of public discontent, he indicated, was going to change his mind. With his sense of history, he was also concerned with the judgments of posterity. "In times like the present," he had warned Congress, "men should utter nothing for which they would not willingly be responsible through time and eternity."[5]

Still, he wavered once—in August 1864, a time of unrelenting gloom for Lincoln, when his popularity had sunk so low that it seemed he could not be reelected. He confessed that maybe the country would no longer sustain a war for slave liberation, that maybe he should not pull the nation down a road it did not want to travel. On August 24, he decided to offer Jefferson Davis peace terms that excluded emancipation as a condition, vaguely suggesting that slavery would be adjusted later "by peaceful means." But the next day Lincoln changed his mind. With awakened resolution, he vowed to fight the war through to unconditional surrender and to stand by emancipation come what may. He had made his promise of freedom to the slaves, and he meant to keep it as long as he was in office.

Here surely is one of the glories of the Lincoln story: a troubled, visionary president contending with an aroused Northern opposition, a determined Southern foe, and his own uncertainties and self-doubts, and yet somehow finding the inner strength to overcome them all. After he won reelection, thanks to timely Union victories and the folly of the Democrats in running a major general on a peace plank in the midst of civil war, Lincoln used all the powers and prestige of his office to get the present Thirteenth Amendment through a recalcitrant House of Representatives (the Senate had already passed it). Lincoln did so to protect his proclamation, for he worried that it might be nullified in the courts or thrown out by a later Congress or a subsequent administration. When the House adopted the amendment, by just three votes more than the required two-thirds majority, Lincoln pronounced it "a great moral victory" and "a King's cure" for the evils of slavery. When ratified by the states, the amendment would end human bondage everywhere in America. Lincoln pointed across the Potomac: "If the people over the river had behaved themselves, I could not have done what I have."[6]

If we are to appreciate what Lincoln did about slavery, as Professor Cox argues, we must view him in the context of what was attainable in the 1860s, a white-supremacist era in which a vast number of Northern whites were hostile to black freedom. In this context, it was Frederick Douglass who perhaps best summed up Lincoln and emancipation. "From the genuine abolition view, Mr. Lincoln seemed tardy, cold, dull, and indifferent, but measuring him by the sentiment of his country—a sentiment he was bound as a statesman to consult— he was swift, zealous, radical, and determined."[7]

NOTES

1. Professor Cox's work, like my own, is part of a growing body of modern scholarship that has reassessed Lincoln's stance toward slavery, blacks, conquered Dixie, Congress, and the so-called Radical Republicans, and that has largely rejected the Randall interpretation. For a discussion of this scholarship, see Stephen B. Oates, *Abraham Lincoln: The Man behind the Myths* (New York: Harper and Row, 1984), pp. 209-10.

2. Unless otherwise cited, documentation for facts and quotations in this essay can be found in Oates, *Abraham Lincoln*, and Oates, *With Malice toward None: The Life of Abraham Lincoln* (New York, Harper and Row, 1977).

3. The expression is from G. S. Boritt, *Lincoln and the Economics of the American Dream* (Memphis: Memphis State University Press, 1978), passim.

4. Mark E. Neely, Jr., "Abraham Lincoln and Black Colonization: Benjamin Butler's Spurious Testimony," *Civil War History* 24 (Mar. 1978): 5-24.

5. Roy P. Basler, ed., Marion Dolores Pratt and Lloyd A. Dunlap, asst. eds., *The Collected Works of Abraham Lincoln*, 9 vols. (New Brunswick, N.J.: Rutgers University Press, 1953-55), 5: 535.

6. Charles M. Segal, ed., *Conversations with Lincoln* (New York: Putnam's, 1961), p. 489.

7. Frederick Douglass, *Life and Times of Frederick Douglass Written by Himself* (reprint of 1892 rev. ed., London: Collier, 1962), p. 489.

203

Lincoln and the Politics of Emancipation: Commentary on "Lincoln and Black Freedom"

ARMSTEAD L. ROBINSON

Of the many trenchant points made in LaWanda Cox's fine paper, I believe that the most significant is her insistence that the slavery issue occupied center stage during the American Civil War. This position conflicts sharply with recent interpretations which tend to downplay the importance of the slavery issue.[1] However, Professor Cox finds able and eloquent support in Abraham Lincoln's assessment of the politics of his day. In his First Inaugural Address, Lincoln asserted that slavery was the cause of the North-South conflict: "One section of the country believes slavery is *right* and ought to be extended, while the other believes it is *wrong* and ought not to be extended. This is the only substantial dispute."[2] Four years of bloody warfare served to strengthen Lincoln's conviction that the resolution of the slavery issue held the key to saving the Union. Thus in his Second Inaugural Address, Lincoln reiterated his earlier contention that slavery had caused the war: "One-eighth of the whole population were colored slaves, not distributed generally over the Union, but localized in the southern part of it. These slaves constituted a peculiar and powerful interest. All knew that this interest was somehow the cause of the war." This analysis of the causes of the war led inexorably to the conclusion that Northern victory required the destruction of slavery and the extension of full civil rights to all Americans:

> If we shall suppose that American Slavery is one of those offences which, in the providence of God, must needs come, but which, having continued through His appointed time, He now wills to remove, and that He gives to both North and South, this terrible war, as the woe due to those by whom the offence came, shall we discern therein any departure from those divine attributes which the believers in a living

God always ascribe to Him? Fondly do we hope—fervently do we pray—that this mighty scourge of war may speedily pass away. Yet, if God wills that it continue, until all the wealth piled by the bond-man's two hundred and fifty years of unrequited toil shall be sunk, and until every drop of blood drawn with the lash, shall be paid by another drawn with the sword, as was said three thousand years ago, so still it must be said "the judgments of the Lord, are true and righteous altogether."[3]

These eloquent sentiments reveal Lincoln's deep personal convictions on the ethical questions raised in Professor Cox's paper. Abraham Lincoln believed that slavery was the moral abomination that had caused the Civil War. And by the time the war ended, he had come to the conclusion that emancipation constituted the sine qua non of Northern victory; futhermore, he came earnestly to hope for the day when all Americans could enjoy "a just and lasting peace."

If we accept the sincerity of these commitments to full citizenship for blacks, how then can we explain the maddeningly enigmatic process through which Lincoln arrived at the emancipation and civil rights views he held at the end of his presidency? After all, Lincoln used his First Inaugural Address both to blame slavery for North-South tensions and also to promise that his administration would not interfere with slavery where it already existed.[4] And while insisting that he believed in universal equality, Lincoln nonetheless urged a delegation of black leaders to support the massive transplantation of American-born blacks to almost any nation other than the United States.[5] To her credit, Professor Cox addresses these contradictions directly and she does so with great skill. Essentially, she argues that Lincoln was a political genius whose deft feel for the public pulse enabled him to sense how quickly he could move the North without jeopardizing the fight to save the Union. According to Professor Cox, Lincoln calibrated the rate of change in his emancipation and civil rights policies to conform to the pace at which public opinion in the Northern states would accept radical alterations in the status of blacks. Thus Lincoln resolved, says Professor Cox, to push forward "as nearly as we can" toward the realization of his own ethical ideals.[6]

This is a subtle and powerful formulation. However, I doubt that we can fully unravel the enigmas surrounding black freedom by focusing solely on the limitations imposed by Northern racial attitudes.

For in order to resolve the contradictions in these policies, Professor Cox's argument asks us to conceptualize Lincoln as a detached and objective analyst of changing Northern racial attitudes, an analyst who skillfully moderated the injection of new racial policies so as to keep change moving forward without fatally traumatizing the patient. And yet, if Lincoln could urge black leaders to accept a standard of civil liberty inferior to any standard he would dare to ask whites to accept, how then can we escape the conclusion that this inferior standard would have led to the separate-but-equal doctrine that justified second-class citizenship for blacks in the 1890s? In short, it seems clear that by allowing himself to be constrained by the ignoble side of Northern public opinion, Lincoln revealed the degree to which he shared the racial prejudices of his age. While he was certainly not a negrophobe, Lincoln nonetheless did practice an ideology of racial gradualism which could move with such deliberate speed as to slow the pace of progress toward universal citizenship virtually to nil. In sum, I doubt that we can describe Lincoln as a detached and objective social analyst. And if this is true, it seems unlikely that we can fully explain the paradoxes outlined by Professor Cox while focusing solely on the racial attitudes of Northern society.

In brief I would like to suggest an interpretation derived in no small part from Professor Cox's stimulating paper. If we accept her persuasive argument about Lincoln's skill at pursuing contradictory policy goals while simultaneously keeping in balance a broad range of different interests, why not expand the number of these interest groups to encompass the full spectrum of social groups likely to be affected by both emancipation and civil rights policy? In other words, why not include Southern whites in our tally of the interest groups Lincoln felt compelled to insert into his calculations? Obviously, Professor Cox has already done this to some extent, with her careful attention to Unionists in Civil War Louisiana.[7] However, I am suggesting that the analysis of Lincoln's emancipation and civil rights policy will remain incomplete until we incorporate the perspectives and the interests of slave masters in the border slave states and Unionists in the mountains of the upper South.

Incorporating these groups of Southern whites permits a more fully rounded explanation of the enigmatic character of Lincoln's emancipation and civil rights policies. Lincoln feared that border-state slaveholders would lead their states into the Confederacy if his administration made emancipation a war aim early on during the conflict. Thus, in September of 1861, Lincoln countermanded an emancipation decree tentatively put forward by Gen. John C. Fremont. Lincoln justified his decision by insisting that a precipitate emancipation decree would force Kentucky to secede: "I think to lose Kentucky is nearly to lose the whole game. Kentucky gone, we cannot hold Missouri, nor, as I think Maryland. These all against us, and the job on our hands is too large for us. We could as well consent to the separation including the surrender of the capital."[8] Similarly, I am convinced that the equivocation and delay characteristic of wartime civil rights policies reflected, at least in part, Lincoln's best judgment about the degree of racial equalitarianism mountain yeomen would accept. Their lack of tolerance on these questions is indicated by the sentiments of a mountaineer who insisted, "I'd rather git killed than have all these niggers freed and claimin' they's as good as I is."[9] This comment suggests that almost any civil rights guarantees for blacks would be perceived as dangerously threatening by Southern mountaineers.

Making concessions to the interests of mountain Unionists was critically important to saving the Union because Lincoln recognized, in the aftermath of the disaster at First Bull Run, that the North had to pursue a divide-and-conquer strategy if it wished to defeat the quest for Confederate independence. A conversation with an old friend allowed Lincoln to describe the catalytic role that popular disaffection would have to play if the North expected to defeat the Confederate revolution. The debacle at First Bull Run had apparently persuaded Lincoln that in itself Northern military power could not defeat the Confederacy. The external pressure exerted by superior Northern resources would be most effective when combined with a strategy for fomenting disaffection among Southern whites. Lincoln directed this destabilization strategy at the major social cleavage among Southern whites, namely, the contradictory interests of the mountain yeomanry as opposed to those of the low-country slaveholders. In short, Lincoln believed that an ideological appeal to the democratic ideals of the Southern yeomanry would help to alienate the Confederate government from the nonslaveholders who constituted the Southern popular majority.[10]

I am suggesting that we take Lincoln at his word. When he insisted that what he did or declined to do in relationship to slavery was done or not done solely in order to save the Union, Lincoln offered a candid explanation for the enigmatic character of his emancipation and civil rights policies. Lincoln saved the Union by mobilizing the resources of Northern society and by turning the constituent parts of Southern society against themselves; he appealed to blacks' interest in destroying slavery, to border-state slaveowners' interests in preserving slavery, and to mountain yeomen's interest in protecting their own liberties. He sought, in short, to undermine the Confederacy from within. And in doing so, Lincoln reaffirmed the centrality of the slavery issue for the era of the American Civil War.

NOTES

1. Eric Foner, "The Causes of the American Civil War: Recent Interpretations and New Directions," *Civil War History* 20 (1974): 197-214.

2. Roy P. Basler, ed., Marion Dolores Pratt and Lloyd A. Dunlap, asst. eds., *The Collected Works of Abraham Lincoln,* 9 vols. (New Brunswick, N.J.: Rutgers University Press, 1953-55), 4: 268-69.

3. Ibid., 8: 332-33.

4. Ibid., 4: 262-63.

5. Ibid., 5: 370-75.

6. LaWanda Cox, *Lincoln and Black Freedom: A Study in Presidential Leadership* (Columbia: University of South Carolina Press, 1981).

7. Ibid. For an exhaustive study of Lincoln's policy toward reconstruction in wartime Louisiana, see Peyton McCrary, *Abraham Lincoln and Reconstruction: The Louisiana Experiment* (Princeton, N.J.: Princeton University Press, 1978).

8. Basler, *Collected Works of Lincoln,* 4: 531-33.

9. Tom E. Terrill and Gerrold Hirsch, eds., *Such as Us: Southern Voices of the Thirties* (New York: W. W. Norton, 1979), p. 61.

10. For a fuller treatment of these issues see Armstead L. Robinson, *Bitter Fruits of Bondage: The Demise of Slavery and the Collapse of the Confederacy* (forthcoming).

PART III

The Psychohistorian's Lincoln

☆　☆
☆

CHAPTER 8

LINCOLN'S QUEST FOR UNION:
Public and Private Meanings

CHARLES B. STROZIER

LINCOLN'S STORY fades into legend. As a result, we are probably better informed about the trivial anecdotes and more confused about the significant events of his formative years then about those of any figure in American history. Most of us know—or think we know—a good deal more about his rail-splitting or his absentmindedness than we do about the shape of his personality, especially the sources of his periodic, paralyzing bouts of depression; what gave meaning to his relationship with his wife and his children (and what difference it makes); and what made him a uniquely fitted leader for a nation rent by discord. In suggesting some tentative answers to these and related questions, I have drawn upon a considerable body of documentary evidence. Throughout, my approach is avowedly psychohistorical: that is, I have attempted to apply concepts from psychoanalytic theory critically and unobtrusively to bring the evidence alive in some new ways.

"God bless my mother," Lincoln told his law partner, William Herndon, in 1850. "All that I am or ever hope to be I owe to her." This simple, direct, and perhaps eternal human sentiment had particular poignancy for Lincoln because he believed his mother was illegitimate. This statement to Herndon was one of the few times Lincoln mentioned his mother. He and Herndon were riding in a buggy to court in Menard County to handle a suit that raised the issue of hereditary traits. Lincoln said his mother, Nancy, was the illegitimate daughter of Lucy Hanks and a well-bred Virginia farmer or planter. From this Virginian, Herndon remembered Lincoln saying, came all the traits—his power of analysis, logic, mental activity, and ambition—that distinguished him from the Hanks family. He even appeared to believe that "illegitimate children are oftentimes sturdier and brighter than those born in lawful wedlock." Having unburdened himself, Lincoln became quiet and was "sad and absorbed. The buggy moved on but not a word was spoken. His words and melancholy tone made a deep impression on me. It was an experience I can never forget."[1]

Herndon seemed to feel that Lincoln carried "a millstone tied to his neck" with the knowledge of his mother's illegitimacy. But here Herndon went beyond reporting, which he did well, and turned to interpretation, which he usually botched. For rather than shame, Lincoln felt a secret pride in his clouded past. On the confessional buggy ride, after telling Herndon of Nancy's illegitimacy, Lincoln continued: "Did you ever notice that bastards are generally smarter, shrewder, and more intellectual than others? Is it because it is stolen?"[2] The distant and mysterious "Virginia planter" thus gave Lincoln a genetic explanation for the profound differences between him and his crude, illiterate, low-born family. "He told me," Herndon reported at another point, "that his relations were *lascivious, lecherous,* not to be trusted."[3] The workings of fantasy seldom follow the rules of logic. Thus Lincoln failed to question his implicit distinction between his angelic, genetically "high-born" but illegitimate mother and the rest of his crude, lascivious, and lecherous—but legitimate—relations (except for Dennis Hanks). It seems that as a child, Lincoln had worked out a rather elaborate genetic myth that both explained and nourished his separateness from his family and environment.

Little else is known about Lincoln's mother. Because she is so obscure, Nancy has inspired poetry that has become, for better or worse, part of the record. "She believed in God," wrote Sandburg, "in the Bible, in mankind, in the past and future, in babies, people, animals, flowers, fishes, in foundations and roofs, in time and the eternities outside of time; she was a believer, keeping in silence behind her gray eyes more beliefs than she spoke."[4] Lincoln's own account of Nancy in his 1860 autobiographical statement is sparse indeed. "Getting back into Kentucky, and having reached his twenty-eighth year, he [Thomas] married Nancy Hanks—mother of the present subject—in the year 1806." Lincoln added simply that his mother was from Virginia and that relatives of hers "of the name of Hanks, and of other names, now reside in Coles, in Macon, and in Adams counties, Illinois, and also in Iowa."[5] The accounts of Nancy by those who knew her differ in detail but are remarkably consistent in tone and overall impression. "She was a tall slender woman," wrote John Hanks, "dark-skinned, black hair and eyes, her face was sharp and angular, forehead big. She was beyond all doubts an intellectual woman, rather extraordinary if anything."[6] A neighbor in Indiana, William Woods, who knew Nancy for a year and a half before her death in 1818, also noted how "very smart, intelligent, and intellectual" Nancy was.[7]

Nancy's character can never be fully known. Contemporary observers tended to remember distantly that "Nancy Hanks was as above Thomas Lincoln as an angel is above mud." There is so little to go on that "her face and figure waver through the myths of time and rumor."[8] For Dennis Hanks she was warmly affectionate, never out of temper, and immovably calm. Another theme in the sources notes Nancy's "habitual sadness" and stresses the "primitive Baptist doctrine of fatalism in which she gloried."[9] She was definitely a Baptist, and Baptists then, and sometimes now, were indeed "primitive" in the sense of firm belief in the Bible and basic moral principles. However, such fundamentalism does not necessarily carry with it sadness; on the contrary, it may foster the quiet peace of someone in touch with God. It would seem that Nancy was a remarkably intelligent woman who responded warmly and empathically to Lincoln during his earliest years, nourishing him with rich emotional supplies into his late infancy. This is the psychological message one gets from people like Dennis or John Hanks and it was implied in Lincoln's own memory of his mother when he told Herndon of her angelic quality. Certainly, one suspects that Lincoln's adult strengths—his flexibility, empathy, humor, and creativity—derived from a close, loving relationship with his mother.

But ambivalence affects any relationship. As a young man (twenty-nine years old) Lincoln wrote a humorous letter to his good friend and maternal figure, Mrs. Orville Browning, on April Fool's Day, 1838. The letter mocks his recent unsuccessful courtship of Mary Owens, whom he could not behold without "thinking of my mother; in this, not from her withered features, for her skin was too full of fat, to permit its contracting in to wrinkles; but from her want of teeth, weather-beaten appearance in general, and from a kind of notion that ran in my head, that *nothing* could have commenced at the size in infancy, and reached her present bulk in less than 35 or

213

40 years."[10] In this letter Lincoln used the image of his mother as a kind of baseline for ugliness. It is true of course that Lincoln called Sarah Lincoln "mother," as he was later to refer to Mary after they had children. But unconsciously "mother" for Lincoln also had to mean Nancy. Perhaps she was that ugly. Certainly the only form of dentistry in those days was extraction, and on her deathbed she may have looked suddenly old and withered to her young son. The endurance of this image in Lincoln suggests it carried some sense of childhood disappointment with his mother. In a part of himself he seemed not to trust her.

The story of Lincoln's father begins in obscurity. The major questions center generally on his competence and possible impotence. These were causally related for Herndon: Thomas was hopelessly incompetent because at some point for some reason he lost his potency. Herndon was at his worst in handling the primary sources of this question, but he did not invent the story out of whole cloth. Dennis Hanks reported that Thomas and Nancy had no other children after Abraham's birth. The cause was said to be "a private matter."[11] (Hanks was wrong about dates here, for there was a third child, Thomas, born in 1811 or 1812; he died after a few days.) Herndon variously gathered reports that Thomas had castrated himself, had one testicle the size of a pea, had two testicles the size of peas, had always been sterile, or had the mumps and then became sterile.[12] Herndon pondered to himself: "But you say that Thomas Lincoln went in swimming and the people saw his manhood was taken out; granted, and yet no witness fixes the date."[13] Herndon never wavered from the idea that Thomas at some point became sterile. In 1886 he told his coworker Jesse Weik to be sure to confirm this issue with Dennis Hanks: "When you see him, ask him, in a roundabout way, if Thomas Lincoln was not castrated because of the mumps when young. Dennis told me this often and repeated it."[14] For Herndon, Thomas Lincoln's sterility became a crucial factor in his theory of Abraham's illegitimacy as well as a useful explanation for the physiological basis of Thomas's "utter laziness and wont [sic] of energy." The problem, Herndon wrote, "is due to the fact of fixing."[15]

Research in the early twentieth century, however, uncovered some new information on Thomas Lincoln. This revisionist work has effectively stripped away the myths surrounding the despicable figure created by the early commentators. Thomas was not in fact improvident, slow, terribly lazy, incompetent, dull, or dumb. He was interesting enough, among other things, to attract two apparently outstanding women to be mothers to his children. The revisionist research, however, has been fundamentally misplaced. It has assumed that a grasp of what Thomas was actually like will clarify our understanding of his infinitely more important son. Ironically, Lincoln's mental picture of his father was a good deal closer to Herndon's characterization than observers have wanted to acknowledge. There is little congruence between the three-dimensional figure of the "real" Thomas and Lincoln's psychological conception of him. All the evidence suggests that Lincoln retained some residual admiration and love for his father but basically grew up with an abiding sense of disappointment with and alienation from him. He struggled mightily with his inner picture of his father, a picture shaped by the distortions of unconscious wishes and fantasies.

Most of the hard evidence indicates that in Lincoln's mind Thomas *was* an illiterate, irresponsible n'er-do-well; a man who chased rainbows but never managed to find any pots of gold; a typical low-born product of the frontier that Lincoln worked hard to escape and to which, once he had escaped, he never returned. Nowhere does Lincoln ever say anything good about Thomas—a reticence that contrasts strikingly with his openly expressed idealization of Nancy and his deep affection for Sarah. Benjamin Thomas came up with an interesting (if strained) interpretation of this aloofness: it reflected Lincoln's "fundamental honesty"; he disliked his father and therefore remained aloof, the only "honest" position to assume.[16]

In fact, Lincoln made clear his negative feeling toward his father, who never quite came up to his own standards. Thus Lincoln, in his 1860 autobiographical statement, described Thomas as a "wondering, laboring boy" who grew up "literally without education. He never did more in the way of writing than to bunglingly sign his own name."[17] Some twelve years earlier, in response to a question from a relative, Lincoln also stressed his father's ignorance: "Owing to my father being left an orphan at the age of six years, in poverty, and in a new country, he became a wholly uneducated man; which I suppose is the reason why I know so little of our family history. I believe I can say nothing more that would at all interest you." It seemed to pain Lincoln to realize how dull his father was, which tells more about Lincoln's

215

driving ambition than it does about Thomas's character. As a boy, Lincoln had aspirations beyond his grasp.[18]

Lincoln's intellectual style and his interest in books created frequent conflicts with his father. Dennis Hanks noted that Thomas sometimes had "to slash him for neglecting his work by reading."[19] His inquisitiveness also irritated Thomas: "When strangers would ride along and up to his father's fence, Abe always, through pride and to tease his father, would be sure to ask the stranger the first question, for which his father would sometimes knock him a rod."[20] This teasing seemed calculated to displace Thomas, who could only respond with anger. Sarah, however, who was undoubtedly more understanding of Thomas, provides a different perspective: "As a usual thing, Mr. Lincoln never made Abe quit reading to do anything if he could avoid it. He would do it himself first." Thomas was sensitive to his own educational deficiencies and wanted "his boy Abraham to learn, and he encouraged him to do it in all ways he could."[21] Lincoln, one suspects, understood these ambitions in his father and played on them. He was "rude and forward" as Dennis noted, teasing, testing, provoking his father by continuing to read when he knew he should be working. Up to a point, Thomas tolerated, even encouraged, his son's independence, but young Lincoln often seemed to push him too far. Then came a whipping, and in Dennis Hanks's phrase, Lincoln would drop "a kind of silent unwelcome tear."[22]

Nancy bore Thomas three children in rapid succession. Sarah, her firstborn, came in 1807, and Abraham, born in 1809, grew up with her. Eventually, in 1828, Sarah died as a young woman in childbirth. Two or three years after Abraham's birth (there is no way to be more precise) his brother Thomas arrived and "died in infancy," as Lincoln was to say. The baby was buried in a small grave within sight of the cabin. Later, after his father died in 1851, Lincoln filled in his genealogy in the front of the family Bible. For some reason he forgot to enter the birth of the short-lived boy.[23] After 1811 or 1812 (whenever Thomas was born) Nancy bore no more children, though she lived until 1818. Nancy's childbearing pattern departed from that of the typical frontier woman who bore a child every two years or so. We do not know whether the limited size of Nancy's family was due to Thomas's alleged sterility, some physical problem of Nancy's, marital indifference, or control. But the pattern of few children apparently

216

influenced Lincoln; he and Mary rigorously controlled the size of their family.

The Lincolns stayed only briefly at Abraham's birth site near Hodgenville, then moved some two miles to Knob-Creek. Here Lincoln lived until he was seven, growing rapidly, absorbing the culture of his environment. He and his sister attended for short periods two "A-B-C schools" kept by Zachariah Riney and Caleb Hazel. Of his education Lincoln had a somewhat deprecatory view (which tended to put his self-made success in a better light): "There were some schools, so called," he told Jessie Fell. "But no qualification was ever required of the teacher, beyond *readin', writin',* and *cipherin',* to the Rule of Three. If a straggler supposed to understand Latin, happened to sojourn in the neighborhood, he was looked upon, as a wizard. There was absolutely nothing to excite ambition for education."[24]

In 1816 Thomas decided to move to Indiana. "This removal," Lincoln commented, "was partly on account of slavery; but chiefly on account of the difficulty in land titles in Kentucky."[25] Thomas genuinely opposed slavery and had broken from his local Baptist church during the debate over that institution. The antislavery group Thomas was associated with established a separatist church, "which not only renounced human bondage but eschewed all written creeds and official church organizations, relying on the Bible as the sole rule of faith." In 1816, Thomas and Nancy Lincoln joined the Separatist Church and prayed with its antislavery ministers. However, the more important reason for the move to Indiana was, as Lincoln himself said, the confusion over land titles. Dennis Hanks said it was untrue that the existence of slavery in Kentucky had anything to do with the move to Indiana. He felt Thomas wanted to better his material condition by buying land at the cheap price of $1.25 per acre, which he could obtain in Indiana.

So the Lincolns moved west after packing up their few belongings in an old wagon. At first life went well in Indiana. Lincoln, "though very young, was large of his age, and had an axe put into his hands at once." The household soon expanded with the addition of Thomas and Elizabeth Sparrow, two of Nancy's relatives, and Dennis Hanks, the illegitimate eighteen-year-old son of another aunt. Lincoln and Sarah occasionally attended more A-B-C or "blab" schools, the sum total of which "did not amount to one year." Lincoln went to school, he said, "by littles," but what he acquired he held onto with pride.

217

"He was never in a college or Academy as a student," Lincoln wrote of himself, "and never inside of a college or academy building till since he had a law-license." After he left home in 1831 he studied English grammar and later, as a United States congressman from 1847 to 1849, began to read and master the six books of Euclid. He regretted his "want of education," but the pride of the self-made man shines through when the presidential candidate, who was soon to write some of this country's best prose, noted how "imperfectly" he knew English grammar and that "what he has in the way of education, he has picked up."[26]

Lincoln listened with the same energy that sparked his interest in books. As a child, he occasionally went to church, and when he did, he listened closely to the sermon. At home, later, to the delight of the children, he would mount a stump of log and humorously repeat the sermon almost word for word.[27] Sarah noted how young Abe "was a silent and attentive observer" who never spoke or asked questions until the person he was listening to left. Then he had to understand everything, "even to the smallest thing, minutely and exactly; he would repeat it over to himself again and again, sometimes in one form and then in another, and when it was fixed in his mind to suit him, he became easy and he never lost that fact or his understanding of it." The intensity here is remarkable. Lincoln seemed driven, and his listening, like his reading, had a certain compulsive quality to it. Not to grasp something was impossible. Indeed, "Sometimes he seemed perturbed to give expression to his ideas and go mad, almost, at one who couldn't explain plainly what he wanted to convey." Herndon later encountered the same intensity in the adult Lincoln, whom he once described as "persistent, fearless and tireless in thinking." Herndon would greet Lincoln on the street, for example, but Lincoln, lost in thought, would appear not even to notice his friend. Some hours later, he might say: "Billy, what did you say to me on the other side of the square this morning as we passed?"[28]

In the fall of 1818 there were tears to shed. Lincoln's mother, Nancy, and Thomas and Elizabeth Sparrow died of "milk sickness," a disease cows periodically caught from poisonous root and then transmitted through their milk. The deaths left Thomas Lincoln alone to care for his nine-year-old son and eleven-year-old daughter. Within a year he married Mrs. Sarah Bush Johnston of Elizabeth-Town, Kentucky, a widow with three children: Elizabeth, twelve; John D., ten;

and Matilda, eight. Now the Lincoln household was much larger than ever before: two adults, three boys (counting Dennis Hanks), and three girls. The parents and girls occupied two beds on the first floor and the boys slept in the loft. There is some suggestion of temptation and sexual excitement in this household menagerie, for within a year the twenty-one-year-old Dennis Hanks married Elizabeth Johnston and moved to a cabin a short distance away.

Sarah was a gentle woman who helped young Lincoln adjust to the painful loss of Nancy. Dennis reported that Sarah "had been raised in Elizabeth-Town in somewhat a high life," but adapted easily to the rugged life near Little Pigeon Creek in Indiana. The year or so between Nancy's death and Sarah's arrival was difficult for the Lincoln household. The speed with which Thomas found a second wife suggests his loneliness. Dennis reported that when Sarah arrived, "Abe and his sister were wild, ragged and dirty . . . she soaped, rubbed and washed the children clean, so that they looked pretty, neat, well, and clean. She sewed and mended their clothes, and the children once more looked human as their own good mother left them."[29] On Friday, September 8, 1865, Herndon visited Sarah and recorded her memories of Lincoln. Her account is honest and informative, warm and yet free of sentimentality. "His mind and mine, what little I had," she said, "seemed to run together, more in the same channel." Herndon recalled that as he was leaving, "she arose, took me by the hand, and wept, and bade me goodbye, saying: 'I shall never see you again, and if you see Mrs. Abraham Lincoln and family, tell them I send them my best and tenderest love. Goodbye, my good son's friend, farewell.' "[30]

Lincoln loved his stepmother. As a lawyer in Springfield, he occasionally visited Sarah, who lived about ninety miles away, near Charleston, Illinois. (She saw him every year or two, she told Herndon.) The most emotional visit to his stepmother was the one Lincoln made just before leaving Springfield for Washington in 1861. According to Ward Hill Lamon, who made the trip with him, "The meeting between him and the old lady was of a most affectionate and tender character. She fondled him as her own 'Abe' and he her as his own mother."[31] Joshua Speed, Lincoln's closest friend in the late 1830s and early 1840s, later spoke of Lincoln's great fondness for Sarah. Lincoln's wife, Mary, echoed this sentiment in a letter of December 19, 1867, to Sarah: "In memory of the dearly loved one,

219

who always remembered you with so much affection, will you not do me the favor of accepting these few trifles?" In Sandburg's evocative terms, Sarah became "one of the rich, silent forces" in Lincoln's life.[32]

As a young man in his twenties, from 1831 to 1837, Lincoln lived and worked at a variety of jobs in New Salem, Illinois. His many activities were necessarily part-time affairs. And they were supplemented by occasional stints at splitting rails, working at the mills, harvesting, and tending store for Samuel Hill. After December 1834, Lincoln served as a local agent for the *Sangamo Journal* and regularly clerked at the polls on election day. He even spent the better part of one winter working at Isaac Burner's still. Between these diverse and not particularly demanding duties, he only gradually came to make creative use of his free time. Until 1834 he was too intimidated by his lack of education to begin the study of law. Even after John T. Stuart encouraged him to start reading law, he did it selectively, though carefully. He had access to the law books of H. E. Dummer and Stuart and could have delved into Stuart's fine personal library. The books were available, but he was not ready for them. Only after joining the legislature did Lincoln achieve any consistent success. He was elected in 1834, 1836, 1838, and 1840. But even his service in the legislature was a part-time activity.

During the New Salem years, Lincoln was, in short, undirected and unfocused, charming and well-liked by his neighbors, but singularly unsuccessful in most ventures he undertook. He had failed in a series of enterprises and had faced two lawsuits on account of his personal debts. He fell into surveying as he did splitting rails or delivering mail or working at the still—by chance, as opportunity beckoned and the need to survive demanded. Even in his most rewarding activity in these years, serving in the legislature, he felt his way cautiously and with some serious errors in judgment.

Lincoln's long, stumbling search for satisfying work with which to supplement his political career may in part have been simply a reflection of his lack of a formal education. But his experimentation may also have been part of a larger search for personal coherence and integrity, a search that theoretically makes sense in psychoanalytic conceptualizations of identity. Sigmund Freud, as an old man, was asked what defines normality. He replied with the terseness characteristic of his old age: "Lieben und arbeiten" (to love and to work).

220

Individuals must discover for themselves how to love and to work. An inability to love precludes working that is free from compulsive fastidiousness; and the commitment to professional activity that realizes one's potential and risks failure flows from a firm sense of sexual identity. Youth is challenged from many directions. There is a forward movement that must meet the needs of society. There are as well inner expectations that draw on enduring childhood issues of self-cohesion. Work and career focus a large part of these concerns; love, social relating, and sexual identity constitute other important aspects of the emerging self.

Lincoln's possible but unlikely romantic involvement with Ann Rutledge remains in doubt. His first documented romance was with Mary Owens, "an amiable, attractive Kentucky girl of considerable culture."[33] It was a curious affair, and the complicated way he dealt with her foreshadows his tortured courting of Mary Todd. As he told her in breaking off his relationship: "I can not see you, or think of you, with entire indifference," a phrasing that cast his supposedly affectionate feeling into a double negative. He continued: "I want in all cases to do right, and most particularly so, in all cases with women." Doing right in this case, Lincoln suggested, probably meant leaving her alone. If that was her desire, he urged her simply not to answer the letter. Such a solution to their "romance" forced her to act and made Lincoln the passive recipient of her decision. He then made the same point again with great emphasis: "Do not understand by this, that I wish to cut your acquaintance. I mean no such thing. What I do wish is, that our further acquaintance shall depend upon yourself . . . if you feel yourself in any degree bound to me, I am now willing to release you, provided you wish it; while, on the other hand, I am willing, and even anxious to bind you faster, if I can be convinced that it will, in any considerable degree, add to your happiness."[34]

Lincoln, with apparent disregard for himself, desperately feared hurting Mary. At all costs he sought to make her happy, and if his actions hurt her he was hurt even more himself. He loved ambivalently, and at the point of marriage, with its potential of intimacy, he withdrew in a clumsy, if genuine, expression of sympathy for Mary's feelings. As she later wrote to Herndon, "Mr. Lincoln was deficient in those little links which make up the chain of a woman's happiness—at least it was so in my case."[35]

Two years later Lincoln first met and was captivated by the

221

spritely, well-educated, and charming Mary Todd. James C. Conckling, a young lawyer from the East and a graduate of Princeton, described this Mary as "the very creature of excitement."[36] Lincoln courted her vigorously and successfully throughout 1839 and 1840. Each of her three extant letters from these two years mentions him, and the third one dwells at some length on marriage.[37] Apparently, before the end of 1840, Lincoln and Mary were engaged. Lincoln was then thirty-one. He had some useful experience as a lawyer behind him and was making a respectable income. He had made a mark in the legislature and was generally esteemed by friends and colleagues throughout Springfield. Still, he was something of a social upstart in Mary's snobbish circle, which centered on the home of Ninian and Elizabeth Edwards, the kind of people whom, in his first impression of Springfield in 1837, he had referred to as "flourishing about in carriages here."[38] His fiancée was probably the most desirable unmarried woman in Springfield. Yet suddenly, in a move that perplexed all his friends — and was to baffle historians and biographers — he broke off the engagement on January 1, 1841.

Lincoln, it seems, feared intimacy and had steered clear of heterosexual union in two relationships. But his inner conflicts over intimacy cannot be fully grasped by examining his courtship of Mary Todd alone. Of even greater significance is his relationship with Joshua Fry Speed, whose patient friendship during these crucial years first aggravated Lincoln's conflicts, then served as the vehicle for their resolution. Joshua Speed was an engaging young merchant, who moved from Kentucky to Springfield in 1835. Lincoln's relationship with Speed began on his arrival in Springfield in 1837. Lincoln, only recently admitted to the bar, had neither relatives nor friends on hand to see him through or help him pay his debts. He was probably already acquainted with Joshua Speed and certainly familiar with Speed's store. He went directly there and asked how much it would cost to buy the material for a bed. Speed made the calculation and told Lincoln it would cost a total of $17.00. As Speed later reported to Herndon, Lincoln asked for the money on credit until Christmas but in such a sad tone as to elicit Speed's sympathy.

> The tone of his voice was so melancholy that I felt for him.
> I looked up at him, and I thought then as I think now, that
> I never saw so gloomy and melancholy a face. I said to him:

"The contraction of so small a debt, seems to affect you so deeply, I think I can suggest a plan by which you will be able to obtain your end, without incurring any debt. I have a very large room, and a very large double bed in it; which you are perfectly welcome to share with me if you choose." "Where is your room?" asked he. "Upstairs" said I, pointing to the stairs leading from the store to my room. Without saying a word, he took his saddlebags on his arm, went upstairs, set them down on the floor, came down again, and with a face beaming with pleasure and smiles exclaimed "Well Speed I'm moved."[39]

In 1838 Speed and Lincoln were joined in their room above the store by William Herndon, who later reported: "Lincoln, Speed, and I slept together for two or three years, i.e., slept in the same room, I being Speed's clerk; and Lincoln sleeping with Speed."[40] For a time Charles R. Hurst joined the dormitory, sleeping in a separate bed. Life in the store centered on open and congenial discussion and was pervaded by a rough maleness that sharply distinguished it from the sophisticated and slightly effete atmosphere of the coterie that met in the Edwards' home.

Joshua Speed was the only intimate friend Lincoln ever had. Ward Hill Lamon, in his 1872 biography, was the first to make this point. The only quarrel with this assertion later came from a jealous Herndon, who also wanted to be considered an intimate friend of Lincoln.[41] In fact the difference was complete. Lincoln liked Herndon but treated him condescendingly: he always called him "Billy," while Herndon called him "Mr. Lincoln." To Speed, Lincoln wrote: "You know my desire to befriend you is everlasting—that I will never cease, while I know how to do anything."[42] Even Herndon had to admit Lincoln and Speed were unusually close.[43] Speed was an attractive young man, affable, kind, and easygoing. Ruth Painter Randall mentions his Byronic eyes and characterizes him as a rake,[44] though the sources do not bear this out.[45] On the contrary, Speed seems to have been as innocent of sex as Lincoln, and when he began seriously courting Fanny Henning, whom he later married, Speed reported: "Strange to say something of the same feeling which I regarded as so foolish in him took possession of me and kept me very unhappy from the time of my engagement until I was married."[46]

It would appear, therefore, that Lincoln and Speed's close relationship centered on their similar and reinforcing conflicts. Their sleeping in the same bed for three and a half years may have intensified their closeness and aggravated their conflicts. It is probable that such close male contact during the years of Lincoln's greatest heterosexual tension heightened the difficulty he found in securing intimacy with a woman. The period during which Lincoln slept with Speed began and ended with unconsummated female relationships, first with Mary Owens and then with Mary Todd. Speed provided an alternative friendship that neither threatened nor provoked Lincoln. Each of the two men found solace in discussing their forebodings about sexuality. Their intimate maleness substituted for the tantalizing but frightening closeness of women.

Though it was common for men to sleep together then, there may have been significance for Lincoln in the fact that at the point of his greatest sexual tension and conflict, he shared a bed with his closest friend. The broken engagement with Mary Todd exactly coincides with the separation of Lincoln and Speed. On that same fateful day, January 1, 1841, Speed sold his store,[47] and he and Lincoln separated, leaving their common bed.[48] This separation apparently threw Lincoln into a panic that shook his fragile sexual identity. In this state his fear of intimacy with a woman was revived, and he broke his engagement with Mary. One point is worth stressing, namely, that Lincoln's conflicts and fears operated at an unconscious level. He was only dimly aware of his conflicts as he struggled to find his identity.

Abandoned by Speed and abandoning Mary, Lincoln fell into a severe depression. He slowly recovered, though as late as June, Mary Todd noted that she had not met him in the "gay world for months."[49] Speed remained in town until May and probably helped meliorate Lincoln's mood. Then Speed left for Kentucky to settle his family estate (his father had died). Lincoln, emotionally unfit to be alone, went on a long visit to Speed's home, where he was welcomed warmly as a member of the family. In September Speed accompanied him back to Springfield and remained there until the end of 1841, although he was anxious to return to Louisville, where he had recently begun to court the lovely Fanny Henning. Speed was full of self-doubts about marriage, just as Lincoln had been. Lincoln seemed almost to welcome the appearance of his friend's dilemma, so similar to his own. After Speed's departure Lincoln proffered advice in frequent letters (Speed's letters in reply have been lost). Lincoln wrote: "I know what the painful point with you is, at all times when you are unhappy. It is an apprehension that you do not love her as you should."[50] A month later: "I am now fully convinced, that you love her as ardently as you are capable of loving. Your ever being happy in her presence, and your intense anxiety about her health, if there were nothing else, would place this beyond all dispute in my mind. I incline to think it probable, that your nerves will fail you occasionally for a while; but once you get them fairly graded now, that trouble is over forever."[51]

Lincoln projected his own attitudes and conflicted feelings onto Speed, through whom he vicariously reexperienced the drama he had twice played out in the previous decade. Lincoln related to Speed's difficulties in courtships with an intensity and involvement that suggests he saw Speed as a mirror of his own inner experience. "I now have no doubt," Lincoln told Speed, "that it is the peculiar misfortune of both you and me, to dream dreams of Elysium far exceeding all that anything earthly can realize." Both also felt the same anxieties. Lincoln encouraged Speed to ease his "nervous temperament" and simply let himself love Fanny: "Say candidly, were not those heavenly black *eyes* the whole basis of all your early reasoning on the subject?" Lincoln told him that his deep fears for Fanny's health should at least reassure him of the "truth" of his "affection for her." He even suggested: "The almighty has sent your present affliction expressly for that object." He concluded: "Why Speed, if you did not love her, although you might not wish her death, you would most calmly be resigned to it."[52] This juxtaposition of love and death suggests a morbid fascination with the destructive potentiality of sex.

At the news that Speed finally was wed, Lincoln experienced feelings that he revealed to Speed in a letter of February 25, 1842: "I received yours of the 12 written the day you went down to William's place, some days since; but delayed answering it, til I should receive the promised one, of the 16 which came last night. I opened the letter with intense anxiety and trepidation—so much that although it turned out better than I expected, I have hardly yet, at the distance of ten hours, become calm." With clear relief Lincoln continued: "I tell you, Speed, our *forebodings,* for which you and I are rather peculiar, are all the worst sort of nonsense."[53]

The letter of February 25 suggests that when Speed at last actually consummated his relationship with Fanny—and the sky did not fall in—Lincoln was liberated from his fear of marriage. Speed experienced what Lincoln could only fantasize about. He served as a kind of emotional proxy for his conflicted friend. Speed thus proved therapeutic. Within months Lincoln began secretly to meet with Mary Todd again, and on November 4, 1842, the two were wed.

As this personal drama unfolded Lincoln was well aware of the significance for him of his relationship with Speed. He had reported to Speed the "sleepless vigilance" with which he followed Speed's courting of Fanny. When Speed thanked him for his help, Lincoln responded that he was not sure he deserved gratitude for his role, since he had been "drawn to it as by fate." He explained: "I always was superstitious; and as part of my superstition, I believed God made me one of the instruments of bringing your Fanny and you together, which union, I have no doubt He had fore-ordained."[54]

For the rest of his life Lincoln retained affectionate feelings for Speed. He considered naming his first son Joshua, but in the end he and Mary chose Robert. He wrote Speed of problems with his children, something he never mentioned to anyone else. In a letter in 1855, he unburdened himself to Speed on the complexities of his feelings about the political turmoil in the country. As president, he appointed Speed's brother, James, to his cabinet. Occasionally the Lincolns and Speeds visited each other, though Mary apparently had little enthusiasm for such visits. In the White House Lincoln once warmly welcomed Speed and talked of old times.

After February 25, 1842, however, Speed had begun to lose emotional significance for Lincoln. Lincoln's letters became fewer and more formal. When Lincoln took care of some continuing legal matters associated with the sale of Speed's Springfield store, the letters the two exchanged contained little except matters of business. Though in 1843 Lincoln had considered naming his first son Joshua, in 1846 he delayed for eight months to inform Speed of Eddie's birth. In 1848 the two even got angry with each other over a lost note that affected a case. Once Lincoln was through with his own crisis of courtship, Speed had little to offer and the friendship faded away.

By the 1840s Lincoln had "made it" in the cherished American sense. He was far beyond his rural roots and rapidly emerging as a sought-after lawyer and political leader among Illinois Whigs. He owned a nice home, had married well, and children were entering his life in regular intervals of three to four years. The first photograph of

226

Lincoln, taken in 1846, nicely captures the contentment of a successful man with a promising future. He would often joke of his "poor, lean, lank, face."[55] In this picture at least there is a hint of bourgeois self-satisfaction in the slight tilt of the head and jaunty thrust of the chin. He seems to be a young man who expected to be taken seriously.

Two points are quite well documented in Lincoln's relationship with Mary. The first is that from the outset Lincoln developed a powerful attachment for his vivacious young wife. A week after the wedding (November 4, 1842) he ended a business letter with the cryptic note, "Nothing new here, except my marrying, which to me, is a matter of profound wonder."[56] Later the following spring, James C. Conckling met Lincoln in Bloomington and reported that he had "found Lincoln desperately homesick and turning his head frequently towards the south."[57] After the stress of their tumultuous courtship, Lincoln seemed to embrace marriage fervently, to find deep needs for love and devotion satisfied in Mary. Separation came as a painful experience.

It is equally clear that by the 1860s Lincoln believed Mary bordered on insanity and required a patient, humane tolerance. He watched her collapse after Willie's death in 1862. When her sister's help proved futile, he exerted a measure of control and told her she must restrain herself or he would have her committed. He carefully and discreetly exposed the fraudulent psychic medium to whom Mary turned in the spring and summer of 1862. Somewhat later he reportedly talked openly about Mary's problems when confronted with evidence of a schemer who had used friendship with Mary to further some illegal business. "The caprices of Mrs. Lincoln, I am satisfied, are the result of partial insanity," he said once to a visiting reporter, and asked whether her malady was "beyond medical remedy to check before it becomes fully developed."[58]

These two ends of the spectrum frame the essential issues in Lincoln's complicated relationship with Mary. From the beginning she met some important needs in Lincoln, but her own problems gradually diminished her central emotional position in his life. These problems were sufficiently severe to cause Lincoln himself to see her as nearly insane. The psychological movement along this emotional spectrum occurred erratically and is difficult to place in chronological sequence. Nevertheless, there is a marked change in all facets of Lincoln's life with Mary around 1854. The coincidence of this dating with larger political events is hardly accidental. It suggests that a multitude of private and public concerns prompted an emotional reordering of Lincoln's self-organization at this time.

The sources do not allow a complete reconstruction of the rhythm of daily life for the Lincolns. One can gain only glimpses of this little world cunningly turned in on itself. The formality of the dining room and the parlors suggest a rigorous scheduling of domestic behaviors. Dinner was probably normally served at the same time each night, and an evening pattern of talking, reading, and then sleeping kept to. There is a sense in which Lincoln deviated somewhat from the script. To Mary's dismay he lounged on the floor at times, answered the door with his tie loose, and allowed himself to slip into distant worlds of thought and perhaps periodic depression. Money matters were divided. Lincoln, who from the mid-1840s on earned a very respectable $1200-$1800 a year, bought his own rather expensive suits and ties and handled such matters as the purchase of the new carriage, but he left the responsibility for food, children, and household in Mary's hands. He certainly paid the bills and probably gave Mary adequate pocket money to run the house. He also allowed her to use various charge accounts in town. In the 1840s these expenditures seemed within reasonable bounds. There is no reason to suspect tension over money, though Mary's delight in material possessions may have helped her endure Lincoln's active and lucrative work on the circuit.

Lincoln's absences from his home are a crucial and highly controversial issue in grasping the rhythm of his life with Mary. No discussion of Lincoln and Mary, their home and children, or indeed the deeper meanings of Lincoln's thought can ignore his mature pattern of distancing and separation. The facts are fairly clear; their meaning ambiguous. Two interests, law and politics, pulled him away. The pull of politics was erratic and obviously regulated by outside factors. The more constant pull on Lincoln was the circuit. Unlike most other lawyers, Lincoln was unique in his practice of attending every court on the circuit and remaining until the end.

However, a subtle shift occurred in the pattern of Lincoln's absences in the early years of his marriage—they lengthened. In the early days of his marriage he seldom stayed away more than two weeks and intentionally broke up longer trips into two- and three-week units.

By 1850, however, he took five long trips that lasted one, four, four, six, and one weeks, in that order.

After the mid-1850s Lincoln again altered the rhythm of his travels, quite dramatically increasing both the frequency and duration of his trips. Several factors contributed to the change. He was more noted and therefore in greater demand as a lawyer. He was also more centrally engaged in political activities, which meant more short visits throughout the state to speak. It all crowded in. In these years the travel was made easier by the railroads, which by the mid-1850s had a fairly extensive set of routes throughout Illinois. The existence of the railroads, however, did not seem to bring Lincoln home more often; it just took him away more frequently. During 1856, for example, Lincoln was away from home a total of nearly twenty weeks.

The evidence of Lincoln's absences from home suggests a number of important conclusions. It seems that during the first decade or so of his marriage, Lincoln wrestled with his conflicted intimacy of Mary and home. He needed to leave often but took emotional sustenance from the episodic refueling he received at home. To push this idea somewhat further, it seems probable that Lincoln embraced the periodicity of his relationship with Mary, the closeness-separation-closeness that defined its contours. In the early years at least he thought of her while absent but thought of being absent while with her. This kind of complex tie to Mary carried with it a deep devotion and fidelity; the stories of Lincoln's sexual capers are ludicrously apocryphal. But conflict created a need for regulated distance from Mary. The background for such a pattern was perhaps Lincoln's childhood experience of the death of his mother and the resulting need to repeat that loss and his desire for recovery in minute doses as an adult. To "lose" Mary when he departed for the circuit evoked significant feelings of dread and, probably more often, depression in Lincoln. He needed the circuit life, however, both to support his material aspirations and to free him temporarily from a transference figure of such potent significance. Once separated, however, Lincoln seemed desirous of returning and reestablishing ties with Mary. He was apparently away no more than absolutely necessary.

Lincoln's shifting field of vision after 1854 had enormous consequences for the country; it also tended to leave Mary alone, abandoned to meet her mounting needs without emotional resources. Deep childhood wounds reopened in Mary as the distance between husband and wife increased. His perception of her insanity, which was undoubtedly partly true, also perhaps carried a measure of desire on his part. His essential human kindness kept him near her, and she could never have survived without it. But in another sense her insanity filled the emptiness Lincoln created as he expanded his vision. The change around 1854 represented a complex shift from a conflicted private world of meanings that never worked themselves out to a public arena of political rhetoric that Lincoln domesticated in his imagery of the house divided. The personal issues for Lincoln proved remarkably continuous as he translated his private experience into an idiom that made sense of much larger concerns. After 1854 Lincoln turned outward and attempted, as Erik Erikson might say, to solve for all what he could not solve for himself alone.

In politics, too, Lincoln shifted his vision after the early 1850s. One can trace this most effectively by comparing positions he took in the 1840s on three major issues with his stance roughly a decade later.

As a representative in the Thirtieth Congress (1847-49), Lincoln came out strongly against the Mexican War; he tried to introduce a bill in Congress to abolish the slave trade in Washington, D.C.; and he worked against Henry Clay and for Gen. Zachary Taylor in the 1848 presidential struggle. Lincoln was, in other words, antiwar, antislavery, and anti-Clay. In each case he either failed completely to accomplish his objectives or met with only partial success. The country was joyfully militaristic, especially the South, and welcomed the huge acquisitions of the 1848 Treaty of Guadalupe Hidalgo with Mexico. In terms of slavery, Lincoln succeeded only in identifying himself with extremists without altering the slave trade at all. He badly misjudged both his support and the strength of the opposition. And in working against Clay Lincoln managed to acquire the smell of a traitor without any offsetting advantage; Zachary Taylor, who beat Clay for the nomination and won the election, proved singularly unresponsive to Lincoln's requests for a position in the new administration. In each case, it seems Lincoln chose the wrong issue at the wrong time in the wrong place. It took years to undo the damage. It was a mark of Lincoln's greatness that he acknowledged to himself the extent of his failure as a congressman and pulled back gracefully to reflect, grow, change for some five years. When his next opportunity came in 1854, he was not unready for the challenge. Neither he nor the country was ever again quite the same.[59]

Lincoln's "Spot Resolutions" were introduced in the House of Representatives on December 22, 1847. In legalistic language Lincoln tried to force President Polk to admit that the actual spot where fighting began was in Mexico, not the United States; if true, that made the United States the aggressor. The first two of Lincoln's eight "interrogatories" directed President Polk respectfully to inform the House of Representatives, first, "whether the spot of soil on which the blood of our *citizens* was shed, as in his messages, was, or was not, within the territories of Spain, at least from the treaty of 1819 until the Mexican Revolution," and second, "whether that spot is, or is not, within the territory which was wrested from Spain, by the Mexican Revolution."[60] Lincoln over-lawyered himself in these interrogatories, which treated Polk as though he were a humble witness on the stand. The technique of asking detailed, probing questions to which only affirmative or negative answers can be given and then from those answers reconstructing a logically ordered chain of events is really appropriate only for the courtroom. In the complex world of parties and politics and the formalized tensions between Congress and the executive, the device Lincoln was using to unmask Polk was inappropriate. Lincoln felt that we were the aggressors in the Mexican War and that the whole venture was unjust and imperialistic. He should have said so in ways he uniquely could.[61]

In the end the worst indignity of all occurred—no one really seemed to hear or care. The interrogatories themselves suffered the fate of inattention. Polk blandly ignored them and left it to prowar Democrats in the House to reply condescendingly to Lincoln's charges. Not one Whig rose to his support. Lincoln was isolated and alone with his righteous pretentions. Lincoln suffered this indignation in silence, though there are hints of a depression in his April 16, 1848, letter to Mary, which began, "In this troublesome world, we are never quite satisfied" and went on to lament how much he hated to stay in his old room by himself directing documents.[62] Lincoln had unleashed his wish for power, recognition, dominance, and fame. The forum had been the political arena, a public setting, where he had made an inauspicious showing. The resulting inattention Lincoln experienced was a blow of the first order. He responded in pained depression, quietly withdrawing from the fray. He expressed his feelings only to

231

Mary, though to her the idiom was personal and private rather than public and political. Public and private were as yet apart, unintegrated. Lincoln had reached beyond his grasp.

The second major initiative Lincoln took as congressman was to attempt an abolition of slavery in Washington itself. All sensitive observers, including some Southerners, agreed that it was unseemly to allow slaves to be publicly traded in the nation's capital. There is no indication that Lincoln reacted in horror to the sight; indeed, there is no indication at all of his feelings on the matter. The bill he tried to introduce on January 10, 1849, therefore, came as something of a surprise.

Lincoln's bill in 1848 drew essentially on his formulation of slavery reform in 1837. He moved slowly but seldom forgot the past. He apparently drafted his measure sometime in the fall of 1848 with the support of people like Joshua Giddings. He also referred on the House floor to fifteen leading citizens who supported his measure; when challenged for their names he chose not to produce them. The claim suggests Lincoln went to some trouble to line up support for his bill. It was also perhaps true that his support was more fragile than he realized. The explicit reason he gave later for quietly dropping the matter was that he lost the support of his former backers.[63] The measure went absolutely nowhere. Lincoln first read the bill to the House on January 10, 1849, as a "proposition" which he intended to submit. Three days later he gave further notice of his intention to introduce the bill, but he then never brought it up.

Lincoln's support of Henry Clay had long been at the center of his political beliefs. But there were many things to consider in 1848. Once in Washington Lincoln probably realized quickly how weak Clay's base of support really was. In the aftermath of a war it was also desirable for the Whigs to have a military hero as standard-bearer. Furthermore, Zachary Taylor appeared to hold views Lincoln could support. At least Lincoln could see enough flexibility in Taylor to allow for the implementation of Whig policies. He realized, however, that he could not be too sure. In a pro-Taylor speech Lincoln gave in Congress on July 27, 1849, he avoided defending Taylor and instead spent most of his time ridiculing the Democratic candidate, another general, Lewis Cass.

Lincoln worked hard for Taylor in the campaign and spent a good deal of time stumping Massachusetts, where he made a good impression. He argued strenuously that the central issue of the campaign was the extension of slavery. On this issue Taylor himself was perhaps vague, but the Whigs were clearly opposed to it; Cass and the Democrats supported extension. Thus both candidates in some ways lacked luster, but one leaned toward evil, the other toward essential Whig positions. Furthermore it would be disastrous for Conscience Whigs and abolitionists to support Martin Van Buren's third-party candidacy in the Free Soil party: that would serve only to draw off support from Taylor and ensure the election of Cass. In the end Taylor won the election, including Massachusetts. Illinois, however, went for Cass, though Lincoln's district stayed with Taylor.

Lincoln's anti-Clay stance in 1848 seemed to make political sense. Yet his position took its psychological toll and left him with a sense of regret for precipitously abandoning his ideological idol. Clay died on June 29, 1852. One week later Lincoln delivered a moving eulogy to Clay in the Hall of Representatives of the state capitol. It was one of only four eulogies Lincoln ever delivered and certainly the only one with real emotion. The speech, which extended to some fifty-five hundred words, extolled Clay's "mighty mind," his "gallant heart," the "mighty sweep of that graceful arm," and the "magic of that eloquent tongue." In the speech Lincoln detailed the positions Clay took on crucial issues, particularly slavery. As Lincoln pointed out, Clay, as an owner of slaves, detested the institution of slavery. It was the kind of ambiguity that Lincoln believed democracy had to tolerate. "Cast into life where slavery was already widely spread and deeply seeded, [Clay] did not perceive, as I think no wise man has perceived, how it [slavery] could be at *once* erradicated, without producing a greater evil, even to the cause of human liberty itself." Lincoln concluded his speech with particularly effusive praise for the central place of Clay in our history. "But Henry Clay is dead. His long and eventful life is closed. Our country is prosperous and powerful; but could it have been quite all it has been, and is, and is to be, without Henry Clay? Such a man the times have demanded, and such, in the providence of God was given us. But he is gone, let us strive to deserve, as far as mortals may, the continued care of Divine Providence, trusting that, in future national emergencies, He will not fail to provide us with instruments of safety and security."[64] This eulogy, in other words, seemed a kind of personal atonement for having opposed Clay politically for the Whig presidential nomination.

Lincoln's three initiatives as congressman had all failed. In the private years between 1842 and 1854, Lincoln's one important foray into politics and the public world beyond the self was his term in Congress. His sense of failure in that effort must be measured against his absorption in the private concerns of his relationship with Mary, raising a family, building his career as a lawyer. It was a decade-long period of consolidation with sights focused intently inward. It seems he tried fleetingly to find a public self too soon. The public issues at that point were only marginally his own. There was no coincidence, no merging, of public and private issues in 1848, only disjunction.

In contrast it all came together in the 1850s. Lincoln knew immediately in 1854 that the issue of slavery's extension and its threat to the Union was his issue, one he could creatively engage and wrestle to the ground. His eloquent speech in Peoria fully attests to his grasp of the deepest implications of the passage of the Kansas-Nebraska Act. And yet in formulating his position he struggled several years for an appropriate metaphor; until he found it, a certain groping, even indecision and confusion, characterized his thinking.

At first he tried two oddly inappropriate metaphors. In his Peoria speech of 1854 Lincoln strove to explain why the founders were so circumspect in their treatment of slavery. He noted that they had to strike a compromise and so included both recognition of and protection for slavery; but they did so reluctantly. The Constitution, Lincoln pointed out, never once actually used the word "slave." Instead, the slave is spoken of as a "person held to service or labor." Similarly, the African slave trade is described as "the migration or importation of such persons as any of the states now existing shall think proper to admit." And Lincoln continued: "Thus, the thing is hid away in the Constitution, just as an afflicted man hides away a wen or a cancer, which he dares not cut out at once, lest he bleed to death; with the promise, nevertheless, that the cutting may begin at the end of a given time."[65] Lincoln here captured the defacement of slavery in the body politic but failed to enlarge on cancer's striking capacity to spread. The metaphor thus lost its most impressive and vital element.

He also stumbled around in the Peoria speech with animal imagery that linked slaves to hogs. "Equal justice to the South, it is said, requires us to consent to the extending of slavery to new countries. That is to say, inasmuch as you do not object to my taking my hog to Nebraska therefore I must not object to you taking your slave. Now I admit this is perfectly logical if there is no difference between hogs and negroes."[66] In his passage Lincoln made the connection between slaves and hogs in order to refute it. He then followed the metaphor with a curious reference to the "snaky" contact with detested slave dealers. Elsewhere as well in 1854 animal metaphors pervaded his thinking. "The ant," Lincoln wrote in July, "who has toiled and dragged a crumb to his nest, will furiously defend the fruit of his labor against whatever robber assails him. So plain, that the most dumb and stupid slave that ever toiled for a master, does constantly *know* he is wronged."[67] The economic meanings of this comparison are readily apparent. But the metaphor also suggests that the slave is a kind of a lowly animal who deserves at least the few crumbs it can drag to the nest.

These agricultural metaphors and animal images built logically on Lincoln's earliest experience on the frontier. In many respects his idiom remained agricultural. He talked of turkeys to express his deepest childhood memories. He joked endlessly about dogs, pigs, cows, and other beasts. His letters abound in references to the wild kingdom. When he was exhausted, Herndon said, Lincoln liked to lie down on the floor and "play with a little dog or kitten to recover." James Gourley, a neighbor, noted that Lincoln tended his own cow and "loved his horse well."[68] And in a sense the once shaded but then despoiled trees of the Lyceum speech in 1838 became the timbers of the house divided twenty years later. It seems he often expressed the deepest and most complex meanings in the metaphors of his rural youth. Slavery's extension, however, was not an issue he could capture in these familiar ways. It was too immediate. His profound sense of the nation's dilemma required a different metaphor, one he found of course in that of the house divided. He left behind the wens, cancers, hogs, cows, and horses of earlier speeches. The notion of the house divided was what he sought. It blended his private self to public concerns in a uniquely creative way. It was a metaphor with personal integrity.

Lincoln's quest for union took many shapes. At first the issues were purely personal and often conflicting; at the end, the public realm swallowed up the enlarged self. In between—where this study concentrates—public and private concerns blended in creative ways.

The story of Lincoln's personality and character has its own special interest. The personal lives of few historical figures have, in fact, attracted so much attention. In that story, generations of Americans have tried to find themselves. There was adversity in the poverty and lack of opportunity. There was conflict with the father, with sexuality and intimacy within the self. There was sadness in the struggle with death and a lifelong pattern of depression. There was determination and hard work. There was unaccountable skill as the young boy defined his separateness from his rural environment and the man grew in stature after each defeat. There was wonderful humor. There was empathy. There was creativity.

Childhood themes merged with adult concerns of love and work. The young man juggled many roles before finding cohesion and integrity in his identity as a lawyer and politician. He worked hard at loving, first in courtship, then in a deeply satisfying but complicated relationship with his wife, Mary. Over the course of a decade he tried to find a viable role as husband and father. But his closeness alternated with inner demands for being apart, separate, and idealized. Mary in turn gave much, perhaps most of all the confirmation that he could love genuinely and father children. But their close relationship and enclosed home held their own divisions. Their intimacy, one might say, was always potentially explosive.

After 1854 Lincoln discovered, remarkably enough, that his private concerns found reflection in the country as a whole. His own ambivalent quest for union—with his dead mother, his bride, his alienated father—gave meaning to the nation's turbulence as it hurtled toward civil war. It took time for Lincoln to bridge the two exactly. He needed the right metaphor. In the idea of a house divided, Lincoln found a way of creatively enlarging his private concerns to fill the public space. When he found it there was resonance.

Until the presidency, however, Lincoln hardly spoke for the nation. He defined the issues of the Union—and disunion—but until late in the 1850s he was in many respects only a Midwestern politician dwarfed by Stephen Douglas in his own state, even in his own town. In retrospect the extent to which Lincoln had his finger on the pulse of the nation after 1854 is much clearer. Lincoln expressed then the deep and underlying issues for everyone in the troubled country. It was a confusing time, when suspiciousness slipped into paranoia, when few were touched, as Lincoln put it in his First Inaugural Address, by the better angels of their nature.

Lincoln the president rose to new heights as he led the North toward victory, and as soon as that was secured, began to lay the groundwork for healing the wounds of war. He died, of course, before Reconstruction, which makes it futile to speculate what he might have done. But it is not frivolous to guess that he purposefully shaped his heroic image to fit a nation longing for unity and greatness. The image he shaped dissolved struggles over father, fatherhood, and founders. It put him in touch with God. And it gave America its greatest hero.

NOTES

1. William H. Herndon and Jesse W. Weik, *Herndon's Life of Lincoln*, with introduction and notes by Paul M. Angle (Cleveland: World Publishing, 1930), pp. 2-3. Note also three Herndon letters to Ward Hill Lamon, Feb. 24, 1869; Feb. 25, 1870; and Mar. 6, 1870; in Emanuel Hertz, ed., *The Hidden Lincoln* (New York: Viking Press, 1938), pp. 59, 62-72.

2. Herndon to Ward Hill Lamon, Mar. 6, 1870, in Hertz, *The Hidden Lincoln*, p. 74.

3. Herndon to Ward Hill Lamon, Feb. 25, 1870, in Hertz, *The Hidden Lincoln*, p. 63.

4. Carl Sandburg, *Abraham Lincoln: The Prairie Years*, 2 vols. (New York: Harcourt Brace, 1926), 1: 13.

5. Roy P. Basler, ed., Marion Dolores Pratt and Lloyd A. Dunlap, asst. eds., *The Collected Works of Abraham Lincoln*, 9 vols. (New Brunswick, N.J.: Rutgers University Press, 1953-55) 4: 61.

6. John Hanks's statement to Herndon, n.d., Hertz, *The Hidden Lincoln*, p. 345; cf. Nat Grigsby to Herndon, Sept. 12, 1865, ibid., pp. 353-54.

7. William Woods's statement to Herndon, Sept. 15, 1865, in Hertz, *The Hidden Lincoln*, p. 364.

8. Herndon to Truman H. Bartlett, Oct. 1887, in Hertz, *The Hidden Lincoln*, p. 208; Albert Beveridge, *Abraham Lincoln, 1809-1858*, 2 vols. (New York: Houghton Mifflin, 1928), 1: 15.

9. William E. Barton, *The Life of Abraham Lincoln*, 2 vols. (Indianapolis: Bobbs-Merrill, 1925), p. 14; Stephen B. Oates, *With Malice toward None: The Life of Abraham Lincoln* (New York: Harper and Row, 1977), p. 5.

10. Basler, *Collected Works of Lincoln*, 1: 118.

11. Dennis F. Hanks to Herndon, June 12, 1865, in Hertz, *The Hidden Lincoln*, p. 275.

12. Herndon to Ward Hill Lamon, Feb. 25, 1870; Charles Friend to

Herndon, Aug. 20, 1889; Herndon's notes to himself, n.d., in Hertz, *The Hidden Lincoln*, pp. 63, 341, 393-94.

13. Herndon's notes to himself, n.d., ibid., p. 393.

14. Herndon to Jesse Weik, Jan. 1, 1886, ibid., pp. 118-19.

15. Herndon's notes to himself, n.d., ibid., p. 393. For years Herndon wrestled with the issue of the exact timing of castration but never doubted the reality of the event. He never seemed to note the distinction between castration and induced sterility from mumps. See Herndon to Truman H. Bartlett, Sept. 30, 1887, ibid., pp. 205-7.

16. Benjamin P. Thomas, *Abraham Lincoln: A Biography* (New York: Alfred A. Knopf, 1952), p. 134.

17. Basler, *Collected Works of Lincoln*, 4: 61.

18. Ibid., 1: 456; Lincoln retained a disdain for the symbols of ignorance generally. He once described a legal matter thus: I am "bored more than enough about it; not the least of which annoyance is his cursed, unreadable, and ungodly handwriting." Ibid., p. 445.

19. Dennis F. Hanks's statement to Herndon, June 13, 1865, in Hertz, *The Hidden Lincoln*, p. 280.

20. Ibid., p. 278.

21. Sarah Lincoln's statement to Herndon, Sept. 8, 1865, ibid., p. 351.

22. Dennis F. Hanks's statement to Herndon, June 13, 1865, ibid., p. 278.

23. Basler, *Collected Works of Lincoln*, 4: 61; 2: 94.

24. Ibid., 3: 511; 4: 61.

25. Ibid., 4: 62.

26. Ibid.

27. Sarah Lincoln's statement to Herndon, Sept. 8, 1865, in Hertz, *The Hidden Lincoln*, pp. 351-52. Compare Matilda Moore's statement to Herndon on the same day [not published in Hertz], Herndon-Weik Collection, Library of Congress, Washington, D.C.

28. Sarah Lincoln's statement to Herndon, Sept. 8, 1865; Herndon to Weik, Nov. 12, 1885; Herndon to Cyrus O. Poole, Jan. 5, 1886; in Hertz, *The Hidden Lincoln*, pp. 351, 99, 120.

29. Dennis F. Hanks to Herndon, June 13, 1865, in ibid., pp. 280-81.

30. Sarah Lincoln to Herndon, Sept. 8, 1865, in ibid., p. 353.

31. Ward Hill Lamon, *The Life of Abraham Lincoln, from His Birth to His Inauguration* (Boston: J. R. Osgood, 1872), p. 463.

32. Justin G. Turner and Linda Levitt Turner, eds., *Mary Todd Lincoln: Her Life and Letters* (New York: Alfred A. Knopf, 1972), pp. 464-65; Sandburg, *Abraham Lincoln*, 1: 50.

33. Thomas, *Abraham Lincoln*, p. 56.

34. Basler, *Collected Works of Lincoln*, 1: 94-95.

35. Mary S. Vineyard [Owens] to Herndon, July 22, 1866, in Hertz, *The Hidden Lincoln*, p. 303; Herndon quoted the entire letter in his book; see Herndon and Weik, *Hendon's Life of Lincoln*, p. 119.

36. James C. Conckling to Mercy Levering, Sept. 21, 1840, Illinois State Historical Library, Springfield, Ill., in James C. Conckling Papers.

37. Turner and Turner, *Mary Todd Lincoln*, p. 21.

38. Basler, *Collected Works of Lincoln*, 1: 78.

39. Joshua F. Speed, "Incidents in the Early Life of A. Lincoln," memorandum to Herndon, n.d. [after 1865], Joshua Speed Collection, Illinois State Historical Library, Springfield, Ill.

40. Herndon to Ward Hill Lamon, Feb. 25, 1870, in Hertz, *The Hidden Lincoln*, pp. 65-67.

41. Lamon, *Life of Abraham Lincoln*, p. 483; Herndon to Jesse Weik, Jan. 22, 1887, in Hertz, *The Hidden Lincoln*, p. 159.

42. Basler, *Collected Works of Lincoln*, 1: 269.

43. Herndon wrote that "on the love question alone Lincoln opened to Speed possibly the whole." Herndon to Weik, Jan. 22, 1887, in Hertz, *The Hidden Lincoln*, p. 159.

44. Ruth Painter Randall, *The Courtship of Mr. Lincoln* (Boston: Little, Brown, 1957), pp. 11-17, variously characterizes Speed as "the frequent lover" (p. 42); as having a "pleasing personality" (p. 12); as "apt to fall in love with practically every pretty girl he encountered" (p. 12); as having a "handsome Byronic face" (p. 12); and as "that Don Juan of Springfield, Joshua Speed" (p. 43).

45. To call Speed a "frequent lover" and a "Don Juan" confuses mild flirtations with sexually consummated relationships. All the evidence indicates the former. Note Mary Todd to Mercy Ann Levering, Springfield, Dec. 15, 1840, in Turner and Turner, *Mary Todd Lincoln*, p. 20; Lincoln to Speed, Jan. 3, 1842, in Basler, *Collected Works of Lincoln*, 1: 266; and the two references to Sarah Richard in Lincoln to Speed, Feb. 3, and Mar. 27, 1842, in Basler, *Collected Works of Lincoln*, 1: 268, 282. As I argue here, Speed seemed to have the same kind of sexual conflicts as Lincoln, which in part explains their friendship.

46. Speed memorandum to Herndon, Nov. 30, 1866 [not published in Hertz], Herndon-Weik Collection.

47. Speed wrote to Herndon on Sept. 17, 1866: "I sold out to Hurst 1 Jany 1841. And came to Ky in the spring" [not published in Hertz], Herndon-Weik Collection. Also note the weekly announcements in the *Sangamo Journal*, beginning January 8, 1841: "The co-partnership heretofore existing between JAS. Bell and Joshua F. Speed is this day dissolved by mutual consent . . . January 1, 1841." A separate announcement noted the formation of the partnership Bell and Charles R. Hurst, as of January 1, 1841.

48. Mary Todd wrote to Mercy Ann Levering in June 1841: "Mr. Speed, are former most constant guest has been in Kentucky for some weeks past, will be here next month, on a visit perhaps, as he has some idea of deserting Illinois, his mother is anxious he should superintend her affairs, he takes a friends privilege, of occasionally favoring me with a letter, in his last he spoke of his great desire of once more inhabiting this region & of his

possibility of soon returning—." Turner and Turner, *Mary Todd Lincoln*, p. 27.

49. Mary Todd to Mercy Ann Levering, June 1841, in ibid., p. 27.

50. Basler, *Collected Works of Lincoln*, 1: 266.

51. Ibid., 1: 269.

52. Ibid., 1: 280, 265-68.

53. Ibid., 1: 280.

54. Ibid., 1: 282, 289.

55. Ibid., 2: 506.

56. Ibid., 1: 305.

57. James C. Conckling to his wife, Apr. 18, 1843, Illinois State Historical Library, Springfield, Ill., in James C. Conckling Papers.

58. Ruth Painter Randall, *Mary Lincoln: Biography of a Marriage* (Boston: Little Brown, 1953), p. 316.

59. There is an old view (which began with Herndon) that Congressman Lincoln honorably but stupidly opposed the Mexican War, lost support of his central Illinois constituency, and was forcibly retired to circuit work in 1849. See Herndon and Weik, *Herndon's Life of Lincoln*, pp. 219-36; Basler, *Collected Works of Lincoln*, 1: 51, n. 9. Nearly every detail of this interpretation has been shown wrong. It was a good position from Maine to Illinois to oppose the war, though the party was divided on the issue. See Mark Neely, "Lincoln and the Mexican War: An Argument by Analogy," *Civil War History* 24 (1978): 5-24; see also Brian C. Walton, "Elections of the Thirtieth Congress," *Journal of Southern History* 35 (1969): 186-87. There is also no indication (beyond Herndon's own complaint to Lincoln) that Whigs back home in the district took offense at his opposition to the war, and if they did it failed to register in newspapers, letters, or diaries that have survived. Only the stridently Democratic press made that charge. See Gabor Boritt, "A Question of Political Suicide: Lincoln's Opposition to the Mexican War," *Journal of the Illinois State Historical Society* 67 (1974): 79-100; Compare, for example, the comments of the *Register* on Jan. 21 and Mar. 10, 1848, in Herbert Mitgang, ed., *Abraham Lincoln, a Press Portrait: His Life and Times from the Original Newspaper Documents of the Union, the Confederacy and Europe* (Chicago: Quadrangle Books, 1971), pp. 55 and 57, with the same paper on Oct. 27, 1848, in Basler, *Collected Works of Lincoln*, 2: 11-13. Nor, finally, is it true Lincoln retired from politics between 1849 and 1854, in the sense of having abandoned involvement in it altogether. He held no elective office but remained important in party affairs throughout the state.

60. Basler, *Collected Works of Lincoln*, 1: 420-22.

61. John P. Frank, *Lincoln as a Lawyer* (Urbana: University of Illinois Press, 1961), pp. 105-10. Lincoln never entirely abandoned his fondness for interrogatories, though he learned to use them more effectively, for example, in the 1858 debates with Douglas. It is also worth noting that the use of interrogatories was quite common in this period and reflected the legal cast of politics.

62. Basler, *Collected Works of Lincoln*, 1: 465.

63. Ibid., 2: 22n.
64. Ibid., 2: 132.
65. Ibid., 2: 274.
66. Ibid., 2: 264.
67. Ibid., 2: 222.
68. Herndon and Weik, *Herndon's Life of Lincoln*, p. 343; James Gourley's statement to Herndon, in Hertz, *The Hidden Lincoln*, p. 384.

Commentary on "Lincoln's Quest for Union"

JEAN BAKER

In his psychohistorical quest for Lincoln, Charles Strozier has provided us with a new Lincoln. And this is as it should be on the 175th anniversary of our sixteenth president's birth. The evidence Strozier uses is familiar. For Lincoln remains the most studied of our national leaders, and the relevant sources were long ago excavated and evaluated. Thus along with Lincoln's other biographers Strozier draws on the patchy details of Lincoln's early years — the death of his mother, his constrained relations with his father, his close friendship with his bedmate Joshua Speed, and his courtship with Mary Todd, as well as his better-documented public life. In *Lincoln's Quest for Union*, the book from which his paper is drawn, Strozier forgoes any claim that his is the only Lincoln. In fact, in an unusual admission for a biographer, he confesses that "the real Lincoln remains obscure for me." Nonetheless he presents here a fresh perspective on an old subject.[1]

To be sure, there have been other efforts to understand Lincoln's inner life. With his depression, withdrawals, and death dreams, the sixteenth president makes an inviting target for psychoanalysis. His partner Billy Herndon began all this when, impatient over postassassination efforts to transform his apple-chewing, joke-telling friend into a great historical character, he tried to preserve Lincoln the human being. Untroubled by the need for any analytic framework of personality development, Herndon simply attached a number of contradictory adjectives to his former law partner. Herndon's Lincoln was sensuous, cool, selfish, practical, firm, indifferent — and so on. Later Louis Warren, the foremost authority on Lincoln's early years, dealt with only the external events of Lincoln's frontier boyhood in Kentucky and Indiana. Along with his generation Warren believed that parental influence was exerted genetically, before a child was born, and accordingly he placed little emphasis on the family relationships considered so critical by Strozier.[2]

In the post-Freudian age Pierce Clark dealt with Lincoln's emotional life as a series of melancholic episodes, while in a lesser-known study, Edward Kempf argued that the president's depressions were caused by that famous horse's kick to the head that rendered ten-year-old Abraham unconscious. For Milton Shutes, a physician writing in 1957, the key to understanding Lincoln's psyche was not that he had syphilis (as Herndon believed), but his fear, common among Victorians, that he might have it. None of these studies connected Lincoln's private life with his public activities, although later George Forgie used Lincoln's supposed oedipal conflict with his father as a mirror for his generation's relationship with the founding fathers. Recently Dwight Anderson concentrated on Lincoln's persistent death dreams.[3]

What distinguishes Strozier from previous psychological studies is his effort to connect Lincoln's inner strivings with his public actions. Hence Strozier's book is aptly subtitled *Public and Private Meanings,* and indeed the larger contribution of this paper is to make clear that efforts to understand the internal life of public figures must not ignore their external preoccupations. Working in the same tradition as Erik Erikson in his studies of Luther and Gandhi, Strozier argues that in the 1850s Lincoln found reflected in the division of his country his own private concerns.

To make his point, Strozier rigorously applies the theories of Heinz Kohut's *The Search for the Self,* in which the quality of the infantile empathic environment shapes the adult personality. Happily, Strozier's psychological conceptualization does not intrude on his narrative, and we are spared what sometimes distracts in psychohistory, that is, discussions of narcissism, horizontal and vertical psyche splits, mirror transferences, and even that old standby, cathexis. Indeed Strozier works successfully on both sides of the hyphen between psycho and biographical, and his rendering of Lincoln's private and public life is sensitive, well researched, and well written.[4]

By using Kohut's ego psychology, Strozier is able to synthesize Lincoln's personal strivings toward an integrated personality and his public expression. Throughout his youth and early manhood, Strozier's Lincoln suffered from low self-esteem, or as Kohut might have said, a fragmented self bruised by a mother's death, insufficient schooling, early business failures in New Salem, awkwardness with women, and political defeats. In time (and it is in *due* time, for Lincoln was in his forties) Lincoln "blended his private self to public concerns in a uniquely creative way." His quest for union (the union here of his conflicted self as well as that of his country) eventually led to a therapeutic transcendence expressed in the famous house divided speech in June of 1858.

This speech, which scholars have previously dissected in terms of its radicalism and representation of hardening views among Republicans, can now be seen as emerging from Lincoln's personal experiences and feelings. Earlier Lincoln had employed other metaphors, usually related to animals, to express his concerns about the spread of slavery. But in what Strozier calls his "rhetorical domestication of politics," Lincoln neatly fused his private self with his public convictions. Thereafter his effectiveness as a leader trying to restore the union of his nation flourished amid the revolution of his former private stumblings.

As is often the case with psychobiography, Strozier's evocative conclusions sometimes rest on slender evidence and tortured extrapolations. He must, in order to follow Kohut, make Lincoln's early life neither too secure nor insecure, for if there was too much of the latter, Lincoln's psychic structure would have tipped over into narcissism and grandiosity. (In that case the house divided speech might have been a Lincoln version of Cassius Clay's verbal assaults on slaveholders). And had Lincoln been too secure, there would have been no conflict and perhaps no interest in politics.

As evidence of Lincoln's early distress Strozier relies on Herndon. Now Herndon, it seems to me, is every Lincoln scholar's reserve army—available to make a point when he agrees with whatever conclusion we wish to establish, but having been so often discredited, easily dismissed when we disagree. Thus Strozier uses Herndon to develop Lincoln's relationship with his mother, but disregards him when Herndon reports on Lincoln's sexuality.

Moreover, Strozier presents a version of the Todd-Lincoln courtship that suits his theory but not necessarily the facts. On that fatal first of January 1841 he has an agonized Lincoln—unready for the intimacy of marriage—break off his engagement with Mary Todd. First of all, the term engagement is misleading, for it conjures up firm resolves, diamonds-are-forever rings, and modern understandings. As Ellen Rothman has recently argued, nineteenth-century court-ships were frequently interrupted, only to be resumed later. Placed in the larger framework of American social history, this disrupted romance had nothing to do with Lincoln's fragmented self, but much to do with his generation's fears about supporting a wife and children.[5]

In fact, a good case can be made that Mary Todd ended their courtship by continuing to flirt with one of her old suitors, Edwin Webb, thus rousing Lincoln's ire. Indeed such narcissistic injuries are often followed by the depression that Lincoln suffered in 1841. Now if Mary did the jilting, then Strozier's carefully constructed argument that Lincoln was not psychically ready for marriage is shaken, if not destroyed.

Also critical to Strozier's exposition is the depiction of Lincoln's perception of his wife's supposed insanity. The data for this is mis-matched to the period of Lincoln's quest for internal harmony in the 1850s. All of it comes from the war years, at which point Lincoln's creativity had been established. It is very unlikely that Lincoln — "the most close-mouthed man" Herndon knew — would have discussed his wife's caprices with a mere acquaintance. Nor would he have used the term "partial insanity" as William Woods, in an account from 1887, indicated.[6]

Like most psychohistories, Strozier's argument depends on tim-ing, in this case of Lincoln's private and public quests for unity. Yet it seems too perfect a synchronism that Lincoln's triumphant assertion of personal equilibrium would coincide with his nation's. Granted a need for self-cohesion that is not tied to any life stage; granted the private conflicts and public failures of Lincoln's life in the 1830s and 1840s; still it seems too pat to have Lincoln conveniently discover after 1854, "that his private concerns found reflection in the country as a whole." He was forty-five; why had he not done so earlier?

Moreover in his effort to explain Lincoln's house divided speech, Strozier overlooks the rationalist explanation for a powerful antislav-ery statement. Lincoln meant to oppose what he saw as a growing Southern conspiracy to nationalize slavery. This is what most of the text is devoted to; hence, if we are going to accept Strozier's psy-chological conceptualization, it must be applied to all parts of the speech.

Finally, having established the healthy self-respect that enabled him to become a great leader, what are we to do with the Lincoln of the 1860s? Surely his reaction to his son Willie's death and his death-wish dreams suggest another emotional crisis. And if Strozier's analogy is a two-way street, how does the public responsibility of leading a nation to reunion affect the president's need for order and control in his private life? And so I would hope that Charles Strozier would take his Lincoln—a Lincoln whose quest for union he has so provocatively and eloquently depicted—another step into the reestablishment of union, personal and public.

NOTES

1. Charles Strozier, *Lincoln's Quest for Union: Public and Private Meanings* (New York: Basic Books, 1982), p. xii.

2. Louis Warren, *Lincoln's Parentage and Childhood* (New York: Century, 1926).

3. See chapters 9 and 10 in this volume and also L. Pierce Clark, *Lincoln: A Psycho-Biography* (New York: Scribner's, 1932); Milton Shutes, *Lincoln's Emotional Life* (Philadelphia: Dorrance, 1957); George Forgie, *Patricide in the House Divided: A Psychological Interpretation of Lincoln and His Age* (New York: Norton, 1979); Dwight Anderson, *Abraham Lincoln: The Quest for Immortality* (New York: Knopf, 1982); Edward Kempf, *Abraham Lincoln's Philosophy of a Common Sense* (New York: New York Academy of Sciences, 1965).

4. Heinz Kohut, *The Search for the Self: Selected Writings of Heinz Kohut, 1950-1978*, 2 vols., ed. Paul Ornstein (New York: International Universities Press, 1978).

5. Ellen Rothman, *Hands and Hearts: A Social History of Courtship* (New York: Basic Books, 1982).

6. Jean H. Baker, *Mary Todd Lincoln: A Biography* (New York: Norton, 1987).

Commentary on "Lincoln's Quest for Union"

HERMAN BELZ

Professor Strozier's study of Lincoln is, as he states, "avowedly psychohistorical." It is therefore fair to evaluate his work in light of recent discussion among psychohistorians concerning the direction the field of psychohistory must take if it is to make a genuine contribution to historical and scientific knowledge. Professor Strozier has been a leading participant in this discussion, and in a recent essay summarizes its central conclusion. No single issue is of greater concern to psychohistorians, he writes, than how to go beyond a focus on individual biography. Citing his mentor Heinz Kohut, Professor Strozier insists upon "the necessity of understanding collective behavior for psychohistory to avoid the curse of triviality."[1]

Judged in relation to this goal, Professor Strozier's study is notably unsuccessful. One chapter in his book, "The Group Self and the Crisis of the 1850s," attempts to go beyond individual biography and explain how a collective paranoia, expressing its exaggerated notions of absolute rightness that held together "the fragmenting nuclear self," generated a pervasive anger that plunged the nation into civil war. I concur with the judgment of the *Journal of American History* that this chapter, which may be described as warmed-over revisionism dressed up in the language of psychohistory, is "perverse."[2] Significantly, none of this chapter appears in Professor Strozier's summary of his book for this conference.

Less ambitiously, Professor Strozier attempts to go beyond individual biography by arguing for a connection between Lincoln's psychological makeup and development, and events in the 1850s. The thesis of the book, as I understand it, is that Lincoln's course of action in the sectional struggle reflected conflicts within himself and in his private household, and that his success in pursuing this course of action was owing to the fact that his inner problems had their coun-

247

terpart or equivalent in the society as a whole. Professor Strozier appears to be saying that but for his internal conflicts, Lincoln would not have turned outward into public life, would not have taken the specific positions he did, and would not have met with the widespread public approval that placed him in the White House. Things would not have come together in the 1850s, there would have been no "resonance" between Lincoln and the people, if his private experience had not prepared him to deal with the public concerns of the Civil War generation.

While I would not deny that Lincoln's public and private lives were connected, in the sense that his ability and inclination to pursue a political career were affected by his personal state of mind and domestic situation, it is not clear to me that the specific stands he took were decisively shaped or influenced by the inner conflicts that Professor Strozier describes, or that his psychological problems were mirrored in problems that the nation faced.

Professor Strozier presents Lincoln as a young man who, lacking inner coherence and psychologically unsure of his identity, met with difficulties in work and in love relationships. With his marriage in 1842 a period of inward consolidation began in which Lincoln, while pursuing a political and legal career, "wrestled with his conflicted intimacy of Mary and home." This inner struggle continued until 1854, when Lincoln shifted his field of vision from "a conflicted private world of meanings that never worked themselves out" to the world of politics and society. He discovered that "his private concerns found reflection in the country as a whole." "A multitude of private and public concerns," Professor Strozier writes further, "prompted an emotional reordering of Lincoln's self-organization." Turning outward, Lincoln tried "to solve for all what he would not solve for himself alone."

With all due respect, these conclusions strike me as portentous and obscure. Professor Strozier is not simply saying that by propelling him more fully into public life after 1854 Lincoln's psychological struggles had an obvious historical significance. Rather, by implication and inference, he is arguing for a correspondence or merging between Lincoln's life course and the life course of the society. Lincoln's private concerns may be clear enough, if we accept Professor Strozier's analysis, but what were the concerns of the country as a whole that reflected those of the Illinois lawyer-politician? Or, what problem did

Lincoln try to solve for American society which at a personal level he was unable to resolve for himself? Neither in his paper nor in his book, except for the discredited chapter on the group self of the 1850s, does Professor Strozier attempt to provide the kind of "stage-state" analysis of the life and mind of the community as a whole that his central conclusions would seem to require.

Presumably Professor Strozier is saying that Lincoln sought inner coherence in a formal framework of matrimonial union, as American society, in the framework of constitutional union, struggled to achieve inner coherence and integrity in the face of debilitating divisions caused by the existence of slavery. To this it may be objected that society is not an organism, that it has no subjective existence, that it has no individualistic drives related to those which characterize the stages of human development.[3] But setting aside the question of the validity of the analogical reasoning on which Professor Strozier's conclusions implicitly rest, could we not with equal authority posit a different explanation of Lincoln's actions and events in the 1850s?

Could we not say that the central issue for Lincoln and his generation was freedom rather than union, or, to be more precise, that it was freedom rather than the order and control that Professor Strozier regards as the practical meaning of union, and he says was "the defining characteristic of Lincoln's adult life?"[4] The sectional antagonists of the 1850s pursued their different ends on the assumption that the Union would continue. We can see in retrospect that their actions subjected the Union to pressures which ultimately were unbearable, and the Union was broken. Then began, among Northerners at least, a quest for union, or re-union. Before 1861, however, antislavery and free soil partisans struggled to enlarge the sphere of freedom, while Southerners struggled to protect slavery, which in their view was the basis of local liberty.[5]

Professor Strozier states that "Lincoln knew immediately in 1854 that the issue of slavery's extension and its threat to the Union was his issue." He further contends that the "confusions, contradictions, and specious distinctions built into Lincoln's thought about the interrelated issues of slavery and racial equality in the 1850s reflected the fact that his primary concern lay elsewhere—with the preservation of the Union." One might ask why, if Lincoln was so concerned with union, he assumed the leadership of an exclusively sectional party, the very existence of which threatened national unity. More to the point, Professor Strozier fails to consider that for Lincoln and his antislavery cohorts union signified not order, organization, control, and restraint, but personal and political liberty as expressed in the Declaration of Independence. Liberty was the "apple of gold," Lincoln wrote on the eve of the war, to adorn and preserve which the Union and the Constitution were made as "the picture of silver" around it.[6]

As for Lincoln's psychological struggles, Professor Strozier concludes that he was unable to solve the problem of achieving inner coherence, and so shifted his attention to public affairs. But could we not say that after 1854 Lincoln resolved any lingering identity problems and successfully came to terms with some basic realities in his life? Resigned to staying married, he stopped wrestling with his conflicted and ambivalent feelings about his wife and possible intimacy with her, and threw himself more fully into his career. He got a house with separate bedrooms, stopped having sex with his wife, and stayed away from home for much longer periods of time. He thus liberated himself from the restrictions of domesticity in order to perform larger works in the world of politics and society. One might say that Lincoln, achieving personal autonomy and independence, negotiated a mid-life crisis in a highly constructive and positive manner.

Professor Strozier's account is most historically satisfying when, rather than trying to go beyond the individual, he confines himself to what a fellow practitioner in the field describes as "essentially a biography."[7] Except for the notorious "turkey story," so devastatingly criticized by Professor Fehrenbacher,[8] most reviewers agree that Professor Strozier throws useful light on Lincoln's childhood, his relationship with his mother and father, his search for a career, and his romantic involvements and marriage. Professor Strozier's treatment of these subjects is by and large persuasive because it employs psychological concepts and language that have passed into our contemporary culture and discourse. We are all of us, if not Freudians, then at least Eriksonians, or some variation thereof. Accordingly, there is a "resonance," to use one of Professor Strozier's formulations, when we read: "For Lincoln it was precisely this loss of self that most threatened him. He could not go beyond himself because he had not fully consolidated the bases of his sexual or work identity. He lacked an inner coherence or identity that would permit him to transcend himself and reach out to another."[9] We think we know what this means, not in a technical sense perhaps, but in an everyday emotional sense.

Professor Strozier's accomplishment in explaining Lincoln—and it is a considerable one—represents not the application of a method, or even of special insights available only to the trained professional. Rather, as Jacques Barzun has written in his critique of psychohistory, it results from the filtering out of psychological teachings and hypotheses into "words and ideas which form a kind of shorthand so commonly used that we take the words themselves as explanation."[10] Much of Professor Strozier's account passes what Barzun says is the test of the biographer's explanatory power: can someone with life experience understand Lincoln's character? "Does the description given make us visualize, sympathize, regret?"[11] Professor Strozier's book frequently succeeds at this level, and to the extent it does it advances our understanding of Lincoln as an individual. It does little, however, to promote our understanding of the public Lincoln.

The value of individual life histories is disputed within the psychological community. Most psychologists, seeking scientific laws of human behavior, take the view that "if you can't generalize from these studies of individual lives, what's the point of doing them?"[12] Other psychologists—proponents of what is called the idiographic approach—are concerned with individual cases rather than the search for general laws of social science. Notwithstanding his quest for the group self, Professor Strozier's study illustrates the latter approach. Historians who are wary of psychohistory can perhaps take comfort in the consideration that idiographic accounts like Professor Strozier's, although they are not intended to, reinforce a humanistic view of history as the study of unique events caused by the actions of individual men and women.

NOTES

1. Charles B. Strozier, "Heinz Kohut and the Historical Imagination," *Psychohistory Review* 7 (Fall 1978): 38. See also Fred Weinstein and Gerald M. Platt, "The Coming Crisis in Psychohistory," *Journal of Modern History* 47 (June 1975): 202-28.

2. Robert H. Abzug, review of *Lincoln's Quest for Union: Public and Private Meanings*, by Charles B. Strozier, in *Journal of American History* 70 (Sept. 1983): 418-19.

3. See Bertram Wyatt-Brown, review of *Lincoln's Quest for Union*, in *American Historical Review* 88 (in Oct. 1983): 1970.

4. Professor Strozier writes: "One might even argue that Lincoln's search for order was the defining characteristic of his adult life, public and

251

private, and that his failure to find effective order domestically prompted an analogous engagement with larger issues in the community." *Lincoln's Quest for Union: Public and Private Meanings* (New York: Basic Books, 1982), p. 139.

5. Shomer Zwelling, in *Journal of Psychohistory* 11 (Fall 1983): 291-94, notes Professor Strozier's failure to take into account the concern for freedom in the Civil War era.

6. Roy P. Basler, ed., Marion Dolores Pratt and Lloyd A. Dunlap, asst. eds., *The Collected Works of Abraham Lincoln*, 9 vols. (New Brunswick, N.J.: Rutgers University Press, 1953-55), 4: 168-69.

7. Zwelling, *Journal of Psychohistory* 11 (Fall 1983): 291.

8. Don E. Fehrenbacher, "In Quest of the Psychohistorical Lincoln," *Reviews in American History* 11 (Mar. 1983): 14-16.

9. Charles B. Strozier, "The Search for Identity and Love in the Young Lincoln," in *The Public and the Private Lincoln: Contemporary Perspectives*, ed. Cullom Davis et al. (Carbondale: Southern Illinois University Press, 1979), p. 12.

10. Jacques Barzun, *Clio and the Doctors: Psycho-History, Quanto-History and History* (Chicago, University of Chicago Press, 1974), p. 32.

11. Ibid., pp. 67-68.

12. William McKinley Runyan, *Life Histories and Psychobiography: Explorations in Theory and Method* (New York: Oxford University Press, 1982), p. 6.

CHAPTER 9

QUEST FOR IMMORTALITY:
A Theory of Abraham Lincoln's Political Psychology

DWIGHT G. ANDERSON

A FEW DAYS BEFORE his assassination, Abraham Lincoln told of having a dream which, he said, "has got possession of me and, like Banquo's ghost, it will not down." In the dream, Lincoln heard "subdued sobs" downstairs in the White House, as if a number of people were weeping. He left his bed and went from room to room in search of the mourners, but saw no one until entering the East Room. "There I met with a sickening surprise. Before me was a catafalque, on which rested a corpse wrapped in funeral vestments. Around it were stationed soldiers who were acting as guards; and there was a throng of people, some gazing mournfully upon the corpse, whose face was covered, others weeping pitifully. 'Who is dead in the White House?' I demanded of one of the soldiers. 'The President' was his answer; 'he was killed by an assassin!' "[1]

Lincoln's observers have always assumed that this dream foreshadowed his own death by assassination. The dream, however, did not reveal the identity of the dead president. As recorded at the time by his personal aide, Ward Hill Lamon, who claimed detailed accuracy for his account, Lincoln said the face of the corpse was covered. Moreover, Lincoln himself seemed specifically to rule out the possibility that he was the dead president by later telling Lamon, who was distressed by Lincoln's disregard for his own safety, "For a long time you have been trying to keep somebody—the Lord knows who—from killing me. Don't you see how it will turn out? In this dream it was not me, but some other fellow, that was killed. It seems that this ghostly assassin tried his hand on someone else."[2]

If not Lincoln, who was the dead president? The only other

possibility suggested by the contextual evidence is that the president of Lincoln's dream was George Washington and Lincoln his "ghostly assassin." That this possibility is also suggested by an examination of Lincoln's personal psychology and political history lends credence to this assumption. For George Washington, it can be shown, provided Lincoln with an imaginary father whom he both emulated and defied, and finally, by ceremonial apotheosis, elevated to divine rank. If the guilt that Lincoln experienced in achieving this symbolic victory over Washington haunted him like Banquo's ghost, it also provided the psychological basis for Lincoln's refoundation of political authority in the United States.

Lincoln's personal psychology became bound up with the history of the nation through the influence of Mason Locke Weems's *Life of Washington*. This book, which Lincoln read repeatedly as a youth, offered him two contradictory models of political success. One was that of Washington himself, who according to Weems achieved his great stature because of his private virtues. The other was that of a "cunning, ambitious, unprincipled" man who would seek greatness on "the ruins of public liberty"—the figure against whom Washington warned the nation in his Farewell Address. Lincoln followed both models sequentially. At first he sought political success by upholding Washington's advice and example; failing there, he seized upon the alternative, eventually presiding over the destruction of Washington's Union, and becoming the very tyrant against whom Washington had warned. Sublimating guilt into political authority, Lincoln took Washington's place as the father of his country.

Reduced to its barest essentials, this theory of Lincoln's political psychology seems cryptic, eccentric, and immodest. Adorning it with appropriate historical evidence and scientific disclaimers does not altogether dispense with these objections. The reason is that this conception of Lincoln, despite its Freudian appearance, does not depend upon a general theory of human psychology; nor can it claim, primarily because of its apparent Freudianism, the sanction of a dominant school of historiography. But novelty can offer rewards as well as risks. In this case, the payoff is a theory whose explanatory utility more than compensates for its oddity. The major risk involved, a speculative conclusion about the influence of Weems's book on Lincoln's speech to the Young Men's Lyceum of Springfield in 1838, seems well worth taking.

Weems's *Washington* may have been the only book Lincoln personally owned as a young man. According to contemporary sources, he borrowed a copy of it from a neighbor when he first learned to read at age fifteen, and then paid for it by a day or two of labor after it was damaged by rain. He read this and the few other books available to him repeatedly, often memorizing entire passages word for word. One source reported that Lincoln read Weems at age twenty, suggesting the likelihood that he continued to peruse the book over a period of several years.

In presenting his life of Washington, an ersatz epic best known for its whimsical anecdotes about young George, Weems said he was concentrating on his private virtues "because in these every youth may become a Washington."[3] And like Weems's Washington, Lincoln was industrious and self-educated, eagerly engaging in the "noble pursuit of knowledge." Like Washington, whose word, according to Weems, was accepted as law among his fellows, and whose athletic prowess was unequaled, Lincoln developed the reputation among his young friends for great physical strength and courage, and became their acknowledged leader, adjudicating their disputes, restraining their mischievousness, but also standing with them against outsiders. Like Washington, Lincoln could not tell a lie—his name was a "synonym for fair dealing"—and he thus became a respected judge in athletic contests, one whose word was never questioned. Like Washington, Lincoln controlled what Weems called the "malignant passions" of hatred and revenge by his use of reason; he had "no ears to hear horrid oaths nor obscene language"; he had "no leisure for impure passions nor criminal amours"; and he "enjoyed that purity of soul which is rightly called its sunshine."[4] Like Washington, Lincoln became a surveyor, and volunteered to help put down an Indian uprising, achieving a position of command which he hoped to parlay into a political position, and like Washington, he was unsuccessful in doing so.

It would appear that in Washington, Weems provided Lincoln with a model of self-discipline by which he could escape the wretched conditions of his early social life. When Lincoln was seven years old, his father sold his holdings in Kentucky for whiskey so as to avoid litigation, and drifted into Indiana by raft on the Ohio River, searching for a new homesite for his wife, Nancy, and their two children. They eventually settled in a sparsely populated, malarial swamp region where vegetation was so dense sunlight could barely penetrate it. The Lincolns lived the first year in an open-sided lean-to made of poles and brush, and provisioned themselves with wild game. The following year a small cabin was built and some land was cleared, but living conditions remained crude. There was no sanitation, and disease was widespread. Nancy's aunt and uncle, who joined the Lincolns and occupied the lean-to, died within eighteen months of their arrival. A neighbor woman, attended to by Nancy, also became sick and died. Shortly thereafter, Nancy herself was stricken with the disease and died. Following her death, Albert J. Beveridge reports, living conditions deteriorated even further: "For the Lincolns 1819 was a year of squalor — mostly flesh for food, unfit water, wretched cooking, no knives or forks, bare feet, bodies partly clad, filthy beds of leaves and skins."[5]

These bestial circumstances were unrelieved by social life. The people of the area were illiterate, unkempt, unruly, and superstitious. Beveridge, the Progressive, describes social relations as "loose and undisciplined," by which he meant that alcoholism, slander, assault, adultery, divorce, bigamy, and rape were quite common. Lincoln went to school briefly at age ten, but did not return until four or five years later when he learned to read. Home life and physical comfort improved markedly under the influence of his stepmother; but Lincoln did not get along well with his father, who treated him roughly and appeared to favor his stepson to Abraham. At least one family member doubted whether "Abe loved his farther [sic] Very well or not. . . . I Don't think he Did." A possible explanation for this abrasive father-son relationship is that contemporaries described Lincoln as "lazy," i.e., disdainful of farm work and bookish.[6] In any case, Lincoln left his family at the earliest opportunity, upon reaching his majority, and seldom saw them again.

If Weems's Washington provided Lincoln with a model of private virtue and self-control by which he could overcome the deadly conditions of his youth, he nevertheless remained compelled by memories of his childhood experiences. Following a campaign trip to Indiana in 1844, Lincoln attempted a poetic rendering of his boyhood home. The poem revealed not only a close association in Lincoln's mind

between love and death, but perhaps even the unconscious love of
death.

> My childhood's home I see again,
>   And sadden with the view;
> And still, as memory crowds my brain,
>   There's pleasure in it too.
>
> O memory! thou midway world,
>   'Twixt earth and paradise,
> Where things decayed and loved ones lost,
>   In dreamy shadows rise.
>
> And, freed from all that's earthly vile,
>   Seem hallowed, pure, and bright,
> Like scenes in some enchanted isle,
>   All bathed in liquid light.[7]

Lincoln set the scenes of his childhood through several stanzas
that expressed his sense of loss at the recognition of how time had
brought change and death to the familiar which now could live on
only in his memory. But for Lincoln, memory did not recall or recollect; it "hallowed"—it freed "things decayed and loved ones lost"
from "all that's earthly vile" and transformed them into "scenes in
some enchanted isle." Memory, in other words, sublimated actual
death into symbols of immortality, and regenerated actual social life
into an elysian community. It would appear that Lincoln's poetry, in
symbolically transcending death, also inevitably celebrated it.

In the second part of his 1844 poem, Lincoln expressed the view
that more horrible than death itself was the living death of insanity.
But the effect of his poetry was to belie his stated attitude toward
insanity. Here the subject was an insane man, Matthew Gentry, "a
rather bright lad" who became "furiously mad" at age nineteen, and
then "gradually settled down into harmless insanity."

> But here's an object more of dread
>   Than aught the grave contains—
> A human form with reason fled,
>   While wretched life remains.
>
> Poor Matthew! Once of genius bright,
>   A fortune-favored child—
> Now locked for aye, in mental night,
>   A haggard mad-man wild.

Through the next four stanzas Lincoln recounted a grisly scene of domestic violence. After maiming himself and attempting to kill his parents, Matthew had his arms and legs bound by frightened neighbors, to which he responded with cries of rage and maniacal laughter.

> And when at length, tho' drear and long,
> Time soothed thy fiercer woes,
> How plaintively thy mournful song
> Upon the still night rose.
>
> I've heard it oft, as if I dreamed,
> Far distant, sweet, and lone —
> The funeral dirge, it ever seemed
> Of reason dead and gone.
>
> To drink its strains, I've stole away,
> All stealthily and still,
> Ere yet the rising God of day
> Had streaked the Eastern hill.[8]

The poet did not explain why he had found Matthew's "mournful song" so compelling, but perhaps in that faint echo of Matthew's rage he heard something of his own protest against the squalor, misery, violence, and death of frontier society. Perhaps in that desperate cry could be heard his own longing for the elysian community envisioned in the first part of the poem. In any case, it is clear that if Lincoln feared the death of reason more than death itself, he nevertheless identified with Matthew's song. It is also clear that in the years preceding his return to Indiana, Lincoln's powers of rational self-mastery had been tested in full, and sometimes found wanting. Indeed, he had been compelled by the funeral dirge of reason dead and gone on more than one occasion.[9]

The characterological influence of Weems's Washington on Lincoln can only be assumed, but the intellectual influence can be demonstrated. In his book Weems presented Washington as the founder of a new political family, regenerated through the violence of a civil war and the blessings of God. Washington's paternal authority, which depended upon his renunciation of a crown at the war's conclusion, is embodied in his Farewell Address—an excellent summary of Federalist political thought—which Weems reprinted in full. Much of the remainder of the book was devoted to the embellishment of Washington's advice, in which Weems emphasized the need for obedience to the law and preservation of the Union; constant vigilance to the dangers posed by ambitious, unprincipled men; and the establishment of "true religion." All these themes found their way into Lincoln's 1838 address to the Young Men's Lyceum, a speech that can be read as a rebuttal to Washington's Farewell Address.

Speaking on "the perpetuation of our political institutions," the twenty-eight-year-old Illinois state legislator began by invoking Washington: "We find ourselves in the peaceful possession of the fairest portion of the earth, as regards extent of territory, fertility of soil, and salubrity of climate. We find ourselves under the government of a system of political institutions, conducing more essentially to the ends of civil and religious liberty, than any of which the history of former times tells us." It was the duty of contemporary Americans, Lincoln said, to transmit both the land and the political institutions "to the latest generation that fate shall permit the world to know." But how should this duty be performed? At what point would dangers arise?[10]

Dismissing the possibility of invasion from abroad, Lincoln identified three potential dangers to existing institutions. First was the increasing incidence of mob violence which threatened public order and governmental legitimacy. The remedy he proposed was that all Americans take the pledge of 1776 in behalf of the Constitution and its laws: "As the patriots of seventy-six did to the support of the Declaration of Independence, so to the support of the Constitution and Laws, let every American pledge his life, his property, and his sacred honor." While implying that the Constitution was not yet sacred, Lincoln also suggested how it might become so:"Let reverence for the laws . . . become the *political religion* of the nation; and let . . . [everyone] sacrifice unceasingly upon its altars."

A second danger envisioned by Lincoln was that of an evil genius who would destroy inherited institutions in order to gratify his ambition. Arguing that the founding fathers had preempted the field of virtuous glory, Lincoln dramatically asked whether new men of ambition would be satisfied with simply maintaining a political order created by others. He was certain they would not. While men could always be found who would be satisfied with a seat in Congress or even the presidency, these positions would never satisfy an "Alexander, a Caesar, or a Napoleon." "Towering genius disdains a beaten path," said Lincoln. "It thirsts and burns for distinction; and, if possible, it will have it, whether at the expense of emancipating slaves, or enslaving free men."

Finally, Lincoln argued that political institutions were threatened by the loss of revolutionary values. For the previous generation of Americans, the meaning of the Revolution was obvious: it could be read in the mangled limbs and scars of loved ones who had been participants in that struggle. With the passing of that generation, Lincoln said, the unity created by revolutionary passions would be lost unless those "living histories" of sacrifice could be replaced by his generation. "Reason, cold, calculating, unimpassioned reason, must furnish all the materials for our future support and defense." Lincoln did not explain how a community created by revolutionary sacrifice could be replaced by reason alone; nor did he specify how materials derived from reason could produce reverence for the Constitution. He thus ended the speech rather ambiguously, inviting his fellow citizens to partake of George Washington's immortality by upholding his advice and example: "That we remained free to the last; that we revered his name to the last; that, during his long sleep, we permitted no hostile foot to pass over or desecrate his resting place; shall be that which to learn the last trump shall awaken our WASHINGTON."

Lincoln concluded his Lyceum speech, as he began it, by invoking Washington. But this son was clearly no passive receptacle for the faith of the fathers. In addressing the major theme of the Farewell Address, the maintenance of political institutions, Lincoln implied that the Constitution was not yet sacred but could become so by adopting a political religion. In taking up Washington's admonition against the dangers of "cunning, ambitious, and unprincipled men," Lincoln seemed to project himself into the very role against which he warned his audience: a towering genius who would destroy inherited institutions rather than suffer the death of political obscurity.[11] Finally, in appealing to reason as the basis for future support, Lincoln also suggested that something more apocalyptic than respect for Washington's advice might be necessary. His final words were: "Upon these let the proud fabric of freedom rest, as the rock of its basis; and as truly as has been said of the only greater institution, *'the gates of hell shall not prevail against it.'* "

The ambiguity in Lincoln's attitude toward Washington's legacy, as reflected in his Lyceum speech, found a corresponding expression in his political career. At first he sought to distinguish himself by upholding Washington's advice and example, perhaps even consciously emulating Washington's character. After his virtuous efforts were both ignored and ridiculed, he entered a prolonged period of despondency. When he finally emerged from this brooding moratorium, he did so with a revolutionary vengeance. In the debates with Stephen A. Douglas, beginning in 1854, and again as president-elect in 1861, Lincoln reiterated themes from his Lyceum Address, including the warning against his own possible malevolence. The 1850s thus marked the emergence of a new Lincoln, one who apparently would emulate not Washington, but the cunning, ambitious tyrant against whom Washington had warned. A constant factor in both modes of identity, however, was the fear of death.

Lincoln finished his one term in the House of Representatives in 1849 a disillusioned and disappointed man. He foolishly had hoped to so distinguish himself on a national level as a virtuous leader that he might be swept back into office by popular demand—despite his pledge not to seek reelection.[12] His scrupulous critique of President Polk's justification for the Mexican War, however, had been ignored by friends and ridiculed by opponents. Public meetings in his home district branded him a traitor and, because of his insistence that Polk specify the precise "spot" where violence first occurred, "the Ranchero Spotty of one term."[13] Adding injury to insult was Lincoln's failure to receive a significant appointment in General Taylor's administration, though he had worked diligently to secure Taylor's nomination. To make matters worse, the Whigs lost their safe Seventh District seat to a Democrat in 1848.[14]

The conditions for Lincoln's disillusionment were created by his rebuke of Polk for failing to meet Washingtonian standards of virtue. In his first important speech on the House floor, Lincoln accused Polk of deception and immorality in his conduct of the war. By attempting "to prove, by telling the *truth,* what he could not prove by telling the *whole truth,*" said Lincoln, the president had forced him to examine the official justifications for the war. What he discovered was that Polk's account of where the violence first occurred was "from the beginning to end, the sheerest deception." Thus, said Lincoln, let the president answer the queries which had been put to him by the "spot" resolutions. "Let him answer, fully, fairly, and candidly. Let him answer with *facts*, and not with arguments. Let him remember he sits where Washington sat, and so remembering, let him answer, as Washington would answer."[15]

It is hard to believe that Lincoln could have expected this speech to "distinguish" him in the ways he hoped, but there can be no doubt about his seriousness. He defended his vote on an antiwar resolution by asking his unsympathetic law partner, William Herndon, "Would you have voted what you felt you knew to be a lie?" If your only alternative "is to tell the *truth* or tell a *lie*," said Lincoln, "I cannot doubt which you would do."[16] Such a passionate commitment to truth-telling suggests the degree to which Lincoln sought to emulate Weems's Washington. Washington could not tell a lie; thus Polk, who sits where Washington sat, should not be permitted to tell a lie. Lincoln could not tell a lie either, but he apparently had forgotten Weems's implicit corollary: Washington did not have any friends.

Branded a Benedict Arnold by constituents and ignored by Whig colleagues in the capital, Lincoln returned to Springfield in 1849, apparently feeling that his political career was ended. He spent much of the next five years in mourning at its passing. According to the testimony of his closest associates during this time, he became childishly dependent upon the indulgence and generosity of others; he regularly fell into periods of depression, marked by occasional manic outbursts, in which he was oblivious to everyone around him; and he was filled with self-pity and helpless rage. It was not simply political failure that sent Lincoln into this emotional decline, however; he remained a viable candidate among local party leaders who urged him to seek reelection to Congress in 1850. Rather, the public reaction to his Mexican War speech was a repudiation of the Weemsian model of political action by which greatness was promised to those who emulated Washington's private virtues. And when Lincoln finally roused himself from his brooding moratorium in 1854, he in turn repudiated the legacy of Weems's Washington.

Lincoln began his attack on Douglas's idea of popular sovereignty by quoting a poem: "Fools rush in where angels fear to tread." The virtuous Lincoln had been ignored and humiliated; now, it would appear, the foolish Lincoln—the "Ranchero Spotty of one term"— fixed upon a new field of ambition. "Our republican robe is soiled," he said, and must be repurified "in the spirit, if not the blood, of the

Revolution."[17] For the next six years, as Lincoln repeatedly challenged Douglas on the issue of slavery, he reiterated themes from his Lyceum speech, including an implicit warning against his own possible malevolence.

Identifying his personal ambitions with the cause of "the oppressed of [his] species," Lincoln attacked the constitutional system which had placed both himself and the slave in political bondage. His warning against the consequences of this enslavement echoed the one he had made twenty years earlier. When you have "extinguished" a man's soul, he said, "and placed him where the ray of hope is blown out in darkness like that which broods over the spirits of the damned; are you quite sure the demon which you have roused *will not turn and rend you?*" He warned that people's acceptance of this system of bondage made them "the fit subjects of the first cunning tyrant who arises." Then he added: "And let me tell you, all these things are prepared for you with the logic of history."[18] Lincoln said he wanted to be neither slave nor tyrant;[19] but the logic of history that damned him to political obscurity also roused a demon who would become a tyrant rather than accept that fate.

Lincoln's warnings against himself in the 1850s were well concealed. His most memorable statement of the period, the house divided speech, was a masterful stroke of political calculation and literary guile. The assertion that the government cannot endure permanently half slave and half free—that it will become "*all* one thing, or *all* the other"—implied the inevitability of civil war. In the argument that followed, Lincoln maintained that there was a national conspiracy to extend slavery into free states and reopen the African slave trade.[20] At the very least this was a gross exaggeration; at most, a deliberate disregard of the truth. The speech, however, did serve Lincoln's larger political purposes. By predicting that the nation would become either all free or all slave, he enhanced his standing among party radicals. Always a man with solid Whig credentials, Lincoln thus succeeded in maneuvering himself into a position as "the second choice of everybody" at the presidential nominating convention in 1860.

The house divided metaphor was a stroke of genius in another way as well. Diabolically clever in its political effect, the metaphor had exactly the opposite cultural effect by anticipating and disarming the assumption that Lincoln acted from demonic motives. To a Bible-reading people Lincoln presented himself not as a satanic destroyer, but as Jesus who healed with divine power. Matthew 12:22-28 provided the biblical context for understanding the cultural significance of a house divided.[21] In this passage, Jesus heals "one possessed with a devil, blind and dumb." The people are amazed, but the Pharisees accuse him of using satanic powers. Jesus responds: "Every kingdom divided against itself is brought to desolation; and every city or house divided against itself shall not stand." If Satan cast out Satan, Jesus said, he is divided against himself and his kingdom shall not stand. Lincoln's assertion that he did not expect the house to fall, but that it would cease to be divided, implied that he, like Jesus, "cast out devils by the Spirit of God." So artfully concealed was Lincoln's demonic cunning in this context it acquired meaning only as a sign that "the kingdom of God is come unto you."

Lincoln's warnings against himself as president-elect, though equally subtle, were more explicit. On his way to Washington, D.C., for the inauguration, he addressed the same question he posed in his Lyceum speech: "Shall the Union and shall the liberties of this country be preserved to the latest generation?" Once again his answer was the same: "When the people rise in masses in behalf of the Union and the liberties of their country, truly it may be said, 'the gates of hell shall not prevail against them.' "[22] He also began to articulate a theology appropriate to the political religion he called for in 1838. Invoking divine authority for the first time in his public speeches, Lincoln appealed for the assistance of the God of Washington, the God who had "never forsaken" the American people. Yet at the same time he assured his audiences that God's justice would prevail, he repeated his earlier warnings against malevolent political leadership, even explicitly identifying himself as the source of possible harm: "Should my administration prove to be a very wicked one, or what is more probable, a very foolish one, if you, the PEOPLE, are but true to yourselves and to the Constitution, there is but little harm I can do, *thank God!*"[23]

The same warning was incorporated into his inaugural address. Again, immediately following his statement that God's justice would surely prevail by the judgment of the American people, Lincoln noted that the framers of the government had given public servants "but little power for mischief." Then he said: "While the people remain patient, and true to themselves, no man, even in the presidential chair, by any extreme of wickedness or folly, can very seriously injure the government in the short space of four years.''[24] If nothing else, the sequence of these two statements would seem to indicate that in Lincoln's mind there was a close association between the attempt to establish his divine authority and his capacity for wickedness and folly. Apparently two elements of the Lyceum speech were now being combined into one; the evil genius would realize his ambition by establishing a political religion. If there were folly in such ambition, it was of the same sort Lincoln exhibited in 1854 when he said that fools rush in where angels fear to tread.

When Lincoln maneuvered the South into firing the first shot at Fort Sumter, he succeeded in replicating the conditions that provided Polk with a rationale for his Mexican adventure. After Sumter, the issue was no longer an abstract constitutional argument about secession, but overt aggression against the United States. This meant, as Stephen Douglas put it, that there could be no neutral ground between patriotism and treason. Lincoln could well understand that definition of the issue on the basis of his own experience in 1847-48. But this "Benedict Arnold" of the Seventh Illinois district now sat where Polk had sat, and answered potential criticisms of his policy as Polk would have answered them. He responded with arguments rather than with facts, attempting "to prove by telling the *truth,* what he could not prove by telling the *whole truth."* In the end, it was Lincoln, far more than Polk, who felt that "the blood of this war, like the blood of Abel, [was] crying to Heaven against him.''[25]

Following the fall of Sumter, Lincoln arrogated to himself unprecedented and virtually dictatorial powers as president.[26] His July 4, 1861, message to Congress was concerned primarily with receiving legislative sanction and public support for his assertion of these extraordinary powers. He asked to be given the "legal means for making this contest a short, and a decisive one." But his message also suggested that the conflict involved more than simply a suppression of Southern "treason." Proclaiming it "essentially a People's contest," Lincoln said that Union forces struggled to maintain the principle of the Declaration of Independence. He thought the sacrifices involved would not be prohibitive: in monetary terms, less per person than the cost of the Revolutionary War.[27]

Lincoln's references to the Revolution were not merely rhetorical formalities. From 1854 to 1861 he repeatedly had insisted that the principles of 1776 not be abandoned in the attempt to save the Union. He had even called for a sacrificial cleansing of the nation's institutions, and urged that the Declaration of Independence be readopted.[28] As president-elect, despite his legal obligations to a constitutional order that sanctioned slavery, he continued to appeal to revolutionary principles. The one new element in his preinaugural speeches was that he began to define himself as a divine instrument for preserving the legacy of 1776. At Trenton, New Jersey, on the eve of Washington's birthday, he gave a startling synthesis of his previous speeches which echoed the themes of his Lyceum Address. Appropriately, he started the speech by recalling his reading of Weems's account of the Revolution:

> I recollect thinking then, boy even though I was, that there must have been something more than common that those men struggled for. I am exceedingly anxious that that thing which they struggled for; that something even more than National Independence; that something that held out a great promise to all the people of the world to all time to come; I am exceedingly anxious that this Union, the Constitution, and the liberties of the people shall be perpetuated in accordance with the original idea for which that struggle was made and I shall be most happy indeed if I shall be an humble instrument in the hands of the Almighty, and of this, his almost chosen people for perpetuating the object of that great struggle.[29]

What is so surprising about Lincoln's many preinaugural appeals to divine authority is that prior to assuming his presidential role, he had never before made such an appeal. An admitted freethinker as a young man, and never a member of any church, Lincoln had been accused of religious infidelity during his campaign for Congress in 1846. His carefully worded response (which told no lies) denied only that he was an "open scoffer at Christianity." He did not say that he never had denied the divinity of the Scriptures, as he had been accused, but only that he never had denied their "truth." He did not say he had given up his belief in the "doctrine of necessity," but only that he had "left off" arguing it. Had Lincoln suddenly become converted between the time of his election and his inauguration? It seems rather unlikely.[30]

A more probable explanation of the change in Lincoln's theological views can be found in his statements of presidential purpose. As he left Springfield, he bid his friends farewell with ominous finality: "I now leave, not knowing when or whether ever I may return, with a task before me greater than that which rested upon Washington. Without the assistance of that Divine Being who ever attended him, I cannot succeed. With that assistance, I cannot fail." He expanded upon this thought two days later by saying "Without a name, perhaps without a reason why I should have a name, there has fallen upon me a task such as did not rest upon the Father of his country." For support in that task, he said, he looked to the American people and "that God who has never forsaken them."[31] According to Weems, Washington too had once been a man without a name, and had achieved a new legitimacy for himself and his countrymen through the divine blessing that accompanied participation in a civil war. Whether or not Lincoln had this model in mind, his invocation of the national deity produced the same effects in 1861 as it had in 1776. It provided a source of authority that transcended a disputed political tradition, and thus provided a means of justifying a fratricidal war and expiating guilt.[32]

Throughout the war, Lincoln sought to vindicate the justice of a God who, as he put it, "could have either saved or destroyed the Union without a human contest," but who nevertheless let the contest proceed. He explained the discrepancies between his stated intentions and actual events as evidence of divine power. As he said in 1864, "So true is it that man proposes, and God disposes." Lincoln had proposed a short and decisive contest in which he would seem morally blameless for defending the Union, and the Constitution would be sanctified through some small amount of sacrifice. He proposed only to save the Union, as he told Horace Greeley in a well-known 1862 letter, not to either save or destroy slavery. But in saving the Union he found it necessary to destroy slavery—just as he found it necessary to resupply Sumter to avoid "national destruction." "God alone can claim it," said Lincoln. "If God now wills the removal of a great wrong, . . . impartial history will find therein new cause to attest and revere the justice and goodness of God."[33] Though men could recognize what happened in the past, they could not claim to have directed it, and therein lay a source of hope for the future. For therein lay proof, as Lincoln said in 1865, that the Almighty has purposes of his own.

Hope for the future depended not only on recognizing God's justice, but also on re-creation of the past. If Lincoln gained his authority in part by controlling events so as to make them appear beyond the control of anyone but God, he also gained it by interpreting the meaning of events so as to provide a source of political regeneration. His most authoritative interpretation of the war's meaning was the Gettysburg Address, the best-known speech in American history. The theme of the speech was that of sacrificial death and rebirth leading to immortality. The Civil War, he said was a test of whether this or any nation born of revolution and dedicated to revolutionary ideals could survive. By their sacrifices, Union forces had preserved the ideals of 1776. As a result, their immortality was assured. At the same time, their noble action provided an inspiring example to others so that the nation might be founded anew, and its immortality assured also.

The speech was a perfect synthesis of secular and religious themes. In a cultural milieu that viewed the war as divine punishment for the sin of slavery, Lincoln offered an interpretation that promised atonement and deliverance from sin. Since the "wages of sin is death," the war threatened to end the life of a nation just as it actually inflicted death upon the citizens. But the sacrifices of those who were without sin themselves, who nobly gave up their lives that the nation might live, promised to redeem the sins of the fathers. By the common recognition of their sacrifice, which was secured by Lincoln himself at Gettysburg, a new spiritual community was created in which the nation might be reborn to a life everlasting. That Lincoln was Paul before he was Christ helped to ensure that his own death would be properly interpreted.

The Gettysburg Address was directly responsive to the major themes of the Lyceum speech. In 1838 Lincoln called upon his fellow citizens to take the pledge of 1776 in behalf of the Constitution so that reverence for the laws could become the political religion of the nation. At Gettysburg he provided the sacramental rite by which this could be accomplished without acknowledging any discrepancy between the Declaration of Independence and the Constitution. By interpreting the war as a reenactment of the struggle of 1776, he transformed a dispute over the meaning of the Constitution into a regenerative act. And by asking the people to dedicate themselves to this struggle, he was in effect requiring that they take the pledge of

1776 without seeming to do so. In the process, his reason presided over events on the battlefield so as to transform death and destruction into symbols of immortality, thereby providing new "living histories" of revolutionary sacrifice. Never have the dead been better loved.

Lincoln's remarks at Gettysburg also recall his warning against a "towering genius." In the earlier speech he raised the question of whether new men of talent and ambition, who would inevitably come along after the Revolutionary generation, could gratify their ruling passions simply by maintaining an edifice erected by others. His answer was prophetic: most certainly they cannot. It was Lincoln who fulfilled his own prophecy; for by appearing to defend and maintain the Union, he actually was transforming it. By refounding the Union on the basis of the Declaration of Independence, Lincoln put himself in Washington's place as the father of his country.

Lincoln was always careful to emulate the style of Washington, especially his modesty and humility. During his early years, he apparently modeled himself on the father of his country. On his way to Washington, D.C., to assume the presidency, he used the first president as the standard by which to assess the task that lay before him. Once in office, he invoked Washington's legacy as a source of authority. Yet after proclaiming Washington's birthday as a national day of celebration in 1862, to be marked by public readings of the Farewell Address, Lincoln made virtually no further reference to Washington. It was as if Washington had suddenly ceased to exist. And in a way he had: the proclamation of his birthday as a national holiday signified his apotheosis, and thus his removal from the seat of authority—a place thereafter to be occupied by Lincoln himself.

There are several intriguing aspects to Lincoln's statement that his dream of the dead president haunted him like Banquo's ghost. First is the identification suggested by Lincoln between himself and Macbeth. He had long been an admirer of this Shakespearean tragedy; telegraph operators often noticed him carrying a worn copy of the play, and he had written in 1863, "I think nothing equals Macbeth."[34] Following his triumphant visit to Richmond in April 1865, he had read aloud from the play, dwelling at length on a particular passage: "The lines after the murder of Duncan, when the new king falls a prey to moral torment, were dramatically dwelt on. Now and then he paused to expatiate on how exact a picture Shakespeare here gives of a murderer's mind when, the dark deed achieved, its perpetrator already envies his victim's calm sleep."[35] Lincoln's observers, by naively assuming that he was making a comparison here between the Confederacy and Macbeth,[36] have overlooked the more plausible parallel between Lincoln and Macbeth: both were fascinating characters, capable of great goodness but driven by ambition to defy the gods; men entrapped by "necessity" in a process of violence, but who had the intelligence to foresee the consequences of their acts, and the sensitivity to accept the burdens of guilt that lesser men might have ignored.

The obvious similarity between Duncan and George Washington strengthens the assumption that Lincoln saw himself as Macbeth. When Macbeth is contemplating the assassination of Duncan, he considers the reasons for not going through with it. He is, after all, both Duncan's kinsman and subject. "Besides," Macbeth says, "this Duncan/Hath borne his faculties so meek, hath been/So clear in his great office, that his virtues/Will plead like angels . . . And pity. . . Shall blow the horrid deed in every eye,/That tears shall drown the wind." By comparison, Macbeth has only his "vaulting ambition" to sustain him. There was, in addition, the inescapable implication of guilt in Lincoln's statement that his dream haunted him like Banquo's ghost: the ghost is but a projection of Macbeth's guilt. More important, in terms of understanding Lincoln's anxieties, Banquo's ghost is also a reminder of the witches' prophecy that it is Banquo's paternal authority, rather than Macbeth's, that is to be perpetuated. But if Lincoln, like Macbeth, feared that the monuments created by his bloody hand would not last, his anxieties must have been calmed somewhat by the other literary reference he recalled as he told about the dream of the dead president: the biblical story of Jacob's dream.

In telling about his dream, Lincoln said, "After it occurred, the first time I opened the Bible, strange as it may appear, it was at the twenty-eighth chapter of Genesis, which relates the wonderful dream Jacob had."[37] The wonder of Jacob's dream was that the God of Abraham and Isaac appeared to him in it and promised that Jacob's paternal line would be extended and blessed, even though he was not the legitimate heir. Born holding onto Esau's heel, Jacob had forced Esau to relinquish his birthright as the firstborn son, and succeeded in deceiving their father, Isaac, so that the father's blessing, rightfully Esau's, was given to Jacob instead. Jacob's dream held out the promise of immortality to Jacob and his descendants, though Jacob lived in fear that Esau would someday seek his revenge.[38]

A thematic link between Banquo's ghost and Jacob's dream is provided not simply by guilt over acts of usurpation, but also by anxiety about legitimacy and fear that symbols of immortality might be destroyed. It was a theme that Lincoln well understood. If he could view himself as Macbeth, tortured by guilt for his crimes, he could also recall himself as Banquo, the loyal and virtuous subject. If he could conceive of himself as Jacob, the unscrupulous pretender, he could also imagine himself as Esau, the firstborn and legitimate heir. In other words, if he could see himself as the cunning tyrant against whom Washington had warned, he could also recollect his identity as Weems's Washington, upholder of virtue and constitutional order. The fool had entered fields where angels feared to tread; but, in the end, the "better angels" of his nature seemed to prevail.[39]

It was with "malice toward none and charity for all" that Lincoln wanted to bring the war to an end. He proposed to end it, as he said in 1864, by the "Christian principle of forgiveness on terms of repentance."[40] His Second Inaugural Address, which combined pity for all with compassion for the guilty, transformed his own guilt into a doctrine by which all might be forgiven. Whether or not Lincoln intended to cast himself in the role of Christ, his contemporaries were more than willing to draw the parallels. By his death, Lincoln became the savior of the republic, one who, by his sacrifice and atonement, redeemed the sins of the fathers and gave to the nation a new life, a life everlasting.

NOTES

1. Ward Hill Lamon, *Recollections of Abraham Lincoln, 1847-1865*, ed. Dorothy Lamon Teillard, 2nd ed. (Washington, D.C., 1911), pp. 116-17.

2. Ibid., pp. 117-18.

3. Mason Locke Weems, *The Life of Washington*, ed. Marcus Cunliffe (Cambridge, Mass.: Harvard University Press, 1962), p. 5.

4. The quotes are from Weems describing Washington. Corresponding descriptions of Lincoln from contemporary sources are cited by Albert J. Beveridge, *Abraham Lincoln, 1809-1858*, 2 vols. (New York: Houghton Mifflin, 1928), vol. 1, chs. 2 and 3.

5. Ibid., 1: 57.

6. Ibid., 1: 51, 54n.

7. Roy P. Basler, ed., Marion Dolores Pratt and Lloyd A. Dunlap, asst. eds., *The Collected Works of Abraham Lincoln*, 9 vols. (New Brunswick, N.J.: Rutgers University Press, 1953-55), 1: 378.

8. Ibid., 1: 384.

9. The most significant of these apparently occurred early in 1841 when Lincoln broke his engagement with Mary Todd. At the time Lincoln was Whig floor leader in the Illinois House and had proven himself to be an effective legislative manager. For six weeks, beginning with the new year, Lincoln attended irregularly and failed to exercise leadership on key party issues. His friends became so concerned about his depression, they removed razors and knives from his room, fearing he might commit suicide. Beveridge, *Abraham Lincoln*, 1: 288-97. Since the broken engagement coincided exactly with the departure of Joshua Speed, with whom Lincoln shared a bed, Charles B. Strozier has suggested that Lincoln's behavior was due to unconscious fears about his sexual identity. *Lincoln's Quest for Union: Public and Private Meanings* (New York: Basic Books, 1982), p. 44. Another possible explanation is that, following the pattern of his mother and sister, and perhaps Ann Rutledge, Lincoln feared he could love Mary Todd only if she were dead, and thus transformed into an object to be hallowed in memory. This possibility is implicit in Lincoln's correspondence with Speed on the subject of marriage. Basler, *Collected Works of Lincoln*, 1: 265, 267-68. See also Dwight G. Anderson, *Abraham Lincoln: The Quest for Immortality* (New York: Alfred A. Knopf, 1982), pp. 90-91.

10. Basler, *Collected Works of Lincoln*, 1: 108-16.

11. Edmund Wilson was the first to recognize the possible significance of Lincoln's warning against a "towering genius." He wrote: "It is evident that Lincoln has projected himself into the role against which he is warning" his audience. *Patriotic Gore: Studies in the Literature of the American Civil War* (New York: Oxford University Press, 1966), p. 108. Wilson's assumption has been challenged recently by George B. Forgie (see chapter 10 of this volume and *Patricide in the House Divided: A Psychological Interpretation of Lincoln and His Age* [New York: W. W. Norton, 1979]), and other writers following his lead. Forgie argues that since Lincoln so closely resembled the ambitious genius he described, "only a man completely unconscious of what he was doing would have presented it" (p. 85). Using the concept of projection in a psychoanalytical sense, he speculates that Lincoln created the tyrant "out of undesirable wishes he could not recognize in himself" which he "expelled and then reified . . . into the image of the bad son" (p. 86). Strozier, *Lincoln's Quest for Union*, also adopts this interpretation (p. 60). Forgie concludes that Stephen A. Douglas was the "bad son" of the Lyceum speech whom Lincoln was psychologically predisposed to recognize and destroy (pp. 250, 262). The basic problem with this interpretation is that by assuming that Lincoln's career was one of "lifelong filiopiety" (p. 85), Forgie overlooks the transformation of Lincoln's political identity in the 1850s. See Anderson, *Abraham Lincoln: The Quest for Immortality*, pp. 99-122.

12. Basler, *Collected Works of Lincoln*, 1: 431.

13. Debate among historians about the actual political effects of Lincoln's Mexican War speech has obscured the more important issue of how Lincoln personally responded to these attacks. Clearly, William Herndon's view that Lincoln committed political suicide with his antiwar speech is incorrect in all respects. See Gabor Boritt, "A Question of Political Suicide? Lincoln's Opposition to the Mexican War," *Journal of the Illinois State Historical Society* 67 (1974): 79-100. While adopting a solid Whig position on the war, Lincoln was disappointed that his speech was not more widely circulated: "He had tried to distinguish himself by speaking up in Congress. His constituents had not rejected his message: they simply had not heard it at all." Mark E. Neely, Jr., "Lincoln and the Mexican War: An Argument by Analogy," *Civil War History* 24 (1978): 24. Beveridge is usually blamed for the assumption that Lincoln's antiwar position was politically ruinous. See Boritt, p. 83, and Paul Findley, *A. Lincoln: The Crucible of Congress* (New York: Crown Publishers, 1979), p. 217. Unlike his critics, however, Beveridge does offer an explanation for Lincoln's failure to seek political office in the early 1850s by presenting a picture of his psychological devastation in the face of perceived political failure. Beveridge, *Abraham Lincoln*, 1: 493 and ch. 9.

14. Basler, *Collected Works of Lincoln*. 1: 467-68, 474; Beveridge, *Abraham Lincoln*, 1: 442, 493. This outcome may have been personally embarrassing to Lincoln, but it did not diminish his standing among Illinois Whigs. See Findley, *A. Lincoln*, pp. 212-16.

15. Basler, *Collected Works of Lincoln*, 1: 439.

16. Ibid., 1: 446-47.

17. Ibid., 2: 265, 270.

18. Ibid., 2: 382-83, 3: 95.

19. In an undated and otherwise unidentified fragment from the 1850s, Lincoln expressed what he called "my idea of democracy": "As I would not be a *slave*, so I would not be a *master.*" Ibid., 2: 532. This statement would appear to reflect the same moral ambiguity found in the Lyceum Address.

20. Ibid., 2: 461-68.

21. I am indebted to Charles Strozier for calling this passage to my attention, though he does not make this interpretation of its significance.

22. Basler, *Collected Works of Lincoln*, 4: 193-94.

23. Ibid., 4: 199, 204, 220-21, 226, 197.

24. Ibid., 4: 260.

25. Ibid., 1: 432, 439. Lincoln's explanation of the circumstances surrounding the Sumter expedition appears to be less than candid. The best account is Richard N. Current, *Lincoln and the First Shot* (Philadelphia: Lippincott, 1963), which concludes that Lincoln maneuvered the South into having either to accept defeat or initiate violence, and that he did so with the expectation that violence was probable.

26. These included the following: calling out the state militias and asking for volunteers without congressional authorization; proclaiming a blockade of Southern ports, an act of war; increasing the strength of regular armed forces and spending federal funds without legislative approval; sus-

pending the writ of habeas corpus. See Richard M. Pious, *The American Presidency* (New York: Basic Books, 1979), pp. 57-58.

27. Basler, *Collected Works of Lincoln*, 4: 431-32, 438-39.

28. Lincoln's Peoria speech of October 1854 set forth the essentials of his position. See ibid., 2: 247-83.

29. Ibid., 4: 236.

30. Ibid., 1: 382; Lincoln did mention to Noah Brooks in 1864 "a process of crystallization" going on in his mind immediately following his election in 1860, but he distinguished between this process and a "change of heart." See F. B. Carpenter, *Six Months at the White House with Abraham Lincoln* (New York: Hurd and Houghton, 1866), p. 189.

31. Basler, *Collected Works of Lincoln*, 4: 192, 204.

32. The Continental Congress almost officially adopted the Puritan Covenant in 1775. See Perry Miller, "From the Covenant to the Revival," in *Religion in American Life*, ed. James Ward Smith and A. Leland Jamison, 4 vols. (Princeton, N.J.: Princeton University Press, 1961), vol. 1, *The Shaping of American Religion*, pp. 322-69. The covenant served to justify fratricide and allay the "guilt and danger and distress" that the Congress in 1776 said "frequently overwhelmed" those who attempted to overturn a country's constitution. See Bernard Bailyn, *The Ideological Origins of the American Revolution* (Cambridge, Mass.: Harvard University Press, 1967), p. 154.

33. Basler, *Collected Works of Lincoln*, 5: 403-4; 7: 301; 5: 388; 7: 282.

34. Ibid., 6: 392.

35. Charles Adolphe de Pineton, Marquis de Chambrun, *Impressions of Lincoln and the Civil War: A Foreigner's Account* (New York: Random House, 1952), p. 83.

36. For example, see Benjamin P. Thomas, *Abraham Lincoln: A Biography* (New York: Alfred A. Knopf, 1952), p. 512.

37. Lamon, *Recollections of Abraham Lincoln*, p. 115.

38. Genesis 28:12-17; 32:11.

39. Lincoln referred to "better angels" at the close of his First Inaugural Address: "The mystic chords of memory . . . will yet swell the chorus of the Union, when again touched, as surely they will be, by the better angels of our nature." Basler, *Collected Works of Lincoln*, 4: 271.

40. Ibid., 7: 169.

Commentary on "Quest for Immortality"

ROBERT V. BRUCE

Professor Anderson's paper, and his book too, make fascinating reading. He writes with fervor, sonority, and frequently with eloquence. His imaginative ingenuity, if it were to be construed as he construes Lincoln, might be called demonic cunning or diabolical cleverness. Yet his argument does not convince me. Of course, inferences about the unavowed inner motives of a man long dead are not subject to proof or disproof. But they are subject to the test of Occam's razor. Even if Anderson's thesis fits the known facts, is it the only one that does? If not, is it the simplest and most straightforward of the possible explanations? Or must it twist and turn, patch and embroider, shift its ground and trifle with its terminology?

Unfortunately I see more examples of such tortuosity in Anderson's paper than I can adduce in some brief comments. But here are some specimens. The paper begins with Lincoln's reported dream of finding an assassinated president in the East Room. Although Anderson reads into many of Lincoln's other statements something different from or even opposite to their surface meaning, he shifts his ground here to accept without question Lincoln's contention that he could not have been both observer and victim. Yet Lincoln could well have been simply reassuring his wife and himself. Besides, in dreaming of or trying to conceive of our own deaths, we are necessarily the observers as well as the observed. Nevertheless Anderson assumes that the dead president in the dream was not Lincoln, that "the only other possibility suggested by the contextual evidence" was George Washington, and that Lincoln was the assassin. He then asserts that Washington was Lincoln's "imaginary father." But perhaps the dream corpse was that of Lincoln's real father, whom he imagined to be president. Perhaps it was William Henry Harrison or Zachary Taylor. More likely it was Lincoln himself, despite his anxious denial. These

275

are suppositions no more farfetched than Anderson's. To choose the most bizarre of several possible interpretations because it fits the thesis, and then to use it as evidence for the thesis, is at least semicircular reasoning.

A key element in Anderson's conjectures is Lincoln's Lyceum Address of 1838. In analyzing it, Anderson makes some puzzling statements. For example, he finds it strange that Lincoln did not "specify how materials derived from reason could produce reverence for the Constitution." I fail to see how one would go about "specifying" such a process, or why reverence cannot be founded on reason. But Anderson uses this rhetorical twist to find some otherwise unspecified ambiguity in Lincoln's summons to emulate Washington. Here and elsewhere, furthermore, Anderson makes much of Lincoln's call for a "political religion," investing Lincoln's phrase with a far broader meaning than the rather commonplace one warranted by the context, namely, adherence to legal process rather than mob action. Anderson also states that Lincoln "suggested that something more apocalyptic than respect for Washington's advice might be necessary." Lincoln, however, actually said that "general intelligence, sound morality, and, in particular, a reverence for the constitution and laws," would be entirely sufficient. These things do not seem apocalyptic, though a cynic might consider them improbable. Such contortions and acrobatics are unnecessarily strenuous, it seems to me, as against taking the speech simply as the high-flown rhetoric of an aspiring young politician.

The crux of Anderson's analysis of the Lyceum speech, however, is his conjecture that in warning against a "towering genius" who might pull down the republic to win greater distinction, Lincoln was revealing his own long-term contingency plan. I concede the possibility that the young Lincoln momentarily fantasized himself in that role. We all have our daydreams, and playing Napoleon in fancy might well have been among those of an ambitious young political leader. But such a notion in Lincoln's mind, if he ever entertained it, seems far more likely to have been a vagrant fantasy than a serious game plan. Besides, if Lincoln had been serious about the idea, he would not have deliberately betrayed himself, as Anderson says he did repeatedly over many years. I note also that in his book Anderson leans heavily on Lincoln's Lyceum remark, as to the glory of Washington, that "the game is caught; and I believe it is true, that with the catching, ends the pleasures of the chase." Yet Anderson himself concedes that until his political doldrums more than ten years later, Lincoln continued to engage vigorously in that chase. So Lincoln evidently did not, in fact, share the attitude he warned against in others, at least not in 1838 or for years afterward.

But time propels me to the bottom line, which Anderson properly defined in his remark that if his thesis seems "cryptic, eccentric, and immodest," that shortcoming is outweighed by its "explanatory utility." The problem is that most of what he purports to explain never happened. Anderson sees Lincoln as "presiding over the destruction of Washington's Union." I have always supposed that it was Jefferson Davis who presided over the destruction of the Union, and Abraham Lincoln who presided over its restoration. The Union, after all, was pulled down before Lincoln became president, and so far as I am aware, his only part in provoking its dismantling was in being a Republican and getting elected president. I would suggest, therefore, that Professor Anderson now investigate whether Ruffin, Yancey, Rhett, and other redhot secessionists also belonged to the Mason Weems fan club. As to the resultant war, Anderson says that Lincoln "had proposed a short and decisive contest" in which the Constitution would be "sanctified through some small amount of sacrifice." What is Anderson's authority for this statement? Civil War newspapers would have headed it "Important if True."

Was Lincoln a tyrant, as Anderson asserts? If Lincoln did, like the evil genius of his Lyceum Address, belong "to the family of the lion," it was surely as a pussycat. What sort of tyrant would so meekly resign himself to being deposed by popular vote in a wartime election, for example? To explain the suspension of habeas corpus, the enlargement of the regular army, the proclamation of a blockade, and the irregular disbursement of modest sums for military needs in time of massive and unprecedented rebellion, is it really simplest to suppose that Lincoln, deranged by a diet of Weems, venerated Washington so much that he murdered him posthumously with an overdose of apotheosis? I think not.

Despite my doubts, as I said to begin with, I cannot prove Professor Anderson wrong. Perhaps Lincoln did secretly harbor all the notions ascribed to him. If Professor Anderson chooses to believe that, I have no objection. In matters intellectual there are many possible worlds. In the worlds of Freud and Anderson, as in that of

Gilbert and Sullivan, things are seldom what they seem. I happen to feel more at home in a world where things are often what they seem. Fortunately, thanks to Washington and others, this is a free country, so we may all take our choice.

Commentary on "Quest for Immortality"

MARCUS CUNLIFFE

Several aspects of Dwight Anderson's speculations put him in good company among psychohistorians (though for skeptics such as Jacques Barzun, there is of course no such thing as "good company" in the realm of psychohistory).[1] Thus, recent scholarship has emphasized the symbolic prominence of George Washington, as exemplary parent and emblem of union for the American republic. Garry Wills's *Cincinnatus* (1984) is an instance of such work.

Parson Weems as biographer (or promoter-iconographer) of Washington is attracting more attention, and more favorable attention, than ever before. Wills notes how spiritedly in Weems's anecdotes the imaginary and the imaginative are interwoven. Daniel Boorstin, Michael Kammen, and Lawrence J. Friedman are among historians who have discussed the role of Mason Locke Weems in establishing the folkloric lineaments of George Washington. Weems and Washington receive sophisticated treatment, too, within a literary-philosophical context, in Jay Fliegelman's *Prodigals and Pilgrims* (1982), which analyzes eighteenth-century resistances to patriarchal authority.[2]

Links between Washington and Lincoln have long been perceived. Their rivalrous preeminence is apparent from a succession of polls of great presidents, in which these two are nearly always in front of everyone else, but in which Lincoln has displaced Washington as number one—the "first American," as J. R. Lowell called him in 1865, in a somewhat different sense of primacy from Henry Lee's tribute to Washington as "first in war, first in peace, and first in the hearts of his countrymen." The two men were paired not long ago in a twenty-cent postage stamp commemorating the National Archives: Lincoln was a man in black with a stove-pipe hat, Washington a featureless profile in pure white. The Washington-Lincoln connection has been ingeniously argued in George B. Forgie's *Patricide in the*

House Divided (1979) as well as in his paper in the present volume (Chapter 10).

Moreover, Forgie and others, in stressing the fierce ambition and yet self-doubts of Lincoln, have followed Edmund Wilson in attaching great significance to the Springfield Lyceum Address of 1838, in which (it has been contended) Lincoln unwittingly reveals his own dreams of despotic glory.[3]

So Dwight Anderson is not a lone heretic but a contributor to a richly intriguing debate about the psychological motivations of Lincoln and his generation. I am in broad sympathy with psychobiographical inquiries; and Lincoln is a man of such complexity, active in an era of such tormenting difficulty, that it seems not only valuable but almost essential to consider him from all possible angles. A recurrent question about psychohistory is whether it imposes a monocausal or otherwise rigid interpretation upon the phenomenon it studies. Mr. Anderson claims his theories do not depend on any specific psychological approach. That being so, there may be a further question: does a particular interpretation pay adequate regard to other types of evidence that may weaken it even if they do not refute it? On this latter score I do have some doubts about Dwight Anderson's assertions. A glance at two examples of historical context may serve to make the general point. They concern, first, the Springfield Lyceum speech and, second, the evidence for believing that a reading of Weems was crucial for Lincoln's view of himself vis-à-vis George Washington.

In recreating the context of the 1838 Lyceum Address, it is important to remember what David Donald pointed out in an influential essay in the 1950s: that Lincoln was not merely a busy politician but a convinced and enthusiastic Whig politician, who supported one Whig presidential candidate after another, starting with Henry Clay in 1832, until the demise of the party in the 1850s. In Whig doctrine, Andrew Jackson was a reckless and overweening autocrat. We may think the charge exaggerated. But there is no reason to doubt that Clay and his companions took it seriously. In an 1832 Senate speech, Clay said of Jackson: "We are in the midst of a revolution, . . . tending rapidly towards a total change of the pure republican character of the Government, and to the concentration of all power in the hands of one man." Gov. Erastus Root of New York, writing to congratulate Clay, asked: "When will the mad career of the 'military chieftain' be checked?" Seconding Clay, John C. Calhoun said: "The Senator from

Kentucky read a striking passage from Plutarch, descriptive of Caesar forcing himself, sword in hand, into the treasury of the Roman commonwealth. We are in the same stage of our political revolution." The man who tried to assassinate Jackson in 1835 thought of the president as a usurper or false king. Nathaniel Beverley Tucker's fantasy novel *The Partisan Leader* (1836) was produced by a Southern Whig anxious to prevent the election of Martin Van Buren to succeed Jackson. He projects American politics into the late 1840s: Van Buren has been president for twelve years, and intends to perpetuate his rule; the White House is known as the nation's "palace."[4]

Why not suppose, then, that the Whig Abraham Lincoln, invited to speak in Springfield early in the first term of the Democrat Van Buren (which some regarded as in effect Jackson's third term), naturally had "King Andrew" in mind? No doubt he had other things, too, on his mind, including possibly his own political aspirations, and a wish to make an impression as a deep and cultivated thinker, elevated above crude partisanship, by serving up the conventional wisdom of the decade with the requisite allusions—including Caesar, and also Napoleon Bonaparte, who had such a compelling if ambiguous hold upon the American imagination. Perhaps Jackson, not Washington, was Lincoln's unconscious as well as conscious role model? According to the artist Charles Alfred Barry, who did a life portrait of Lincoln in 1860, his sitter's head was markedly "Jacksonian," and Lincoln thought the portrait a "true likeness."[5]

A possible implication is that by the time Lincoln was a man, George Washington had ceased to exercise any *vital* influence upon American imaginations. Perhaps his renown was too amorphously large to stimulate people or make them feel he could be challenged. In Emerson's words, "Every hero becomes a bore at last . . . 'Damn George Washington!'" was (he said) one understandable reaction. Perhaps the truly challenging figures for the Lincoln age-cohort were of the generation or two between his and Washington's—Jackson, Webster, Calhoun, Clay, Zachary Taylor, and maybe Polk. For Lincoln, Clay was "my *beau ideal* of a statesman," whose political wreck may have been for Lincoln more immediately moving and instructive than the dignified triumphs of the Pater Patriae.

What then of Weems? The direct evidence is confined to a speech made by President-elect Lincoln to the New Jersey legislature, on his zigzag railroad journey from Springfield to the nation's capital: "May

I be pardoned if, upon this occasion, I mention that away back in my childhood, the earliest days of my being able to read, I got hold of a small book, such a one as few of the younger members have ever seen, 'Weem's [*sic*] Life of Washington.' I remember all the accounts there given of the battle fields and struggles for the liberties of the country, and none fixed themselves upon my imagination so deeply as the struggle here at Trenton, New Jersey."

There is no other recorded mention of Weems in Lincoln's letters and speeches. There are references to Lincoln's encounter with Weems in Albert J. Beveridge's biography, based on the testimony of Lincoln acquaintances taken by Herndon and others. The reliability of such testimony is open to doubt; it is in any case fragmentary; and it raises the possibility that Lincoln, who was slow in learning to read, did not come across Weems until he was twenty years old—not exactly the "child" alluded to in his New Jersey remarks, or in Anderson's paper.[6]

Consider again the circumstances of this address. Lincoln is making the whistle-stop journey of a little over two weeks, in February 1861, through parts of Illinois, Ohio, New York, New Jersey, and Pennsylvania. Again and again he repeats a slightly labored, ingratiating joke about his own unhandsomeness, contrasted with the beauty of the ladies who have turned out to see him ("I have the best of the bargain"). Again and again he admits deprecatingly that many or most of the people in each audience voted for another candidate. Throughout he is the politician, feeling his way, by turns maladroit and canny. His longest speech, curiously unstirring, is in Pittsburgh, on the subject of a protective tariff. He is at pains to accept invitations from state legislatures, in Albany and Harrisburg as well as Trenton. He seizes every opportunity to appeal to the local pride of his listeners. "Good old Cincinnati" is all he can manage in that city. In Albany he speaks of his "diffidence" and "awe" in face of "the history of this great state, the renown of those great men who have stood here." In Philadelphia, Lincoln pays tribute to Independence Hall, "the consecrated walls" where "the Declaration of Independence was framed, and the Constitution." He addressed no fewer than six audiences, briefly or more substantially, in various parts of Pennsylvania, in one day—February 22, 1861. Only once did he mention that it happened to be Washington's birthday; and that was apparently in response to someone else's allusion to the date and its significance.

In this context of political activity, the mention of Weems begins to look rather workaday, and perfunctory. What can Lincoln find to say about Trenton that is more apropos than the "good old Cincinnati" type of remark? His memory fishes up the assault on Trenton made by Washington—the most noteworthy occurrence in the town's history up to 1861, and an event of the Revolutionary War familiar to everyone. Why speak of Weems? Probably because that was where Lincoln had first read of the battle. Perhaps too, out of a politician's instinct to be anecdotal and folksy; to disclaim any but the most basic knowledge of past history. In Trenton, he claims to have been struck by how the struggle for liberty occurred *there*: "I recollect thinking . . . , boy . . . though I was, that there must have been something more than common that those men struggled for." Next day, in Philadelphia, he uses the new locale for the same purpose: "I have often inquired of myself, what great principle . . . it was that kept this Confederacy so long together" (again, universal liberty).[7]

In other words, Lincoln psychobiography must also take into account the day-to-day imperatives of his trade, and the external circumstances of the gathering crisis of the Union. That is not the entire story. The commanding stature of the founding fathers, sectional antagonisms, the fear of disunion, penitential religious angst (heightened by the persistence of slavery), covert doubts as to the soundness of the democratic creed: all have a part in the story, together with elements in Lincoln's individual makeup. To bring them into a satisfactory relationship is a tall order. Dwight Anderson has commendably not allowed the problems to intimidate him. But in at least two cases—those of the Springfield Lyceum Address and the Weems life of Washington—the interpretative burden seems too great for the evidence to carry.

NOTES

1. Jacques Barzun, "The Muse and Her Doctors," *American Historical Review* 77 (Feb. 1972): 36–64; David E. Stannard, *Shrinking History: On Freud and the Failure of Psychohistory* (New York: Oxford University Press, 1980); and for a well-balanced selection, Robert J. Brugger, ed., *Our Selves / Our Past: Psychological Approaches to American History* (Baltimore: Johns Hopkins University Press, 1981).

2. Garry Wills, *Cincinnatus: George Washington and the Enlightenment* (Garden City: N.J.: Doubleday, 1984); Daniel J. Boorstin, "The Mythologizing of George Washington," in *The Americans: The National Experience* (New York:

Random House, 1965); Michael Kammen, *A Season of Youth: The American Revolution and the Historical Imagination* (New York: Oxford University Press, 1978); Lawrence J. Friedman, "The Flawless American," in his *Inventors of the Promised Land* (New York: Knopf, 1975); Jay Fliegelman, *Prodigals and Pilgrims: The American Revolution against Patriarchal Authority, 1750-1800* (Cambridge: Cambridge University Press, 1982). See also Marcus Cunliffe, *George Washington: Man and Monument*, rev. ed. (New York: Mentor, 1982); Mason Locke Weems, *The Life of Washington*, ed. Marcus Cunliffe (Cambridge, Mass.: Harvard University Press, 1962); the same author's review article on Wills's *Cincinnatus* in the *New York Review of Books*, Oct. 12, 1984; and Barry Schwartz, *George Washington: The Making of an American Symbol* (New York: Free Press, 1987).

3. Edmund Wilson, *Patriotic Gore: Studies in the Literature of the American Civil War* (New York: Oxford University Press, 1962); George B. Forgie, *Patricide in the House Divided: A Psychological Interpretation of Lincoln and His Age* (New York: W. W. Norton, 1979), pp. 83-87; David B. Davis, *Homicide in American Fiction: A Study in Social Values* (Ithaca, N.Y.: Cornell University Press, 1957), pp. 237-90; Marcus Cunliffe, *Soldiers and Civilians: The Martial Spirit in America, 1775-1865* (Boston: Little, Brown, 1968), pp. 392-404.

4. David Donald, "Abraham Lincoln: Whig in the White House" (1959) in his *Lincoln Reconsidered: Essays on the Civil War* (2d ed., enlarged; New York: Vintage, 1960), ch. 10; Marcus Cunliffe, *American Presidents and the Presidency* (New York: McGraw-Hill, 1986), pp. 149-56. The nationwide controversy over the "expunging resolution," finally accomplished by Sen. Thomas Hart Benton in January 1837, should also be taken into account in assessing Lincoln's warning to the young men of Springfield, Illinois.

5. On Barry's portrait see Harold Holzer, Gabor S. Boritt, and Mark E. Neely, Jr., *The Lincoln Image: Abraham Lincoln and the Popular Print* (New York: Scribner's, 1984), pp. 50-56. On Lincoln, Van Buren, and the Lyceum speech see Major L. Wilson, "Lincoln and Van Buren in the Steps of the Fathers: Another Look at the Lyceum Address," *Civil War History* 29 (1983): 197-211.

6. Roy P. Basler, ed., Marion Dolores Pratt and Lloyd A. Dunlap, asst. eds., *The Collected Works of Abraham Lincoln*, 9 vols. (New Brunswick, N.J.: Rutgers University Press, 1953-55), 4: 235-36; Albert J. Beveridge, *Abraham Lincoln, 1809-1858*, 2 vols. (New York: Houghton Mifflin, 1928), 1: 76.

7. Basler, *Collected Works of Lincoln*, 4: 191-245. The Pittsburgh speech is reproduced in ibid., 4: 210-15. Richard Cohen's humorous column for Sept. 14, 1984 (*Washington Post*, p. A23), takes the form of a memo of advice to the Democratic presidential candidate Walter Mondale on how to improve his campaign "message." One suggestion is to "pose on a battlefield. Most of the European ones have already been used by Reagan, so choose an American one—maybe Trenton. That way you could identify yourself with George Washington, point out that the battle took place on Christmas Eve and hit the religious angle as well. Also don't forget that Trenton is in New Jersey, a swing state with 17 electoral votes."

CHAPTER 10

LINCOLN'S TYRANTS

GEORGE B. FORGIE

We are striving to maintain the government and institutions of
our fathers, to enjoy them ourselves, and transmit them to our
children and our children's children forever.
—Abraham Lincoln, August 31, 1864

Many free countries have lost their liberty; and *ours may* lose hers;
but if she shall, be it my proudest plume, not that I was the *last*
to desert, but that I *never* deserted her.
—Abraham Lincoln, December 26, 1839

AMONG LEADING Northern political observers in the late 1850s two
distinct apprehensions prevailed about the likely direction of the in-
tensifying conflict over slavery. The first was that the chronic sectional
division over the issue would, if not arrested, lead to secession and
then civil war. Uncountable numbers of Northerners, in other words,
warned against a calamity that was eventually approximated by events.
The second apprehension was that the so-called slave power (a group
seldom precisely delineated but understood to comprise the leaders
of the slaveholding class operating through the Democratic party)
would, if not arrested, extend its political domination over the entire
nation, spreading and eventually nationalizing slavery itself in the
process. This second expectation, especially common among members
of the Republican party before and even during the Civil War, is less
well known now because what was feared did not occur.

These two versions of crisis appear inconsistent with each other.
People who saw only the grasping hand of the slaveholder stood
positioned, so to say, with their backs turned to the possibility of
secession. In fact these opposing expectations were rooted in different
assessments of the nature of the slavery conflict, and led to differing
policy proposals for dealing with it. People who feared the Union was
at stake tended to see the crisis as unnecessary (although they did not

always consider sectional differences to be superficial). To them it was the work of agitators both opposing and defending slavery and of shortsighted politicians who took them too seriously. They consequently looked for formulas to push the issue aside without pushing either section to an overwhelming sense of insecurity in the process. People who saw a determined slave power at work were naturally more distrustful of compromise, which itself was seen as a device for Southern gains, and looked for ways to block aggression permanently.

Between 1854 and 1860, as Abraham Lincoln rose from relative obscurity to national prominence and power, he did not identify himself with either of these two broad understandings. As he moved from the edge of the slavery conflict to its center, he seemed to go out of his way to avoid interpreting the slavery problem as a sectional issue. The man whose election as the first Republican president in 1860 precipitated the secession of several Southern states did not acknowledge until almost the last minute that the crisis of the Union might culminate in secession. Indeed he seemed reluctant even to concede that the Union was in crisis. Lincoln's frequent assertion that "I do not expect the Union to be *dissolved*—I do not expect the house to *fall*," is well enough known.[1] It is perhaps less well appreciated that he did not associate himself with the second view of events either. References to the "slave power" are among the most common staples of Republican rhetoric before the Civil War, but it appears from the record that Lincoln did not use the term during that period.[2]

If Lincoln did not claim as his own the prevailing perceptions of the course of political events, how in fact did he interpret it? This question is easy enough at least to begin to answer because on no other subject did he speak and write so frequently between 1854 and 1860, especially during the campaign in 1858 for the Senate seat held by his longtime Democratic rival in Illinois politics, Stephen A. Douglas. There were variations, some of which I will note, in his own assessment, but the overall consistency of his view means that it is not difficult to make the following summary.

The framers of the republic built their institutions of popular government upon a central doctrine, enunciated in the Declaration of Independence, that all men are created equal and possess certain inalienable rights, among which is the right to liberty. They believed accordingly that slavery is wrong. But they found the institution existing among them, and they could not have gotten rid of it at once

286

without producing greater evils. They did however mark it for eventual extinction and moved to cut off the African slave trade and to prevent slavery from moving into United States territories then free of it. The public mind rested then and for a long time afterward in the belief that slavery was doomed ultimately to disappear.

This situation changed abruptly in 1854. A group of political leaders, among whom Lincoln named Stephen A. Douglas, Franklin Pierce, James Buchanan, and Roger B. Taney, implemented a plot to transform a local and decaying institution into one that was national and perpetual. To reach their goal they moved in a series of measured, stealthy steps. First, the bulk of the remaining, unorganized area of the Louisiana Purchase, once closed to slavery, was reopened to it, if the people there wanted to have it among them. This was accomplished in the epochal Kansas-Nebraska Act of 1854. Then, after an interval in which the public mind adjusted itself to this change, the Supreme Court was understood to open all territories to slavery, regardless of the wishes of the people there. This was accomplished in the epochal Dred Scott decision of 1857. The next step, likely to be taken at any time, would dismantle barriers keeping slavery out of states that did not want it. But even this deed was probably not the plotters' final object. Their ultimate project was the subversion of republican institutions, to be replaced by despotism.[3]

Lincoln insisted that "all these things are prepared for you with the logic of history." But whether what was prepared would also be served depended on further expressions of popular will. Returning politicians like Douglas to high office would be read by the plotters as acquiescence in their schemes so far, and license to proceed further. The future thus turned on manifestations of popular regard for liberty. "Our reliance is in the *love of liberty* which God has planted in our bosoms," Lincoln was reported to say during the Senate campaign. "Destroy this spirit, and you have planted the seeds of despotism around your own doors. Familiarize yourselves with the chains of bondage, and you are preparing your own limbs to wear them. Accustomed to trample on the rights of those around you, you have lost the genius of your own independence, and become the fit subjects of the first cunning tyrant who rises."[4] What Lincoln saw at risk, then, was not the Union but the liberty of white Americans. A cunning tyrant, not the aggression or the departure of the South, was the danger to be guarded against.

287

Although Lincoln expressed these themes again and again, he varied and even contradicted them on occasion. Indeed, he set his analysis up as a kind of moving target. He did not know that a conspiracy existed, he said, but he believed that it did. He attributed certain intentions to Douglas, but he insisted he was saying nothing about his motives. He left it unclear whether Douglas was the leader of a conspiratorial gang, or the puppet of one.[5] At times, Lincoln appeared to contradict his conspiracy charge by asserting that Douglas was also thinking up ways to deny slaveholders their constitutional right to carry their slaves into the territories.[6] Accompanying positions at once precise and ambiguous was a range of attitudes toward Douglas himself. It is not clear that Lincoln ultimately regarded Douglas as incorrigibly evil, amoral, or a sinner who might yet repent—or any of these things. He could accuse Douglas of great crimes (what could be worse than destroying the republic of the fathers?) and then engage in banter with "my friend the judge." He actually said afterward that he had made the house divided speech "with the most kindly feeling towards Judge Douglas."[7] His language almost begs modern observers to dismiss with that oxymoron "just politics" a matter that Lincoln insisted he took quite seriously.

If we keep our eyes fixed for the time being on the dominant pattern of Lincoln's analysis, we see that his version of crisis differs from those mentioned earlier in at least two conspicuous respects. First, both leading versions assumed the sectional nature of the slavery conflict. To be sure, they disagreed completely on the nature of Southern intentions. In the first case the South would secede and disappear. In the second the slave power would take over and impose its will. Still, in both cases the focus was upon the intentions of Southerners. Of the four conspirators named by Lincoln, only one—Taney, of Maryland—resided in a slave state. The others were Northerners. The bond among the men was leadership in the Democratic party.

Second, the other two crises were understood by their interpreters to be deeply rooted in American society, or chronic, or both. For example, the point of the famous "irrepressible conflict" passage in a speech William H. Seward gave in 1858 on the "designs of the slaveholders" was that the slavery controversy arose from antagonistic labor systems, themselves traceable to geographical variations, and hence was not only sectional, but fundamental. "Those who think that it is accidental, unnecessary, the work of interested or fanatical agitators, and therefore ephemeral, mistake the case altogether. It is an irrepressible conflict between opposing and enduring forces." Lincoln once said he agreed with the irrepressible conflict idea.[8] In fact he and Seward did share the stated expectation that, in Seward's language, the United States would eventually become "either a slaveholding nation, or entirely a free-labor nation."[9] Historians have accordingly tended to link the irrepressible conflict speech with the house divided speech, with which it was nearly contemporaneous. But in fact the differences between the speeches are as interesting as the resemblances. Unlike Seward, Lincoln spoke of a conflict that was, if not "accidental," at least "unnecessary"; the work of men who, if not "fanatical," were at least "interested"; and one he said he hoped would prove "ephemeral." The crisis of the house divided was among the most repressible of crises. It began in 1854. It was the work of a small group of Democrats. Remove them from office, replace them with Republicans, and the crisis would pass.

If we can accept the premise that Lincoln's expressed understanding of the crisis facing the nation was idiosyncratic, indeed perhaps unique, the question becomes one of accounting for that. I wish to present three complementary answers to this question.

First, the case Lincoln made helped to deal with a constellation of immediate practical challenges he faced in Illinois politics. Lincoln had two immediate, connected goals. He sought election to the Senate, and he wanted to preserve, vindicate, and strengthen the Republican party. Between Lincoln and these objects stood a showdown with Stephen A. Douglas. It had been foreseeable since 1855, when Lincoln narrowly lost his first bid for the Senate, that he would get one more chance, this one against Douglas. Here was the proverbial opportunity of a lifetime, but anyone looking at the situation realistically would probably have concluded that Lincoln's chances for success were not good.

Whatever opprobrium had attached itself to Douglas as a result of his sponsorship of the Kansas-Nebraska bill had been largely dissolved in the acclaim he was receiving by 1858 for successfully leading the congressional fight that effectively blocked the admission of Kansas to the Union as a slave state. That Douglas's opposition was based on a procedural issue — he opposed the controversial Lecompton constitution because the will of the people of Kansas was not properly consulted, not because it was proslavery — was surely less noticed by

289

LIBRARY ST. MARY'S COLLEGE

the voters of Illinois than its practical result: Kansas, when it eventually joined the Union, would enter as a free state. The outcome of this latest crisis over slavery in the territories called into question the Republican party's reason for being, or at the very least made it harder to see a difference between the two parties on the leading question of the day. No one could be certain in 1858, after the party turmoil of the preceding four years, that the Republican party would not prove as transitory as several others that had organized themselves quickly in response to some event or other and then as quickly disappeared. Lincoln was a founder of the Republican party in Illinois and had cast his lot with it. His pride and ambition were linked to the immediate electoral prospects of the party and to keeping it, like the republic, true to the precepts on which it was founded. Thus bound up with his desire to win high office was the necessity of maintaining the vehicle that might carry him there.

This meant emphasizing and even exaggerating the differences between the Democratic and Republican parties as a way of legitimizing the latter. In particular Lincoln had to make as clear as he could his sense of the moral difference between the positions of the parties on slavery. Yet he understood that he could not reply on a moral argument alone. He believed that people needed to feel that policies they were being asked to repudiate were not only morally wrong but practically undesirable as well.[10] The prospect of the nationalization of slavery was effective in this respect. By the late 1850s the idea of the spread of slavery implied to probably a majority of Northerners the decline of infested areas into the dreary realm of social blight and economic stagnation. Politically, slavery promised to wither democracy and open the gates to the usurpations of a brutish aristocracy. These images were sufficiently familiar by the late 1850s that they needed only to be intimated to be vividly imagined. Further still, the spread of slavery into Illinois meant the spread of blacks into a state that had always discouraged their presence. Lincoln was reported by a local newspaper to have warned voters in Carlinville, in southern Illinois: "Sustain these men and negro equality will be abundant, as every white laborer will have occasion to regret when he is elbowed from his plow or his anvil by slave niggers."[11]

A second explanation might be called that of the intentional, strategic misreading of the situation. It is probably safe to say that of all observers of the political scene in the 1850s, Lincoln stood among

290

those least subject to delusion. He did not require instruction on the origins of the slavery crisis, its sectional configuration, or on what lay in store if the South (for which he always claimed a certain sympathy) should conclude that remaining in the Union was incompatible with its most fundamental interests. To continue the slavery controversy on its by now familiar course promised only to rend the Union, now that the credibility of compromise solutions had been drastically undermined by the Kansas-Nebraska Act. Lincoln dismissed as unacceptable the radically alternative solutions to the slavery issue — secession or abolition. With solutions that were both realistic and acceptable seemingly ruled out, the sensible thing to attempt was the redefinition of the very nature of the crisis.

Like contemporary advocates of popular sovereignty and later so-called revisionist historians, Lincoln appeared to believe that the practical question at hand involved what white Americans thought and were prepared to do about slavery more than it involved the institution itself. He looked forward to the death of slavery, but he acknowledged he had no program for abolishing it. He sought nothing more in this respect, he said, than the restoration of a policy he claimed had prevailed as recently as the start of 1854. This in turn was the key to the more important object of putting the (white) public mind at rest about slavery. Agitation over slavery, the only issue in Lincoln's experience that ever really threatened the Union, presupposed that the future of slavery was up in the air. Once the public mind understood that the fate of slavery had been a closed question for three quarters of a century, that opening the question was a short-term aberration, and that it was a closed question once again, the agitation would cease.

The misreading of Douglas was equally intentional, in this view. Lincoln, who had been well acquainted with Douglas since the 1830s, knew that his antagonist was no participant in a conspiracy to destroy liberty. But a conflict understood as attitudinal required a psychological resolution. If returning Douglas to the Senate abetted the projects of the conspirators, presumably defeating him would thwart them. Lincoln imposed the structure of electoral ritual upon a sectional conflict, with the apparent aim of transforming the latter. Partisan conflict moved along a familiar course toward a predictable resolution almost always decisive yet bearable, and cathartic yet peaceful. Defeating Douglas would signal popular determination to return the slavery issue to the ground on which Lincoln kept insisting it had been successfully dealt with until 1854. As political calm had prevailed up to that time, so it could prevail again. The purpose of pretending Douglas was a villain was to make him in fact a scapegoat. The accumulated tensions of many years could be focused on him. With the symbolic murder of his political defeat, these agonies could be dissipated harmlessly. But there was no time to lose. Once parties became fully congruent with sectional lines, it would be too late.

There is at least one additional explanation available. It reaches backward from these immediate political and strategic concerns to observe that the crisis Lincoln saw after 1854 was consistent with— indeed it summarized, dramatized, and exploited—images of danger he had been evoking on and off for twenty years at least, and that he had probably begun to formulate even earlier.

The political culture into which Lincoln's generation was born was that of the last phase of the founding age of the republic. The men who had rebelled against Great Britain, created the Union, won the war for independence, and written the Constitution—the set of heroes known to Lincoln's generation as "our fathers"—continued to dominate American political life into the nineteenth century. (Jefferson was in his last weeks as president when Lincoln was born.) This simple fact of birth near the American beginning permanently marked the political consciousness of Lincoln's generation. The virtue of the fathers, the purity of their actions, and the wisdom of their prescriptive laws made the founding itself something of a god which hovered over the nineteenth century constantly posing a single question: is this new order going to last or not? The founding deed as inescapable point of reference and definer of the central question for the succeeding age is probably not better illustrated than in the beginning of the Gettysburg address: "Four score and seven years ago our fathers brought forth. . . ." Registering that length of time was a way of getting one's bearings before dealing with the question whether a nation "conceived in Liberty, and dedicated to the proposition that all men are created equal" could "long endure."[12]

Probably at no time between the 1770s and 1865 could this question be answered with overwhelming confidence by a realistic observer. Certainly it was asked with urgency during the extended moment in which the fathers departed from the stage. Americans of the new generation arriving to succeed them had invested nothing of themselves in the Revolution, did not experience it, could not recall it, and thus knew it only in the misshapen corpus of myth. The transition from one set of leaders to another must have terrified patriotic bystanders, but the means to make it bearable and even smooth were readily seen. The fathers could not be prevented from dying, but they could be made immortal. In the first third of the nineteenth century, determined publicists with various designs set to work with ingenuity to spread to the boundaries of literacy a message so vivid and simple that it is hard to imagine how any child with access to printed words could have missed it.

The message said essentially this: In the virtuous character of the founders of the republic could be found the explanation for the wondrous set of events that led to its birth. Virtue would likewise prove the key to its preservation. To maintain inherited institutions and transmit them intact to the next generation, the sons were obliged to imitate the fathers, especially George Washington, who, in his character fully as much as in his achievements, surpassed all other leaders in the history of the world. American children should learn to pronounce the word "Washington" as soon as they were able to talk, and study the founder's life as soon as they were able to read. They should "reverence and copy his godlike virtues." They should "bow their hearts before heaven, and in a spirit of pious patriotism fervently ask 'make me like Washington.'" The hopes associated with this project, summarized in verse by Thomas Dunn English, were towering:

> Oh! may the youths of this free land,
> Columbia's proudest rising sons,
> Become with every virtue fraught
> A race of God-like Washingtons.

God-like Washingtons: virtue, as always, was to be its own reward, but not necessarily the only reward. The child who built his character on the model of Washington was encouraged to try to win the same prize he did: immortal fame. One writer expressed a common enough understanding when he said in 1840 that the path was open for any young man to become if he could "the Washington of his age."[13]

Now here was a myth if ever there was one, as even the slightest reflection could have revealed at the time. Precisely because the fathers had been heroes, their sons did not need to be, and could not be, heroes. As a Whig journal observed, a "heroic age . . . never comes to a nation but once."[14] If its achievements are preserved by virtuous men, there is no need of another. Americans of Lincoln's generation could be urged to imitate Washington, and they could be promised fame if they did so. But the Jacksonian 1830s clearly revealed that a stable democracy dedicated to impersonal social progress, a society that counted among its more pressing concerns tariff rates, the provenience of bank charters, and the funding of internal improvements did not demand a "race of God-like Washingtons" or even another generation of heroes. To a youth like Lincoln who was both ambitious and highly perceptive, the endless biographies, eulogies, and patriotic orations on the revolutionary fathers would perhaps have succeeded not so much in demonstrating the need for heroic virtues as in calling attention to a society so arranged and so destined that it did not require those virtues, did not inspire them, and, indeed, could find no place for them at all. Moreover the commonplace virtues it could find room for were hardly likely to be celebrated or even noticed by posterity, whose eyes were more likely to fix on the inherited gift and its creators than on its mere transmitters.

Surely the sensible way for public figures to deal with this set of historical circumstances was to accept and even rejoice in it, which is what Martin Van Buren, for example, did when he entered the presidency in 1837.[15] He observed that he was the first president born after the Revolution. He understood that the heroic age of the republic was over, and he made much of the fact in an optimistic way. The Union and the Constitution had not only survived but actually thrived on the various challenges pessimists had prophesied would soon do it in: territorial expansion, population growth, political factions, and the ill wishes of foreign nations. Now the fathers' inspired system could be managed by workaday political professionals like himself, as long as they kept the faith. Trials no doubt lay ahead, but surely no worse than the ones already experienced and surmounted.[16]

It is just here, during Van Buren's administration, that we first take extended note of Lincoln in connection with this transition, for he presented a commentary on the subject in a speech he delivered to the Young Men's Lyceum, in Springfield, in January 1838.[17] Like Van Buren at his inaugural, Lincoln appeared in this speech to understand and accept the role history had dealt to modern political leadership. But from the same point of departure, the Democratic president and the young Whig legislator went off in different directions. Looking at the same set of facts, Van Buren was on the whole complacent while Lincoln was wary.

The danger to republican institutions lay in the possible combination of two different orders of passion. Lincoln suggested that although historical conditions fluctuate—and the difference between then and now was stark—human nature does not change. Therein lurked imminent danger. During the Revolution the passions of ordinary Americans were directed toward the British. That enemy, having been defeated, was no longer of concern. But the baser passions of humans, being natural, remained. They revealed themselves disturbingly in the lawlessness of mob violence which increasingly characterized town life in Jacksonian America.

The second, more elevated passion was ambition for distinction. In every age, Lincoln believed, talented men appear on the political scene looking for ways to make names for themselves. During the revolutionary era the project of founding a nation provided an outlet for this ambition. Although that opportunity was gone, there was no reason to suppose ambitious men would not continue to appear. Once they did, Lincoln imagined, there were just three tasks they might consider undertaking.

One was the enterprise of founding. That task was barred by history. The house—or "political edifice of liberty and equal rights" as Lincoln called it here—was already built. The second task was preservation. The nature of ambition made that course unsatisfying to the ambitious. Men like President Van Buren might be content to tread epigonically in the path of heroes, but not the kind of figure Lincoln was describing. "Towering genius disdains a beaten path. . . . It *scorns* to tread in the footsteps of any predecessor, however illustrious." That left the third task—destruction. Not because it was necessarily the most desirable course but rather because it was the only one left, the drive of the ambitious, talented figure would head toward tyranny. With "nothing left to be done in the way of building up" the edifice, and unable to find gratification in "supporting and maintaining an edifice that has been erected by others," the ambitious man in search of distinction "would set boldly to the task of pulling down" the edifice.[18]

It was in combination and only in combination that these two different kinds of passion posed a threat. The danger of mob violence

295

lay less in its direct results than in its corrosive effects on the people's regard for their institutions. Uncontrolled violence called into question the ability of existing governments to perform their indispensable function of providing security for life and property, and thus opened the gates to a tyrant, who would be blocked otherwise. Since tyranny could not triumph without the invitation of the people as reflected in the behavior of mobs, their lawlessness was as patricidal as the ambition of the destructive genius: "Let every man remember that to violate the law, is to trample on the blood of his father."

Just what or whom Lincoln had in mind in his specter of the dangerously ambitious figure has been the subject of considerable surmise ever since Edmund Wilson suggested in *Patriotic Gore* that Lincoln had "projected himself into the role against which he [was] warning."[19] Whether or not one is willing to accompany Wilson that far, we have him to thank for pointing out what now seems obvious enough: Lincoln had himself in mind when he composed the entire speech. The only outlets for ambition he invites others to consider are those narrow political channels he knew himself to be suited for by talent and desire. One would never know from this speech that a nineteenth-century man might be remembered in the twentieth for writing a novel about a whale or an essay on nature, for inventing the telegraph or the phonograph, or for building huge empires in petroleum, railroads, or steel. Of course Lincoln had himself in mind when he made this early speech, but surely he would say (did it not go without saying) that he could never intentionally play the role of destroyer. Consciously he was fully prepared, good son that he saw himself to be, to tread in the footsteps of others—in his case men like De Witt Clinton and especially Henry Clay. These were men who, unlike the fathers, could be readily imitated.

But in addition to the implied renunciation in this presentation, one senses desire. There are at least two sound bases for saying so. One is the possibility that Lincoln, without being aware of it consciously, envied and resented the fathers as much as he revered them. One of the most famous short assessments of Lincoln's character is William H. Herndon's remark that "his ambition was a little engine that knew no rest."[20] The founders—whom Lincoln implied were more fortunate and competent than meritorious and inspired—had gathered in all the prizes of renown, leaving none for nineteenth-century political leaders. Lincoln had been preempted, and he knew it. Although his filial respect would most likely have hidden feelings of hostility toward the fathers, it would not necessarily have obliterated them. Such feelings, unacceptable and hence unrecognizable, might have been projected upon some completely imaginary being. In other words, patricidal desire, always hidden from view, surfaced in the disguised form of a desire to defend the fathers' institutions and laws from a patricide. But this possibility by its very nature cannot be verified by the evidence without great assistance from inference. It arises from oedipal logic—plausible logic to my mind—applied to the facts rather than from the facts themselves, and thus is best labeled speculative.

Another inference is based on logic of a different kind. The prophecy of the tyrant was unconditional. The man would appear. Whether or not he would succeed would depend on the devotion of the people to their institutions and laws. Thus, Lincoln was not looking to the prevention of the emergence of this figure. He was looking to stop him after he appeared.

The psychological reassurance that this structured expectation might have provided is apparent, for it implied a formula for achieving towering distinction in a post-heroic age while remaining a good son of the fathers. To recognize and confront and defeat such a villain, to "frustrate his designs,"[21] to save the edifice of liberty the fathers had built—would not that deed be rewarded with renown? Given that, is there not some likelihood that a prophecy of the sort Lincoln made would tend to be self-fulfilling? If one's chances for distinction depended on the appearance of a dangerous villain, would not the son who is both good and ambitious be doubly prepared to recognize such a figure when he appeared, and even go in search of him if he did not appear? And if the tyrant did not spring up from the dynamics of history as Lincoln explained them, would he then not only have to be imagined, but also invented?

To consider that Lincoln at least sensed this solution to the problem of ambition in a post-heroic age helps make sense of his recurrent tendency to imagine himself struggling defensively against the enemies of liberty—in the role, in short, of a savior. On more than one occasion he made dramatic public statements in which he portrayed himself in the role of the defender of liberty in its last redoubt, prepared even to martyr himself regardless of whether the sacrifice would serve any defensive purpose. One example is especially conspicuous because in the context in which he made it, the remark was gratuitous and incongruous. Nearly two years after he appeared at the Lyceum, at the end of a long and rather technical presentation on a complex subject (the subtreasury proposal) to a small audience in Springfield, Lincoln abruptly turned to a warning that the republic was in grave danger of succumbing to tyranny. The Democratic administration of Van Buren—who was himself an "evil spirit"—was a "great volcano . . . belching forth the lava of political corruption" which threatened to overrun everything in its path. If the country should lose its liberty, Lincoln said, his proudest boast would be "not that I was the *last* to desert, but that I *never* deserted her." Never did he feel more noble than "when I contemplate the cause of my country, deserted by all the world beside, and I standing up boldly and alone and hurling defiance at her victorious oppressors." Nothing—not the prospect of failure, chains, torture, even death—would deter him.[22]

The sensible way to treat the Lyceum warning is neither to attempt to explain it away nor to mystify it by speculating that Lincoln somehow anticipated his later career. The significance of the speech is that in it Lincoln related his own conflicting desires—the humble ones in one corner and the grandiose in the other—to the structure of his broad understanding of politics and the processes of history. Ambition and understanding shaped and focused each other, and both proved exceedingly durable.

In the style of its prose, the Lyceum speech, which Lincoln gave when he was just twenty-eight, does not match the unforgettable speeches he gave between 1858 and 1865. But the earlier speech does resemble the later ones in certain other respects: in its structure (the noting at the outset where speaker and audience are located in time, the pivotal warning that the fate of popular government is still an open issue, the hopeful conclusion that popular government will endure); in its reverent inclination to use the fathers and their legacy as the standard for assessing the value of anything to come along since; in its conspicuous avoidance of any remark that could be taken as anti-Southern; in its sense that tyranny rather than disunion is the great danger to be guarded against; and in its insistence that popular dedication to liberty is the key to the survival of republican government. These were not the concerns of a single occasion but designs in the pattern of a whole life.

It was perfectly natural, then, that Lincoln tended to interpret the political upheavals of the 1850s, events he did not anticipate and over which he had next to no control, through the secure, informing frame of his preexisting understanding. It would be surprising if he had suddenly abandoned one mental universe for another. Lincoln was accustomed to expect danger in the form of tyranny and not secession. He was accustomed to see this danger emanating from the Democratic party and not from a disaffected section. (He had once been a Southerner; he had never been a Democrat.) In the 1850s as in the 1830s, the depth of popular devotion to liberty was the key to whether the tyrants would prevail. In all these areas his house divided analysis ran true to form.

The match of perception to expectation was never exact. Lincoln's predisposition conditioned the way he saw events; it hardly blinded him to them altogether. But even the variations from his habitual formulations attest to their lingering hold. The imagined villain, we recall, would tear down the fathers' temple of liberty. Douglas's methods were covert. He "shirks the responsibility of pulling the house down, but he digs under it that it may fall of its own weight." Again, the imagined villain was described as a towering genius, with caesarian ambition. Lincoln surely never considered Douglas a genius, and he once acknowledged that Douglas's ambition was not more intense than his own.[23] He could not force his "friend, the judge" into a caesarian mold, and he did not try. Imagined danger arrived in a single figure; actual danger arrived tagged with the names of four men. Despite differences of detail, however, the danger then was the same as the danger now. The preformulated remedy matched the one that should now be applied.

The immediate practical object toward which many of Lincoln's post-1854 political statements pointed was election to the Senate. Indeed, the scarcity of clues he provided about what he would actually do once he got there encourages underscoring the point. Probably with most politicians running for office, the goal of election naturally overshadows the prospect of incumbency. With Lincoln, incumbency was not merely obscured; it appears to have been an idea that barely occurred to him, as Douglas seemed to sense at the time.[24] Winning the seat rather than having the seat was Lincoln's great desire. More than that, it was important to win the seat in a certain way—by moving to resolve heroically a crisis created by a tyrannical challenge to inherited institutions. The accusation of conspiracy that Lincoln drew up accorded with this object. Adopting the interpretations of crisis more widely held than his own might have worked as well as his own did in his quest for office. But he had objects in view in addition to holding office. The alternative understandings did not speak to these requirements as well, or at all.

That Lincoln's pattern of perception and expectation was falsified by events did little to undo it. The crisis he expected did not occur. Those that did occur were those he said he did not expect. But even when the related issues of disunion and emancipation became his to resolve, he did not abandon his customary habits of thought. Instead he employed them in dealing with the problems they had helped hide from his view. There is, indeed, a connection between Lincoln's pattern of perception and his celebrated prose, as if nothing but the contemplation of ultimate political values could inspire the greatest art. He needed to see the emancipation of the slaves as more than liberation. "In *giving* freedom to the slave, we assure freedom to the free—honorable alike in what we give, and what we preserve. We shall nobly save, or meanly lose, the last best, hope of earth."[25] He needed to see the war for the Union as more than a righteous struggle for territorial and constitutional integrity. The Civil War presented the question, as mob lawlessness had in the 1830s and Douglas had in the 1850s, whether popular government conceived in liberty would last or die. Indeed, from the beginning to the very end of his career, it is probably true that the only cause that ever fully engaged his energies was the threat of the extinction of liberty.

NOTES

1. Roy P. Basler, ed., Marion Dolores Pratt and Lloyd A. Dunlap, asst. eds., *The Collected Works of Abraham Lincoln*, 9 vols. (New Brunswick, N.J.: Rutgers University Press, 1953-55), 2: 461.

2. Ibid., 2: 232. The Bloomington, Illinois, *Weekly Pantagraph*, Sept. 20, 1854, reported Lincoln using the phrase "slaveholding power" in a speech there on September 12. But it is impossible to say where paraphrase stops and direct quotation begins in this summary of the speech.

3. Basler, *Collected Works of Lincoln*, 2: 492, 514, 521, 548; 3: 18-21, 89-90, 95, 233, 255-56, and passim.

4. Ibid., 3: 95.

5. Ibid., 2: 549-50; 3: 18, 232-33; 2: 525-26.

6. On this see Don E. Fehrenbacher, *Prelude to Greatness: Lincoln in the 1850's* (Stanford: Stanford University Press, 1962), pp. 121-42.

7. Basler, *Collected Works of Lincoln*, 2: 485, 2: 512.

8. George E. Baker, ed., *The Works of William H. Seward*, 5 vols. (Boston: Houghton Mifflin and Co., 1884), 4: 294, 292; Basler, *Collected Works of Lincoln*, 4: 50.

9. Baker, *Works of Seward*, 4: 292. On differences between the rhetoric of Lincoln and Seward, see Fehrenbacher, *Prelude to Greatness*, p. 74.

10. See, for example, Basler, *Collected Works of Lincoln*, 2: 351.

11. Ibid., 3: 78.

12. Ibid., 7: 23.

13. *Eulogies and Orations on the Life and Death of General George Washington, First President of the United States of America* (Boston: Manning and Loring, 1800), p. 41; "To Whom Does Washington's Glory Belong?" *Southern Literary Messenger* 9 (1843): 589; Thomas Dunn English, "Young Washington's Reply to Gov. Dinwiddie," *Casket* 12 (1837): 385; "Bulwer," *Southern Literary Messenger* 6 (1840): 405.

14. "Memoirs of the Administrations of Washington and John Adams," *American Whig Review* 4 (1846): 614.

15. Major L. Wilson has noted the striking points of contact between the rhetoric of Van Buren and Lincoln in "Lincoln and Van Buren in the Steps of the Fathers: Another Look at the Lyceum Address," *Civil War History* 29 (1983), 197-211.

16. James D. Richardson, comp., *A Compilation of the Messages and Papers of the Presidents, 1789-1897* (n.p., 1898), vol. 3, pp. 313-16.

17. The text of the Lyceum speech is in Basler, *Collected Works of Lincoln*, 1: 108-15.

18. I have here brought together for my own purposes passages from different places in the speech.

19. Edmund Wilson, *Patriotic Gore: Studies in the Literature of the American Civil War* (New York: Oxford University Press, 1962), p. 108.

20. Quoted in Hofstadter, *American Political Tradition*, p. 92.

21. Basler, *Collected Works of Lincoln*, 1: 114.

22. Ibid., 1: 178-79. See also 2: 547; 4: 240.

23. Ibid., 3: 205, 2: 382-83.

24. Ibid., 3: 266. "I thought that you desired to hear us upon those questions coming within our constitutional power of action. Lincoln will not discuss those. What one question has he discussed that comes within the power or calls for the action or interference of an United States Senator?" Ibid., 3: 266.

25. Ibid., 5: 537.

Commentary on "Lincoln's Tyrants"

KENNETH M. STAMPP

Professor Forgie's paper is more reaffirmation than reformulation of the general argument of his provocative and in some respects provoking book, *Patricide in the House Divided*. I found only three modifications. First, he advances with less certitude the idea that Lincoln envied and resented the fathers of the republic, conceding now that this is at most "speculative," a possibility arising not from the facts but from "oedipal logic." Second, he is a trifle more ambiguous about the significance of the warning in Lincoln's Lyceum speech that a tyrant might emerge to threaten American liberty. Edmund Wilson claimed that Lincoln "projected himself into the role against which he was warning," thus betraying his own overweening ambition. Forgie seems to have distanced himself a little farther from Wilson's position, but he is still quite certain that Lincoln "had himself in mind" when he wrote the speech and that he revealed "his own conflicting desires." Finally, he does not repeat his book's stunning suggestion that Lincoln's pursuit and "symbolic murder" of Douglas "set in motion a sequence of events that might not otherwise have occurred"—events that "led to power for Lincoln but also to war." I trust the omission was deliberate and not merely due to lack of space.

However, these modest revisions are not sufficient to remove my doubts about Forgie's explanation of Lincoln's role in the crisis of the 1850s. According to him, Lincoln shared the apprehensions of neither those who feared secession and civil war nor those who feared the aggressions of the Slave Power. Rather, from the time of his Lyceum speech of 1838, he admonished his countrymen to guard against another danger—that is, the subversion of their liberties by some ambitious and "cunning tyrant" who would "set boldly to the task of pulling down" the republican edifice which the fathers had built.

At what point Lincoln first became apprehensive about the danger of secession and civil war is not easy to determine, but I think it is clear that he did express concern during the 1850s about proslavery aggression and its ultimate goal. He may not have used the term "Slave Power," but if one accepts Forgie's definition—that is, "the leaders of the slaveholding class operating through the Democratic party"—his house divided speech is one of the most concise Republican descriptions of the Slave Power at work. Lincoln advised those who doubted its ultimate intent to nationalize slavery to study the course it had been following and "trace the evidences of design, and concert of action, among its chief bosses, from the beginning." Perhaps we cannot prove that the Kansas-Nebraska bill, the Dred Scott decision, and the Lecompton fraud are the results of "preconcert," he said: "But when we see a lot of framed timbers, different portions of which we know have been gotten out at different times and places and by different workmen—Stephen, Franklin, Roger and James, for instance—and when we see these timbers joined together, and see that they exactly make the frame of a house . . . we find it impossible not to *believe* that Stephen and Franklin and Roger and James all understood one another from the beginning."[1]

Moreover, Lincoln did not view the crisis as simply "the work of a small group of Democrats," for he implicated Southern slaveholders as well. In a letter to Joshua F. Speed of Kentucky he noted that "decent" slaveholders talk about justice in Kansas, but

they never *vote* that way. Although in a private letter, or conversation, you will express your preference that Kansas shall be free, you will vote for no man for Congress who would say the same thing publicly. No such man could be elected from any district in any slave state. . . . The slave-breeders and slave traders are a small, odious and detested class, among you; and yet in politics, they dictate the course of all of you, and are as completely your masters, as you are the masters of your own negroes.[2]

Nor did Lincoln claim that political calm had prevailed until the repeal of the Missouri Compromise in 1854. In his debate with Douglas at Alton he reviewed the various crises caused by slavery.

How many times have we had danger from this question? Go back to the days of the Missouri Compromise. Go back to the Nullification question, at the bottom of which lay this same slavery question. Go back to the time of the annexation of Texas. Go back to the troubles that led to the Compromise of 1850. . . . Is it not this same mighty, deep seated power that somehow operates on the minds of men, exciting and stirring them up in every avenue of society? . . . Is that irresistible power which for fifty years has shaken the government and agitated the people to be stilled and subdued by pretending that it is an exceedingly simple thing, and we ought not to talk about it?[3]

In short, though Lincoln did not regionalize morality or view slaveholders as evil, he did describe the aggressive action of proslavery forces as the most dangerous threat to the republic and to the liberties of the American people.

If the American people did not stand up to that threat and resist proslavery aggression, they would ultimately pave the way for the tyrant who would take from them their own liberties. It was in this context that Lincoln asked his white audience,

when you have made it forever impossible for Negroes to be but the beasts of the field . . . are you quite sure the demon which you have roused *will not turn and rend you?* . . . Our defense against tyranny is in the preservation of the spirit which prizes liberty as the heritage of all men . . . . Destroy this spirit, and you have planted the seeds of despotism around your own doors. . . . Accustomed to trample on the rights of those around you, you have lost the genius of your own independence, and become the fit subjects of the first cunning tyrant who rises.[4]

Clearly, as Forgie contends, Lincoln did perceive the potential threat of an ambitious "towering genius" to American liberty, but he linked that danger to proslavery aggression. The Slave Power was the primary danger; the "cunning tyrant" would have been but the offspring of its triumph.

Of course, in Forgie's view, this does not dispose of the problem of the tyrant, because he also relates it to the frustrations of ambitious young men in a "post-heroic" age, when all battles had been won, independence secured, and the republican edifice firmly established. "Oedipal logic" tells us that the sons, at least the ambitious ones, resented the fathers, and Lincoln, we know, was extraordinarily ambitious. His Lyceum speech may or may not have betrayed his own suppressed ambition to be a Caesar, but Forgie does not doubt that when he wrote it he was thinking of himself. Lincoln, like other ambitious sons, was not content to perform the mundane tasks involved in preserving and managing the system created by the fathers. Suppressing whatever wish he may have had to destroy their work, his "patricidal desire . . . surfaced in the distinguished form of a desire to defend the fathers' institutions and laws from a patricide." Here was a role that the ambitious Lincoln could savor: "to save the edifice of liberty the fathers had built—would not that deed be rewarded with renown?" Then would not the prophecy of a patricidal son "tend to be self-fulfilling?" Would not Lincoln, in his search for distinction, recognize the patricidal son when he appeared, "and even go in search for him?" But if the patricidal son could not be found, would Lincoln then not have to invent him? Forgie's answers to these hypothetical questions, piled one on the other, are Yes, Yes, Yes, and Yes.

However, one must ask whether these conjectures provide the most plausible explanation of Lincoln's Lyceum speech. Is it reasonable to read into the extravagant rhetoric of a young man of twenty-eight "designs in the pattern of a whole life," as Forgie does? He offers in support of his conjectures only a few subsequent pledges by Lincoln to sacrifice all in defense of American liberty and Herndon's remark that Lincoln's ambition "was a little engine that knew no rest." Is it valid to apply "oedipal logic" to Lincoln, who was in fact not a son but a *grandson* of the founders of the republic? Grandsons, we know, have a far easier time with grandfathers than with fathers. A whole generation of ambitious men stood between Lincoln and the founders—Calhoun, Webster, John Quincy Adams, Van Buren, Jackson, and above all, Henry Clay, who was Lincoln's idol and role model. Why not apply "oedipal logic" to one of the true sons—to Calhoun, for example, who seemed to have a good deal of trouble with the fathers and who, according to one of them, James Madison, posed a considerable threat to the edifice they had built? Perhaps Calhoun projected his patricidal desires on others, for his favorite posture was as defender of the Constitution against Northern politicians who threatened to destroy it. But if someone of Lincoln's generation is to be interpreted with "oedipal logic," a better subject might be one of the Southern secessionists who really did set about to destroy the work of the founders. Might not this logic be applied more successfully to Jefferson Davis than to Lincoln?

I think it is quite appropriate for historians to speculate about the psychological implications of Lincoln's speeches, state papers, and private letters. But the speculation ought not to do great violence to the man revealed in a mass of empirical data. Lincoln is not a shadowy historical figure whose character must be studied primarily through the textual exegesis of a single speech. His collected works fill nine fat volumes, and the corpus of this material simply does not square with Forgie's portrait of Lincoln as the tyrant hunter. To start with his Lyceum speech and the reality of his ambition and conclude with such a portrait is to make a gigantic leap from fact to fancy.

A Lincoln scholar must at least consider a more obvious explanation of the Lyceum speech, as several commentators suggested at a session of the American Historical Association in December of 1984.[5] In that speech Lincoln warned that the mob violence of the Jacksonian era might have a corrosive effect on American political institutions, thus paving the way for an ambitious tyrant. About that he was explicit. Unfortunately, we have no way of knowing whether he had in mind a specific person of towering ambition; but if he did it would surely be plausible to suspect that the person was Andrew Jackson, who had retired from the presidency only the year before. The Whigs had labeled Jackson a tyrant—King Andrew I—and Lincoln was an ardent Henry Clay Whig. Or, alternatively, he might have had in mind the "cunning tyrant" who had destroyed the first French Republic in the very recent past.

The "towering genius" described by Lincoln would never have been content merely to be a United States senator or a constitutional president. Yet, in 1838, even these goals must have seemed far beyond the grasp of this young, ambitious, but still obscure Illinois legislator. Twenty years later they did seem to be within his reach. Significantly, presidential power, when in his hands, not only fulfilled his ambition but was almost more than he could bear.

NOTES

1. Roy P. Basler, ed., Marion Dolores Pratt and Lloyd A. Dunlap, asst. eds., *The Collected Works of Abraham Lincoln*, 9 vols., (New Brunswick, N.J., 1953-55), 2: 462-66.

2. Ibid., 2: 32.
3. Ibid., 3: 310-11.
4. Ibid., 3: 95.
5. Richard N. Current read the formal comments of Gabor S. Boritt, who could not be present. Current added his own comments, as did Don E. Fehrenbacher and Kenneth M. Stampp.

Commentary on "Lincoln's Tyrants"

Major L. Wilson

Professor Forgie's paper deals primarily with the rhetoric and not the reality of the house divided, that is, with Lincoln's perception of political events in the 1850s and not the events themselves. It demands of the reader some knowledge of these events from the Kansas-Nebraska Act to the election of 1860. A full appreciation of the paper also requires an acquaintance with his book, *Patricide in the House Divided,* which was published in 1979 and honored with the Allan Nevins Award. The following comments focus on what I take to be three important points in the paper: (1) that Lincoln's strategic view of events was distinctive if not unique, (2) that his ideological perspective had been articulated two decades earlier in his Lyceum Address, and (3) that a psychological analysis of the address yields new insight into his motivation.

First of all, Professor Forgie argues that Lincoln's perception of events during the sectional controversy of the 1850s was "idiosyncratic, indeed perhaps unique." Most Northern spokesmen interpreted the course of events in one of two ways: as leading either to secession and civil war or to the goal of a slave power conspiracy to make slavery national. For Lincoln, by contrast, the ultimate tendency of events, the end most to be feared, was not secession or even slave power ascendancy but, beyond that, "the subversion of republican institutions." The slave power could attain its goal, he assumed, only if and when the people lost that virtue and love of freedom on which the republic reposed. At issue was not freedom for slaves but the possible enslavement of the free.

Even more striking was the difference over political strategy. While others saw conflict in profoundly sectional if not irrepressible terms, Lincoln defined the crisis strictly along party lines and deemed it eminently repressible. In his view, accordingly, a few Democratic leaders—Douglas, Pierce, Buchanan, Taney—began a conspiracy against freedom in 1854 with the Kansas-Nebraska Act. This measure lifted the earlier ban on slavery north of 36° 30′ and gave to settlers the right to adopt slavery if they wanted it. Three years later, after the public mind had grown accustomed to a policy of retreat from freedom, the Supreme Court ruled in the Dred Scott case that the Constitution carried slavery into all territories. The next step of the conspiracy would be another court decision carrying slavery into free states as well, thus making slavery entirely national. With the public mind now totally debauched, a "cunning tyrant" would soon appear to end all pretense of republican freedom. Happily, Lincoln's analysis of the crisis along party lines prescribed a peaceful means for resolving it: let Republicans drive Democrats from office at the next election on a platform reaffirming the pure and primitive principles of the republic. The crisis would then be met and passed.

This interpretation of events constituted a rhetorical strategy of great practical value, for it served Lincoln's dual purpose in 1858 to defeat Douglas for the Senate and to strengthen the new Republican party. By emphasizing, even exaggerating, the differences between Republicans and Democrats he could make Douglas appear to be an enemy of the republic and its salvation only one election away. In this strategy, however, Lincoln was not as idiosyncratic as Professor Forgie claims. Republicans elsewhere confronted Democratic foes in similar ways; and Democrats in turn warned voters of the threat to freedom posed by the Republican party. Indeed, as the recent studies of Michael F. Holt, J. Mills Thornton, and Jean H. Baker among others suggest, the "electoral ritual" Lincoln performed was one that exhibited a basic pattern of two-party politics since the Jacksonian period. In this pattern a concern for the security of republican institutions provided Americans with a "framework of perception" for judging events. A successful appeal to the voters thus depended upon the skill of politicians at "identifying and crusading against antirepublican monsters." Sharing the same general strategy, the two parties differed only over the specific way to define the "antirepublican plot."[1] Two-party competition in the North still kept the electoral ritual relevant for Lincoln. In the Lower South, by contrast, one-party politics inescapably led to a definition of conflict in stark sectional terms, making Lincoln's party the antirepublican monster and secession the only way to restore republican ideals.

The second point in the paper deals with the broader ideology out of which Lincoln's rhetorical strategy in the 1850s arose. Professor Forgie shows that Lincoln's republicanism had been articulated at least by 1838 in the address he delivered at the Springfield Lyceum entitled "The Perpetuation of Our Political Institutions." The young Lincoln professed to share with his "post-heroic" generation a reverence for the heroic fathers and a sacred obligation to preserve the temple of liberty they had built. Republics, all agreed, were very fragile and in need of constant tending. In the 1830s Lincoln warned of two dangers. One was the "mobocratic spirit," manifested in widespread rioting and violence, which threatened to undermine the republican foundation of ordered liberty. The second and related danger was Caesarism. Lincoln here predicted that some "towering genius" would arise with a "ruling passion" for fame that could not be appeased by the mere task of preservation. Unwilling to build on the work of the fathers, he would rather exploit public disorder and tear it down. It was this same "pattern of perception" or "mental universe," Professor Forgie believes, through which Lincoln interpreted events in the 1850s.

Once more, however, the claim for the distinctiveness of Lincoln's outlook must be qualified. A growing body of studies on "republicanism" shows how deeply imbedded it has always been in American political culture. A central feature of this outlook was, to use Daniel Walker Howe's phrase, "a conspiracy paradigm."[2] Americans from an early day believed that their institutions began in a state of essential perfection. Consequently, any problems arising at a later point in time were essentially moral and not structural, problems that evinced a design by evil men to corrupt and overthrow the republic. The basic political task for each generation was therefore to isolate any conspirators and restore the nation to its original idea. Thus, the revolutionary fathers foiled a ministerial conspiracy under George III; Jefferson rallied freemen against the monarchical designs of Federalists; Jackson slew the Monster Bank; Whigs warned against the caesarian menace of Jackson; and abolitionists, proslavery Southerners, and Antimasons pointed to other dangers. Lincoln's eloquence and moral earnestness surely made his views somewhat distinctive and unique; yet seen in a broader context, his tyrants look very much like the tyrants of other Americans.

A final point in the paper — the one scholars associate most closely with Professor Forgie — is his psychological interpretation of the house divided. One needs to read his book, along with Lincoln's Lyceum Address, in order to appreciate the full force of this interpretation. The address, in his view, was not only a formulation of republican ideology; it was also a profound study of ambition in a "post-heroic" age. Driven by a "ruling passion" for fame, Lincoln unconsciously identified with the "towering genius" against whom he warned. Along with his professed love for the fathers was a hatred of them because their heroic actions had left nothing heroic for ambitious sons to do. Lincoln resolved the conflicting claims of filiopiety and ambition by projecting onto an "evil son" his own patricidal impulses and by preparing himself, as the "good son," to save the house of the fathers. In the crisis of the 1850s Douglas could be easily fitted into this pattern of expectations. Indeed, he had to do little more than "pass across Lincoln's established field of vision" in order to appear as the evil son; the "emotional charge from within" shaped Lincoln's view far more than the actions and character of Douglas.[3] By electoral victory over Douglas, Lincoln could "symbolically slay" the evil son and thereby share the glory of the founders.

Any brief summary cannot do justice to Professor Forgie's book, and most reviewers have rightly found much to praise.[4] If the study of history is an ongoing task of rethinking the past, one great virtue of historical thought is its speculative richness. Judged in this way, *Patricide* is an original, exciting, and highly suggestive study. It compels the reader to reexamine the question of Lincoln's ambition; it also provides new perspectives on the entire antebellum culture. Style is another merit, for the book is written in sparkling, elegant, and jargon-free prose. But as a book purporting to explain the coming of the Civil War, it has not persuaded most of the critics. Psychology provides flashes of insight, but it should not be allowed to give basic structure to an account of the past. The historical imagination must be disciplined by evidence; and evidence speaks more directly to conscious motives of interest and ideology than to the unconscious. A psychological approach, by contrast, necessarily leans heavily on speculation and inference.

In the paper before us, Professor Forgie defends the value of "oedipal logic," yet he does recognize some of the problems raised by critics. The influence of his critics can also be seen in his reassessment of the Lyceum Address. While his book places greater emphasis on a psychological reading of the address, his paper gives greater attention to the ideological component and integrates the two in a more balanced way. Lincoln, he thus concludes, "related his own conflicting desires . . . to the structure of his broad understanding of politics and the processes of history." Ambition and ideology acted upon each other. Lincoln was ambitious and very adept at political strategy, but he was also profoundly shaped by republican ideals.

NOTES

1. Michael F. Holt, *The Political Crisis of the 1850s* (New York: John Wiley and Sons, 1978), pp. x, 5; J. Mills Thornton, *Politics and Power in a Slave Society: Alabama, 1800-1860* (Baton Rouge: Louisiana State University Press, 1978); Jean H. Baker, *Affairs of Party: The Political Culture of Northern Democrats in the Mid-Nineteenth Century* (Ithaca: Cornell University Press, 1983).

2. Daniel Walker Howe, *The Political Culture of the American Whigs* (Chicago: University of Chicago Press, 1979), p. 80. Two articles by Robert E. Shalhope—"Toward a Republican Synthesis: The Emergence of an Understanding of Republicanism in American Historiography," *William and Mary Quarterly*, 3d ser., 29 (1972): 49-80; and "Republicanism and Early American Historiography," ibid., 39 (1982): 334-56—survey the studies of republicanism in the early republic and invite historians to project studies further into the nineteenth century.

3. George B. Forgie, *Patricide in the House Divided: A Psychological Interpretation of Lincoln and His Age* (New York: W. W. Norton, 1979), pp. 263ff.

4. Among the most perceptive reviews are Richard H. Sewall, *Reviews in American History* 8 (1980): 52-56; Richard N. Current, *Journal of Southern History* 46 (1980): 438-40; Gabor S. Boritt, *American Historical Review* 85 (1980): 213-14; David Brion Davis, *New York Review of Books* 26 (Oct. 25, 1979): 23-26.

PART IV

The Assassination

☆ ☆
☆

CHAPTER 11

THE LINCOLN MURDER CONSPIRACIES:
The Assassination in History and Historiography

WILLIAM HANCHETT

IN THE AMERICAN CIVIL WAR men and women on both sides believed they were struggling to uphold basic American traditions and ideals, and on both sides they were right, for the Constitution itself defined the divided loyalties, one to the states, one to the union of states. "There never existed any other government against which treason was so easy," declared the New England novelist Nathaniel Hawthorne, "and could defend itself by such plausible arguments." The federal system, he continued, "has converted crowds of honest people into traitors, who seem to themselves not merely innocent, but patriotic, and who die for a bad cause with as quiet a conscience as if it were the best."[1] Hawthorne never doubted who were the traitors and who were the patriots, which the bad cause and which the best, but neither did the people on the other side.

Since both sides were in fact loyal to fundamental American principles, there were necessarily large numbers of men and women in each section who sympathized with the objectives of the other. Northern Copperheads, or citizens of states that did not secede who supported the Confederacy, and Southern Unionists were despised as traitors by most of the people of their sections, and were sometimes the victims of persecution and abuse. They saw themselves, of course, as true patriots and, depending upon circumstances, the more daring and committed of them gave open or covert support to the cause in which they believed. Naturally, the dominant power in each section sought to strengthen its friends amidst the enemy. A well-financed Confederate mission operating out of Montreal and Toronto, cities

315

of intrigue throughout the war, sought to aid the Confederate cause by exploiting the North's internal divisions and growing war weariness. Confederates in Canada planted anti-Lincoln articles in the press, encouraged Copperheads to spread defeatism and commit acts of sabotage, organized raids across the border and an attempt to burn the city of New York, and planned or undertook other acts of the kind.

It was easy for Copperheads to feel virtuous in their opposition to Lincoln and his policies, for many Democrats loyal to the Union, and even some Republicans, also opposed them. Lincoln suspended the writ of habeas corpus and held without charge thousands of citizens in what became known as "American Bastilles"; he tried civilians alleged to be guilty of ill-defined "disloyal practices" before military commissions instead of in civil courts; he suspended the publication of newspapers; he issued a proclamation confiscating billions of dollars' worth of private property. Such actions were justified, he insisted, as fit and necessary war measures. But critics like the chief justice of the U.S. Supreme Court disputed his reasoning and denounced him for disregarding Constitutional restraints and making his will the limit of his power. Lincoln appeared to be acting like a dictator, reminding many Americans in both sections of one of their most cherished political principles: "Resistance to Tyranny Is Obedience to God."

Ironically, the policy that aroused the most emotional reaction against Lincoln was the same policy for which he was at the time and later most honored, the emancipation of slaves. Good political arguments were raised against emancipation; four slave states of the Upper South had not seceded, and throughout the North there was vigorous objection to interfering with what was considered a local institution. The South, on the other hand, was united in its determination to protect slavery. Opponents of the policy therefore insisted that emancipation would prolong the war by further dividing the North and strengthening unity in the South.

But the most extreme attacks on Lincoln's emancipation policy were racially motivated. Prejudiced whites feared that if the slaves were freed, ignorant black hordes would invade the North, displacing white workers and defiling the section's relative racial purity. Ultimately, the white race would be mongrelized, and that would be the end of American greatness. When Lincoln issued his Emancipation Proclamation—having decided that emancipation would shorten, not lengthen, the war and at the same time rid the nation of the only institution that had ever threatened its existence—the negative response was about as strong as the positive. The *Chicago Times* called the president's action "a monstrous usurpation, a criminal wrong, and an act of national suicide." The proclamation, said the *Times*, "will be known in all history as the most wicked, atrocious, and revolting deed recorded in the annals of civilization."[2]

Among the factors that caused Lincoln to adopt emancipation as a war measure was the huge reservoir of manpower it would make available to the army. But the recruitment of black soldiers infuriated many whites, who felt it degrading for whites and blacks to wear the same uniform and who objected to the idea that the Union might be dependent upon "niggers" for its salvation. Other whites in both sections viewed the turning of docile slaves into armed warriors as an invitation to a massive slave insurrection and the massacre of thousands of innocent women and children. They saw such barbarism as only too characteristic of the Lincoln administration, which had thrown out the time-honored rules of war and adopted the ruthless tactics of total war.

To his enemies, North and South, Lincoln was thus a modern Attila waging war against the sacred principle that governments derived their just powers from the consent of the governed. He had seized dictatorial powers in the face of explicit constitutional prohibitions, and was pursuing a policy with regard to slavery which would pollute the white race and thwart the country's true destiny. In addition, he was himself uneducated and uncouth, a drunkard who spat tobacco juice and blew his nose frontier-style through his thumb and forefinger.

Among the good Americans who hated Lincoln was the popular young actor John Wilkes Booth, a border-state Copperhead from Maryland. Sometime during the summer of 1864, Booth decided that he could do more than serve the Confederacy as a spy and smuggler of medicine. Languishing in Northern prisoner-of-war camps were many thousands of Confederate soldiers whom the United States refused to exchange for its own soldiers held in the Confederate States because it could afford the loss of manpower and the South could not. Booth determined to save the South by freeing some or all of these prisoners. He would capture Lincoln on the road to the Soldiers' Home outside

the city limits of Washington, rush him through the pro-rebel coun-
tryside of southern Maryland to a boat on the Potomac, and deliver
him to the authorities in Richmond to be held for ransom. Even if
the United States refused to exchange the prisoners for the president,
it was bound to make some important concession, and the very daring
of the coup would revitalize the South's sinking morale.

Convinced that his plan was feasible and legitimate as an act of
war—certainly legitimate in the kind of war Lincoln was fighting—
he recruited a small band of Confederates and Copperheads to help
him. He all but gave up his profession, playing only twice during the
early 1865 season, both times in Washington. He traveled to Montreal,
almost certainly to confer with rebel leaders. He purchased horses,
guns and ammunition, and handcuffs, and spent himself poor in the
partial support of his men. But the winter months passed and there
was nothing but talk of heroic deeds. In March Booth almost caused
the breakup of his group by proposing seriously to kidnap Lincoln
in his box in the theater instead of on the open road. A few days
later he actually led his men out the Seventh Street road to ambush
the president as he returned to the city from a theatrical performance
at a hospital, only to learn what he could have read in the newspapers,
that Lincoln was attending a ceremony honoring an Indiana regiment
at Booth's own hotel. Some of the conspirators drifted off. Later in
the month Booth sought futilely to recall them for still another attempt
to capture. This time he discovered the president was out of town.

If Booth had ever been a mature and determined leader of a
daring conspiracy, he was now only a humiliated, frustrated, and
depressed Southern patriot who sought with brandy to deaden the
pain of his own failure and of the South's approaching collapse. His
zeal for the South and his abhorrence of what the North was doing
to it were inflamed by Lincoln's visit to Richmond on April 4, 1865.
There, in the city that had been the capital of the Confederacy and
in which Booth had played over a hundred times in 1859 and 1860,
the Yankee president was received like a god by mobs of newly freed
blacks who wept and knelt before him and cried out their blessings
in gibberish. It was a depraved spectacle, Booth thought, and the
portent of things to come. A week later he and two fellow conspirators
were at the White House when the president spoke on Reconstruction
policy from a second-story window. When they heard him say he
favored enfranchising literate Southern black men and those who had

318

served in the army, Booth exclaimed in disgust, "That means nigger citizenship. Now, by God, I'll put him through. That is the last speech he will ever make."[3]

But it was not just simple racism that turned Booth from an unsuccessful kidnapper into a successful assassin. Most Americans assumed that the April 9 surrender at Appomattox was decisive, that the war was as good as over; but many Southern patriots did not. Robert E. Lee had surrendered only 22,000 men; Joseph E. Johnston's rebel army was still in the field, and at least 100,000 additional soldiers were scattered through the Confederacy. Had he not believed the South would continue to fight, Booth told a Southern officer who assisted him during his attempt to escape, "he would not have struck the blow as he did."[4]

At noon on April 14 Booth stopped for his mail at Ford's Theatre and learned that Lincoln and Ulysses S. Grant planned to occupy the presidential box that evening. Lincoln and Grant together! The commander in chief and the general in chief!

Perhaps Booth had already decided to murder Lincoln if he got the chance. Perhaps the decision came to him only now, when he discovered he had an opportunity to kill at the same time the two men chiefly responsible for the South's imminent defeat. Perhaps the prospect of this twin killing led his despairing mind to imagine the effect upon the Union of the killing of still more of its leaders, and perhaps this vision, in turn, caused him to experience a thrilling resurgence of hope for his beloved Confederacy. So many men had been sacrificed, why not the officials who were responsible for all the killing and for the merciless destruction of Southern rights and institutions? They were the guilty ones and their deaths would end the war.

Early in the afternoon Booth arranged for an evening meeting with at least three of the members of the kidnapping conspiracy who were still in town, and then busied himself preparing for the assassinations of Lincoln, Grant, Vice President Andrew Johnson, Secretary of State William H. Seward, and possibly Secretary of War Edwin M. Stanton. He would save the South by bringing down the government of the United States, leaving the country leaderless and bewildered. And he would redeem himself.

Grant's plans changed and he did not appear at the theater. But Booth did. After shooting Lincoln point-blank in the back of the head,

319

he vaulted over the railing of the box to the stage below, catching his right spur in the folds of a flag, and fracturing the fibula of his left leg when he landed. "Sic semper tyrannis!" he cried before making his way upstage left and out a door in the rear of the theater. Thus always to tyrants! One of the conspirators talked his way into Seward's bedroom and nearly succeeded in knifing the secretary to death as he lay in bed. Pulled away, he wounded four other men and dashed down the stairs and into the street. The conspirator who was supposed to kill Johnson made no attempt to do so. Two unknown individuals who may have been potential assassins tried unsuccessfully to approach Grant and Stanton. Booth's assassination conspiracy, apparently conceived and executed on the spur of the moment, thus resulted in the death of Lincoln alone.

"Damn the rebels!" swore Secretary of the Navy Gideon Welles when he heard the news, "This is their work."[5] It was the most common and most natural reaction, and before dawn on April 15 evidence linking Booth — recognized by many theatergoers — to Richmond was discovered, apparently confirming the quick assumption that the assassination was the product of a grand conspiracy of Copperheads and Confederates. In Booth's hotel room officers found a letter advising Booth to postpone some sort of enterprise and recommending that he "go and see how it will be taken at R——d." In addition, they found a Confederate secret cipher which proved to be keyed to a deciphering device recently taken from the abandoned office of the Confederate secretary of state in Richmond.

Responsibility for the investigation of the assassination fell to Joseph Holt, judge advocate general of the U.S. Army and head of the War Department's Bureau of Military Justice. A loyal Kentuckian, Holt had denounced supporters of secession as "maniacs and monsters," and advocated the severe punishment of "rebels and traitors." As judge advocate general, he acted as the principal agent through whom Lincoln extended military control over civilian prisoners, the practice that had been so widely condemned as unconstitutional in the North and that had helped convince Booth Lincoln was a tyrant. Now, after the assassination, Holt was in charge of collecting and evaluating the evidence that would be used before a military commission in the trial of the "maniacs and monsters," the "rebels and traitors," responsible for Lincoln's death.

Within a week Holt found what he had expected to find, and on

April 24, just ten days after the shooting, Secretary Stanton made it public: "This Department has information that the President's murder was organized in Canada and approved at Richmond." This sensational charge was made official on May 2 when President Johnson issued a proclamation stating that the murder of Lincoln and attempted murder of Seward had been "incited, concerted, and procured" by Jefferson Davis and five Southern leaders in Canada, and offering large rewards for their arrest. Davis was captured in Georgia later in the month and imprisoned at Fort Monroe, Virginia.

Booth was killed by a soldier at the time of his capture near Bowling Green, Virginia, on April 26, but on May 10 eight civilian friends of his were formally charged before a military commission with having combined in the assassination conspiracy with him and the individuals named in the president's proclamation. At the end of June all were found guilty. Four were sentenced to terms in prison, and four were hanged. Among the latter was Mrs. Mary E. Surratt, owner of the house in Washington where some of the conspirators had met, and the mother of John H. Surratt, a Confederate courier and close associate of Booth, who escaped to Europe. There were rumors that Johnson would extend special clemency in her case, but he did not and she met her fate with the others on July 7.

Even while the trial was in progress, a flood of letters and affidavits denouncing the principal government witnesses as liars and imposters was published in Canadian newspapers and reprinted in the United States. Disturbing as these attacks were, they were only to be expected from rebels and their Canadian friends, and some of the alleged perjuries could be explained or rationalized away. Yet they did shake Stanton's confidence in Holt's evidence, and just two weeks after the hanging of the four condemned for having conspired Lincoln's death with Davis, Stanton supported the cabinet's decision to try Davis for treason, not assassination, and in a civil not a military court.

There proved to be more difficulties involved in trying Davis for treason in a civil court than the cabinet had anticipated, for Confederate soldiers had been treated as belligerents and given the protection of the laws of war. Could their commander in chief now be tried as a traitor? Many Republicans thought not. In addition, the U.S. attorney general gave it as his opinion that Davis would have to be tried in the federal circuit court in Virginia, where any jury impaneled would be so biased in his favor as to make conviction an impossibility.

For these reasons the administration did not pursue its decision to try Davis and looked, instead, for a way by which it could release him with a minimum of embarrassment. In November Stanton withdrew the offer of rewards for the other confederates named in the president's May 2 proclamation. He later stated that he had done so because he was convinced the men were out of the country and if they were apprehended it would be by government officials in the line of duty. Maybe so, but the withdrawal was more likely an indication of his loss of faith in the evidence against them.

Unaware of Stanton's shift in position and recognizing the futility of trying Davis for treason in a Southern civil court, many Republicans assumed President Johnson was protecting the ex-Confederate leader in exactly the way his Reconstruction policies were protecting the Southern states. In the spring of 1866 the House Judiciary Committee therefore undertook its own investigation of the assassination. Holt appeared before the committee, his confidence in the evidence collected by his bureau apparently unshaken. He restated the case against Davis which had been made at the conspiracy trial, and supplemented it with incriminating depositions from eight new witnesses in whose integrity he said he had complete confidence.

His confidence was misplaced. The new depositions proved to be fictions created by one of the government's chief witnesses at the 1865 conspiracy trial, a scoundrel who was seeking personal revenge against Davis. This man was tried and convicted of perjury and the suborning of perjury, and sentenced to prison. But he insisted that the testimony he had given to the military commission the previous year had been true, and in this matter the beleaguered judge advocate general continued to support him.

Despite the disgrace of the government witness, the Judiciary Committee concluded that Davis was probably privy to the events leading to Lincoln's death, recommended that the War Department continue its investigations, and urged that Davis and the others named in the president's May 2 proclamation be tried without further delay. In a well-publicized minority report, the Democratic member of the committee denounced the majority report and charged that far from being members of the conspiracy against Lincoln, Davis and the others were themselves victims of a conspiracy designed to save the reputations of "certain officers" of the government who had made reckless accusations and then proceeded to manufacture the evidence to support them. It was an accusation to which Holt had certainly left himself—and Stanton—vulnerable, but it is probable that he was the victim of his witness's lies rather than a party to them. The witness had enjoyed a remarkably successful wartime career of deception and self-promotion in Richmond, Washington, and Canada, and in Holt's papers are letters and reports from him which seem marvelously plausible and convincing even today.

During the war Andrew Johnson had talked very much like a Radical Republican. But as president he permitted the former leaders of the Confederacy to continue in political power in their states and sanctioned passage by the Southern legislatures of laws that made a mockery of the Emancipation Proclamation and the Thirteenth Amendment. He was so partial to the ex-rebels that by 1867 Republicans were far more interested in removing him from office than in bringing Jefferson Davis to trial. During hearings to determine if the president had committed an offense for which he could be impeached, the House Judiciary Committee heard testimony from Lafayette C. Baker, chief of the War Department's detective police during the war, that was all Johnson's worst enemies could have desired. Baker swore that he had seen and could obtain wartime correspondence between the president and Davis and other Confederates that proved Johnson had been a rebel spy. As the only one who could be said to have profited from the assassination, some Republicans had already wondered if Johnson might have had an understanding with Southern leaders and been maneuvered into the vice-presidential nomination in 1864 and the presidency in 1865 as part of an intricate conspiracy by which the South could win in peace the protection against the national government denied it by defeat in war. But Baker was unable to produce the sensational letters or any evidence that they had ever existed, and within a short time it was he, not Johnson, who was exposed. As two exasperated members of the committee exclaimed, "It is doubtful whether he had in any one thing told the truth, even by accident."[6]

In one thing, however, Baker did tell the truth to the Judiciary Committee. He revealed that at the time of his death Booth had been carrying a pocket diary. When the diary was produced, Baker startled the committee by testifying that pages had been cut out of it during the two years since he had last seen it, years in which it had been in the custody of the executive branch. "Who spoliated that Book?"

cried Representative Ben Butler of Massachusetts with a gesture toward the White House. Who did Booth expect to succeed to the presidency "if the knife made a vacancy?"[7]

Shrugging aside the fact that Johnson had been himself an intended victim of the assassination conspiracy, Congress established a special committee to see if it could establish a link between the president and the conspirators. The committee did its best, but it did not bother to report, and Butler later conceded that there was no case against Johnson.

By releasing Jefferson Davis from prison in May 1867 the government admitted that there was no case against him, either. The rebel leader promptly departed for a vacation in Canada, the last place a guilty man would have wished to visit.

The release of Davis naturally raised questions about the justification of the 1865 prosecution, conviction, and punishment of the eight individuals with whom he was supposed to have conspired. So, too, did the 1867 civil trial of John H. Surratt, who had been discovered serving as a private in the papal guard at the Vatican. The jury, standing eight to four in his favor, was dismissed, and in 1868 all charges against him were dropped.

At John Surratt's trial was produced the long-rumored petition of clemency for Mary Surratt signed by five of the nine members of the military commission. President Johnson denied ever having seen the petition—which had also been omitted from the published record of the conspiracy trial approved by the War Department—although he conceded that he and Holt had discussed the possibility of commuting Mary Surratt's sentence to life imprisonment. Holt claimed that he and Johnson had discussed the petition specifically and that it had been before the president when he signed the order of execution. The public could not be sure who was telling the truth, but the knowledge that a majority of the commission had recommended that Mary Surratt be spared caused many people, chiefly Democrats, to think of her as a martyr to Republican vindictiveness.

When at the end of his presidency Johnson pardoned the conspirators who had been sent to prison, it attracted no public outcry and little notice, proof that the Confederate grand conspiracy theory mapped out by Holt and originally accepted by Stanton was dead.

But not quite dead, for many Union men and women who bore the psychic scars of a hundred battlefields and one theater could never rid themselves of the suspicion that the rebel leaders responsible for waging war against the United States must also have been responsible for the killing of Lincoln. That a case had not been made did not mean there was no case. In 1901 Osborn H. Oldroyd, a Union veteran who had lived for ten years with his collection of Lincolniana in the Lincoln home in Springfield and who would ultimately live for nearly thirty in the house on Tenth Street in Washington where Lincoln died, expressed these long-lingering misgivings. "Had the military court reached out a little farther in its investigations," he wrote in his popular descriptive history of the assassination, "I believe it would have implicated many persons holding positions of power and authority in the service of the Confederate Government."[8] By the 1980s some serious researchers agreed that Confederate leaders might have been involved at least in Booth's kidnapping conspiracy.

Perhaps no event in their history stirred and has continued to stir the American people so much as Lincoln's assassination. In a sense, Lincoln was the last casualty of the Civil War, and if his death was not the result of a grand conspiracy, it was all the more meaningless and unnecessary, and therefore all the more tragic. Once the trauma of Ford's Theatre tuned out the static of partisanship, it was suddenly recognized that Lincoln had been a supremely successful president. Against staggering odds, he had preserved the Union and the principle of democratic government, and he had destroyed slavery. Yet he had been denounced continually as a failure. Critics had cursed him both for usurping power and for failing to exercise power, and his person and personality had been ridiculed and disparaged. The extraordinary idealization of Lincoln that took place in the generation after the war was in part a way by which those who had underestimated or scorned him could expiate their regret or guilt. Popular veneration was encouraged for their own purposes by Republican leaders and hagiographic biographers, but it was nonetheless real, and the mysteries of Lincoln's mind and character lent credibility to his emergence as the central figure of a new secular religion. Thus the wartime president, who had been just as controversial as the political and social controversies that divided and subdivided his country, was transformed into a revered figure somehow above politics and worldly strife.

In the reputation of Lincoln's murderer there was an opposite and almost equal reaction. The end of the grand conspiracy theory meant, by default, that the assassination had been the result of a simple conspiracy organized by John Wilkes Booth. Where Booth had earlier been accorded a certain respect as a Confederate agent or else dismissed with the contempt due a hired gunman, he was now alone held responsible for Lincoln's death. That meant that he alone had to bear the hatred of increasing millions of Americans who were discovering that they loved Lincoln. As Lincoln's image rose to the heights of a national diety about whom nothing too good could be thought or said, Booth's image sank to the level of a demon about whom there *was* nothing good to be thought or said. Only an evil or insane person would kill a god. Therefore Booth had been evil or insane—and a second-rate ham actor, as well.

Winning sides get to write the history, or at least the first histories. Through sympathetic historians and publicists, the Republican party was thus able to establish itself as the vehicle through which the sainted Lincoln had saved the Union and freed the slaves, and to stigmatize its Democratic opponents as anti-Lincoln rebels and Copperheads. By the end of the century, however, the Democrats had regrouped and counterattacked by revising Republican assessments of Civil War era leaders and issues. The triumph of the revisionist movement was closely related to the prompt reunion of North and South. In the interests of restoring intersectional harmony, many Republicans joined in the critical reevaluation of their party's postwar, post–Lincoln policies, and ended up repudiating them and the leaders associated with them. The nation was reunited by revisionist historians in a bipartisan orgy of recrimination against the "excesses" of Radical Reconstruction. David M. Dewitt, who served as a Democrat in the U.S. House of Representatives in the 1870s and in the New York state legislature in the 1880s, introduced anti-Radical revisionism into the history of Lincoln's assassination.

In two powerful volumes, *The Judicial Murder of Mary E. Surratt* (1895) and *The Assassination of Abraham Lincoln* (1909), Dewitt presented the first systematic accounts of the assassination as a simple conspiracy. Because he was revising the War Department's hapless grand conspiracy charge, he was necessarily anti–War Department, and that meant that his severest criticism was reserved for Secretary of War Stanton, rather than Judge Advocate General Holt (who, however, did not escape lightly). In place of the vigorous and efficient, if admittedly somewhat irascible, secretary so much admired by Republicans, Dewitt portrayed Stanton as an unstable coward who panicked under pressure. His job the night of Lincoln's murder was to mollify public hysteria; instead, every action he took seemed designed to magnify it. His quick assumption that the attacks on Lincoln and Seward were parts of a Confederate grand conspiracy and his subsequent official statements to this effect fixed the false idea in the minds of the Northern people and helped create the desire for vengeance which set the tone for Reconstruction.

Among the major offenses for which Dewitt excoriated Stanton was the government's insistence at the conspiracy trial that assassination, not kidnapping, had been Booth's intention from the beginning. One of the conspirators had referred to the plot to kidnap Lincoln at the time of his arrest, and another later amended his confession to include kidnapping. Booth himself made two references to kidnapping in documents possessed by the government, and one of the government's own witnesses testified that Booth had sought his assistance in an effort to capture the president. But at the time of the conspiracy trial, there were good reasons to doubt the reality of a plot to kidnap. Most of the conspirators said nothing about one, and the story Booth told to the government witness was considered to be only a ruse, since Booth had known that this man would have recoiled in horror from a conspiracy to kill. Given the facts of Lincoln's murder, Seward's near murder, knowledge that Johnson was to have been murdered, the incidents suggesting that Grant and Stanton were to have been murdered, too, and the early evidence apparently implicating the Confederate leadership in these awful matters, it was not unreasonable for the War Department to treat talk about a conspiracy to kidnap originating with the actor Booth as trivial and ridiculous, a "silly device" to fool the government.[9]

Revisionist Dewitt also argued at length that the petition of clemency for Mary Surratt had been withheld from President Johnson by War Department treachery. Although this conclusion was based exclusively upon conjecture, it was so plausible and so forcefully stated that practically every writer since has accepted it, even though it is by no means the only conclusion that could be drawn from the facts. Whoever was responsible for the fate of the petition, Dewitt's case against Stanton was every bit as crude and malicious as he claimed

Stanton's case against Mary Surratt had been. Closing his eyes to the myriad individuals, problems, and uncertainties with which Stanton had to deal in the chaotic weeks following Lincoln's death and the simultaneous end of the bitter Civil War, he contended that with Booth dead and John H. Surratt missing, the secretary's "one supreme aim" was to hang Mary Surratt.[10] With revisionist fervor, he slanted every-thing against Stanton, conceding nothing to the turbulence of the times, permitting the secretary no honest misjudgments, and dealing his reputation a blow from which it has not yet recovered.

The first book on the assassination as a simple conspiracy in which there was some effort to be fair was Clara Laughlin's *The Death of Lincoln* (1909). A writer on the staff of *McClure's Magazine*, Laughlin approached the subject like a journalist going after a big story. She interviewed surviving principals and searched magazine and news-paper files for articles and documents unknown to a new generation, and reprinted some of them as appendices. Unlike Dewitt, she did not denounce or ridicule Stanton for not knowing from the beginning that only a simple conspiracy was involved, and although the military trial of the conspirators looked "hideously unfair" to her, she de-scribed it in its historical setting and concluded that it was probably as fair a trial as was possible under the circumstances. Nevertheless, her portrait of Stanton as a man of overpowering hatreds was almost as unfriendly as Dewitt's, and she accused the secretary of entertaining special hatreds for Southern women and Roman Catholics, a charge— already old in 1909—with no more substance behind it than Mary Surratt's Southern origins and Catholic religion.

Far more surprising was Laughlin's sympathetic, even flattering, description of Booth. Beginning in the 1890s, actors and actresses had begun to publish scattered reminiscences in which they revealed that Lincoln's assassin had not been at all the fiend imagined by the public. He had been, on the contrary, talented and warmhearted, and was remembered fondly for many acts of kindness on and off stage. By the time Laughlin wrote, Lincoln's position as the nation's most beloved hero was so secure that it was possible for her to portray Booth as the charming young man his friends and family had known. If he committed a monstrous deed, she declared, it was because he had been "cruelly misguided" and thought Lincoln was a tyrant.[11]

Equally sympathetic was actor Francis Wilson's *John Wilkes Booth: Fact and Fiction of Lincoln's Assassination* (1929), still the only book-

length biography of Booth. Intimately acquainted with members of the Booth family and with Booth family history, Wilson knew that brutality was no part of John Wilkes's nature. His crime, therefore, had been out of character, committed in a state of temporary insanity induced by his extreme depression at the South's impending subjugation and the failure of his own plans to prevent it, and by a "sudden exaggeration of hereditary imbalance."[12]

If the Laughlin and Wilson portraits of Booth marked the beginning of a trend that would eventually change the image of the assassin and lead to a more sophisticated understanding of the furies let loose by the Civil War, the trend was abruptly halted by *Myths after Lincoln* (1929), by Lloyd Lewis, a Chicago newspaperman. Published the same year as Wilson's biography and far more widely read, *Myths after Lincoln* showed the relationship between the public's worshipful attitude toward Lincoln and the dying god figure found in popular mythologies since antiquity. The dying god was the "one hero brighter and more beautiful than the rest, [the] one dear, friendly god who had sacrificed his life for the race." When Lincoln ascended into immortality, he took Booth with him, for dying gods had often been the victims of treachery and conferred upon those who had betrayed them an immortality of infamy. Booth was America's demon-hero, and so long as Lincoln was revered, he was destined to be reviled.

Although Lewis was well aware of the difference between the mythological Lincoln and the historical Lincoln, he made no effort to distinguish between the mythological Booth and the historical Booth. In fact, his chapters on Booth and his conspiracies, grouped under the general title "The American Judas," exceed in vituperation any extended analysis of Booth ever published. Drawing freely upon his imagination and disregarding well-established facts, Lewis described Booth perfectly as the evil genius of the American past, thus making a contribution to folklore if not to history. Unfortunately, he called his folklore biography.

By the time *Myths after Lincoln* was published, anti-Radical revisionism had become the new orthodoxy, and Lewis did not fail to insult Stanton with the by now routine charges. The secretary was a coward, he became unbalanced in the presence of danger and death, he was power mad, and he was fanatically anti-Catholic. But Lewis did add something new by suggesting that as early as the day after the assassination Stanton knew the shooting was only "the fool exploit

of a disgruntled actor." The secretary proceeded to blame it on Jefferson Davis so that the Radicals, "Lincoln's enemies," could seize control of the government.[13] One might suppose that knowing the assassination was a simple conspiracy but for political purposes announcing it was a grand conspiracy would be the most despicable outrage imaginable against Stanton. But Otto Eisenschiml, another Chicagoan and friend of Lewis, imagined something worse, as we shall see.

An entirely new Booth made his debut in the literature of Lincoln's assassination in Philip VanDoren Stern's *The Man Who Killed Lincoln* (1939). Although in reality a novel, the book was generally received as nonfiction, and Stern, a New York writer and editor, himself described it as "my first historical work." He claimed to have invented only conversations and five minor incidents. In fact the book's major hypothesis—that Booth killed Lincoln because he identified him with his own father, whom he hated—was also Stern's invention. Not one of the books listed in his bibliography lends the idea any support whatsoever, and several help to establish the exact opposite. The fact is that Booth, who was fourteen years old when his father died, loved and admired him deeply, and was in turn his father's favorite child. Nevertheless, psychiatrists, amateur and professional, responded eagerly and predictably to Stern's nonsense, regaling each other with explanations of the assassination that featured Booth's hatred for his father or brothers or both, and other tensions originating in the family circle, which had been, in truth, loving and close.

One psychological theory is worthy of consideration if only because it originated with journalist Stanley Kimmel, author of the fact-filled *The Mad Booths of Maryland* (1940): Booth shot Lincoln because he was losing his voice and recognized that his career on the stage was drawing to a close. A member of a great acting family who had reveled in the applause of standing-room-only audiences all across the country, he was now faced with the prospect of oblivion. It was this dread, wrote Kimmel, that "drove him to that act of madness. There can be no doubt that this was the underlying cause of his determination to kill Lincoln."[14]

It is true that John Wilkes, unlike his older brothers, had not served a stage apprenticeship under his father, the great tragedian Junius Brutus Booth, and had not been taught how to project his voice without straining his vocal chords. The result was occasional hoarseness and the cancellation of some performances. But there is no evidence that Booth believed his career was ending, and he would have been a rare twenty-five-year-old to believe it was. In the fall of 1864, when he began to devote himself so fully to the kidnapping conspiracy, he sent his theatrical wardrobe to Richmond (through Canada), where he expected to join it and use it. Among the last things he said to one of his friends the following spring, when the kidnapping scheme had been abandoned, was that he planned to return to his career on the stage. Kimmel's overstated theory trivializes Booth and is unworthy of the impressive research on the Booth family apparent in his book.

Far more convincing an explanation of the assassination is offered by George S. Bryan in his classic *The Great American Myth* (1940). Like Stern a New York writer and editor, Bryan devoted nearly a hundred pages to Booth's evolution from a high-spirited young boy, proud of his famous family and confident of his own future, into the angry, quick-tempered fanatic who shot Lincoln. He followed Booth's theatrical career in greater detail than Kimmel, and accorded the actor a greater degree of success and recognition. More important, he showed how closely Booth identified himself with the pro-Confederate sympathies of his native Baltimore and Maryland.

It is no coincidence that Bryan, who wrote the best analysis of Booth as a youth, actor, conspirator, and assassin, should also have written the best analysis of the assassination as a simple conspiracy. As he observed, the assassination had from the first become "involved in a tangle of disorder and error, of falsehood and credulity, from which it has not yet been set free."[15] If he had had the influence he deserved, Bryan would have gone a long way toward setting it free, for he genuinely sought the truth and the tone of his writing was judicious and unemotional. Unfortunately, *The Great American Myth* was published just after Eisenschiml revolutionized the subject of Lincoln's murder with an entirely new grand conspiracy theory, entangling the assassination in new "disorders and errors, falsehoods and credulities," and reducing Booth once again to the secondary role of hired gunman. The public was far more interested in the sensational Eisenschiml thesis than in Bryan's sober analysis of Booth's simple conspiracy, and the result was that Bryan had very little influence at all.

Trained as a chemist in his native Austria, Otto Eisenschiml made a fortune as a businessman in Chicago in the 1920s, and thereafter devoted himself to the study of the Civil War until his death in 1963. Why did Booth shoot Lincoln, he wondered, disbelieving that the actor had turned assassin out of either a mad desire to avenge the South or a vainglorious one to be hailed as the last champion of the lost cause. As he saw it, "A great political crime was committed without an adequate motive."[16]

In attempting to discover what had motivated Booth, Eisenschiml engaged in the most thorough and imaginative search for assassination-related materials yet undertaken. He prided himself upon discovering in dusty files in the War Department the documentary evidence, now known as "Investigation and Trial Papers Relating to the Assassination of President Lincoln," collected by Joseph Holt's Bureau of Military Justice in 1865 (although these documents had been consulted by previous researchers). He purchased private collections of papers of individuals involved with the assassination or its aftermath, and with the help of a research staff he turned up hundreds of relevant government documents, memoirs, and magazine and newspaper articles, many of them never before studied. As he and his assistants sifted through these thousands of pages, he later recalled, a pattern began to emerge. As the pattern "grew in size and distinctness, we became almost frightened at the form it was taking. Could it be that Lincoln's murder had been an inside job?"[17] After years of work, Eisenschiml revealed in his *Why Was Lincoln Murdered?* (1937) that the pattern did indeed show the assassination to have been an inside job. In fact, Lincoln's murder had been masterminded by Secretary of War Stanton!

Eisenschiml's hypothesis was that Stanton and other Radical leaders had arranged the assassination because they opposed the president's compassionate Reconstruction program and wished to substitute a policy that would make the South pay for its rebellion and assure the permanent supremacy of their party. In addition, according to Eisenschiml, Stanton believed that with Lincoln dead he would emerge as the nation's most popular hero and be rewarded with the presidency.

No fairminded person, let alone a scientist striving for scholarly objectivity (which is how Eisenschiml repeatedly characterized himself) could possibly maintain that this pattern emerged from the evidence. It did not. It was imposed upon the evidence, which was stretched and twisted to establish the pattern. A few examples of how Eisenschiml manufactured his case against Stanton by asking leading and misleading questions must suffice:

Why did the War Department not take the strictest measures to protect the president?

Why did Stanton deny Lincoln the escort he had requested to the theater on the fatal evening?

Why was the guard who deserted his post outside Lincoln's box never punished?

Why was the telegraphic service out of Washington interrupted at about the same time as the assassination?

Why did Stanton send out telegraphic orders blocking all the roads out of Washington except the one Booth took?

When Booth's coconspirators were captured and held in prison for trial, why were they silenced and cut off from communication with the world by being forced to wear canvas hoods over their heads?

These are shameful questions. They imply a complicity that honest answers do not justify, and they establish a prejudice against Stanton that is extremely difficult to overcome. Consider:

Presidents cannot be strictly protected unless they want to be. Despite frequent and urgent pleas from Stanton and others, Lincoln did not want to be.

Stanton denied Lincoln the officer whose company he had requested because he did not want Lincoln to go to the theater. The officer was to have been a guest inside the box, not a guard outside of it, a distinction Eisenschiml blurred by referring to him as an "escort."

The guard who took a seat so he could watch the play, a member of the Washington metropolitan police force, was tried before the police board. The case was dismissed, perhaps because Parker could show he had not been ordered to remain at the door to the box, where, in fact, it had not been the habit to station a guard; perhaps the board recognized that Parker would have had no reason to deny Booth entrance to the box, Lincoln's interest in actors and the theater being well known.

Only the commercial telegraph between Washington and Baltimore went out of operation. Other commercial lines and the military lines were not interrupted.

Stanton could not order the blocking of the road Booth took out of Washington because there were no telegraph facilities along it or at the end of it. He did notify the nearest telegraph stations.

The conspirators were not silenced or denied communication with the world. Each was interrogated repeatedly by civilian or military authorities, and each was represented by counsel at the conspiracy trial. Those who were hanged spent their last nights in the company of family or clergy; those sentenced to prison had unlimited opportunities to talk both in prison and after their pardons.

The suggestion that Stanton hoped to succeed Lincoln as president was pure fiction. Never a popular figure, he cared nothing for popularity and never held an elective office.

Analyzed point by point, Eisenschiml's grand conspiracy simply falls apart. Eisenschiml freely admitted he could not prove his case against Stanton because it was based exclusively on circumstantial evidence, thereby winning for himself a reputation for fairness. But he never admitted that he had tampered with the circumstantial evidence, which is what he did when he asked questions that inferred sinister answers he knew were not warranted. For reasons that have not yet been explained and may be inexplicable, he abandoned the scientific principles he claimed to be applying—he abandoned even the simplest rules of fair play—and then justified himself by explaining he was only advancing a hypothesis. The title of his book, he pointed out, was *Why Was Lincoln Murdered?* not *Why Lincoln Was Murdered.* The sophistry may have salvaged his self-respect, and it fooled the American people into thinking he was an honest man.

An immediate hit, the book was a selection of the Book-of-the-Month Club and enjoyed a large sale as a paperback. More important, all or parts of the thesis were picked up by writers who understood the market value of stories of conspiracy and betrayal involving the nation's best-loved hero, and who eagerly searched for additional facts and incidents by which to arouse suspicion against Stanton and the Radicals. The revisionist books these writers consulted necessarily reinforced the anti-Stanton bias taken from Eisenschiml (who had consulted the same books) and added credibility to Eisenschiml's conclusions. Viewing the assassination from revisionist perspectives, the popularizers saw Eisenschiml's grand conspiracy as but the logical climax of Radical extremism and hostility toward Lincoln. That is how they passed it on to their own readers. They publicized the Eisenschiml thesis so extensively in books, in articles in newspapers and mass-circulation magazines like the *Reader's Digest* and later *Playboy*, and in radio and television dramatizations, that it is probable that within a generation a majority of the people who had any opinion at all about the assassination had come to believe it: Lincoln had been a victim of an evil plot by Stanton and other government officials he had trusted.

Even writers who adhered to the traditional, simple conspiracy theory were influenced by Eisenschiml and perpetuated features of his argument. In *The Day Lincoln Was Shot* (1955), the most popular of all books on the assassination, Jim Bishop, for example, noted that Stanton had sent out telegraphic warnings along all the roads out of Washington except the one Booth took, but offered no explanation. He presented Stanton as a frightened fool who recognized by 3:00 A.M. the day after the assassination that he was pursuing only one man; he made the charge of a grand conspiracy in order to save face. Bishop, and virtually every other writer after 1937, also accepted Eisenschiml's idea that the War Department had known about Booth's kidnapping conspiracy but allowed the conspirators to remain at large because it was not averse to having Lincoln become the victim of violence.

If the general public bought the Eisenschiml thesis in whole or in part, professional historians—who were not much interested in the assassination—did not, although one leading Lincoln scholar and a professor of history at Harvard University were at least temporarily mesmerized. Recognizing that *Why Was Lincoln Murdered?* and most of Eisenschiml's subsequent books were captious and perverse, historians said so to each other in reviews in their journals, but until recently no one ever attempted a close analysis of the techniques employed by Eisenschiml in his case against Stanton. Had it not been for his success with the public, an exposure would not have been worthwhile, for scholars have more important things to do than to occupy themselves with every fool theory that comes along. But it was precisely because historians ignored Eisenschiml that his thesis was able to obtain such a powerful hold over the public imagination.

In the literature of Lincoln's assassination there are many crackpot theories which have won and held their coteries of true believers. There is the theory that Booth was not captured and killed on a farm in Virginia, but escaped to live in Europe or India or Oklahoma or California. At least twenty men confessed to Booth's crime, and for years a Booth mummy was an attraction at county fairs across the country. There is the theory that the assassination was plotted by the Roman Catholic church, which saw Lincoln, the Protestant champion of democracy and emancipator of slaves, as an obstacle in its struggle for world mastery. Were not some of the conspirators Catholic? Was not John Surratt serving in the Vatican at the time he was discovered? There is the theory that Lincoln was the victim of a conspiracy of international bankers, who objected to his protectionist policies and wanted him removed so that they might dominate the American economy. There is the theory that Lincoln was killed by the officer who was his guest at Ford's Theatre; Booth, who happened to be in the box at the time, became frightened and fled. About the only theory of the assassination that has not been seriously proposed, historian William C. Davis has remarked, is that Lincoln, bored with the play, shot himself.

Such theories are generally recognized for what they are, and for the most part they are harmless. But the writers inspired by Eisenschiml popularized a theory equally absurd, which was generally accepted as the truth, and which, because it deceived the American people about one of the most important events in their history, was not harmless. To compound their influence—and Eisenschiml's— most of the popularizers of the Eisenschiml thesis were reputable, if uncritical, writers whose books were published by respected and responsible houses.

It is not surprising that the irrationality and sensationalism of writing on the assassination should have led in the 1960s and 1970s to the appearance of a large number of "documents" and transcripts of "documents" apparently manufactured to prove the Eisenschiml thesis. A much advertised and widely sold paperback book, *The Lincoln Conspiracy* (1977), by David Balsiger and Charles E. Sellier, Jr., and a simultaneously released feature-length film of the same title, brought this material to the attention of a very large audience. But far from becoming the triumphant capstone of Eisenschiml's work, *The Lincoln Conspiracy* was one of the factors that finished off the Eisenschiml thesis for good. For professional historians—most notably Davis for *Civil War Times Illustrated* and Harold M. Hyman for the Abraham Lincoln Association—assumed their critical responsibilities and exposed the hoaxes upon which it was based. In doing so they also helped to establish that the Eisenschiml thesis was itself a hoax.

336

Another factor that helps to explain the sharp decline in the public's interest in Eisenschiml is a profound conceptual shift which took place within the historical profession in the 1960s. During the civil rights revolution of that decade—sometimes referred to as the Second Reconstruction—the nation was torn by many of the same conflicts it had experienced in the post–Civil War period. The intrusion of the federal government into areas traditionally left to the states in order to bring about the civil equality of all citizens was precisely what the Radical Republicans had attempted a hundred years before. These long-maligned leaders now began to seem more heroic (if premature) than villainous; their objective had not been to punish or humiliate the South but to safeguard the results of the war and give meaning to the freedom won by the ex-slaves. A fresh examination of the sources showed that on these vital matters there had been no major differences between Lincoln and the Radicals, certainly no irreconcilable ones. There would have been no reason, therefore, for Stanton or any other Radical to plot the president's murder.

The perspectives and insights of future historians will change again. But even a revival of anti-Radical revisionism, remote as it seems at the moment, is not likely to revive Eisenschiml's theory of a War Department grand conspiracy, for that explanation of the assassination is now too clearly seen to be a fraud and a libel on the reputation of a great secretary of war and true friend of Lincoln.

NOTES

1. As quoted in Jack Lindeman, ed., *The Conflict of Convictions: American Writers Report the Civil War* (Philadelphia: Chilton Book Co., 1968), p. 79.

2. As quoted in Robert S. Harper, *Lincoln and the Press* (New York: McGraw Hill, 1951), p. 258.

3. U.S., House of Representatives, "Impeachment of the President," *House* Report no. 7, 40th Cong., 1st sess., 1867, serial 1314, p. 674; and George Alfred Townsend, *Katy of Catoctin* (New York: Appleton, 1886), p. 490, 490n.

4. M. B. Ruggles, "Pursuit and Death of John Wilkes Booth," *Century Magazine*, 33 (Jan. 1890): 445.

5. As quoted in Thomas Reed Turner, *Beware the People Weeping: Public Opinion and the Assassination of Abraham Lincoln* (Baton Rouge: Louisiana State University Press, 1982), p. 46.

6. *House Report* no. 7, 40th Cong., 1st sess., 1867, p. 111.

7. U.S. Congress, *Congressional Globe,* 40th Cong., 1st sess., Mar. 26, 1867, p. 363.

8. Osborn H. Oldroyd, *The Assassination of Abraham Lincoln* (Washington: O. H. Oldroyd, 1901), p. vi.

9. *The Assassination of President Lincoln and the Trial of the Conspirators,* comp. Benn Pitman, facsimile ed. (New York: Funk and Wagnalls, 1954), p. 390.

10. David M. Dewitt, *The Judicial Murder of Mary E. Surratt* (Baltimore: John Murphy and Co., 1895), pp. 105-6.

11. Clara Laughlin, "The Last Twenty-Four Hours of Lincoln's Life," *Ladies Home Journal,* Feb. 1909, p. 54.

12. Francis Wilson, *John Wilkes Booth: Fact and Fiction of Lincoln's Assassination* (Boston: Houghton Mifflin, 1929), p. 35.

13. Lloyd Lewis, *Myths after Lincoln* (New York: Readers Club, 1941), p. 62.

14. Stanley Kimmel, *The Mad Booths of Maryland,* 2nd ed., rev. and enl. (New York: Dover Publications, 1969), pp. 262-63.

15. George S. Bryan, *The Great American Myth* (New York: Carrick and Evans, 1940), p. xi.

16. Otto Eisenschiml, *Why Was Lincoln Murdered?* (New York: Grosset and Dunlap, 1937), pp. 379-80.

17. Otto Eisenschiml, *Without Fame: The Romance of a Profession* (Chicago: Alliance Book Corp., 1942), p. 349.

Commentary on
"The Lincoln Murder Conspiracies"

James M. McPherson

The assumption that "great events have great causes" is one to which historians might not subscribe but which seems to be widely held among the public. A corollary to this assumption might be stated as follows: great events that are also horrible or traumatic must be the result of a conspiracy. Not a simple conspiracy, but a grand conspiracy, a conspiracy involving people of power or wealth, a conspiracy whose consequences affect the lives of millions and alter the course of history.

Assassinations and wars provide the most fertile ground for theories of grand conspiracy. All of us are probably familiar, at least in a general way, with some of the many grand conspiracy theories that have been advanced to explain the Kennedy assassination. A number of such theories have also popped up to explain those other two traumatic assassinations of the 1960s, of Robert Kennedy and Martin Luther King, Jr. But it was the events of a century earlier, the Civil War and the assassination of Lincoln, that have proven most traumatic and consequential in American history and that have probably spawned the greatest number of conspiracy theories. First there was the slave power conspiracy. Secession was seen as a grand conspiracy of fire-eaters, the men whom historian Lee Benson some years ago labeled "Southern Bolsheviks." Then we have had the grand Copperhead conspiracy to undermine the Northern war effort, and its subsidiary theory, the Northwest conspiracy to detach the Midwestern states from the Union and ally them with the South. Then of course there was the grand conspiracy theory that Jefferson Davis and other Confederate leaders engineered Lincoln's assassination. John A. Logan, the Union wartime general and postwar Radical Republican, neatly packaged all of these theories along with a few others for good measure in a book about the Civil War appropriately entitled *The Great Conspiracy*.

But Logan and his fellow Radicals did not escape the tarbrush of conspiracy theories themselves. Indeed, even among serious historians until quite recently the Radicals were viewed as the most conspiratorial of all great conspirators in the Civil War era. For Charles Beard and others, they were the front men for Northern industrialists who wanted to cripple the power of Southern agrarians in the interest of fostering Northern industrial domination. For James G. Randall and the early T. Harry Williams, among others, the Radicals constituted a cabal of Jacobins conspiring to undermine Lincoln's generous policies toward the South. For a whole host of historians, the Radicals were responsible for driving the South into secession in 1861 and preventing a sane reconstruction of the Union after 1865, all in the interest of promoting their own political power and the domination of Northern industrial capitalism. And then there is the most persistent of the modern conspiracy theories of Lincoln's assassination—that it was engineered by Secretary of War Stanton on behalf of a clique of Radicals who wanted the soft-hearted president out of the way so they could reconstruct the South in their own harsh manner.

Within the Confederacy there were plenty of cabals and intrigues: Joe Brown and the Georgians against Jefferson Davis on the issues of states' rights and civil liberties; West Virginia and east Tennessee Unionists against secession; the antiwar Heroes of America in North Carolina; and so on. But somehow none of these seems to have achieved the status of a grand conspiracy like those of the Copperheads or Radicals in the North. And of course we have no grand conspiracy theories of the assassination of Jefferson Davis—for what would seem to be an obvious reason. But for those of you who might be disappointed about this, cheer up—one is on the way. The second volume in novelist John Jakes's trilogy on the sectional conflict was published with the title *Love and War*. If you think that title means that all's fair and anything goes, you are right. The melodramatic plot includes a substantial conspiracy by Confederate insiders to assassinate Davis. Sound enticing? You have not heard the best yet. ABC created an eighteen-hour television miniseries based on this and the preceding novel in the trilogy, *North and South*. The original script produced by Warner Brothers for ABC made the assassination conspiracy even more central to the plot and added to it a scheme to establish a

Southwest Confederacy west of the Mississippi stretching to California. Since millions of viewers probably acquired their notions of Civil War history from this television melodrama, we are indebted to ABC's nay-saying historical consultant for saving us from a new video-enshrined assassination theory.

Perhaps a Davis assassination conspiracy would have been welcome diversion from the troublesome plague of Lincoln conspiracies. Using William Hanchett's superb study of these conspiracy theories as a guide, I have counted about a dozen that we might dignify with the label of grand conspiracy—as distinguished from the simple conspiracy of Booth and his small-time hangers-on that actually happened. First there was the theory of a Confederate conspiracy to kill Lincoln. This had several variants and sometimes has included Northern Copperheads—whose alleged role became in some interpretations a separate though related theory. Third, the notion developed that Andrew Johnson was somehow involved, perhaps as the prime mover. Fourth was the persistent idea that the man killed in the burning barn was not Booth, and that the War Department—for any of several attributed reasons—conspired to cover up that fact. Then there has been the long-running theory of a Catholic conspiracy, put forth in dozens of books and articles during the past century. There has also been a theory that a consortium of international bankers headed by the Rothschilds plotted the assassination to weaken the United States for their takeover of its economy. Another theory attributed the dark deed to domestic bankers and businessmen who wanted to get rid of an obstacle to their exploitation of the South—or perhaps for some other reason. Then there is the idea that Secret Service Chief Lafayette Baker was involved in any of several ways, perhaps in conjunction with Stanton and leading Radicals, perhaps not. And of course there is the most popular conspiracy interpretation—the Stanton theory. This has developed an almost infinite number of variants since Eisenschiml's day, including attribution of participation in the plot at one level or another by Secretary of State Seward, Lincoln's friend and bodyguard Ward Hill Lamon, and yes, Mary Lincoln herself—who presumably did it for the insurance. David Balsiger and Charles Sellier's notorious book and movie, *The Lincoln Conspiracy,* manage without blushing to incorporate most of these theories into one superconspiracy interpretation, which, they tell us breathlessly, is based on discoveries of shocking new evidence that enables them to tell all to an anxiously waiting world. These entrepreneurs add quite a few new twists of their own to old theories in a manner that implicates dozens of prominent officials and businessmen in both North and South in several concurrent plots to assassinate Lincoln. They also favor us with the revelation that one group of backers of the original kidnapping plot were Maryland planters and Dr. Samuel Mudd, who resented Lincoln's suppression of civil liberties in Maryland and thought kidnapping was just the thing to stop it.

I do not need to belabor the obvious point that these theories are false as well as ludicrous. William Hanchett and other scholars have exposed them as well and thoroughly as it can be done. The question I want to focus on is not the truth or falsity of these theories, but rather what has made them so popular among so many people. The myths of a people can tell us a great deal about their culture. Conspiracy theories are a form of myth. A promising frontier of research might lie in a study of these conspiracy theories for clues to popular and political culture during the years since the assassination. Some of you are probably familiar with David Donald's intriguing essay "Getting Right with Lincoln," in which he shows how all manner of political leaders, reformers, radicals, and reactionaries since 1865 have found it useful or necessary to cite Lincoln on behalf of their particular positions. Lincoln has become a touchstone for just about any question one can think of; quoting Lincoln became as important as quoting the Bible; it has been important to "get right" with Lincoln. I have had personal experience of this. A few Februaries back I gave a Lincoln's Birthday talk to the Lincoln Club of Wilmington, Delaware. Afterward a reporter for a local radio station interviewed me. The first question he asked was: "If Lincoln were alive today, what position would he take on abortion and the budget deficit?"

If Lincoln's life and thought are a touchstone for questions of politics and morals today, the manner of his death can also become a touchstone for the darker, negative aspects of popular culture. The Catholic conspiracy theory of the assassination, for example, might furnish material to the historian to measure and analyze anti-Catholic sentiment among groups that believed the theory. The Confederate conspiracy theory reflected anti-Southern sentiment growing out of a bitter and all-consuming war. The relationship between the Andrew Johnson conspiracy theory and Reconstruction politics is obvious. An analysis of the international banker and Rothschild theory might tell us what the author of this theory and his intended audience thought about bankers, especially Jewish bankers. The Stanton/Radical theory is rich with ambivalence and irony when used for its insights on popular attitudes from the 1930s to the 1960s. This theory became popular among some liberals of the New Deal era who saw the Radical Republicans as a front for big business and were willing to believe that they murdered Lincoln. On the other hand, the theory found favor with some Southerners and conservatives and racists who saw the Radicals as self-righteous Jacobins out to destroy the South and equalize the races. The possibilities are endless. What was CBS's motivation in putting on the television docudrama in 1972 called *They've Killed Lincoln?* Who went to the movie or read the book *The Lincoln Conspiracy* in 1977? Was there a pattern? If so, what does it tell us about popular culture? There are some hints and suggestions of the interrelations between conspiracy theories and popular culture in Hanchett's book. One of the most fascinating is his reference to the rise of something of a Booth cult among certain young people in the 1970s, who called themselves Boothies. This has been the subject of an article in the *Journal of American Culture;* this is the kind of work I would like to see more of; this is the sort of thing I am suggesting as a new frontier of research on the Lincoln assassination grand conspiracy theories.

CHAPTER 12

BEWARE THE PEOPLE WEEPING

THOMAS REED TURNER

THE LINCOLN ASSASSINATION is so surrounded by myth, sensation-alism, and falsehood, that beginning to unravel the truth of what really happened is no easy task. Difficulties notwithstanding, what can actually be known about that event and its aftermath?

The most obvious point is that the assassination did not occur in the calm historical vacuum that is portrayed by so many authors, but at the end of an extremely costly and bitter Civil War that was one of the most divisive events in our history. Many contemporaries did not view Lincoln as a godlike figure, as William Hanchett has explained, but as a leader who had to deal with controversial problems in tumultuous times. Lincoln had often been threatened with violence during the course of the war, and while the timing of the attack may have caught people by surprise, the idea that someone might harm the president was certainly not foreign to them.

The week preceding Lincoln's death had been a week of joy and celebration. The end of the war brought great rejoicing accompanied by fireworks, speeches, and parades. Some even began to call for leniency toward the ex-Confederates. Against this background, the assassination seemed all the more traumatic, an evil betrayal.

These feelings rapidly turned into calls for revenge, particularly directed against those thought to be sympathetic to the assassin's act. A most gripping description of the violence that erupted was recorded in an unknown source by Melville Stone, the general manager of the Associated Press: "I made my way around the corner to the Matteson house . . . [,] very soon I heard the crack of a revolver, and a man fell in the centre of the room. His assailant stood perfectly composed with a smoking revolver in his hand, and justified his action by saying: 'He said it served Lincoln right.' There was no arrest, no one would have dared arrest the man. He walked out a hero. I never knew who he was."[1] Other individuals also recorded carrying pistols to take their revenge against anyone who spoke ill of the dead president. The times are hardly normal when men are shooting each other on the street and escaping punishment, and others are contemplating similar action.

Next revulsion set in against what was mildly criticized as Lincoln's policy of being too lenient toward rebels and traitors. Many of the Radical Republicans greeted the ascendancy of Andrew Johnson to the presidency as the beginning of an era of harshness. Some seemed to be particularly pleased that if Lincoln had to die, at least Johnson was the proper person to succeed him. The Radicals have been blamed for stirring up the public hatred of the South, yet it was natural for Northerners to assume Southern involvement in the president's death. Indeed since Lincoln and Secretary of State William Seward were assaulted almost simultaneously, the attacks appeared to be a well-organized conspiracy, the last dying gasp of the Confederacy. Secretary of the Navy Gideon Welles, not prone to such utterances, blurted out: "Damn the rebels, this is their work."[2]

Several government officials were so convinced that the Confederates were about to capture Washington, that they abandoned their first impulse to rush to the bedside of the dying president and, instead, were paralyzed to inaction by their fear. Chief Justice Salmon Chase, recalling the tramping outside his window of the guards who were sent to protect him, wrote, "It was a night of horrors."[3]

Though the public was convinced that the South was involved, the proclamation issued by President Johnson accusing Jefferson Davis and several other Confederates of being behind the murder caused a profound sensation. There was very little caution expressed in accepting such charges. Newspapers that had been hinting that Davis and Confederates in Canada had engineered Lincoln's death now gloated that they had been correct.

While it has long been certain that the Confederate government had nothing to do with the assassination, Southern reaction to the murder was mixed. It is true that there were some genuine expressions of sorrow, typified by the comment of the *Richmond Whig* on April 17: "The heaviest blow which has ever fallen upon the people of the South has descended."[4] There were also many mass meetings held, as well as statements of sympathy from ex-Confederate leaders and even by those who privately recorded their feelings in their diaries.

However, there were many Southerners who actually rejoiced at Lincoln's death, the same way Northerners might have had it been Davis. The *Texas Republican* of April 28 said that men would thrill to Lincoln's killing "from now until God's judgment day," while the *Galveston Daily News* spoke of martyrdom for Booth. Even many years later there were those who believed Booth to be a Southern hero.[5]

The reaction of Jefferson Davis himself fell something short of deep sympathy. To his Secretary of the Navy Stephen Mallory he managed the rather lame assessment that, "I certainly have no special regard for Mr. Lincoln; but there are a great many men of whose end I would much rather have heard than his." In his memoirs he added that while he could not mourn for Lincoln, his death was "a great misfortune to the South." This comment is revealing in that mourning for Lincoln in the South often centered around anxiety over Johnson's Reconstruction policy rather than genuine grief about the dead president. It took some time for Lincoln to be converted to a national and Southern figure.[6]

Secretary of War Stanton can hardly be accused of artificially manufacturing anti-Southern feelings, and one of the most unfortunate legacies of the assassination has been the innuendo that has so tarnished Stanton's reputation. The truth is that he, along with Lincoln's friend Marshal Ward Hill Lamon, was one of the few presidential advisors who constantly worried about safety and warned Lincoln to be cautious. However, like most presidents, Lincoln was a fatalist who thought he could not spend his life worrying about his personal safety. On the occasion of his second inauguration, when Stanton had tried to strengthen his guard, Lincoln had told the war secretary, "If it is the will of Providence that I should die by the hand of an assassin, it must be so."[7]

With the war ended, most of Lincoln's friends, including Lamon, breathed a sigh of relief that the danger had passed. While Stanton shared these feelings, to a degree, it should not be forgotten that on the day of the assassination, it was Stanton who was still concerned enough for the president's safety that he was urging him not to go to the theater that evening.

Stanton was also one of the few cabinet members intimate enough with the president that they exchanged folksy letters concerning everything from the weather to great affairs of state. And it was Stanton who had a cottage next to Lincoln's on the grounds of the Soldier's Home, where the two men played with each other's children and enjoyed each other's company.

This real Stanton, not the caricature created by his enemies, conducted the pursuit and capture of the assassins and, judged by his contemporaries, he did a more than adequate job. With many other government officials immobilized by fear, people in 1865 marveled at his ability to take charge in an extreme moment of crisis. Several eyewitnesses at the Petersen House, including Assistant Secretary of War Charles A. Dana, wrote glowing tributes to his efficiency. They did not see the out-of-control dictator later portrayed by various writers, but a man who functioned well under very trying circumstances.

While Stanton has been accused of being slow in the pursuit of the assassins, that charge does not stand up to careful investigation either. With all that Stanton had to do that fateful night, the four and a half hours it took to identify Booth positively as the assassin does not appear to be an inordinately long amount of time. Claims that Stanton was slow in releasing Booth's name to the newspapers, as if he were engaging in some sort of cover-up, are nonsense. His task was to notify the detectives and military commanders who would pursue the assassins, and he did this rapidly and effectively. In fact, his hesitancy to publish far and wide Booth's name as the assassin may indicate that he was trying to avoid whipping up the public frenzy that his critics have accused him of doing anyway.

Given the trauma of the assassination, the pursuit of the assassins could not have been as easy as later writers have wished. There were reports from many geographic areas that Booth had been seen, often disguised as a woman. Sometimes unfortunate Booth look-alikes were apprehended and then released with the admonition that anyone looking as much like Booth as they did would be wise to stay off the streets at present. Some of these individuals narrowly avoided bodily harm, although one newspaper humorously tallied up the numbers of those caught in the dragnet.

One popular theory was that Booth had never even left Washington. A letter claiming that Booth had been seen in women's clothes on E street between Eleventh and Twelfth streets brought the seizure of the entire block and a house-to-house search. Even the Washington postmaster, S. J. Bowen, communicated to Stanton his belief, and that of his friends, that Booth was still in the city and that every house should be searched.

While some of the evidence that reached the government appeared to be false or the work of cranks, a great deal of time and energy had to be expended in checking it out. No matter how suspicious the lead, it would have been extremely embarrassing not to have pursued the information and to have discovered that Booth was thereby allowed to escape.

Even Booth's audacity in giving his name as he crossed the Navy Yard Bridge, leading out of Washington, caused confusion. Whether Booth did this on purpose or accidentally, it caused many people to believe that Booth had accomplices who were trying to mislead the authorities as to his true direction of flight. Few seemed inclined to believe that a shrewd assassin would have been foolish enough to give his real name.

Many contemporaries would not have been very much surprised had the assassins escaped altogether, given a wooded and swampy area and a sympathetic populace. One need only be reminded that in 1963 Lee Harvey Oswald was not apprehended at the site of the shooting of John F. Kennedy, or that in 1968 James Earl Ray, who was convicted of killing Dr. Martin Luther King, Jr., eluded his pursuers for many weeks.

Despite all of the confusion involved, the authorities did manage to strike Booth's trail and, on April 26, 1865, he was shot and killed in the tobacco shed of farmer Richard Garrett near Port Royal, Virginia. Booth's death, however, raised many other questions, including how the authorities managed to pinpoint his exact location. While Lafayette Baker claimed that an elderly black informant had provided the break in the case, S. H. Beckwith, telegraph operator for General Grant, had been dispatched to the area to aid Major James O'Beirne, whose forces were tracking the assassin. It was apparently the information relayed by Beckwith that led Baker's detectives, along with a troop of cavalry, to Booth's hiding place. The importance of Beckwith's role is revealed by the fact that he was granted a $500 share of the reward money.

In fact, had the Baker forces not discovered Booth, another party under H. W. Smith, assistant adjutant general, was also close on the trail and would likely have made the capture. Col. H. S. Olcott confirmed that Smith had narrowly missed the capture when he wrote to Judge Advocate Joseph Holt: "A party of twenty-five cavalry that we sent under Smith on a tug reached the scene of Booth's death, eleven hours after that occurrence, and would have been there eight hours before it if the steampower of the vessel had not been inadequate. And yet we see Baker made a general and receiving all credit, while the rest of us are not even mentioned in anyway."[8]

The huge rewards offered led to a rather unseemingly scramble among the detectives for their share, but the public in 1865 had great faith that this was the proper means to apprehending the assassin. This public thought it not so unusual that Booth had escaped, and it believed that rewards totaling as much as $100,000 would ultimately cause someone to betray him.

One of the unfortunate aspects of the killing of Booth was the secrecy with which the body was handled. This secrecy fueled rumors that either the government had something to hide, or the corpse was not Booth. The authorities had inadvertently fostered this speculation by allowing a picture to be printed, which appeared in *Frank Leslie's Illustrated Newspaper,* showing Baker's detectives placing the body in a rowboat on the Potomac River and rowing away in the gathering twilight. This led to the belief that the body had been disposed of in the river, when in reality the detectives had secretly rowed back to the Old Penitentiary on the Washington Arsenal grounds and buried the body in an ammunition box. The government's purpose was to prevent Booth's grave from becoming a shrine for those who sympathized with his deed.

With Booth dead, the government arrested eight of his associates, including David Herold, who had been found with him in Garrett's barn. One of the key problems now became the mode of trial for these suspected assassins. President Johnson consulted Attorney General James Speed and received the opinion that the suspects could be tried by a military commission. On May 6, 1865, he appointed such a body.

Few Americans of any era have been very comfortable with military courts for civilians and, in retrospect, Johnson's was an unwise decision. Yet no author has attempted to investigate why, in 1865, the government felt compelled to abandon the time-honored tradition of using civil courts to try civilians.

During the Civil War Lincoln had suspended the writ of habeas corpus; therefore, holding civilians without trial and trying them by military court were not unusual procedures. While historian David Dewitt argued that the trial of Mary Surratt was unprecedented, another woman, Mrs. Bessie Perrine, was actually undergoing a military trial at the same time as Mary Surratt on charges of having aided rebel raiders in July 1864. She was convicted, although President Johnson set aside the execution of her sentence, contingent upon her future good behavior.

To say that military trials were not uncommon is not to indicate lack of opposition to them. Many sensed instinctively that the guilt or innocence of those involved would become confused, and that those convicted by such a court might be made martyrs. Former Congressman Henry Winter Davis sounded like a prophet when he warned Johnson "that the trial of the persons charged with the conspiracy . . . by Military Commission will prove disastrous to yourself your administration and your supporters who may attempt to apologize for it."[9] Perhaps Booth might have lost some of his villainy had he lived to stand trial before a military court.

Another facet of the trial that caused problems was the proposed secrecy. Those who favored a military trial usually did not wish to keep the proceedings secret. Stanton has been criticized for the policy of secrecy, but the evidence seems to indicate that Judge Advocate Holt was responsible for it. Eventually a huge outcry forced the proceedings into the open.

Many people favored a military trial in 1865 not to dispense harsh and vindictive justice but because, with its wider rules of evidence, such a trial was supposed to get more easily to the bottom of the vast conspiracy which the public perceived. As the *Boston Evening Transcript* explained, "A court confined within strictly legal bounds, and never travelling out of the narrow limits of merely technical investigation, could not have developed the full extent of the hideous plot."[10] The court was to serve as a sort of Warren Commission that could investigate all areas and clear up all questions.

The court members have been stereotyped as a vindictive group of army officers who were lusting for blood to avenge Lincoln's death. The actions of two tribunal members, in particular, have fostered this stereotype. Gen. Thomas M. Harris and David Hunter attacked Mary Surratt's lawyer, Reverdy Johnson, as a Southerner unfit to serve as

351

counsel. Later Harris also wrote two books in which he defended testimony that had turned out to be perjured. He also charged that the Catholic church might have been behind Lincoln's death.

However, the actions of the majority of the members do not support the stereotype of vindictive judge. One of the judges, Gen. August V. Kautz, for example, noted that Reverdy Johnson "did the other members great injustice, if he supposed they united with General Harris in his ill advised objection to Lawyer Johnson."[11] Indeed, the court was hardly the bloodthirsty tribunal that has been portrayed.

Nor were the prisoners treated as harshly through the course of the trial as many writers have claimed. While they were initially hooded and kept in chains, both Kautz and Gen. Cyrus Comstock argued against such treatment and the practice was discontinued. A physician visited the prisoners and made recommendations for their comfort. One historian has argued persuasively that by the tenth of June the government had determined that the plot was not as widespread as it had believed and thereafter the prisoners were treated in a more normal manner.

The government also attempted to procure counsel for the accused, an action that has usually not been acknowledged. Letters and telegrams were sent to lawyers requested by the defendants, but obtaining counsel was not a very easy task. In a case so notorious, many lawyers seemed to think that their patriotism would be questioned if they defended those accused of killing Lincoln. Even Joseph Bradley, who successfully defended John Surratt two years later, pleaded pressing professional engagements—in his case a sensational but rather ordinary murder trial.

Several of the lawyers who did take the cases appeared merely to be going through the motions. Observers sensed that the attorneys seemed to be as convinced of the guilt of their clients as the prosecution was. Even Reverdy Johnson, who was praised for his handling of the defense of Mary Surratt, actually did little in a concrete way for that unfortunate woman. He prepared a brief against the jurisdiction of military courts over civilians but left her defense to others. Similarly, Frederick Stone, who was out of the city, did not read his client David Herold's defense but left that job to court reporter James Murphy.

One other myth that should be dispelled is that the accused were tried by a military court so that they might be prevented from testifying in their own behalf. While it is true that they did not testify, in 1865 the only state that would have allowed testimony in a civil trial for murder was Maine. Thus, it was the status of the law that restricted the testimony, not some conspiracy of silence.

Of those tried, the cases of Mary Surratt and Dr. Samuel Mudd have been the most controversial. Surratt was the first woman hanged by the federal government. John Lloyd, a tenant at her tavern in Surrattsville, Maryland, testified that five or six weeks before the assassination, John Surratt, David Herold, and George Atzerodt had brought weapons, ammunition, a rope, and a monkey wrench to the tavern, and that he, Lloyd, had hidden these items for them. He also alleged that on two occasions, including the afternoon of the assassination, Mary Surratt had told him to have the "shooting irons" ready as they would be wanted soon. Booth and Herold stopped during their flight on the evening of April 14 at Lloyd's to secure one of the weapons and a field glass along with some whiskey before they resumed their flight.

Equally damaging to Mary Surratt was the testimony of her son's friend Louis Weichmann, who boarded with the Surratts in Washington. He testified that on April 14, before Mary Surratt had left for Surrattsville, she had been engaged in a lengthy conversation with Booth. He also told the court that Confederate agents and blockade runners Mrs. Sarah Slater and Spencer Howell had visited the Surratt home, as did a mysterious Baptist preacher, "Mr. Wood" (Lewis Paine), who turned out to be Secretary Seward's assailant. In an affidavit dated August 11, 1865, he added details about Mary Surratt weeping at the fall of Richmond, and implied that she hastened back to Washington from Maryland on April 14 for a meeting with a caller whom Weichmann had not seen, but whom he presumed to be Booth.

In addition, just as the authorities were arresting Mary Surratt and some members of her household, Seward's assailant, Paine, arrived at her door dressed as a laborer. While her defenders claim she had poor eyesight and would not have recognized Paine in this partial disguise, her denial that she had ever seen him, coupled with Weichmann's testimony that he had visited her home, obviously made an unfavorable impression on the court.

It is true that much of the evidence against Mary Surratt might have been viewed as circumstantial had the case been tried in calmer times, but in the heated aftermath of the assassination, a very different picture emerged. Surratt appeared to be an intimate of Booth and a

Confederate supporter, as was her son, who was a Confederate courier and blockade runner. The plot against Lincoln had been hatched in her home. And she seemed to be the stereotypical Southern woman, very capable of plotting the death of the hated Lincoln.

A great deal of blame has been heaped on Louis Weichmann for the death of Mary Surratt. He has been portrayed as a son who, out of fear for his own life, made falsely incriminating statements which sent his adopted mother to the gallows. There is some truth to the portrayal of Weichmann as a coward, for he had written to Judge Advocate H. L. Burnett on May 5 that "you confused and terrified me so much yesterday, that I was almost unable to say anything."[12] At the trial's conclusion, a friend of the Surratt family, John Brophy, said that Weichmann had told him that Stanton and Burnett had threatened him with death if he did not tell all he knew and also that Mary Surratt did not like her son's trips to Richmond or the company that he kept. According to Brophy, Weichmann had agreed to write a letter to President Johnson avowing her innocence if Brophy would carry it to the president.

However terrorized Weichmann may have been in private, on the witness stand he made a very favorable impression. Commission member Gen. Lew Wallace noted how firmly Weichmann stood up under cross-examination. His impression was echoed by several newspaper reporters and even Dr. Samuel Mudd, who indicated that Weichmann seemed inclined to tell what he believed was the truth.

There is also some legitimate suspicion that Weichmann was originally involved in the plot to kidnap Lincoln or was, at least, privy to its details. John Surratt, although he can hardly be considered to have been unbiased, made such charges, leading some authors to argue that the transformation of Weichmann from suspect to star witness was another part of the conspiracy and cover-up.

This view is again erroneous, for such a reversal does not necessarily carry with it sinister implications. Encouraging a witness to implicate his fellow conspirators, for promises of immunity, is a procedure often used in American courts, even if it is a sometimes controversial practice. But as the *San Francisco Alta Californian* said so perceptively in 1865, "If such testimony were not accepted, the punishment of great crimes would be rarer than it is."[13]

The effort to defend Mary Surratt's innocence has been made almost entirely by later writers. Most people in 1865 seemed to believe she was guilty and there is some evidence that they were as much convinced of that guilt by Lloyd's reference to "shooting irons" or Paine's arrival at her home as by the investigators' focus on Weichmann. Weichmann's role in her conviction has been blown far out of proportion.

The other major feature of Mary Surratt's trial was the clemency plea signed by a majority of the court, urging the president to commute her death sentence to life imprisonment because of her age and sex. It is ironic that this allegedly bloodthirsty court should make such a recommendation. If they were really as bloodthirsty as they have been portrayed, they could just as easily have condemned to death all those involved. That they did not do so shows that in arriving at their verdict they weighed the evidence as fairly as they could under the circumstances.

Their request for clemency for Mary Surratt has often been obscured by the president's failure to act on the plea. Andrew Johnson and Joseph Holt waged a bitter battle over whether Holt had even shown the president the clemency plea when he brought the death sentences to be signed. Holt attempted to solicit letters showing that the matter had been discussed by the entire cabinet but he waited until Stanton and Seward were both dead and could not corroborate his story. Other cabinet members who were alive were either hesitant or, in some cases, contradicted Holt, and Johnson staunchly maintained that no plea for clemency had been presented to him.

The entire affair boils down to the truthfulness of the two men, Holt and Johnson, and in this case, the evidence on the whole seems to support Johnson. However, there is additional evidence that Johnson may have seen the plea just shortly after the executions, not many weeks or months later, as he was reminded by one James May in a letter dated September 6, 1873.[14] Johnson was also capable of shading the truth if it suited his political purposes.

In some respects this is also an issue that has been discussed out of context. With the mood of both Johnson and the country in the spring of 1865, the clemency plea might not have had much effect anyway. The president refused to see several relatives of the accused when they came seeking clemency, including Mary Surratt's daughter, Anna. Johnson indicated that Holt had urged upon him that the sex of one of the conspirators should have no bearing on the case and that he had agreed with the judge advocate. Since he obviously con-

355

sidered some of the issues raised in the petition, and rejected them, there is no real indication that he would have changed his mind, although it would have provided him a means to spare her life had he chosen to use it. As late as 1873, however, while campaigning, Johnson still maintained that she had been tried by a legal tribunal and he had seen no reason not to carry out the sentence.

Dr. Mudd is the other alleged conspirator whose case has elicited some sympathy, although not quite to the extent of that for Mary Surratt, since he was not executed. It has been argued that if Booth had not broken his ankle the name of Mudd would never have been heard in conjunction with the case and there is some justification for this view. What caused Dr. Mudd the biggest problem were statements by Louis Weichmann that in January 1865 he had been present at a meeting in the National Hotel where Booth and Mudd had private discussions and drew lines on an envelope. Mudd, himself, admitted that in November 1864 Booth had spent the night at his home when he was in the area buying horses. There was also testimony that seemed to portray Mudd as a Southern sympathizer and raise some question as to how quickly he had alerted the authorities about the two men who had come to his home on April 15. Mudd and his wife claimed that Booth had been disguised with false whiskers, which was why they had not recognized him.

Mudd was saved from the gallows by the lack of reliability of several of the witnesses against him. However, his Southern sympathies, his previous connection with Booth, and his setting of the assassin's leg made formidable evidence against him. It seemed hard to believe that Mudd would not have recognized Booth, and if Booth did wear false whiskers at the Mudds, it was the only place he did so. Why he would have disguised himself to those he knew and not to others is not easy to explain. Even some later writers, most of whom have not believed that Mudd was involved in the murder, have speculated that Booth's horse-buying trips may have been connected with his kidnapping schemes and that Mudd may have been involved in some manner.

The other alleged conspirators have received far less attention than either Mary Surratt or Dr. Mudd and that is probably because their sentences more clearly coincided with a rough form of justice. Lewis Paine, who had attacked Secretary Seward and also wounded several other people, was clearly identified by witnesses as the assailant and seemed to be ready to die for his participation. His lawyer, William E. Doster, who later argued that before a civil court Paine would have been acquitted by reason of insanity, actually did his client more harm than good. When he failed to convince the court that Paine had the physical characteristics of insanity, Doster argued a sort of environmental insanity: he claimed that Paine's Southern background made him believe there was nothing wrong with killing his enemy. This impressed the court unfavorably and, as General Kautz wrote, "It was a rather remarkable defense. The deeds charged were not denied."[15]

Similarly David Herold, who was found with Booth, and George Atzerodt, who had been designated to kill Vice President Johnson, were doomed. Attempts to portray Herold as an inexperienced youth had no more effect than the insanity plea did for Paine. Having aided Booth's flight and having surrendered in Garrett's barn, there was little defense that could be made. Atzerodt admitted that he had been approached to kill Johnson but had not done so. This might have won him some leniency in calmer times but not in 1865.

As for the other alleged conspirators, Edward Spangler ran afoul of the perception that Booth must have had help in the theater, although the fact that he was sentenced to only six years shows that the government's case against him was the weakest. Michael O'Laughlin and Samuel Arnold were previously involved in Booth's plot to kidnap Lincoln, but the evidence of their role in the murder was hardly conclusive and they were sentenced to life imprisonment. While this sentence has sometimes appeared harsh, contemporaries seemed to view their cases under the modern legal term of joint venture. That is, if several people conspired to kidnap and some of the group killed the intended victim, then all of those involved should be punished for the crime of murder.

As in the cases of Mary Surratt and Dr. Mudd, the trials of the conspirators ended much as they probably would have in a civil trial. There was much more discrimination on the part of the military tribunal than might reasonably have been expected. If the clemency plea had been honored, only three people would have died and they were all involved with Booth. A civil jury, composed of some of the same citizens who were carrying pistols to avenge the dead president, could hardly be expected to reach a much different conclusion.

There is one other aspect of the trial that has often been overlooked by those who have focused only on the individual conspirators. There were really two trials occurring simultaneously, since the government went to great lengths to prove its charges of Southern conspiracy.

A great deal of this testimony involved areas considered to be sensational in 1865. Evidence was introduced that Jefferson Davis had prior knowledge of the plot and that he spoke favorably of Lincoln's death. There was also much testimony about general rebel atrocities such as the burning of towns and steamboats. In addition, several Union prisoners testified about the wretched treatment they had received, the overall purpose of such testimony being to show that those who were capable of such brutal behavior were certainly capable of murdering the president.

Particularly fascinating to the public was the introduction of cipher letters, with their hidden meanings, and charges that the Confederates had attempted to spread yellow fever throughout the North by infecting water supplies. This raised the same apprehensions that discussion of chemical and biological warfare do today. As the *New York Tribune* said, "This evidence seemed to send a thrill of horror through all."[16]

There were also several witnesses who testified that Booth had dealings with Confederates in Canada who had provided encouragement and money for the assassination project. The star witness was Sandford Conover, whose real name was Charles Dunham. Conover testified that he had seen Booth and John Surratt in conversation with Confederate commissioners Jacob Thompson and George Sanders. Dispatches were allegedly brought from Richmond indicating that Booth had been chosen to kill Lincoln.

Even before Conover had concluded his testimony rumors arose that there were discrepancies. Weeks later, he then had to be returned to the stand to try to deal with these charges. Conover explained that he had returned to Canada, and under threat of death by the Confederates, he had been forced to retract several of his prior statements. He still maintained that everything he had testified to had been true.

In 1866, during an investigation by the House Judiciary Committee of the charges against Jefferson Davis, it was revealed that Conover's testimony was completely false and that other witnesses who had testified along similar lines had actually been coached by

Conover as to what they should say. These revelations make it appear that Judge Advocate Holt was, at best, once more sadly misled or, at worst, consciously involved in using perjured testimony to try to bring Davis to trial and conviction. Holt once more became involved in a series of efforts to clear his name.

Many authors have not really understood the impact of the Conover testimony. They have focused exclusively on the perjured testimony without realizing how people could be so easily deceived by it. Furthermore, it seemed perfectly plausible to people in 1865 that those who had committed treason against their country, as well as atrocities against prisoners of war, were capable of plotting assassination. When academic historians can be taken in, as some were for a time in the case of the recent Hitler diaries which turned out to be forgeries, perhaps we expect too much of our public officials. Even years later many people believed that if the Conover stories were lies, there was still enough other evidence to make the charges stick.[17]

The final act in the Lincoln assassination drama came with the trial of John Surratt by a civil jury in 1867. It has been argued that the jury's inability to agree about Surratt's guilt, and his going free, proves just how biased the earlier military commission had been. Since the evidence against John Surratt was virtually the same as that against his mother, the son's case has also been used to prove that the mother was the victim of judicial murder.

John Surratt might very well have received harsh punishment had he been apprehended in 1865. However, he escaped, making his way to Canada, England, and the Papal States, where he enlisted as a papal Zouave. He was recognized by a former acquaintance and fellow Zouave, Henry Ste. Marie, who reported his presence to the American minister, Rufus King. As Surratt was about to be arrested at Veroli, Italy, he leaped over a precipice and temporarily escaped. He was finally arrested at Alexandria, Egypt, and sent back to the United States aboard the ship *Swatara*.

The arrest of John Surratt brought some interesting rumors, not the least of which was that Johnson feared his return and trial because he might reveal the president's own involvement in the murder. As evidence was being gathered to impeach Johnson, the Radical Republicans, as well as some of the press, hinted that Johnson had been behind Lincoln's death. Actually Johnson did have some worries along these lines, not because the charges were true, but because he feared the Radicals might offer John Surratt a pardon, and in a desperate attempt to save his own life, he might confess to anything they wanted.

To equate the 1865 and 1867 trials, however, is untenable, since the 1867 trial was held in a much calmer atmosphere. The anger and confusion that had surrounded Lincoln's death in 1865 had naturally abated. The evidence was viewed much more dispassionately and some of the testimony about Southern complicity that had been allowed before the military tribunal was now ruled illegal.

Even in 1867, though, the prosecution's case at first seemed formidable. Sgt. Joseph Dye, who had testified in 1865 that he had seen two men outside the theater with Booth engaged in calling out the time and other suspicious activities, now identified one of these men as Surratt. He added that Surratt's thin, pale face had so impressed him that he afterward often saw it in his dreams. He further claimed that as he and his friend, Sgt. Cooper, were returning to camp, a woman whom he believed was Mary Surratt had raised her window and inquired what was going on downtown.

Other testimony seemed to be equally damaging. Numerous witnesses testified that they had seen John Surratt in Washington on April 14, and Ste. Marie claimed Surratt had confessed to him that he had escaped from Washington on the evening of the murder. Weichmann and Lloyd also repeated their testimony given in 1865, although Weichmann added a few new details, such as Anna Surratt's alleged statement on the morning of April 15 that the death of Lincoln was no more than the death of any Negro in the army. Dr. Lewis McMillan, surgeon of the steamship *Peruvian*, on which Surratt had fled to England, also was brought to the stand and testified that Surratt had admitted murdering some escaped Union prisoners in cold blood and that he said he hoped to live to serve Johnson as Lincoln had been served. All of this seemed terribly incriminating and as the *New York Weekly World* said on July 10, "If the testimony which has thus far been given is not shaken by counter-evidence, and is believed by the jury, it will go hard with the prisoner."[18]

The point is that in 1867 just such counterevidence was presented, which did a great deal to weaken the prosecution's case. Dye's testimony was shaken when stage carpenter James Gifford, actor C. B. Hess, and costumer Louis Carland revealed that they were the group of three men who were in front of the theater. Mrs. Frederika Lambert also testified that she had had an encounter with two soldiers on April 14 similar to the one described by Dye and Cooper. Attempts were made to impeach Weichmann and Lloyd by showing that Weichmann had been intimidated into making the statements he did while Lloyd admitted to being drunk during his encounters with Mary Surratt. There were hints that both these men might themselves have been accomplices of Booth.

There was also testimony from Stephen Cameron, chaplain and sometime Confederate secret service agent, that the surgeon McMillan had told him that Surratt had been in Elmira, New York, on the day of the assassination and then had gone to Canandaigua. Indeed, this line of evidence proved to be the most telling for the defense, for as it became fairly certain that Surratt had been in upstate New York as late as April 13, the prosecution had to alter its tactics. Witnesses were produced to show that it would have been possible to come by train to reach Washington on April 14. However, when that too appeared doubtful, since several parts of the railroad line were out of operation, the last resort was to argue the doctrine of constructive presence. This stated that Surratt was in league with the conspirators and that he might have been in Elmira as part of that plan, perhaps to cause confusion by burning the city or releasing Confederate prisoners. Such connection was not legally convincing and so weakened the case that in 1889 Edward Carrington, one of the prosecutors, admitted that there was no really good evidence that Surratt was in Washington on April 14.

This trial, while not as rancorous as the 1865 trial, did produce a degree of bitterness. Defense counsel Joseph Bradley spoke of vindicating Mary Surratt while District Attorney Carrington took strong exception to the charges that she had been murdered. On another occasion defense counsel Richard Merrick questioned the veracity of prosecution witnesses, stating that some were apt to end up in the penitentiary, which led to a clash in court between witness McMillan and Merrick. The old animosities of the war were also raised, for example, when James Ford, the brother of theater owner John Ford, was questioned as to which side he had supported in the war. At the end of the trial, tempers ran so high that senior defense counsel Bradley and presiding judge George Fisher almost came to blows, and challenges to a duel were issued when Fisher disbarred Bradley.

While the acrimony did provide a certain amount of excitement, the evidence had become so bewildering that it was very difficult to reach a clear decision. The *Baltimore Sun* very prudently cautioned, "The jury will certainly have to exercise a wise judgment in reconciling the great conflict in evidence."[19] Despite some partisan comments at the outcome most people could comprehend why the jury could not agree.

It is wrongheaded to argue that the one overriding factor in the failure to convict John Surratt was his trial before a civil instead of a military court. The jury did not convict John Surratt because the evidence was inconclusive and there seemed to be relatively little desire to retry him. The public appeared content to leave to historians the task of unraveling whatever mysteries still remained.

Unfortunately, historians for over a hundred years have generally been willing to abandon the field to sensationalists and popularizers. Perhaps we are now entering a phase where scholars will give the death of Lincoln the attention it deserves. It is worth noting that one of the preeminent Lincoln scholars of our generation, Richard Current, suggests in his latest book that future Lincoln scholarship is not apt to proceed from the startling discovery of any new large body of Lincoln letters. Rather, advances will come from a careful restudy of materials that have been heedlessly used in the past and the application of the historian's imagination to see new patterns of meaning in already familiar evidence.[20]

The Lincoln assassination well illustrates his point. Too many sensational new revelations have turned out to be frauds for us to believe that many new valid materials will be discovered in the future. But there have been numerous underutilized or misunderstood sources. One example of this is the hundreds of sermons delivered on Lincoln's death. If authors had really read and understood these sermons, with Northern ministers preaching hatred for the South and castigating the Confederates as being behind the murder, they would have had a much better understanding of the forces unleashed by the assassination. Secretary of War Stanton's views may have coincided with those of the ministers, but he was presiding over events that were far beyond his power to control even had he wished to do so.

Another fruitful area of pursuit in the future may be a study of the assassination in the broader context of other American assassinations. The belief that Booth escaped death in Garrett's barn or that a double died in place of Lee Harvey Oswald appear to be too similar to be mere coincidence. Historian Lloyd Lewis suggested many years ago in *Myths after Lincoln* that in death Lincoln became the traditional folk god who was betrayed. In that folk myth tradition the Judas who betrays the folk hero is not allowed to rest but must wander the world alone and friendless until some retribution is made for the crime. Booth and Oswald, having assumed the role of Judas, cannot be seen as dying a simple death, even though the evidence is overwhelming that both died in the manner traditionally portrayed. There appear to be additional similarities surrounding American assassinations that might further illuminate the death of Lincoln.

There are so many layers of myth to be stripped away from Lincoln's assassination and its aftermath that the task is not easy, but progress has been made and can be made in the future. It is high time for academic historians to recapture the ground they have lost, for if the historiography of the Lincoln assassination teaches us anything, it is that we abandon any area of research to the sensationalists and popularizers only at great peril to the truth.

NOTES

1. *Lincoln Lore*, no. 1478 (Apr. 1961); Unidentified newspaper clipping, in Truman H. Bartlett Collection, Boston University.

2. Mrs. M. J. Welles (Typescript), Apr. 14, 1865, in Gideon Welles Papers, Library of Congress.

3. David Donald, ed., *The Civil War Diaries of Salmon P. Chase* (New York: Longman's, Green, 1954), p. 267.

4. *Richmond Whig*, quoted in *New Orleans Times-Picayune*, May 12, 1865, p. 4.

5. Robert S. Harper, *Lincoln and the Press* (New York: McGraw Hill, 1951), p. 360.

6. Stephen Russell Mallory, "Last Days of the Confederate Government," *McClure's Magazine* 16 (1901): 244; Jefferson Davis, *The Rise and Fall of the Confederate Government*, 2 vols. (New York: D. Appleton, 1912), 2: 683.

7. John A. Bingham, "Recollections of Lincoln and Stanton, by Honorable John A. Bingham of Ohio, the Judge Advocate That Tried the Assassins" (Typescript of the originals, compiled by J. L. Conwell and in the possession of Milton Ronsheim), in John A. Bingham Papers, Ohio Historical Society, microcopy, roll 1.

8. H. S. Olcott to Joseph Holt, Sept. 15, 1865, in Joseph Holt Papers, Library of Congress.

9. Henry W. Davis to Andrew Johnson, May 13, 1865, in Andrew Johnson Papers, Library of Congress, microcopy, roll 15; Mark E. Neely,

Jr., "The Lincoln Administration and Arbitrary Arrests: A Reconsideration," *Papers of the Abraham Lincoln Association* 5 (1983): 7-24.

10. *Boston Evening Transcript,* June 23, 1865, p. 2.

11. August V. Kautz, Daily Journal, May 8, 9, 21, 27, June 9, 1865: "Reminiscences of the Civil War" (Typescript), pp. 108-9, in August V. Kautz Papers, Library of Congress.

12. Louis Weichmann to Henry L. Burnett, May 5, 1865, in Record Book, file W, p. 102, National Archives.

13. *San Francisco Alta Californian,* July 20, 1865, p. 2.

14. James May to Andrew Johnson, Sept. 6, 1873, in Andrew Johnson Papers, Library of Congress, microcopy, roll 37.

15 August V. Kautz, Daily Journal, June 21, 1865, in Kautz Papers.

16. *New York Tribune,* May 30, 1865, p. 1.

17. *New York Tribune,* Apr. 23, 1983, pp. 1, 4; Apr. 24, 1983, pp. 1,4; Apr. 25, 1983, p. 1; Apr. 26, 1983, pp. 1, 8.

18. *New York Weekly World,* July 10, 1867, p. 2.

19. *Baltimore Sun,* July 24, 1867, p. 4.

20. Richard Nelson Current, *Speaking of Abraham Lincoln: The Man and His Meaning for Our Times* (Urbana: University of Illinois Press, 1983), pp. 48-49.

Conspiracies, Myths, and the Will to Believe: The Importance of Context

Commentary on "Beware the People Weeping"

JAMES W. CLARKE

As a social scientist interested in historical subjects, I have become very aware of the disturbing ahistorical quality of much social science. It would be easy to conclude, as some have, that this defect is largely symptomatic of the advances in statistical methodologies that characterize the thrust of much of the research for the past three or four decades in the social sciences. But the problem is just as apparent in many nonstatistical studies that either ignore or fail to consider systematically and empirically the context of behavior and events. Nowhere is the problem more apparent than in psychological and psychiatric research that until recently has focused almost solely on personality and dispositional variables as if such characteristics exist in a contextual vacuum. It can also be observed, ironically it would seem, even in some psychohistorical work.

Professor Turner, both in his excellent book and the paper drawn from it presented here, has skillfully exposed the difficulties in the most widely known conspiratorical explanations of the Lincoln assassination.[1] It is apparent that intellectual dishonesty inspired by politics, greed, or slothfulness characterizes a number of those theories. But the real weakness in other honest but unconvincing efforts is the failure to evaluate persons and events in the political context of the nation's only civil war and first presidential assassination and the aftermath of both events. He concludes that "unfortunately, historians have acted as if the assassination occurred in a vacuum and have spent a great deal of time discussing erroneous and irrelevant issues. They have been extremely critical of events that transpired in 1865 and have felt little need to investigate *how* and *why* people reacted the way they did [my emphasis]."[2]

While I share this conclusion, I am compelled to point out that Professor Turner appears to make the same mistake he condemns in the research of others in his own assessment of President Lincoln's assassin, John Wilkes Booth, whom he describes as "a deranged gunman." He implies that the failure to accept this view of Booth appears to be based on some seemingly neurotic compulsion within the body politic to believe in conspiracies. In his words: "There seems to be (as suggested by the 1969 Report of the President's Commission on the Causes and Prevention of Violence) some sort of psychological phenomenon that causes people to see conspiracies behind nearly all assassinations. Somehow it is more satisfying to believe that a president died as the victim of a cause rather than at the hands of a deranged gunman."[3]

If the public tends to "see" conspiracies, authorities and the media seem to possess a comparable tendency to "see" mental impairment and irrationality behind these acts with the same disregard, or selective use, of empirical evidence. It would be difficult to find a better example of such problems than the poorly researched and contextually barren study cited above. Unfortunately, the report of the President's Commission is typical of most of the literature on presidential assassinations.

Like the actions of his contemporaries (Edwin Stanton and Jefferson Davis, for example), John Wilkes Booth's motives and behavior must be evaluated in the appropriate political context—a time of raging emotions and unprecedented turmoil. Instead, our understanding of this assassination has been based on a number of incorrect assumptions about both victim and assassin that are now part of our national mythology, the most important of which is the assumption that Lincoln was the revered leader in life that he became in death. Given this assumption it follows that only a profoundly evil, deranged person could have killed a president so noble and good. Consequently, generations of scholars and writers have used evidence naively or selectively to deify Lincoln and vilify Booth and, as Professor Turner has argued, those thought to have conspired with Booth. To this extent, our public understanding of this event is simplistic and incomplete.

Lincoln's reputation is securely and positively established. It would not diminish that reputation to state that his virtues were not acknowledged to the same extent in life as they have been in death. Nor would it detract from that reputation to recognize that Booth's virtues in life have been ignored or denied while his vices and eccentricities have been magnified or fabricated. The result is an ideologically inspired explanation of this sad event designed to deny the real partisan motives of the assassin and to misrepresent an era. Why?

The answer has to do with the political context of nineteenth-century America and the legitimate concerns of some at that time about whether this diverse new nation could survive as a democracy. Such doubts were chronic as the nation drifted toward civil war and, of course, became acute as that war raged. Moreover, as we know, there were particularly grave and bluntly stated concerns at the highest levels of government and society about President Lincoln's ability to lead the nation through this crisis.

But having survived the crisis, in large part, because of the president's sound judgment and strong leadership, it became necessary to rescue his reputation after his death from the ignominious end to which it had been consigned by his many critics throughout most of his administration. Thus, the Lincoln legend was born as his funeral train slowly wound its way back to Springfield. Qualities for which he had been ridiculed throughout his public life—such as his impoverished rural background and his lack of formal education and manners—were reevaluated and relabeled as basic elements in a new image of the rail-splitting frontiersman who came to epitomize the virtues of hard work, pragmatism, and, of course, honesty so central to America's mythical image of itself. Lincoln's success became in a very real sense America's success, so that now along with Washington and Jefferson, his presence dominates—both literally and figuratively—our nation's capital and history.

By the same token, it was necessary to reevaluate the life of his assassin; to strip from him any endearing qualities and talents that explained the affection and esteem he enjoyed in life; to emphasize his frailties and eccentricities when no real vices were known; and to attribute to him that most contemptible of motives, jealousy, which had reached insane proportions. For only a madman could have killed a president so without fault.

But to do this Booth had to be removed, consciously or unconsciously, from the politics of his day. Because within that context his act was not an insane departure from normality; rather, it was simply an extension of the bloody violence that characterized this period of history and over which his now sainted but once unpopular and widely hated victim had presided. Unfortunately, such distortion of political reality and personal motives was to establish a pattern of politically inspired—as opposed to empirically based—interpretations of these recurring violent events.

In his classic essay "The Will to Believe," William James observed that "as a rule we disbelieve all facts and theories for which we have no use."[4] We replace them with interpretations based more on convenience or tradition than fact. And so national myths are conceived; traditions are established and subsequently amplified as occasion demands until a worldview emerges as so-called conventional wisdom.

The Lincoln assassination marks the beginning of a number of myths that reveal much about our hopes and fears as a nation. One of those fears—so pronounced in 1865—is that this great democratic experiment of ours might fail; that the freedom we cherish might be lost through domestic turmoil and ideological subversion, or even through foreign invasion by an enemy sensing internal weakness. And that fear is expressed, in part, in the way we interpret and explain the assassinations of our political leaders. Thus Booth has become deranged in the popular mind—if not his own—since his death. And sixteen years later when President Garfield died at the hands of the truly deranged Charles Guiteau, this assessment was offered: "The royal world abroad, whose peoples have their own assassins to contend with, must not be furnished reason to conclude that, in [democratic] America, the assassin is moved by the same impulses which control the assassin under monarchical forms of government." To do so, it was explained, would question the "vaunted stability of our government in the estimation of the outside world."[5]

We may assume that the tradition of insane presidential assassins was firmly established in 1901 when anarchist beliefs were officially labeled "delusions" by the psychiatrists who analyzed President McKinley's assassin. As one of them wrote: "Such a monstrous conception and impulse as the wanton murder of the President of the United States, arising in the mind of so insignificant a citizen, without his being either insane or degenerate could be nothing short of a miracle. . . . To assume that he was sane, is to assume that he did a sane act."[6] So in this manner we explained away the destabilizing political threat represented by the socialist-labor movement.

In similar fashion, Sirhan Sirhan's Arab nationalism was dismissed as paranoia by the doctors who attended him. And James Earl Ray's calculated contract killing of Martin Luther King, Jr., has been explained by his most recent biographer as displaced oedipal rage in terms reminiscent of those applied earlier to John Wilkes Booth. And once again, the truth is subverted to sustain the myth.

All this is not to suggest or endorse, heaven forbid, the rationality of assassination in America. Indeed, most assassins and would-be assassins were emotionally disturbed (but sane) persons. It is simply to underscore and extend, perhaps, the issue Professor Turner has raised in his book and paper. It would seem that as scholars, rather than mythmakers — whether the myths have to do with conspiracies or mental derangement — we can do better than we have in assessing and explaining these dark events in the nation's history.

NOTES

1. Thomas Reed Turner, *Beware the People Weeping: Public Opinion and the Assassination of Abraham Lincoln* (Baton Rouge: Louisiana State University Press, 1982).

2. Ibid., p. 252.

3. Ibid.

4. William James, *The Will to Believe and Other Essays in Popular Philosophy* (New York: Dover Publications, 1956), p. 10.

5. Quoted in James W. Clarke, *American Assassins: The Darker Side of Politics* (Princeton, N.J.: Princeton University Press, 1982), p. 6.

6. Quoted in ibid., p. 41.

Commentary on "Beware the People Weeping"

HAROLD M. HYMAN

Upon learning in 1885 of the appearance of still another sensational, baseless published rush to judgment about the Lincoln murder conspiracy, Supreme Court Justice David Davis responded despairingly: "[W]hat is the use of correcting it?"[1] In the century since the justice's statement about the ineffectiveness of history, or perhaps of historians, the flow of exploitations and pseudohistories about the Lincoln murder conspiracy has not abated. Perhaps the Davis-like disgust felt by professional historians at this venal literature, a disgust reflected in scholars' self-exclusion from relevant research, left the field to unprincipled sensationalists and uneducable misrepresenters.

Professor Turner's paper, his book, *Beware the People Weeping,* and William Hanchett's 1983 book, *The Lincoln Murder Conspiracies,* plus the publications of others, signal an end to this century-long domination of the subject by the shrill voices. If so, a question rises, one to which I wish Professor Turner had attended in greater detail: why this tenacious, dainty attitude among scholars, so belatedly lessening? Tentative approaches to answers exist in Turner's, Hanchett's, and others' publications on the Lincoln assassination. Perhaps the following questions deserve further attention.

First, what connections existed between this scholarly distaste for the Lincoln murder theme and the nineteenth-century rise of modern history Ph.D. and law school curricula, a rise occurring just when Justice Davis expressed his despair at history's uselessness? For complex reasons centering perhaps on their self-images as elite guardians of social values and their alleged dedications to then-new social sciences, leaders of both history and law education effectively excluded legal history, including criminal law history, from their respective curricula. This mistake by early paper-chasers suggests that the poet W. H.

370

Auden was perhaps wise in warning, "Never... commit a social science."

Both the law and history disciplines have, happily, been recently rediscovering legal history, and, in it, criminal law history. Their rediscovery increases the possibilities that there may be additional uses in correcting both the record and the derivative interpretations of the Lincoln murder conspiracy. As example of these possibilities, it is reasonable now to ask a second question of the past that has not been fully asked, much less answered: what standards of federal and state justice, both civilian and military, prevailed in mid-1865?

No one knows the answers, because too little research has been completed. But some responsible if partial conclusions exist. They suggest that Professor Turner is on a sound road.

Significant recent research, by Donald Nieman among others, focuses especially on the condition of federal criminal justice during Lincoln's White House years. In brief, such justice was little developed. For example, no federal prisons existed. This is why most of the 18,000 civilian "prisoners of state" imprisoned by the military under Lincoln's habeas corpus suspensions from 1861 to 1865 spent their usually brief periods of incarceration in contrived detention sites, such as Fort McHenry's stockade, and in state prisons.

Likewise, so far as federal criminal law was concerned, the murder of Lincoln was no special crime but an "ordinary" felony. It was also an unpunishable felony, because the federal District of Columbia then used Virginia's criminal statutes, rules of court procedure, and decisional case law. Justice would have been a sure casualty if Lincoln's murderers had been tried in Virginia's legal atmosphere, where the testimony of blacks and of Unionist white witnesses was either formally or informally inadmissible, and where white-only racial tests and elite-only property qualifications screened jurors, lawyers, judges, and peace officers.

Next, we need to look at Professor Turner's interesting point about the Union public's acceptance of military trials for Lincoln's murderers and accomplices. He suggested that this acceptance derived from the public's familiarity, since 1861, with army arrests of civilian security risks. Perhaps. I am intrigued with a differing possibility, one still wanting basic research. Civil War volunteers and conscripts left what was perhaps the least fettered civilian environment of the western world when they put on their bluecoats. And they accepted the rig-

371

orous disciplinary and criminal law standards then prevailing for long-service regulars. By 1865, for hundreds of thousands of bluecoats, multiplied by their families and friends nationwide, experience suggested that military trials were rugged, not rigged: coercive, not lawless.

This popular perception was correct. Military and martial law *were law.* Military law resulted from civilian statutes, the periodic Articles of War required by the Constitution. If a military trial was acceptable for a loyal son or husband, it was certainly good enough for Lincoln's killer, Seward's attacker, and their aiders and abettors.

Permit me here to stress a point Professor Turner touched glancingly. The standards of civilian criminal justice were then not only extremely poor but were also slipping badly, according to unhappy lawyer-patricians. This is one reason why, in 1866-67, in the Test Oath cases, the Supreme Court worried so about state and bar association licensing standards for practicing lawyers and other licensed professionals, and why, in 1870-71, Harvard Law School initiated the paper-chasing curricula that still dominates legal education.

In state lower courts, which tried the overwhelming number of accused criminals, unprofessionalism was common. Many judges and lawyers were self-taught, and not all were Lincolns. Judges and lawyers were frequently illiterate, and sometimes browbeat witnesses, defendants, and jurors. Procedural irregularities and doctrinal deviations were scandalous. Exposures of bribery and other corruptions were frequent. Only in tiny Maine could defendants in states' felony trials testify in their own defense.

As noted, even those standards for criminal law were slipping. Demoralizing newer practices were gaining popularity among a despised subcaste of lawyers, especially recent immigrants with strange surnames, who, because the WASP legal establishment largely excluded them from lucrative property cases, by default took on criminal law practices. According to lawyer-patricians of the 1860s and later, these deplorable newer practices included contingency fees, bail bonding even in capital cases, ambulance-chasing, fee-splitting and other referrals, plea-bargaining, and exploitations of the still novel insanity plea—as was done for one of the Lincoln murder conspirators. States' bar association leaders—and the associations were themselves products of the 1860s—accused un-WASPish lawyers (Germans, Irish, and Jews) of creating this deterioration in the profession. In the 1860s, patricians of the bar began to devise ways of keeping such exotics, plus black men and all women, out of the law schools and practice. Law professors aided this cause by sneering at criminal law, by not teaching it, by not writing criminal law texts or using those in print as textbooks, and by ignoring it in the lists of courses required for a law degree.

Backtracking to 1865, the point is that civilian criminal law was by no means respected, much less revered, even in comparison with military criminal legal procedures and standards. By no means do I extol military justice. I do want to know more about it and all these matters that are part of the context of the Lincoln murder trials.

A last, carping matter. Perhaps Professor Turner has claimed too much in suggesting that in 1865 the public looked on the military court that tried the conspirators as a kind of Warren Commission. My own work suggests that such a role was more likely played by the Congress's joint standing investigating Committee on the Conduct of the War. Since 1861 this committee had helped Lincoln and Congress greatly to maintain civilian controls over the Napoleonic-size Union military establishment that mushroomed after Sumter. To the amazement of America-watchers Karl Marx, Walter Bagehot, and Georges Clemenceau, this huge army disappeared unthreateningly back into civilian life within weeks after Lincoln's death and Appomattox.

Professor Turner is not responsible for coping in his paper with all of my concerns. I know that these are topics for future research and for full examination in a Lincoln bicentennial conference, perhaps on the splendid campus of Gettysburg College. Naturally, I find many reasons for praising Turner's paper, and the derivative questions that it spins off. We are, clearly, chipping away usefully, healthily, if belatedly, at encrusted errors surrounding the Lincoln murder and the trial of the assassins. I thank Professor Turner for his effective chips, and the organizers of the Gettysburg Lincoln conference for making further chipping probable. They have helped us move a step closer to the point that T. S. Eliot described in his last Quartet: "The end of our exploring will be to arrive where we started and see the place for the first time."

NOTES

1. David Davis as quoted in John P. Usher to Ward Hill Lamon, Oct. 13, 1885, Lamon Papers, Huntington Library, San Marino, Calif.

PART V

The Lincoln Biographers

☆　☆
☆

CHAPTER 13

OATES AND THE HANDLINS

RICHARD N. CURRENT

RECENT SINGLE-VOLUME biographies of Abraham Lincoln include
one of the best and one of the worst. Admirable despite serious flaws
is Stephen B. Oates's *With Malice toward None* (1977), some of the
themes of which the author makes more explicit in his collection of
essays subtitled *The Man behind the Myths* (1984).[1] Undeserving of even
faint praise is Oscar and Lilian Handlin's contribution (1980) to the
Library of American Biography, a series of brief, interpretative volumes of which Oscar Handlin is founder and editor.[2]

According to Handlin's specifications, each book in the series is
to illuminate the intersection between the subject's life and the nation's
history. In such terms the Handlins justify their small contribution to
the vast Lincoln literature. They declare that "there is something
more to say," and they are confident that they have said it. "Our
research has uncovered no facts, but it has encompassed all the facts
known," they assert. "And it has provided us with the means of
understanding Abraham Lincoln, his times, and the meaning of both."[3]

Certainly there is room for a new short life of Lincoln, an interpretative one that would do what the Handlins claim to have done.
Such a volume, to justify itself, would need to distill the best of recent
Lincoln scholarship and present the distillation with at least a bit of
dramatic flair and literary grace. This the Handlin book fails to do.
Three-fourths of its pages are given over to a rather plodding, un-
imaginative account of the prepresidential years. The treatment of
the presidency is not only skimpy but poorly organized. In a chaos
of chronology Lincoln's assassination comes before Lee's surrender,
which precedes the 1864 election, which in turn arrives ahead of the
1863 announcement of the 10 percent plan. The ill-told story lacks
any clear and consistent theme or combination of themes, and it
contains all too many dubious or erroneous statements, including

377

opinions once widely believed but now discredited. A couple of examples: Lincoln as an Illinois legislator in 1835 was "swapping railroads, canals, turnpikes, and bridges for votes" to move the state capital to Springfield; he decided not to run for Congress a second time because of the Illinois reaction to his stand on the Mexican War. In sum, the Handlins' volume does not fulfill the promises of its preface, nor does it meet the aim that Handlin himself set for the series.

Oates's Lincoln deserves much more attention than the Handlins'. Indeed, Oates's must be considered as, on the whole, the finest of the one-volume biographies. Among the other notable ones of this century, Lord Charnwood's (1917) and Nathaniel W. Stephenson's (1922) now seem completely outdated and almost quaint.[4] Even Benjamin P. Thomas's (1952) and Reinhard H. Luthin's (1960) appear somewhat old-fashioned by comparison.[5] For instance, neither Thomas nor Luthin included in his index the entry "Frederick Douglass," "Negroes," "race," or "racism." Oates does list these topics in his index, and he gives them considerable attention in his text, in accordance with his announced intention to reveal Lincoln's "racial views in the context of his time and place."

On matters other than race, the Thomas or the Luthin biography may sometimes be more useful, or at least handier, as a work of reference. But Oates is probably somewhat more readable than Thomas and certainly much more readable than Luthin. Not that Oates's style is flawless. He likes slangy expressions (on one occasion Lincoln "wasn't too interested"; on another he "griped"). He uses overfamiliar terms (surely the hatchet-faced, hard-bitten Montgomery Blair would resent the author's chumminess in always referring to him as "Monty"). He mixes his metaphors (someone once "waded into Lincoln's speech . . . with both fists, flaying it"). He falls into misusages ("by-elections" for "midterm elections") and even into malapropisms ("expostulated" for "expounded"). But gaffes of this kind will probably offend no one except perhaps some fussy old composition teacher. Nearly all readers will, no doubt, agree with the jacket blurb, which describes the book as "lyrical, engrossing and thoroughly moving." They are likely to get from it a warm sense of sympathy with Lincoln—and with Mrs. Lincoln—in their many trials.

Unlike the Handlins, Oates has kept abreast of the writing on Lincoln and his times. He avows that in preparing the biography he has "utilized scores of published source materials and unpublished manuscript collections" in addition to numerous scholarly studies. In his reference notes, however, he actually cites very few manuscript sources. Essentially the book is a synthesis of recent scholarship and a remarkably comprehensive one. At some points, where scholarship remains divided or uncertain, the Oates account has an assurance and a precision that the sources hardly warrant. But more about that later.

In *With Malice toward None* the author announces his intention to present the "real Lincoln" in place of the "Lincoln of mythology." He undertakes to carry the exposure further in *Abraham Lincoln: The Man behind the Myths,* which we may view as a supplement to the biography. "In shaping it," he says of the newer volume, "I benefitted enormously from a growing library of modern Lincoln studies. In fact, the last couple of decades have witnessed a veritable renaissance of Lincoln scholarship." Much of this "hasn't reached a broad literary audience. I am addressing that audience, because I want lay readers to rediscover Lincoln as the scholars have."[6]

Oates, then, does not pretend to be offering a strictly original interpretation. Perhaps the most innovative idea in the two books is his characterization of the Radical Republicans as "liberals." According to him, Senators Charles Sumner, Benjamin F. Wade, and Zachariah Chandler "belonged to a loose faction incorrectly categorized as 'radicals,' a misnomer that has persisted through the years." Republicans of this faction "were really progressive, nineteenth-century liberals who felt a powerful kinship with English liberals like John Bright and Richard Cobden."[7] Well, Sumner did feel a certain kinship with Cobden and Bright. He was a free trader, as they and the rest of the English liberals were, but most members of Sumner's faction were protectionists. Some of them, most notably Sumner himself, were to join the so-called Liberal Republican movement of 1872, but they did not refer to themselves as Liberal Republicans in Lincoln's time. For us now to call them liberals is inappropriate and anachronistic.

Oates apparently prefers to call the Radicals "liberals" so as to minimize the difference between them and Lincoln, whom he looks upon as another progressive, nineteenth-century liberal. He agrees with those scholars who see Lincoln as lagging only a little behind, and quickly catching up with, the members of his party who took the most advanced positions in regard to emancipation, black suffrage, and the reconstruction of the seceded states. He is an advocate of what might be called the Donald-Hyman-Trefousse-McPherson-Belz-McCrary-Cox thesis, its foremost proponents being David Donald, Harold Hyman, Hans Trefousse, James McPherson, Herman Belz, Peyton McCrary, and LaWanda Cox.[8] Each of those historians has taken issue with the once generally held belief that Lincoln and the Radicals differed significantly on questions of black rights. To Oates, that belief is the worst of the Lincoln myths, the one that he is at the greatest pains to dispel.

He likens his own interpretation to that of Peyton McCrary and adds: "Several older historians, especially those in or from the South, have faulted McCrary's inescapable conclusions that Lincoln stood with his advanced Republican colleagues on critical reconstruction questions; apparently these historians prefer the mythical version."[9] I do not like to get personal, but I cannot help recognizing myself as one of those "older historians," one who lived for nearly thirty years in the South and, while living there, wrote a review that "faulted McCrary's inescapable conclusions." I now submit that the question whether those conclusions are "inescapable" is, to say the least, open to debate, as is the identity of the historians who "prefer the mythical version" of the events.

Consider what Oates has to say, in *The Man behind the Myths*, about the Emancipation Proclamation. It was, he contends, "a sweeping blow against slavery as an institution in the rebel states, a blow that would free *all* slaves there—those of secessionists and loyalists alike."[10] The fact is that the proclamation did not apply to the rebel states as a whole—not to the areas under Union occupation but only to those still under Confederate control. Even at its most efficacious, the proclamation therefore would fall far short of freeing all the slaves in the rebel states.

Oates quotes the famous passage in Lincoln's December 1862 message to Congress beginning: "Fellow-citizens, we cannot escape history." Then he says: "That message provoked a fusillade of abuse from congressional Democrats, who blasted Lincoln's projected Proclamation as unconstitutional."[11] Thus he gives the impression that Lincoln uttered those eloquent words in support of his forthcoming proclamation. The fact is that Lincoln was urging the adoption of a constitutional amendment that would authorize his favorite emancipation plan. According to this plan, the states themselves would have to free the slaves. They could take their time about it, delaying final freedom until as late as 1900. They would have to compensate the slaveowners but could get financial aid from the federal government. And they would induce the freed blacks to resettle in Africa, Haiti, or some other place outside the United States. This was hardly a plan that the Radical Republicans could approve, and they did not approve it.

"As Union armies pushed into rebel territory, they would tear slavery out root and branch, automatically freeing all slaves in the areas and states they conquered," Oates continues. "By war's end, all three and a half million slaves in the defeated Confederacy could claim freedom under Lincoln's Proclamation and the victorious Union flag."[12] Maybe so. Maybe not. Lincoln himself had doubts about the lasting effect of the proclamation even in the still rebellious areas to which he confined it. On September 22, 1861, exactly one year before he issued his preliminary proclamation, he had defended his revocation of Gen. John C. Fremont's Missouri emancipation proclamation by asking: "Can it be pretended that it is any longer the government of the U.S. — any government of Constitution and laws — wherein a General, or a President, may make permanent rules of property by proclamation?"[13] By September 22, 1862, he had persuaded himself to make permanent rules of property and to base his action on his constitutional authority as commander in chief of the army and the navy. It is very doubtful that the framers of the Constitution, when they made the president the commander in chief, had anything more in mind than to assure the supremacy of the civilian over the military. By the time of the Civil War, some students of the Constitution had begun to argue for a presidential "war power." Today we take that power pretty much for granted, but when Lincoln became the first president to exercise it, its constitutionality was very much in doubt. Would the federal courts approve? Even if they accepted the proclamation as a war measure, what would they think of its efficacy once the war was over? Lincoln did not know the answers to these questions, and neither do we. What we do know is that after Appomattox the future of slavery remained unclear until the final ratification of the Thirteenth Amendment near the end of 1865.

Consider, next, what Oates has to say about the proclamation of December 1863 in which Lincoln announced his 10 percent plan for reconstructing the Southern states. This, Oates declares, "made emancipation the very basis of reconstruction, thus placing him on the side of Sumner and the advanced and moderate members of his party."[14] In fact, it did no such thing. It required that at least 10 percent of a state's voters swear to abide by all congressional acts and presidential proclamations with regard to slavery. As yet, no act of Congress called for complete abolition. The Emancipation Proclamation, as we have seen, exempted those parts of the Confederacy that the Union armies had already recovered—the only parts where reconstruction could possibly begin. By no means did Lincoln's announcement place him on the side of the "advanced" Republicans, the Radicals. They showed their disagreement by passing a quite different reconstruction plan, the Wade-Davis bill, which Lincoln pocket vetoed. Then they denounced him in the Wade-Davis manifesto and plotted to get rid of him as the party's presidential candidate.

Consider, finally, what Oates has to say about Lincoln and black suffrage. "Over the winter of 1864-65," he writes, "Lincoln approved some form of Negro suffrage for other rebel states if Congress would accept his Louisiana regime"—without black suffrage. "But the compromise fell apart because most congressional Republicans opposed even limited Negro suffrage as too radical."[15] Now, even McCrary, whom Oates closely follows, concedes that "there had been some misunderstanding on the precise nature of the compromise."[16] The evidence for such a compromise is unconvincing. One thing seems clear enough: Lincoln insisted on the removal of the black suffrage provision from the proposed reconstruction bill.

Oates sums up his case as follows: "Not only did the historical Lincoln side with Sumner and Stevens on most crucial reconstruction issues; by 1865 he was prepared to reform and reshape the South's shattered society with the help of military force."[17] But the historical Lincoln spoke "with malice toward none, with charity for all," of "binding up the nation's wounds." Thaddeus Stevens talked of compelling Southerners to "eat the fruit of foul rebellion"; of confiscating plantations, driving off the owners, and dividing the land among the freedmen; of revolutionizing the South. Neither Sumner nor Stevens thought the Constitution a hindrance. Sumner held that the Southern states, by seceding, had committed suicide and had reverted to territories. Stevens argued that having been defeated in war, those states were nothing but "conquered provinces." But Lincoln said the question whether they were still states or not, whether they were in or out of the Union, was a "merely pernicious abstraction." The important thing, he thought, was to restore them to their "proper practical relation" with the Union as soon as possible.

Why should we even expect Lincoln to have taken positions as extreme as those of some Radicals in Congress? In the White House he could hardly afford to be so far advanced or so single-minded. He had to hold the North together and direct the war effort so as to achieve a victory that would reunite the nation. He had to act as the president of the Conservatives as well as the Radicals, the Democrats as well as the Republicans, the Southerners as well as the Northerners, the whites as well as the blacks. None of the Radicals represented any such broad constituency. Stevens, for one, had a very narrow power base; he was responsible only to the Republican majority within a small portion of a single state — the Lancaster district of Pennsylvania.

All this is, emphatically, not to suggest that Lincoln leaned toward the other extreme from that of the Radicals. The black historian Lerone Bennett, Jr., was quite unhistorical in denigrating him as a man notable for racism.[18] The antiblack historian J. G. de Roulhac Hamilton, a North Carolinian of the Dunning school, was equally wrong in praising him as one who shared conservative white Southerners' "belief in the natural inferiority of the negro" and who, if he had lived, would have managed to "check the radicals in Congress" so as to save the reconstructed states from the horrors of "Negro rule."[19] James G. Randall was perhaps the greatest of all Lincoln scholars, but he was mistaken in saying that the Radicals were "the precise opposites of Lincoln" and that he planned an "easy reconstruction" but was "confronted with the hateful opposition of anti-Southern radicals."[20] Not Lincoln but his party foes, the Democrats, were the confirmed racists of the North. Not he but they were the true friends of the white supremacists in the South.

Oates and other recent writers who emphasize Lincoln's growing radicalism are much closer to the truth than were the earlier historians who portrayed him as the reluctant destroyer of slavery but the willing preserver of a caste system. There can be no doubt as to the direction in which he was moving during the presidential years. Under the pressure of events he tended to advocate the more and more immediate realization of the promise of equality. But doubts persist as to exactly where he stood at particular times. At various points, as I have just undertaken to show, Oates and like-minded writers make him appear to have been farther advanced than the evidence warrants.

When Lincoln said, in his last public address, that he might soon "make some new announcement," what did he have in mind? Even McCrary recognizes that Lincoln's assassination a few days later "makes it impossible to know precisely what direction his proposed shift in policy might have taken."[21] More than that, it makes it impossible to know whether he was actually contemplating any shift in policy.

This uncertainty has left ample room for speculation among historians, novelists, and politicians ever since Lincoln's death. Consciously or not, they have manipulated his memory to suit their own necessities. Opponents as well as proponents of Radical Reconstruction tried to get him on their side. Later, Southerners appealed to his name to legitimize state laws and constitutional amendments disfranchising and subordinating blacks. Then, as the renewed movement for civil rights gained momentum, sympathetic (white) historians attempted to enlist him in this cause.

Years ago, when William H. Herndon and the preachers were quarreling about Lincoln's religious beliefs, one of the preachers pointed out that "the faith and future of the Christian religion in no wise depends upon the sentiments of Abraham Lincoln."[22] Today we might add that the justice and prospects of the civil-rights movement in no wise depend upon his sentiments. In any case, those who rewrite the past to serve a present cause, no matter how worthy the cause may be, are engaged in the very essence of mythmaking. In destroying the old myth of Lincoln the pro-Southern-white conservative, they are in the process of creating a new myth of Lincoln the most radical of Radicals.

NOTES

1. Stephen B. Oates, *With Malice toward None: The Life of Abraham Lincoln* (New York: Harper and Row, 1977); *Abraham Lincoln: The Man behind the Myths* (New York: Harper and Row, 1984).

2. Oscar Handlin and Lilian Handlin, *Abraham Lincoln and the Union* (Boston: Atlantic/Little, Brown, 1980).

3. Ibid., pp. ix-x.

4. Lord Charnwood, *Abraham Lincoln* (New York: Henry Holt, 1917); Nathaniel Wright Stephenson, *Lincoln: An Account of His Personal Life Espe-*

cially of Its Springs of Action as Revealed and Deepened by the Ordeal of War (Indianapolis: Bobbs-Merrill, 1922).

5. Benjamin P. Thomas, *Abraham Lincoln: A Biography* (New York: Alfred A. Knopf, 1952); Reinhard H. Luthin, *The Real Abraham Lincoln: A Complete One Volume History of His Life and Times* (Englewood Cliffs, N.J.: Prentice-Hall, 1960).

6. Oates, *Man behind the Myths*, p. xiv.

7. Ibid., p. 96.

8. David Donald, *Charles Sumner and the Rights of Man* (New York: Alfred A. Knopf, 1970); Harold M. Hyman, "Lincoln and Equal Rights for Negroes: The Irrelevancy of the 'Wadsworth Letter,' " *Civil War History* 12 (1966): 258-66; Hans L. Trefousse, *The Radical Republicans: Lincoln's Vanguard for Racial Justice* (New York: Alfred A. Knopf, 1969); James M. McPherson, *The Struggle for Equality: Abolitionists and the Negro in the Civil War and Reconstruction* (Princeton: Princeton University Press, 1964); Herman Belz, *Reconstructing the Union: Theory and Practice during the Civil War* (Ithaca: Cornell University Press, 1969); Peyton McCrary, *Abraham Lincoln and Reconstruction: The Louisiana Experiment* (Princeton: Princeton University Press, 1978); LaWanda Cox, *Lincoln and Black Freedom: A Study in Presidential Leadership* (Columbia: University of South Carolina Press, 1981).

9. Oates, *Man behind the Myths*, p.209.

10. Ibid., p. 106.

11. Ibid., p. 109.

12. Ibid., p. 111.

13. Lincoln to Orville H. Browning, Sept. 22, 1861, in Roy P. Basler, ed., Marion Dolores Pratt and Lloyd A. Dunlap, asst. eds., *The Collected Works of Abraham Lincoln*, 9 vols. (New Brunswick, N.J.: Rutgers University Press, 1953-55), 4: 532.

14. Oates, *Man behind the Myths*, p. 140.

15. Ibid., p. 144.

16. McCrary, *Abraham Lincoln and Reconstruction*, p. 288-89.

17. Oates, *Man behind the Myths*, p. 137.

18. Lerone Bennett, Jr., "Was Abe Lincoln a White Supremacist?" *Ebony* 23 (Feb. 1968): 35-42.

19. J. G. de Roulhac Hamilton, "Lincoln and the South," *Sewanee Review* 17 (Apr. 1909): 134-38.

20. J. G. Randall, *Lincoln and the South* (Baton Rouge: Louisiana State University Press, 1946), pp. 119-23.

21. McCrary, *Abraham Lincoln and Reconstruction*, p. 351.

22. James A. Reed, quoted in Richard N. Current, *The Lincoln Nobody Knows* (New York: McGraw-Hill, 1958), p. 54.

CHAPTER 14

VIDAL'S LINCOLN

DON E. FEHRENBACHER

FOR A PROFESSIONAL HISTORIAN, the first question to be asked about Gore Vidal's *Lincoln* is: "What have we here?" Again, as in *Burr, 1876,* and *Washington,* Vidal has blended historical fact with literary invention, but the finished product in this instance might better be called fictionalized history than historical fiction. Subtitled *A Novel,* the book is nevertheless almost entirely about real persons whose depicted words and actions were drawn largely, says Vidal, from the historical record. Of course, as a novelist he felt free to attribute thoughts and motives, invent dialogue, and modify events. Yet he plainly intended the work to have historical as well as literary merit and for that reason submitted it before publication to the scrutiny and criticism of a leading Civil War historian.[1]

Like other writings that mix the techniques of the novelist with those of the historian (such as William Styron's *The Confessions of Nat Turner,* Alex Haley's *Roots,* and the various quasibiographies of Irving Stone), Vidal's *Lincoln* poses a problem for critics with respect to criteria of evaluation. Is historical soundness a matter of central importance, or should a book calling itself a novel be judged simply as a literary creation? Predictably, both the *New York Times Book Review* and the *New York Review of Books* assigned the volume to literary reviewers, neither of whom was an expert on Lincoln and his era. In the *Times,* author and critic Joyce Carol Oates brushed aside the question of Vidal's historical accuracy. "Surely," she wrote with fetching innocence, "the history cannot be faulted, as it comes with the imprimatur of one of our most eminent Lincoln scholars, David Herbert Donald of Harvard." Oates saw the book as one in which the author had subordinated the role of novelist to the role of "historian-biographer," thereby producing "not so much an imaginative reconstruction of an era as an intelligent, lucid, and highly informative transcript of it."[2] In the *New York Review*, Harold Bloom of Yale ventured the categorical statement that no biographer and no other novelist "has had the precision of imagination to show us a plausible and human Lincoln." Vidal, he declared "does just that, and more: he gives us the tragedy of American political history, with its most authentic tragic hero at the center."[3]

Here, then, we have one reviewer virtually classifying Vidal's *Lincoln* as a biography rather than a novel, and another finding it superior to the best nonfictional studies of Lincoln. Furthermore, even from less appreciative critics the principal complaint was that Vidal had written too much history into a purported work of fiction. "His book," said Nicholas von Hoffman, "sticks so closely to the actual chronology of events and has so little of his imagination in it that it merits review by a historian."[4] Yet this widely read interpretation of Abraham Lincoln by a prominent author will receive little if any formal attention from historians and historical journals. That seems not only unfortunate but old-fashioned in an age of blurred literary boundaries when so much history is incorporated into fiction and so much fiction masquerades as history. Perhaps historians should pay closer professional attention to the influence on America's historical consciousness of works such as *Roots, Ragtime, The Armies of the Night,* and Vidal's *Lincoln.*

Of course there are many novels about the life of Lincoln and many more in which he appears as a secondary or background character. One remembers especially Winston Churchill's *The Crisis,* with its chapters on the Lincoln-Douglas debates; Thomas Dixon's *The Clansman,* in which Lincoln vows to expel all blacks from the country; and Irving Stone's *Love Is Eternal,* a workmanlike, sentimental treatment of the Lincoln marriage.[5] There are very few novels, however, that focus on Lincoln's presidential career. The only thing comparable to Vidal's in this respect is a trilogy written in the 1920s by Honoré Willsie Morrow, an Iowan who went to New York as a young woman and, with some early encouragement from Theodore Dreiser, became a successful author and editor.[6] Her Lincoln books were thoroughly researched and well written in a romantic tone, but she had no particular interest in the politics of the Lincoln administration. Vidal, on the other hand, is a man fascinated as well as repelled by the American political game—one who, in his younger years, thought of himself as having presidential potential.[7] Thus it was perhaps inevitable that he should come eventually to writing a book about Lincoln. According to Joseph Blotner, Lincoln has been a dominant influence on the genre of the American political novel, not as a character but rather as the model from which many protagonists have been drawn.[8] Curiously, Vidal's book is the first major political novel making Lincoln himself the central figure.

It is no easy task to evaluate the historical validity of Vidal's *Lincoln* while at the same time recognizing the imaginative prerogatives of the novelist. Without doubt, a work of this kind tends to confuse many readers about what actually happened. For example, Joyce Carol Oates speaks of the "shrewd judgment" made by Stephen A. Douglas that Lincoln as a young man "had already fantasized dictatorial powers." She quotes Douglas as reminding Lincoln in 1861 of words that he had uttered in 1838: "You said that the founders of the republic had got all the glory that there was and that those who come after can never be anything except mere holders of office, and that this was not enough to satisfy 'the family of the lion, or the tribe of the eagle.' " What Oates had apparently failed to realize is that Vidal invented these remarks of Douglas in order to introduce passages from the most notable speech of Lincoln's younger years. She had mistaken fiction for historical fact.[9]

The difficulty of separating history from fiction in the book is compounded by a certain amount of factual error and dubious interpretation on Vidal's part, as well as by the unreliability of some of his sources. When Vidal has Lincoln say, "I was in New Orleans once" (instead of twice); when he declares that the Taylor administration offered Lincoln "no government appointment other than the secretaryship of the Oregon territory" (ignoring the governorship of Oregon, also offered); when he has Douglas winning reelection "decisively" (instead of narrowly) in 1858; when he puts a statue of Jefferson in Lafayette Square and speaks of Robert E. Lee as "the rebel commander" in June 1861 — in each of these instances, it seems fair to assume that he has simply committed an error.[10] But when he makes Elihu B. Washburne one of Lincoln's frequent companions on the judicial circuit, when he causes Lincoln as president-elect to carry "an elaborate file of papers" in his hat, when he pictures Mary Lincoln as having once been in love with Lyman Trumbull, has he likewise fallen into error, or is he engaging in literary invention?[11] Another question to be asked is whether Vidal's prerogatives as a novelist include the right to retail dubious testimony (such as Herndon's maggoty speculation that Lincoln contracted syphilis and infected his family with it), and the right to perpetuate outmoded interpretations (such as the notion that Lincoln in 1858 deliberately adopted strategy calculated to lose the senatorial contest with Douglas in order to win the presidency two years later.)[12]

Although there is also "much good history" in Vidal's *Lincoln,* as Donald has asserted,[13] the mixing of fact, fiction, and error, each difficult for the average reader to distinguish, produces a work seductively unreliable as biography, whatever its value as literature may be. Yet the ultimate question is not whether Vidal has written conventionally sound history, but rather the extent to which he has managed to penetrate the mystery of Lincoln's character and leadership.

The soberness of Vidal's approach to his subject has surprised and disappointed some reviewers who expect more mischief and iconoclasm from "the dancing boy of American letters." One critic, who found the book "literal, solid, and reverent," opened his review with a bit of parody:

> Lincoln, Lincoln, burning on
> In the nation's pantheon—
> A mystery of like degree:
> Did he who made Myra make thee?[14]

It is true that Vidal treats Lincoln with more respect than he accorded Jefferson, for example, in his earlier novel, *Burr.* But while putting aside his cynicism, he has not ceased to be a skeptical observer of politics. He admires Lincoln's skill but seems puzzled by what lies behind it. His treatment, I think, is not so much reverent as tentative. He circles Lincoln quizzically, viewing him from different angles, but seldom trying to get inside the man in the same way that he puts himself inside the minds of Chase, Mary Lincoln, and several other characters. His Lincoln remains something of an enigma throughout the book and perhaps seems all the more believable as a consequence; for the people we know best sometimes prove to be the profoundest mysteries. What Vidal provides more effectively is not an analysis of character but a delineation of leadership—leadership as it was manifested in the relations between Lincoln and the circle of persons most intimately associated with his presidential career. This feature of the novel is, in my opinion, his most valuable contribution to history.

NOTES

1. See Vidal's afterword on p. 659 of *Lincoln: A Novel* (New York: Random House, 1984); also his afterword on pp. 429-30 of *Burr: A Novel* (New York: Random House, 1973).

2. *New York Times Book Review,* June 3, 1984, pp. 1, 36-37.

3. *New York Review of Books,* July 19, 1984, pp. 5-6, 8.

4. *Nation,* June 16, 1984, pp. 744-45.

5. Winston Churchill, *The Crisis* (New York: Macmillan Co., 1901); Thomas Dixon, *The Clansman: An Historical Romance of the Ku Klux Klan* (New York: Grosset and Dunlap, 1905); Irving Stone, *Love Is Eternal: A Novel about Mary Todd and Abraham Lincoln* (Garden City, N.Y.: Doubleday and Co., 1954). See Roy P. Basler, *The Lincoln Legend: A Study in Changing Conceptions* (Boston: Houghton Mifflin Co., 1935), pp. 45-49.

6. Honoré Willsie Morrow, *Forever Free, With Malice toward None:* and *The Last Full Measure* (New York: William Morrow and Co., 1927, 1928, and 1930).

7. Gerald Clarke, "Petronius Americanus: The Ways of Gore Vidal," *Atlantic Monthly,* 229 (Mar., 1972): 50.

8. Joseph Blotner, *The Modern American Political Novel, 1900-1960* (Austin: University of Texas Press, 1966), p. 17.

9. The quotation is from p. 111 of Vidal, *Lincoln.* The reference is to Lincoln's address before the Young Men's Lyceum of Springfield, Ill., Jan. 27, 1838, Roy P. Basler, ed., Marion Dolores Pratt and Lloyd A. Dunlap, asst. eds., *The Collected Works of Abraham Lincoln,* 9 vols. (New Brunswick, N.J.: Rutgers University Press, 1953-55), 1: 108-15.

10. Vidal, *Lincoln,* pp. 9, 11, 28, 72, 186.

11. Ibid., pp. 10, 37, 199.

12. Ibid., pp. 67, 100, 290. See also Vidal's essay on Lincoln in his *The Second American Revolution, and Other Essays* (New York: Random House, 1982), p. 276.

13. Quoted on the jacket of the book.

14. Thomas Keneally, review of *Lincoln: A Novel,* by Gore Vidal, in *New Republic,* July 2, 1984, pp. 32-34.

Contributors

DWIGHT ANDERSON has been a member of the political science faculty at San Diego State University since 1969. He earned his B.A. degree from Montana State University and the M.A. and Ph.D. degrees from the University of California at Berkeley. In addition to his *Abraham Lincoln: The Quest for Immortality* (1982), he has produced a variety of articles and papers on Lincoln, several providing psychological perspectives on the sixteenth president. He has been the recipient of a Woodrow Wilson Fellowship and a research grant from the Lincoln Foundation. His most recent book, coauthored by Nancy Scott Anderson, is *The Generals: Ulysses S. Grant and Robert E. Lee* (1988).

JEAN H. BAKER has developed a career in scholarship and undergraduate teaching at her alma mater, Goucher College, Towson, Md., where she has held the post of Elizabeth Todd Professor of History since 1982. She received her Ph.D. from Johns Hopkins University and has published three books on mid-nineteenth-century American political history, the most recent entitled *Affairs of Party: The Political Culture of Northern Democrats in the Mid-Nineteenth Century* (1983).

PARTICIPANTS OF THE "LINCOLN 175" CONFERENCE AT GETTYSBURG COLLEGE. Photo by Ross Ramer, Gettysburg. *On facing page, left to right: Row 1:* Michael F. Holt, Jean H. Baker, J. Roger Stemen, Harold Holzer, LaWanda Cox, Robert V. Bruce, Jean Holder, Glen E. Thurow. *Row 2:* Harold M. Hyman, Don E. Fehrenbacher, Charles Jarvis, Phillip S. Paludan, P. M. Zall, James W. Clarke, Lloyd Ostendorf. *Row 3:* George B. Forgie, David A. Nichols, Mark E. Neely, Jr., Thomas Reed Turner, Major L. Wilson, M. E. Bradford, David Hein, Dwight G. Anderson. *Row 4:* Charles H. Glatfelter, Richard N. Current, Kenneth M. Stampp, Norman O. Forness, William S. McFeely, William Hanchett, Hans L. Trefousse, James M. McPherson, David B. Potts. *Participants not pictured:* Louis Athey, Robert Bannister, Herman Belz, Robert L. Bloom, Gabor S. Boritt, Marcus Cunliffe, Norman A. Graebner, John T. Hubbel, Stephen B. Oates, Wendy Wick Reaves, Armstead L. Robinson, Charles B. Strozier, and John F. Wilson.

Goucher College has honored her both for her scholarship and for distinguished teaching, and she has received grants from the American Council of Learned Societies, and the Elizabeth Nettle Fellowship. Though her articles, papers, and other scholarly contributions have focused largely on politics, her most recent book is *Mary Todd Lincoln: A Biography* (1987).

HERMAN BELZ, a member of the history faculty at the University of Maryland since 1968, received his B.A. from Princeton University, and his M.A. and Ph.D. degrees from the University of Washington. His specialty is American constitutional history, a field in which he has produced four books, including *Emancipation and Equal Rights: Politics and Constitutionalism in the Civil War* (1978), and his substantial revision of the long-popular Kelly and Harbison college textbook *The American Constitution: Its Origins and Development* (1983). He has published many scholarly articles and delivered numerous papers, frequently on constitutional topics of the Civil War and Reconstruction era. Awards and prizes in recognition of his scholarship include the American Bar Foundation Legal History Merit Research Fellowship, and the Albert J. Beveridge Award of the American Historical Association.

GABOR S. BORITT, Robert C. Fluhrer Professor of Civil War Studies and director of the Civil War Institute at Gettysburg College, received his B.A. from Yankton College in South Dakota, an M.A. at the University of South Dakota, and the Ph.D. at Boston University. Before joining the Gettysburg faculty in 1981, he taught in Boston, Asia, the University of Michigan, Memphis State University, and Washington University. He has been awarded fellowships from the National Endowment for the Humanities, Harvard University, and the Social Science Research Council, and has written numerous scholarly articles. His continuing interest in Lincoln and the Civil War is also demonstrated by his books *Lincoln and the Economics of the American Dream* (1978), and, written in coauthorship, *The Lincoln Image: Abraham Lincoln and the Popular Print* (1984) and *The Confederate Image: Prints of the Lost Cause* (1987).

M. E. BRADFORD has been a member of the Department of English at the University of Dallas, Irving, Texas, since 1967. He received the B.A. and M.A. degrees at the University of Oklahoma and a Ph.D.

at Vanderbilt University. Editorial boards of a number of literary journals have received his services, and in 1978 he became senior editor of *Modern Age*. From 1975 to 1977 he served as president of the Southwestern American Literature Association. His writings focus on American literature, history, and political philosophy, and in these contexts he has produced many articles, edited and contributed to several books, and currently is preparing a book on Faulkner's short fiction, and a study of Abraham Lincoln.

ROBERT V. BRUCE has developed a career combining two scholarly specialties—the Civil War era and the history of American science and technology. He received a B.S. degree from the University of New Hampshire, and an M.A. and a Ph.D. from Boston University. He began teaching in the fields of history and mathematics at the University of Bridgeport and has been on the history faculty of Boston University since 1955. In recognition of his scholarship he has been a Guggenheim Fellow, a fellow of the Henry E. Huntington Library, and a Fellow of the Society of American Historians. The diversity in his writing is reflected in many scholarly articles and chapters in books, both on Lincoln and on scientific matters. He is the author of *Lincoln and the Tools of War* (1956), *1877: Year of Violence* (1959), *Alexander Graham Bell and the Conquest of Solitude* (1973), and most recently, *The Launching of Modern American Science* (1987), winner of the Pulitzer Prize in History, 1988.

JAMES W. CLARKE, Professor of Political Science at the University of Arizona, is a graduate of Washington and Jefferson College and received his M.A. and Ph.D. degrees at the Pennsylvania State University. He served in the Department of Government and the Institute for Social Research at Florida State University before joining the faculty at Arizona. His research in the area of political behavior has produced many articles for professional journals, chapters for books, and papers at political and social science conferences. This line of investigation has involved him in the study of political assassinations, and the publication of a book entitled *American Assassins: The Darker Side of Politics* (1982).

LAWANDA COX, Professor Emeritus of History at Hunter College of the City University of New York, received her B.A. from the University of Oregon, an M.A. from Smith College, and the Ph.D. from

395

the University of California at Berkeley. The field of Reconstruction history has been the focus of her writing in scholarly journals and her frequent participation in symposia and in the sessions of conventions of the major historical associations. With her late husband, John H. Cox, she coauthored *Politics, Principles and Prejudice, 1865-1866: Dilemma of Reconstruction America* (1963), which received the John H. Dunning Prize of the American Historical Association. Her *Lincoln and Black Freedom: A Study in Presidential Leadership* (1981) won the Lincoln-Barondess Award of the Civil War Round Table of New York.

MARCUS CUNLIFFE, long one of the foremost British interpreters of American life, is now University Professor of History at George Washington University in the District of Columbia. He received the B.A., M.A. and B. Litt. degrees from Oriel College, Oxford, and from 1947 to 1949 studied at Yale University on a Commonwealth fellowship. Before moving to the United States he held a professorship in the field of American Studies at the University of Sussex. His books include *Soldiers and Civilians: The Martial Spirit in America, 1775-1865* (1968), *Chattel Slavery and Wage Slavery: The Anglo-American Context, 1830-1860* (1979), and most recently, *American Presidents and the Presidency* (1986).

RICHARD N. CURRENT, the University Distinguished Professor of History Emeritus of the University of North Carolina at Greensboro, is a former president of the Southern Historical Association. After graduating from Oberlin College, he took an M.A. at the Fletcher School of Tufts University and a Ph.D. at the University of Wisconsin. He has served on the faculties of several American colleges and universities, has been a lecturer at institutions in Asia, Latin America, and Europe, and held the post of Harmsworth Professor of American History at Oxford University in 1962-63. His awards include the Bancroft Prize, which he received jointly with J. G. Randall, for *Lincoln the President: Last Full Measure* (1955). His numerous publications on Lincoln have made him a leading interpreter of the sixteenth president, as demonstrated in *The Lincoln Nobody Knows* (1958), and *Speaking of Abraham Lincoln: The Man and His Meaning for Our Times* (1983). His most recent book is *Those Terrible Carpetbaggers: A Reinterpretation* (1988).

DON E. FEHRENBACHER holds the rank of William Robertson Coe

Professor of History and American Studies Emeritus at Stanford University. He received his B.A. from Cornell College, Mt. Vernon, Iowa, and the M.A. and Ph.D. degrees from the University of Chicago. Before a career of three decades at Stanford, he taught at Coe College in Iowa, and in 1967-68 was Harmsworth Professor of American History at Oxford University. Universities at home and abroad have honored him as a special lecturer, and he has also been a National Endowment for the Humanities Fellow, a Huntington-Seaver Fellow at the Huntington Library, and a Guggenheim Fellow twice. His scholarly writing on Lincoln and the era of the Civil War has produced numerous journal articles, essays in books and encyclopedias, and several books, which include *Prelude to Greatness: Lincoln in the 1850's* (1962) and *The Dred Scott Case: Its Significance in American Law and Politics* (1978), winner of the Pulitzer Prize in History in 1979.

GEORGE B. FORGIE has been a member of the history faculty at the University of Texas at Austin since 1974, and prior to that he served on the faculty of Princeton University. He did his undergraduate work at Amherst College and thereafter earned the LL.B., M.A., and Ph.D. degrees from Stanford University, where his dissertation won national recognition in 1973 when awarded the Allen Nevins Prize of the Society of American Historians. From that study came his book, *Patricide in the House Divided: A Psychological Interpretation of Lincoln and His Age* (1979). Mr. Forgie has also been honored twice for excellence in teaching by the University of Texas.

NORMAN A. GRAEBNER, a specialist in American diplomatic history, is the Compton Professor of History and Public Affairs Emeritus at the University of Virginia, where he joined the faculty in 1967 after teaching earlier at the University of Illinois, Iowa State University, and Oklahoma College for Women. He received his B.S. from Wisconsin State Teachers' College in Milwaukee, an M.A. from the University of Oklahoma, and the Ph.D. from the University of Chicago. He has held visiting lectureships at various universities in the United States and abroad, including the Harmsworth Professorship in American History at Oxford. In the course of his career he has published extensively. His books include *Empire on the Pacific* (1955), *Ideas and Diplomacy* (1964), and *America as a World Power: A Realist Appraisal from Wilson to McKinley* (1984).

WILLIAM HANCHETT has had a career of three decades in the History

Department of San Diego State University. He received his undergraduate degree from Southern Methodist University, and the M.A.
and Ph.D. degrees from the University of California at Berkeley.
Before going to San Diego, he taught for short periods at Colorado
State University and the University of Colorado, and served also as
a historian of the United States Air Force. His many articles in scholarly journals reflect his interest in the history of the American West
as well as matters related to the Civil War and Lincoln. He is the
author of two books: *Irish: Charles G. Halpine in Civil War America*
(1970) and *The Lincoln Murder Conspiracies* (1983).

DAVID HEIN, a member of the Department of Religion and Philosophy
at Hood College, Frederick, Maryland, since 1983, earlier taught for
a year in the field of religious studies at James Madison University,
Harrisonburg, Virginia. Both his B.A. and Ph.D. degrees were awarded
by the University of Virginia, and his M.A. by the University of
Chicago. His writings in scholarly journals have treated various issues
in religion, though his most recent work centers on Lincoln. In 1983,
with Hans J. Morganthau, he published *Essays on Lincoln's Faith and
Politics*.

HAROLD HYMAN, the William P. Hobby Professor of History at Rice
University, Houston, Texas, a specialist on legal and constitutional
issues, has devoted much attention to the Civil War and Reconstruction. He received his baccalaureate degree from the University of
California at Los Angeles, and his Ph.D. from Columbia University.
His numerous articles for scholarly journals, his editorial responsi-
bilities, and his papers for professional meetings have earned him
recognition that includes acting as a Fellow of the Center for the
Study of the History of Liberty in America, Senior Fellow of the
National Endowment for the Humanities, and Senior Fulbright Lec-
turer in Japan. For *Era of the Oath: Northern Loyalty Tests during the
Civil War and Reconstruction* (1954) he received the Albert J. Beveridge
Award of the American Historical Association. One of his more recent
works, written with William M. Wiecek, *Equal Justice under Law: Con-
stitutional History, 1833-1880* (1982), is a volume in the New American
Nation series.

JAMES M. MCPHERSON, Edwards Professor of History at Princeton
University, is an authority on the Civil War and on the ensuing history

of the civil rights of black Americans. He received his B.A. from Gustavus Adolphus College, St. Peter, Minnesota, and his Ph.D. from Johns Hopkins University. Since joining the Princeton faculty in 1962, he has also acted as Commonwealth Fund lecturer in American history at the University of London, held several fellowships, and received the Anesfield-Wolf Award. He has published important articles on Lincoln, and his books include *Marching toward Freedom: The Negro in the Civil War* (1968), *The Abolitionist Legacy: From Reconstruction to the NAACP* (1976), *Ordeal by Fire: The Civil War and Reconstruction* (1982), and *Battle Cry of Freedom: The Civil War Era,* Oxford History of the United States, vol. 6 (1988).

MARK E. NEELY, JR., is director of the Louis A. Warren Lincoln Library and Museum in Fort Wayne, Indiana, and the editor of *Lincoln Lore.* He holds a B.A. and a Ph.D. in history from Yale University and taught at Iowa State University before taking his current position in 1972. Though his articles in scholarly journals deal chiefly with Lincoln, he has also addressed subjects focused on intellectual history. He is the author of *The Abraham Lincoln Encyclopedia* (1982) and coauthor of *The Lincoln Image: Abraham Lincoln and the Popular Print* (1984), *The Confederate Image: Prints of the Lost Cause* (1987), and *The Insanity File: The Case of Mary Todd Lincoln* (1986).

DAVID A. NICHOLS chairs the Division of Management at Southwestern College in Winfield, Kansas, where he holds the ranks of Professor of Business and Social Science. He received his M.A. from Roosevelt University and earned a Ph.D. in history from the College of William and Mary. Prior to joining the faculty of Southwestern College, he taught in the Department of History and Humanities at Huron College in South Dakota and also held administrative appointments there and with the State of South Dakota. He has produced journal articles for the fields of both history and management and has written a book entitled *Lincoln and the Indians: Civil War Policy and Politics* (1978).

STEPHEN B. OATES is Paul Murray Kendall Professor of Biography at the University of Massachusetts, Amherst. He received his B.A., M.A., and Ph.D. degrees from the University of Texas at Austin. Focusing chiefly on biography and the era of the Civil War, he has numerous articles, papers, invited lectures, and books to his credit.

Professor Oates's many awards and honors as a scholar and writer include a Guggenheim Foundation fellowship, membership in the Texas Institute of Letters, and the Distinguished Teaching Award of the University of Massachusetts. His book *With Malice toward None: The Life of Abraham Lincoln* (1977) won the Christopher Award for outstanding literature and the Barondess/Lincoln Award of the New York Civil War Round Table; and *Let the Trumpet Sound: The Life of Martin Luther King, Jr.* (1982) received the Christopher Award and the Robert F. Kennedy Memorial Book Award.

PHILLIP S. PALUDAN, a professor of history at the University of Kansas, received his B.A. and M.A. degree from Occidental College in Los Angeles and a Ph.D. from the University of Illinois. Since joining the Kansas faculty in 1968, he has gained increasing recognition as a specialist in the Civil War era and has received awards which include a study fellowship from the American Council of Learned Societies, a fellowship in Law and History in the Harvard Law School, and a Guggenheim Fellowship. In addition to his articles in scholarly journals, he published in 1975 a book entitled *A Covenant with Death: The Constitution, Law and Equity in the Civil War Era*, and in 1981, *Victims: A True Story of the Civil War.*

WENDY WICK REAVES is the Curator of Prints at the National Portrait Gallery of the Smithsonian Institution in Washington, D.C. She studied English and art history as an undergraduate at the University of Pennsylvania and then received an M.A. from the University of Delaware in the Winterthur Program in Early American Culture. She has published articles on portrait prints and has organized many exhibitions, among them "Heroes, Martyrs, and Villains: Printed Portraits of the Civil War" (1982). In 1976 she was elected to the Print Council of America and in 1979 appointed to the Council of the American Museum in Britain, in Bath, England. She is the author of *George Washington, An American Icon: The Eighteenth-Century Graphic Portraits*, published in 1982.

ARMSTEAD L. ROBINSON is a member of the history faculty at the University of Virginia and director of the university's Carter G. Woodson Institute for Afro-American Studies. He received his B.A. degree from Yale University and his Ph.D. from the University of Rochester. Prior to joining the faculty at Virginia he taught at the University of

California at Los Angeles, and at two institutions of the State University of New York, Brockport and Stony Brook. For his scholarship he has received a variety of awards, including the Carter G. Woodson Award of the *Journal of Negro History* and the Ford Foundation's Award for Distinguished Black Scholars in Social Science. His work has appeared in many scholarly publications and includes the forthcoming book *Bitter Fruits of Bondage: The Demise of Slavery and the Collapse of the Confederacy, 1861-1864.*

KENNETH M. STAMPP, Morrison Professor of History Emeritus at the University of California at Berkeley, is a former president of the Organization of American Historians. He was trained at the University of Wisconsin, where he earned the B.S., M.A., and Ph.D. degrees. After teaching a number of years at the University of Maryland, he joined the faculty at Berkeley in 1946, and has also served as a Fulbright lecturer at the University of Munich and Harmsworth Professor of American History at Oxford. His publication of *The Peculiar Institution* in 1956 marked an important milestone in the interpretation of the institution of slavery, and the range of his scholarship is further demonstrated in *The Era of Reconstruction, 1865-1877* (1966) and *The Imperiled Union: Essays on the Background of the Civil War* (1980).

CHARLES B. STROZIER is executive director of the John Jay College of Criminal Justice, The City University of New York. He received his B.A. degree at Harvard and then the M.A. and Ph.D. in history at the University of Chicago, after which he was a research candidate at the Chicago Institute for Psychoanalysis. He is the editor of the *Psychohistory Review,* and has published extensively and delivered many papers on psychohistorical subjects. Much of this work has focused on Abraham Lincoln, and in recognition of his contributions he received in 1981 the Lincoln Library Writer of the Year Award. His book *Lincoln's Quest for Union: Public and Private Meanings* appeared in 1982.

GLEN E. THUROW, a political scientist with a special interest in Lincoln, is a member of the Department of Politics and director of the American Studies Program at the University of Dallas in Irving, Texas. After receiving a B.A. from Williams College, he earned the M.A. and Ph.D. degrees at Harvard University. Thereafter, he taught political science at the State University of New York in Buffalo and the

University of Georgia before going to Dallas in 1974. Much of his scholarly writing deals with the American presidency, and in 1979 he received a National Endowment for the Humanities award for the study of presidential rhetoric. In 1976 he published a book entitled *Abraham Lincoln and American Political Religion.*

HANS L. TREFOUSSE is Distinguished Professor of History at Brooklyn College and at the Graduate Center of the City University of New York. After receiving his B.A. from the City College, he earned an M.A. and a Ph.D. from Columbia University. His honors include a Guggenheim Fellowship and the Distinguished Teacher Award of Brooklyn College. His numerous scholarly articles and books include *The Radical Republicans: Lincoln's Vanguard for Racial Justice and Reconstruction* (1969), *Ben Butler: The South Called Him Beast* (1974), and *Carl Schurz: A Biography* (1981).

THOMAS R. TURNER, a specialist on the Lincoln assassination, has been a member of the history faculty at Bridgewater State College in Bridgewater, Massachusetts, since 1971. He received his B.A., M.A., and Ph.D. degrees from Boston University. Research in his specialty has led to a number of journal articles and an active role in the Lincoln Group of Boston. In 1982 he produced a book entitled *Beware the People Weeping: Public Opinion and the Assassination of Abraham Lincoln.*

MAJOR L. WILSON, a specialist in the antebellum period and American intellectual history, has been a member of the history faculty at Memphis State University since 1964. He received the B.A. degree from Vanderbilt University, an M.A. from the University of Arkansas, and a Ph.D. from the University of Kansas. His interest in American politics and American ideas has resulted in many articles for scholarly journals, essays in anthologies, and in 1974 a book entitled *Space, Time, and Freedom: The Quest for Nationality and the Irrepressible Conflict, 1815-1861.* His most recent work is *The Presidency of Martin Van Buren* (1984).

PAUL M. ZALL is Emeritus Professor of English and American Studies at California State University in Los Angeles. After receiving his B.A. from Swarthmore College, he earned a Ph.D. at Harvard, and thereafter held teaching positions at Cornell University, the University of Oregon, and the University of Washington before taking his post in

California. As an expert on the origins of humor, he has published several books that probe the popular imagination through the medium of humor. Included among these are *A Hundred Merry Tales* (1963), *Peter Pindar's Poems* (1972), and *Ben Franklin Laughing* (1980). His work on Lincoln appeared in 1982 under the title *Abe Lincoln Laughing*.

Index

405

Coles County, Ill., 212

Colonization: Lincoln's method, 184; end of Lincoln's efforts, with Emancipation Proclamation, 200-201; and Lincoln's views on equality, 205; mentioned 97, 197. *See also* Slavery

Colorado, 164

Commander-in-Chief Conciliating the Soldier's Vote on the Battle Field, 73

Common people, 10, 21, 94

Comstock, Cyrus, 352

Conckling, James C., 222, 227

Concordance to Lincoln's writings, xxiii

Confederates: trading with, 98; military officers retain posts, 99; leadership, 193; ex-Confederates, 345, 346; fear that Confederates would capture Washington, 346; mentioned, 198, 199, 201, 206-8, 270, 315, 317-19, 320, 321, 323-27, 331, 340, 341, 345, 346, 353, 354, 358, 361, 380, 381, 382

Confessions of Nat Turner, The (Styron), 387

Confiscation laws, 98

Connecticut, 187

Conover, Sandford, 358-59

Conservatism, 20

Conspiracy against Lincoln: 1865 military trial of suspected assassins, 350-59; 1857 civil trial of John Surratt, 359-62; historians' need to solve this case, 362-63; validity of conspiracy hypothesis, 366; mentioned, xix, 288, 299, 310, 318, 320, 324, 327, 331, 333, 335, 339, 340, 341, 342, 371, 372

Constitution: separates religion from politics, 125; absence of word "slave," 234; mentioned, xxiii, 28, 110, 111, 112, 126, 132, 153, 173, 182, 184, 259, 260, 263-68, 275, 294, 300, 301n24, 305, 316, 372, 381, 382

Continuity in Lincoln's values, xix, 99

Convention of 1860 (presidential nomination): Lincoln's maneuvers, 263

Cooper, Sgt., 360-61

Copenhagen, Denmark, 5

Copperheads, 96, 315-18, 320, 340, 341

Corporations, 92

Corwin, Thomas, 5-6

Cox, LaWanda, xviii, xxi, 121, 197-208, 380

Criminal law, 371-73

Crisis, The (Churchill), 388

Crockett, Davy, 27

Cruikshank, George, 55

Cunliffe, Marcus, xxi, 28

Currency (uniform paper currency), 96

Current, Richard N., xx, 121, 172, 176, 180, 273n25, 362

Currier and Ives, xxiv, xxv, 53, 55, 60, 71, 74-75

Dakota Territory, 154-55, 158

Dana, Charles A., 348

Daumier, Honoré, 50, 55

Davenport, Ia., 3

Davis, Charles A., 27

Davis, David (Judge), 20, 370

Davis, Henry Winter, 351

Davis, Jefferson, xxiv, 10, 99, 201-2, 277, 305, 321-24, 330, 339-40, 346-47, 358-59, 366

Davis, William C., 336

Dawes Act, 172

Dawley, Alan, 121

Day Lincoln Was Shot, The (1955) (Bishop), 335

Death dreams, 242, 243, 253-54, 275. *See also* Religion

Death of Lincoln, The (1909) (Laughlin), 328

Debates, Lincoln-Douglas. *See* Lincoln-Douglas debates

Declaration of Independence, 72, 94, 108, 126, 131-33, 192, 198, 250, 259, 265, 266, 268, 269, 282, 286. *See also* Equality

Delaware, 178

Democracy: Lincoln measures it on an economic basis, 95; slavery's threat to, 290, 308; people's concerns (before and during Civil War) about its survival, 367; mentioned, 99, 110, 140, 284n7. *See also* American Dream

Democratic party: Jeffersonian-Democratic sociopolitical reasoning, 92; Douglas and others plot to make slavery a permanent, nationwide institu-

tion, 287; mentioned, 14, 27, 73, 89, 171, 181, 183, 188, 192, 201, 232, 261, 281, 285, 286, 288, 289, 290, 294, 299, 303, 308, 309, 324, 326, 383
Demon (view of Lincoln), xvii
Department of Mississippi, 152
Depew, Chauncey M., 20
Derby, Earl of, 49, 74
Derby, George Horatio, 27
Dewey, John, 133
Dewitt, David M., 326-28, 351
Dickens, Charles, 50, 119
Dietz, Gottfried, 111
Diggins, John P., xxii
Disraeli, Benjamin, 65, 75
District of Columbia, 371
Divine Being, 267
Divine Providence, 233
Dixie, 197, 200-201
Dixon, Thomas, 388
Dole, William P., 149-51, 158, 160, 162-63
Donald, David H., xx, xxiii, 121, 280, 342, 380, 387, 390
Doolittle, James, 166
Doster, William E., 357
Doubled Images of Lincoln and Washington, The (1987) (Cunliffe), xxi
Douglas, Ann, 27
Douglas, Steven A.: Lincoln's ambivalence toward, 288; mentioned, xviii, xxiv, 9, 10, 21-25, 59, 112, 137, 236, 261-63, 265, 286-89, 291, 299-300, 302-3, 309, 311, 389
"Douglas Polka," 51, 58
Douglass, Frederick, 176, 183, 203, 378
"Douglass [*sic*] Grand March," 58
Dred Scott decision: Lincoln administration repudiates, 184; claim that it makes slavery legal throughout country, 287; mentioned, 23-24, 137, 309
Dreiser, Theodore, 388
Dublin, Thomas, 121
Dummer, H. E., 220
Duncan (*Macbeth*), 269-70
Dunham, Charles, 358
Durant, Thomas J., 179-80
Dye, Joseph, 360-61

Ebony, 177

Economics: Whig-Republican, 92; antislavery battle more important, 94, 95; economic revolution, 95; argument for ending war, 97; mentioned, xix, 116
Edwards, Ninian and Elizabeth, 222-23
1876 (Vidal), 387
Einhorn, Lois, xxiii
Eisenschiml, Otto, 330-37, 341
Election fever, 49
Eliot, T. S., 373
Elizabeth-Town, Ky., 218-19
Ellsworth, Elmer, 71
Elmira, N.Y., 361
Emancipation, xvi, 170, 180, 202, 205, 206, 207, 260, 300, 316, 317. *See also* Slavery
Emancipation Proclamation: timing, 177-78; significance, 197-203; number of slaves it freed, 199; opposition to, 201-2; Lincoln's adherence to it, 202; mentioned, xxii, 28, 62, 71, 72, 108, 172, 179, 182, 187, 316-17, 322, 380, 381, 382. *See also* Colonization
Emerson, Ralph Waldo, 93, 119, 281
England, 49-50, 55, 81, 359
Engle, William, 7
English, Thomas Dunn, 293, 301
"English Pictorial Music Title Pages, 1820-1885: Their Style, Evolution and Importance" (1950) (King), 75
Engravings, xxiv, 50, 52, 54, 62, 65, 69, 70, 72, 73, 74, 76, 77
Equality: economic, 117-18, 119; religion, unity and, 130-31; Union based on principle of, 131; threatened erosion of, as cause of Civil War, 131-32, 134; public opinion must support in principle, 132-33; for nation to endure, equality must become a principle of faith, 133; memory of the founding fathers instills new social conviction, 133; Lincoln's approach ahead of his time, 173; Lincoln's equality measures, 184; conditions facing those fighting for black freedom at end of Civil War, 186-87; acceptance of racial equality as biological fact, 189; in Declaration of

Sociology for the South (Fitzhugh), 119-20
Soldiers' Home, 317, 348
Solon, 110
Soltow, Lee, 117-18
South Carolina, 149
Southern Dream, 97
Spain, 231
Spangler, Edward, 357
Sparrow, Thomas and Elizabeth, 217-18
Sparta (ancient), 110
Speaking of Abraham Lincoln (1983) (Current), xx
Speed, James, 226, 350
Speed, Joshua F., 145-46, 219, 222-26, 242, 303
Spirit of the Times (Porter), 8, 12
"Spot Resolutions," 231, 261, 262
Springfield, Ill., 19, 27, 76, 87, 89, 112, 145, 219, 222, 224, 226, 262, 267, 281, 294, 298, 325, 367, 378
Squatter sovereignty. *See* Popular sovereignty
Stampp, Kenneth M., 175-76
Stanton, Edwin M., 13, 151, 154-55, 185, 319-23, 326-28, 330, 332-35, 340-41, 343, 347-48, 354-55, 362, 366
Staten Island, N.Y., 10
States' rights, 340
Steele, Frederick, 180
Stephens, Alexander, 100
Stephens, L. H., 71
Stephenson, Nathaniel W., 378
Stern, Philip VanDoren, 330
Stevens, Thaddeus, 96, 382
Stone, Frederick, 352
Stone, Irving, 387-88
Stone, Melville, 345
Stowe, Harriet Beecher, 8-9, 14
Strikes, 119, 120
Strong, George Templeton, 8-9
Strozier, Charles B., xvii, 242-51, 272n9, 272n11
Stuart, John T., 220
Styron, William, 387
Suffrage, xix
Sumner, Charles, 82, 379, 382
Supreme Court, 23, 126, 191, 287, 309, 316, 370, 372
Surratt, Anna, 355, 360

Surratt, John H., 321, 324, 328, 336, 352-54, 359-60, 362
Surratt, Mary E., 321, 324, 327-28, 351-57, 360-61
Surrattsville, Md., 353
Swatara, 359
Sylvis, William, 118
Syphilis, 243, 390

Taney, Roger B., 287-88, 303, 309
Tariffs, 91, 96, 110, 120, 121, 282
Taxes: Lincoln's efforts, 91; graduated income taxes, 96; excise, 120
Taylor, Zachary, 6, 7, 230, 232-33, 261, 275, 281
Tennessee, 171, 184, 198, 340
Test, John, 5
Texas, 149-50, 304
Texas Republican, 347
Thernstrom, Stephan, 121
They've Killed Lincoln (1972), 343
Thirteenth Amendment, 112, 172, 181, 182, 199, 202, 381
Thomas, Benjamin P., 215, 378
Thompson, Jacob, 358
Thoreau, Henry David, 119
Thornton, J. Mills, 309
Thurow, Glen E., xix, 144-47
Todd, Robert, 112
Toombs, Robert, 22
Toronto, Ontario, Canada, 315
Transportation: revolution of the 1830s, 89; mentioned, 88
Trefousse, Hans, 380
Trenton, N.J., 100-101, 266, 281-83
Trollope, Anthony, 50
Trollope, Frances, 49
Trueblood, D. Elton, 144
Trumbull, Lyman, 389
Tucker, Nathaniel Beverley, 281
Turner, Thomas Reed, xix, 365-73
Tyranny theme: Lincoln's warnings against himself as president-elect, 264; mentioned, xvii, 66, 263, 280, 287, 296, 297, 298, 299, 302, 304, 309, 316, 317, 320

Uncle Tom's Cabin (Stowe), 119
Union: and liberty, xv-xix; Lincoln's forceful approach to saving Union, 199; both personal and political, 237,